GW00391026

Transregional and Transnational Families in Europe and Beyond

Transregional and Transnational Families in Europe and Beyond

Experiences Since the Middle Ages

Edited by

Christopher H. Johnson,
David Warren Sabean,
Simon Teuscher,
and
Francesca Trivellato

Berghahn Books
New York • Oxford

Published in 2011 by

Berghahn Books

www.berghahnbooks.com

Library of Congress Cataloging-in-Publication Data

Transregional and transnational families in Europe and beyond : experiences since the middle ages / edited by Christopher H. Johnson … [et al.].—1st ed.
p. cm.
Includes bibliographical references and index.
ISBN 978-0-85745-183-5 (hbk)
1. Families—Europe. 2. Kinship—Europe—History. 3. Intergenerational relations—Europe. 4. Europe—Social life and customs. 5. Transnationalism. 6. Ethnicity. I. Johnson, Christopher H. II. Title.
HQ611.T736 2011
306.8509'03—dc22

2010048091

British Library Cataloguing in Publication Data

A catalogue record for this book is available from the British Library

Printed in the United States on acid-free paper.

ISBN 978-0-85745-183-5 (hardback)
ISBN 978-0-85745-184-2 (ebook)

Contents

Figures

Preface

This book is the result of continuing discussions among an international group of historians that during the last decade has been attempting to think through the implications of taking the idea of "kinship" seriously for the history of European societies. The first publication to come out of our discussions was *Kinship in Europe: Approaches to Long-Term Development (1300–1900)*.[1] The point there was to build on the findings of microhistorical studies of kinship in particular temporal and regional settings in order to explore systemic and structural changes in the way webs of kinship relations were constructed from the late Middle Ages to the eve of World War I. That, in turn, called for further exploration, and the next project examined how interconnections between brothers and sisters were patterned within the larger contexts of kinship during the same period (*Sibling Relations and the Transformations of European Kinship, 1300–1900*).[2] The current volume grew out of a series of panels at the 2006 Amsterdam meeting of the European Social Science History Conference and a subsequent workshop at the German Historical Institute in Washington in January 2008. We would like to thank all the participants at the six panels at the 2006 European Social Science History Conference and especially Els Hiemstra, the organizer of the conference, and Antoinette Fauve-Chamoux, the coordinator of the Family and Demography network. The workshop at the German Historical Institute in Washington was made possible by the interim director, Gisela Mettele. Bryan Hart, Richard F. Wetzell, and David Lazar took care of the organization. Among the many colleagues who participated in our discussions we would like to mention Vivian Berghahn, Uwe Israel, Rukshana Qamber, and Dorothee Wierling. Astrid Reinecke provided the illustrations for chapter 5. Daphne Rozenblatt was responsible for compiling and editing the bibliography. We would also like to thank Marion Berghahn for her support in publishing the series on kinship and Ann Przyzycki for her help as editor of the volume.

Notes

1. David Warren Sabean, Simon Teuscher, and Jon Mathieu, eds., *Kinship in Europe: Approaches to Long-Term Development (1300–1900)* (New York, 2007).
2. Christopher H. Johnson and David Warren Sabean, *Sibling Relations and the Transformations of European Kinship, 1300–1900* (New York and Oxford, 2011).

Introduction

Rethinking European Kinship

Transregional and Transnational Families

David Warren Sabean and Simon Teuscher

In the current discussion of ethnic, trade, and commercial diasporas, "circulation," international or global networks, and transnational communities, reference is continually made to the importance of families and kinship groups for understanding the dynamics of dispersion. Not very many of the studies, however, proceed to detailed examinations of those families and kinship groups that are or were scattered across the map, living in diverse cultural, ethnic, or political spaces, and coordinating their activities, maintaining claims upon each other, or carrying on various kinds of reciprocities. We want to suggest a series of analytical tools, themes, and conceptual clarifications that could be useful for opening up fresh discussion.[1]

Many of the chapters in this volume take up the challenge of postculturalism by looking at the way families and kinship groups are formed within the production and circulation of goods. Cultural forms and ways of representing reality cannot be simply set aside—the social imaginary plays a central role in how people relate to each other, of course. But we are not just after the "imaginary." The accent throughout this book is on how ideas circulate within social situations, and on these situations themselves: how and why people migrate, what the consequences are for a particular regime of property devolution, why the demands of state or nation call for particular responses, or what women do when their fathers or brothers change the rules of the game.

To begin a consideration of transnational families, we should be careful not to take the word *family* for granted. It is not a term that has great historical depth even in European history. In the Middle Ages, *familia* referred to those who depended on a lord, and it did not single out his parents, siblings, and children.[2] Until late in the eighteenth century, in most European languages, the *house* was the relevant term to cover relationships that we now capture with the word *family*, and yet it encompassed groups of people, social dynamics, and political rights that are missing in our own vocabulary.[3] When we speak of "international families," we are certainly pushing the boundaries of a concept that was devised to represent a form of social organization that grew up with the nation-state and civil society. Western observers took over the word *family* to talk about themselves and devised the notion of "kinship" to talk about those others who had not yet benefited from modern life and European culture. And the disciplines of sociology and anthropology were put together to parcel out an intellectual division of labor to correspond to the broad map of modern and traditional societies. To the sociology of the family was opposed the anthropology of kinship, and kinship suggested a science devoted to the study of relationships of peoples connected by descent or marriage and a field of obligations, claims, rights, and duties that penetrated or went beyond the boundaries of the nuclear family.

For many years now, European historians have been trying to break down the neat divisions suggested by this older self-understanding of the West and its self-conscious adoption of a linear model of modernization. It turns out that kinship in the sense of connected families and households was and still is central to the dynamics of European societies and that it is quite possible to study kinship in Europe along formal lines, to analyze systematic practices, and to account for regular shifts in kinship structures.[4] Taking up the question of the nature and importance of transregional and international families in European historical experience suggests a recourse to kinship analysis, a lively exchange between history and anthropology, and a fundamentally comparative perspective. It offers the possibility to reexamine European narratives, on the one hand, and, on the other, to transgress European boundaries.

This book grew out of discussions among an international group of historians that during the past decade has been actively attempting to think through the implications of taking the idea of "kinship" seriously for the history of European societies. One of the main strategies was to look at social situations over a long period, this time from the end of the Middle Ages to the beginning of the twenty-first century. And there are many things left out, such as forced mass migration of slavery, ethnic cleansing, deportations, and mostly the complex history of colonialism, in order to concentrate on a particular set of issues. The point, as we will explain below, was to think through the results of research into European families, households, and kinship practices to pose a set of questions for participants to entertain. Rather than contribute to a global consideration of "transnational" families, we would like to add a series of new issues and problems to the debate by reviewing once again experiences from Europe and by placing them in a broader, comparative perspective. In what follows, we will suggest strategies for bringing problems of power, the circulation of property, and structures of relationships to the core of discussions about transregional and transnational families.

Authority, Hierarchy, and Power

The figures of diasporas, international and transregional communities, and networks seldom prompt questions about authority, power relations, hierarchies, formal and informal sanctions, or the kind of socialization of individuals that allows for collectively coordinated strategies. Issues of power in European historical research into the family have most often been associated with (apparently) sedentary settings, in particular with ways of conceptualizing the "house." Two of the most influential ethnographers of the nineteenth century, Frédéric Le Play and Wilhelm Riehl, both stressed paternal authority and its devolution from one generation to the next as the key to understanding how the complex unity of the house could be welded together.[5] Their understandings of the household as a social unit with similar characteristics from the ancient world to the present, of course, were developed from research on noble and large peasant households where attention centered on the dynamics of landed property, inheritance, the patriarchal power of the father/manager, and the moral capacities of the collectivity. The logic of the "stem family" (*famille-souche*) (Le Play) and the "total household" (*ganzes Haus*) (Riehl) grew out of the necessity of maintaining the integrity of the patrimony, which in turn determined power relations within the family.

Otto Brunner borrowed the concept of *das ganze Haus* from Riehl, who thought of the traditional house as a formation where ethical and social life, work, socialization, and welfare and emergency care were all combined together in a complex whole.[6] Without the domination (*Herrschaft*) of the *Hausvater*, Brunner argued, such a set of complex functions could not be held together. Power was the key to Brunner's interpretation of the house: "All relations of dependence in the house were based on the lord of the house [*Hausherr*], who as the directing head created a whole out of them in the first place. … The house [*Oikos*] is a whole which rests on the heterogeneity of its members, who are molded into a unity by the directing spirit of the lord [*Herr*]." In this understanding of rural households, some members had to be sacrificed to the goal of lineal succession and disciplined to collective "responsibility."

The concepts of Le Play and Riehl, who were nineteenth-century conservatives, and of Brunner, a National Socialist, have since been shown to owe a great deal to the nostalgia of an idealized authoritarian rural order that the authors felt was about to be eroded by the individualizing effects of modernity. Nevertheless, their ideas had great influence on the development of social history and provided an important point of departure for historical reflection about the development of innerfamilial hierarchies.[7] At the same time, Le Play, Riehl, and Brunner cemented the problematic notion that questions about authority within families concerned primarily rural settings.

Pierre Bourdieu, who essentially reformulated Le Play, had greater success putting his stamp on the current international ethnographic discussion about the dynamics of the house.[8] Focusing on the social reproduction of stem families in the Pyrenees, he tried to work out the set of practices (*habitus*) that conformed to the logic of the integral perpetuation of the patrimony. At the heart of the system of practices, patriarchal rule ensured the goals of property transmission and class endogamy. The head of the house defined the claims of each member, controlled information, manipulated "rules," and indoctrinated the children, who emerged with strongly interiorized principles of the tradition and schemes of perception that fitted them for the tasks at hand. The oldest son subordinated his interest to those of the line, and younger sons were socially primed to "embrace the traditional values" and "customary distribution of tasks and powers among brothers." As Bourdieu puts it, "the sociology of the family, which is so often depicted as based on sentiment, might be nothing but a specific aspect of political sociology."[9]

This short summary of a particular tradition in European ethnography might seem in the first instance too tied to the rural and the preindustrial world to be of much interest for looking at families that extend themselves across large spaces and are frequently grasped under the notion of "network."[10] We think, however, that drawing from the ethnographic tradition's central focus on how a patrimony disciplines the members of the family is promising. This helps to overcome overly simplistic notions of a transition from traditional "tight" to modern "loose" forms of family organization. Within such a simplistic opposition, international families that in many ways appear to be the epitome of the modern have primarily been looked at as networks but not as structures of dominance and subordination. Authority, discipline, and hierarchy are not matters that disappear with the advent of capitalism.[11] Bourdieu's reformulation of the issues in terms of the material and cultural things that mediate relations, the practices of socialization, and the logics of command and obedience seem fruitful ways of opening up new lines of research. Researchers might well give close attention to the way the allocation not only of land, farms, and castles, but also of capital, credit, and all forms of movable property mediate relations and distribute roles throughout a network of kin spread across extended areas. It might then well turn out to be the fact that many kinds of well-integrated international families are acephalous, but if so, then an account of the "political" practices of such families is all the more interesting.[12]

In chapter 11, Sabean discusses how the Siemens family built a powerful industrial enterprise during the nineteenth century that stretched from England to Russia and Central Asia. Family members as shareholders, managers, technicians, and workers were distributed throughout the family's industrial empire, all coordinated under the authority first of Werner Siemens in Berlin and later by successors chosen from the family. The reproduction of the family network, the practices of familial socialization, the linking of family members through endogamous marriage practices, and the disciplining of family members in the interest of the larger enterprise—all come under the heading of Bourdieu's notion of "political sociology."[13]

Antenhofer (chapter 3) tells a story about the reorganization of a high noble ruling family in the late Middle Ages. But she argues that the securing of the line, the development of primogeniture, and the reconfiguration of devolutionary practices to radically differentiate among siblings were something new. She chronicles the restructuring of the Gonzaga dynasty away from competition among equally qualified lines to the formation of a dominant line, the exclusion of women from succession, the differentiation of the eldest son from cadets, and the development of new forms of patronage. Furthermore, it was precisely in the context of this reorganization and development of new forms of family discipline that the family entered the European stage, creating alliances with the high nobility beyond the Alps and in France. For the quite different context of urban patriciates at about the same time, Teuscher (chapter 4) examines how the practices related to contractions of urban elites, their stability over time, and their "sedentariness" necessitated the mobility of younger sons. His chapter is an examination of the interdependence of property regimes and transregional dispersion and the collective familial strategies that required the disciplined response of family members. He argues that patrician mobility, far from being just the cultural experience that is frequently highlighted in contemporary patricians' own accounts, was lived out in response to economic exigencies. And he critiques the often-held assumption that geographical mobility was incompatible with family cohesion: "Being gone was not a position outside, but inside the family."

It is not enough to consider power and authority as a family-immanent matter alone. Authority within kinship constellations also responds to juridical systems, state power, and social hierarchies, including those of gender. Piterberg (chapter 2) provides an interesting contrast to the European and later Ottoman experience by examining elite political "households" in military patronage states, with the Egyptian Mamluks as his example. There, precisely the problem was always to recreate the elite by *excluding* familial continuity from generation to generation in the holding of office or political power. The political household took in slaves, raised them, manumitted them, and passed power on to them. The children of the grandees had no rights to succession and seldom were able to affect it, blocked at every turn by the clients raised within the house. What the Ottomans effected after the fifteenth century was to combine the logic of the military patronage state with kinship politics by not allowing marriage of ruling families into surrounding elites. Powerful kinship ties were developed across the empire through marrying daughters of the sultan to imperial officers. What emerged in the sixteenth century was the strengthening of the household system with kin ties across the complex space of Ottoman rule.[14] Similarly, Mettele (chapter 8) deals with a fascinating case counter to the kinds of kinship that we usually discuss. With the Moravians of the eighteenth and early nineteenth centuries, she finds dynamics resembling those of kinship groups but in the name of a spiritual kinship, an imaginary order of belonging, networks of aid and solidarity, and rituals of "familial" observance. They always married internally to the group in marriages that were arranged—frequently through the casting of lots. In joining the sect, most people sloughed off their old kinship ties. And marriage among themselves was understood as an important tool for strengthening group cohesion. And through ritual activity, correspondence, and newsletters, they developed what Mettele calls a "narrative community" that came to be seriously challenged by the nascent nation-states.

Gender roles and shifting concatenations of force are a matter taken up for the late twentieth-century Palestinian camps in Jordan and Gaza by Latte Abdallah (chapter 13). There until the 1960s, the family was among the very few institutions that remained in place, and the conditions of its existence in exile put a premium on older values and almost "dictatorial" powers of fathers. Latte Abdallah examines how what looks like an increasing fragmentation of social conditions went along with the step-by-step emergence of women to the head of many families. Both patriarchal power and marriage bonds were weakened as women (mothers, daughters, and sisters) became responsible for sustaining their families.[15] Latte Abdallah's account looks at the dialectic between the public discourse of camp families, the creation of family ideology, ideals of nationhood, and the conditions of exile. In the quite different context of early nineteenth-century bourgeois France, Johnson (chapter 10) looks at the role of powerful women inside a wider constellation of kin: how they maintained familial discipline through a continual flow of correspondence, marriage negotiations, oversight of manners, societal influence, and directing careers. He draws attention to the fact that kinship relationships have to be constantly monitored, created, and sustained by hard work and that particular tasks of this continuous effort are often delegated to or arrogated by one sex or the other. It is only in detailed and concentrated reading of texts that we are able to understand the nuances and costs of social power.

Succession and Inheritance: The Circulation of Property

The notion of "transnational families" provides new difficulties in imagining the social. Most social history until now has anchored analysis in unambiguous spaces, but transnational families can offer the problem of not being "locatable." As Bryceson and Vuorela have argued, the attitudes of transnational families to place are "varied, ambiguous, and subject to change."[16] If "some individual transnationals espouse no origins, no permanent geographical attachments, and no final destinations," what structures them and gives them coherence?[17] Also Osterhammel has argued that one of the problems with operationalizing the concept of "transnationality" is that it can have no social structural substratum.[18] He finds networks, flows, and transfers much too amorphous to build any kind of systematic social history. The terms that one continually encounters are "multilocality," "mobility," "migrancy." If the issue in studying them is "connecting, mixing, and networking," then one way to give form to them is to ask systematic questions about the material and immaterial things that mediate their relations. The advantage of studying kinship is that it can provide a systematic but not territorial definition of whom to include in an examination. How does the understanding of the family vary according to the perceived claims and rights and obligations different members have for each other?

If property in some ways can be analyzed as a system of claims and obligations—as a set of relations around things—then kinship as a set of claims and obligations can be understood as a kind of property system or a bundle of resources. In order to make kinship analytically useful for the study of international families, it cannot be left as an amorphous, ill-defined set of values or vaguely defined networks, but necessitates careful consideration of how it functions and is structured in particular contexts—how rights are distributed, how people are socialized, or as Bourdieu puts it, how the things that mediate relations discipline those gathered around them, on the one hand, and engender particular kinds of knowledge, on the other—a savoir faire, a *habitus*, a particular kind of character formation.

From the early nineteenth century onwards, one major focus for studies of the European family has had to do with the effects of different forms of inheritance on the structures of the family and on regional and local political, social, and economic life. Much of this literature was centered on rural and noble social groups, and quite impassioned arguments about the effects of "closed" vs. partible inheritance practices developed. Large, open villages, with handicraft industries, regional mobility, intensive and innovative agriculture, egalitarian social structures, and small families were associated frequently with partible inheritance practices. Closed systems of inheritance—primogeniture, ultimogeniture, unigeniture—encouraged out-migration, sharp social differences, and a stress on the tight discipline of paternal authority. In such territories, it has frequently been argued, communal institutions were less developed, although recent work on Dutch regions by Hilde Bras and Theo van Tilburg suggests that authoritarian unigeniture practices might elicit stronger neighborly ties and more integrated kin groups.[19]

Comparative research by Bernard Derouet for different French regions has shown that systematic forms of property devolution in France—whether closed or subject to equal division—were not a vestige of an age-old past or a characteristic of a region, but solidified only during the late fifteenth and early sixteenth centuries and became a feature of early modern social development. And further, he has shown that the pattern of property devolution had important implications for political structures, the nature of local and regional social relationships, and the psychological development of individuals.[20] There have been several other important studies of the effects of different forms of property devolution that have raised questions about the way property can mediate quite different kinds of psychosocial behavior. In a study of Basque farming families, Leonard Kasden argued that the eldest son and younger sons were socialized in such a way as to have quite different personality types.[21] The eldest—the one destined to get the farm—tended to be solid, traditional, reflective, and unadventurous. Younger sons, whose destinies sent them across the Atlantic in fishing enterprises or as emigrants, developed what he called "entrepreneurial" personalities. In contrast to this kind of region, with its generations of out-migration, rural Austrians, studied by Sigrid Khera, sharply differentiated between their inheriting elder sons and sons destined to end up in the rural proletariat.[22] As adults, siblings living in the same villages avoided each other, socialized in different circles, and even failed to be integrated into the clientage system of their inheriting siblings. Examples can be multiplied, but the point is that the form of property, the way it is held and distributed, and the way it is passed down the generations needs to be closely examined to understand how people connect to each other, what claims and rights they have on each other, and what obligations and duties they assume for each other. Patterns of distributing and circulating property are in part defined by family structures not only in rural contexts, but also in the contexts of migration and entrepreneurship, and examples such as the Basque case show that in many instances, the two are interrelated.

These considerations suggest that it is very useful to pay attention to the way property and resources mediate relations among international families. Scarce resources such as information can be the medium that makes far-flung merchant families successful. Gujarati families have been the subject of intensive study, for example, and we know that men circulated to Central Asia or to the many parts of the British Empire and beyond, always trying to return to the small region they set off from. Firms were organized and controlled from India, and we have a good overall description of the loyalties and controls and the financial arrangements that allowed the system to work.[23] Where we have far less understanding is with the property relations of the home territory, the circulation of wealth across and down the generations, obligations and opportunities for socialization and training, the work of women and the culture of families in the home base, the selection of those who circulate and those who stay put, the movement of credit and resources among family members, and the kinds of sanctions kin could wield. Space has also to be seen as a resource, and the circulation of resources cannot be abstracted from the issue of how fast and efficiently people themselves could circulate. Just as a historian has to take into consideration the development of different kinds of markets—land, capital, labor, or commodity—to understand the working of partible or unigeniture inheritance, so the observers of international families have to understand means of transportation—pack trains, sailing ships, steamships, postal services, railroads, telegraph, airplanes, telephone, and e-mail. Different diasporas have put different weight upon issues of lineage and descent, and sometimes migratory populations treat kinship itself as a resource.[24] Furthermore, significant issues have been raised in contemporary debates about the integration and assimilation of migrants or their enduring allegiance to a culture and language of origin.[25] Whether migrants come in order to return to their home country or to stay in the new place is ultimately not only a question of culture and individual choice (both fetishes of current debates), but also of property regimes and income strategies of their families. It is precisely when one gets down to specifics, to the details of who gives, receives, and controls resources, whose needs are satisfied and interests taken into account, that we can understand the logic of different social forms. As Markovits suggests, "A network [is] a structure through which goods, credit, capital and men circulate regularly across space, which can vary enormously in terms of size and accessibility."[26] Important in his conceptualization is the understanding that networks are not conceivable apart from the material objects that circulate through them.

Trivellato (chapter 6) provides a model for how to deal with the ways in which the understanding of the family varies according to the perceived claims and obligations members have for each other. Her argument is that one needs to take into consideration the larger structures of families and the place of women in the distribution of resources and the coordination of personal relations. Networks are not subject to a single law, but take shape according to how things and what things move through them and where people are located by age, status, and gender. Trivellato begins her examination by pointing out that studies on the business organization of trading diasporas rarely examine how those were influenced by "specific kinship structures, inheritance practices, and dowry systems." She offers contrasting case studies of Sephardic Jews based in Livorno and Armenians based in Julfa, looking at the specifics of kinship structures and devolutionary practices. Not only does she reassert the family in long-distance trade, but she also shows the mechanisms of how it was done. And she is able to relate the different instruments of kinship—endogamy, dowries, family-based contractual relations—to the spatial distribution of networks, the nature of business ties, the formation of capital, the relative centralization of commercial arrangements, and the reliance on outsiders.

Teuscher (chapter 4) in his study of urban patriciates stresses that the networks of kin creating ties across regions were the outcome of sending nonsucceeding sons on the road. Yet they were supported by their families on their journeys and often passed around among distant kin as they made their way. The key point was to keep them away from the home town and competition for scarce familial goods. In her account of the eighteenth- and early nineteenth-century Ottoman Empire Phanariots (chapter 9), Philliou looks at a political group that constituted itself around the control of a fundamentally scarce good: information. The development of their transregional households, spread throughout the Ottoman Empire during the early modern period, contrasted sharply with other Ottoman elites, who constructed "monoregional" political and social networks. The informational webs composed by relatives in Istanbul, the Danubian principalities, and beyond allowed the Phanariots to control certain key imperial offices, around which they built powerful dynasties. Marriage alliances were largely endogamous and carried out with the intent of developing patronage networks. Their very position as Christians in a Muslim polity determined their eclectic approach to the instrumentalization of family relationships.

Those elites in Europe who occupied territories in between the great powers, France and the Empire, are the subject of Spangler's chapter 7. He deals with European princely families with their own territorial bases who served in the great courts and in competing armies. They had their own houses and clients and in turn served in greater houses and as clients to greater powers. Their patterns of intermarriage, rules of succession, and cultivation of local political and social networks, and the fact that members of the same family were careful to assume high positions with political powers in competition with each other offers important insight into the specifics of Western state formation and nascent nationalism.

In Sabean's (chapter 11) treatment of international entrepreneurial families in Imperial Germany, he deals with the nineteenth-century construction of a particular agnatic lineage configuration. The need for capital, connection, and the placement of children encouraged the widespread practice of endogamous marriage practices, although the strategy always necessitated both near and far marriages.[27] Developing international business enterprise called upon the widespread use of kin. A family rich in brothers like the Siemens or Rothschilds could place their members in many different states, taking advantage of the Russian, English, Ottoman, and Austrian empires.

Patterned, Structured, and Systemic Aspects of Kinship

Recent work on the history of the family in Europe has begun to look carefully at the systemic aspects of kinship cultures and is now at the place where it is possible to map the shifts in kinship structures over time.[28] The key things to keep in mind for the study of international families are that it is possible to give a formal account of kinship and that different forms have significant implications for understanding how groups are created, maintained, reconfigured, and how they persist over time. Many recent case studies from different regions and social settings call attention to two major transitions in the development of European kinship. The first leads from the late Middle Ages into the early modern period, and the second can be traced from the mid-eighteenth century. The fifteenth and sixteenth centuries witnessed a new stress on familial coherence, a growing inclination to formalize patron-client ties through marriage alliance or godparentage, and a tendency to develop and maintain structured hierarchies within lineages, descent groups, and clans and among allied families. These developments were closely connected to processes of state formation and the formalization of social hierarchies as well as to innovations in patterns of succession and inheritance, new forms of delineating and mobilizing property, and novel claims to privileged rights in office, corporations, and monopolies. While the first transition can be associated with an increasing stress on vertically organized relationships, the second one brought about a stronger stress on horizontally ordered interactions. During the early modern period, marriage alliances were sought with "strangers," frequently cemented long-term clientage relations, and created complex patterns of circulation among different political and corporate groups (*Stände, ceti, ordres*) and wealth strata. Beginning around the middle of the eighteenth century, alliance and affinity, rather than descent and heritage, came to organize interactions among kin. Marriages became more endogamous in terms of class, milieu, and consanguinity: marriage partners sought out the "familiar." Among other things, these innovations reflected reconfigurations in political institutions, state service, property rights, and the circulation of capital. In the nineteenth century, enormous energy was invested in maintaining and developing extensive, reliable, and well-articulated structures of exchange among connected families over many generations.

During the eighteenth century, in some areas from the early decades but almost everywhere by around 1750, the structures stressing descent, inheritance, and succession, patrilines, agnatic lineages and clans, paternal authority, house discipline, and exogamy gradually gave way to patterns centered around alliance, sentiment, horizontally structured kindreds, and social and familial endogamy. The progressive dissolution of patrilineal systems of property devolution was probably most prompted by bourgeois concerns, by people whose wealth came to be centered more directly on money, credit, and exchange than on land, monopolies, and birthright, and we can see some of the features that characterized these groups in the nineteenth century already in play with trading diasporas of the early modern period as Trivellato argues in chapter 6. Kinship structures are not dependent variables but innovative and creative responses to newly configured relationships between people and institutions and around the circulation of goods and services. Therefore there could be many different ways of developing patterns of interaction, cultivating networks, and evolving systems of reciprocity. Kinship and the alliance systems of nineteenth-century Europe were crucial for concentrating and distributing capital; providing strategic support over the life of individuals; structuring dynasties and recognizable patrilineal groupings; maintaining access points, entrances, and exits to social milieus through marriage, godparentage, and guardianship; creating cultural and social boundaries by extensive festive, ludic, competitive, and charitable transactions; configuring and reconfiguring possible alliances between subpopulations; developing a training ground for character formation; shaping desire and offering practice in code and symbol recognition; training rules and practices into bodies; and integrating networks of culturally similar people.[29] Along with this closeness based on familiarity came a stronger appreciation of romantic love, emotional accord, and similarity of personality as the basis of legitimate marriage. This was by no means contrary to economic considerations: the flow of sentiment and the flow of money operated in the same channels. Even though we are well aware that the mapping of kinship systems in Europe is just at its inception, it is hard to overlook the central importance of cousin marriages and repeated consanguineal endogamy, homogamy, and familial-centered construction of cultural and social milieus.

There are a number of essays in this volume that take up the issue of kinship structures. Teuscher (chapter 4) investigates some of the practices leading to the structures that were typical outcomes of the first transition. He deals with patricians in German-speaking cities at the end of the Middle Ages, when elites closed off. This came with an increasing pressure to limit the number of sons who could lay claims on their fathers' positions and property. One strategy was to establish hierarchies within families and to shape distinct but interdependent roles between those sons who stayed and those who left, which were important steps towards the development of dynastic structures. These allowed connecting local property to continuous successions of fathers and sons, i.e., to mark property as dynastic property. The local rootedness of dynasties and the continuity of their local property were crucial to patrician self-representation and are therefore still today highly visible for historians.

This rootedness of the dynasty was, however, in part brought about by a less-emphasized mobility of some of the dynasties' unprivileged members, whose life courses were characterized by dislocations, ruptures, and discontinuity.

Hohkamp (chapter 5) argues against a simple genealogy of state-building in Europe based on the linking of primogeniture and territoriality in favor of an understanding of the kinship dynamics of European rulers that not simply reiterates the dominant perspective of succession between fathers and sons, but looks at family organization also from the perspective of sisters, daughters, and aunts. She draws attention to the establishment of dynasties through the politics of marriage exchange and points to the fundamental actions of married sisters as mediators in the political system. She analyzes changes in the structure of marriages, pointing to the integral importance of cousin marriage after the middle of the eighteenth century. She wants a "rethinking of the emergence of modern nations and statehood not so much in terms of centralization around a vertical line of succeeding princes as through the cohesive web of relations-constructed translocalities, regions, and nascent states through the dynamics of kinship."

Spangler (chapter 7) deals with princely families from small territories between France to the West and the German principalities to the East. He takes up the role that these families played in the construction of early modern states and the problems posed for them in the aftermath of the French Revolution and the triumph of the nation-state. A key aspect is that members of the families took high office and high military positions on all sides, with France, Spain, and Austria. During the early modern period, the families divided into multiple lines, marrying back and forth and with other such families as well. Besides serving several sides of the political spectrum, they also developed well-integrated patronage networks in their own territories, so that when these come to be included in one state or the other, they played an important role in integrating the territories into the new states. And like the Phanariots, they served crucial functions as conduits of information, since their members were scattered among the important courts throughout Europe.

The concept of the nation and the discourses of nationalism reinforced the changing structure of the state, as the very nature of political authority came to be redefined; sovereignty was deemed to reside in the "nation," that is, all people living within the boundaries of a given state who putatively shared a national culture. The kinship terminology of patriarchy that legitimated absolutism gave way to a new terminology that privileged horizontal bonds: the brotherhood, *la fraternité* of all (male) members of the nation.[30] The connection between the shifts in the nature of kinship and the character of the emergent polity could not be clearer. In Moya's chapter 1, the author discusses the migration patterns of peoples from the Paleolithic to the present, exploring the precise meaning of "national" in the notion of "transnational families." He argues that migration has always been a fact of human society and points out that humans have the most complex kinship webs in the animal kingdom. What makes transnational migration specific are new forms of political organization operating with clearly delimited spatial entities and rigidly monitored borders—so the phenomenon is at most five centuries old and for many regions of the world only little more than a century old. Moya distinguishes between "cross-communality," "trans-regionality," and "transnationality." All of these are important in mixing populations in specific ways and constructing different kinds of polities, but it is the nineteenth century that first saw the massification of international families. And for the nation-state, these families had integral meaning—they themselves form a mechanism for migration, determine the patterns of migration, and become a self-generating force.[31]

Johnson (chapter 10) considers a slightly different issue, for he argues that the construction of the nation itself is not understandable without the actions of those transregional families who linked the disparate parts of the territorial state to draw the sinews of the nation together.[32] He offers a detailed analysis of the new nineteenth-century alliance system, with the centrality of cousins, and links that to the formation of class and the development of the nation. Interestingly, his families were coordinated by strong older women, much like Chamberlain (chapter 12) finds in the Caribbean, but here where conjugality was strong and mobility was confined to the nation. He points out that the families he deals with in Brittany created a strongly endogamous system of marriage in terms of locality, class, and kin, but balanced that system always with a set of marriages that reached out across space to other bourgeois groups with which they had no prior ties. He sees these two practices as fully complementing each other. So the nation-state both relies on the movement of kin-structured populations to invent itself and sets barriers to those same kinds of families to maintain its new identity.

Rutten and Patel (chapter 14) also deal with structural aspects of kinship in their study of migrants from Gujarat in India to contemporary Britain, some of whom arrived by way of East Africa ("twice migrants"). Coming from a series of villages, hierarchically ordered, the Gujaratis have a long history of migration. Marriage among them is characterized by separate marriage circles organized hypergamously (women marry upward) where differences between high-status and medium-status villages play a central role. Migrants to East Africa and those who went directly to Britain have rather different traditions of maintaining links back to the home society. In Britain, the immigrants remain attached both to Indian culture and to the social relations of where they came from. Like Chamberlain, these authors put great stress on the nature of communication—through phone contact (and probably today through e-mail). Like those from the Caribbean, Gujaratis in Britain maintain contacts with their home villages by frequent travel. And also like them, some of the older generation become "world citizens," spending several months during the year at different locations in Britain, India, North America, and other places where relatives have settled. In the end, Rutten and Patel argue that the two communities—the home villages and the British immigrant community—have to be treated in the same unit of analysis, while at the same time they cannot be considered as a homogenous transnational community.

Chamberlain (chapter 12) uses examples from the Caribbean to discuss a society whose very identity is based on migration. She puts great stress on the systemic aspects of kinship practices, including "serial polygamy," weak conjugal unions, and bilateral descent lines. These are both the result of migration (and slavery) and constitutive of the kind of migration that characterizes families from the region. In this system, there is a powerful place for mothers and grandmothers, such that the kinship system has come to be characterized by "matrifocality."[33] The Caribbean family, Chamberlain argues, has adapted well to migration. Migrants see themselves as having a wide kinship network, and this has played out well in Britain and North America. Those who leave the Caribbean maintain an imagined continuity with it through an emotional attachment and genealogical map of the kin. The fact of migration stretching out over a very long time has become a feature of life in the Caribbean and of the understanding of family.[34] In a quite different context from the Phanariots discussed by Philliou, the circulation of communication is also fundamental for Caribbean family dynamics. And one of the things that is passed on is the *habitus* of migration itself—how to do it.

Strategies

A fundamental question to be asked is whether considerations of the long-term developments in European kinship outlined above offer analytical possibilities for the study of international families as well. Rather than seeing mobility and great geographic spreads as modern or modernizing per se, we should ask whether there might be specific medieval or modern patterns of dispersing family members over extended areas.

Is there a "transnationalism" or "transregionalism" of families that is typical of the fluctuating kin groups of the Middle Ages and a different one or different ones characteristic of the more coherently organized kin groups of the early modern period? A key question is whether empires and nation-states make a difference for transnational families as much of the literature (sometimes idealizing empires) has framed the comparisons between modern and premodern groups. Are the kinship forms of merchant, entrepreneurial, and laboring families found in the nineteenth and twentieth centuries similar to those of political elites and merchants in the medieval and early modern periods?

In taking some of these considerations into the study of transnational families, one strategy might be to examine family members over several generations. Chamberlain has shown that such an approach leads to an understanding of how familial connections can be coordinated and how certain configurations shift from generation to generation.[35] In our account, we have stressed how the kinds of resources available and the structural nature of states and economies themselves both condition how families organize themselves and act as resources that families use for their own purposes. In this respect, we can expect that families are not simply "reactive." An important "resource" is the people themselves, and anthropologists have paved the way for understanding the implications of different forms of marriage, filiation, and exchange. "Rechaining," cross-cousin and parallel-cousin marriages, homogamy, hypergamy, lineages, clans, kindreds, incest prohibitions, affinity, consanguinity, and so forth are all concepts that are invigorating the study of European kinship systems in the past.

On a regional level, Gérard Delille has demonstrated how the formation of the leading dynasties in the center (capitals, courts) of early modern monarchies went along with the emergence of cadet branches that intermarried with local elites in the peripheries and thus tied the latter to the centers. Many researchers have noted that in different epochs, quite extensive reunions of families take place periodically: where relations are reinforced, younger people are acquainted or reacquainted with an extended set of relatives, and, often, the seeds of new marriage alliances are planted (chapters by Chamberlain, Sabean, and Rutten and Patel). Examining an extended family across generations allows a researcher to see how the forms of communication can show a dynamic in structural relationships (Chamberlain, Rutten and Patel). This kind of work also can show ways in which families (and different family members) conceptualize the family, develop certain kinds of identities associated with a lineage or a name or a connection with a central figure, always understanding that patterns of use and ways of modeling relationships are not at all the same thing. Identity itself is a highly problematic concept: we find some dispersed families where members remain strangers where they reside, for whom national boundaries are irrelevant, and where primary loyalties and meanings arise from a nonlocatable network of kin. But there are other situations where families have been broken up through the process of adopting national identities. Chamberlain has stressed the mobility, ambivalence, and contradictoriness of identity in migrant families, and Khater, observing migrants returning to the country of departure with new experiences, skills, and wealth, uses the concept of "kaleidoscopic" identities.[36]

To push the understanding of transnational families to the next level, we will need microanalyses of family interaction over several generations; systematic accounts of socialization, points of cohesion and fission, and distributions of obligations and claims; and close examination of familial norms, values, and representations.[37] It should also be possible to give formal accounts of patterns of exchange and reciprocity, marriage alliances, and the structures of affinity, consanguinity, clientage, spiritual kinship, adoptive and adaptive "relatives," and friendship. These processes can be examined over the range of centuries during which the nation-state emerged, from its incubation in the "states" of medieval cities and principalities and within multi-"national" empires in the sixteenth and seventeenth centuries, through its triumph in the age of national and democratic revolutions of the eighteenth and nineteenth, to its hyperextension in the twentieth, as well as in the contemporary context of its contradictory trajectories as ethnic-regional claims vie with globalization.

Notes

1. Claude Markovits, *The Global World of Indian Merchants 1750–1947: Traders of Sind from Bukhara to Panama* (Cambridge, 2000), 260–61, discusses the concept of "trust," which is the value most frequently ascribed to family business networks. The question is whether trust is embedded in dense kinship networks and is affective or rather a matter of rational calculation. He argues that family and kinship are not "privileged breeding grounds for trust" (262). Witness the frequent conflicts and sibling rivalries. What kinship networks offer are speed and ease of communication and they provide a "dense flow of accumulated information about past behaviour." Trust is not an automatic outcome but the result of process.
2. Dieter Schwab, "Familie," in Otto Brunner, Werner Conze, and Reinhart Kosellek, eds., *Geschichtliche Grundbegriffe: Historisches Lexikon zur politisch-sozialen Sprache in Deutschland* (Stuttgart, 1975), 255–58.
3. Claude Karnoouh, "Penser 'maison,' penser 'famille': residence domestique et parenté dans les sociétés rurales de l'est de la France," in *Études rurales* 75 (1979) :

33–75. And see the discussion on the house in David Warren Sabean, *Property, Production and Family in Neckarhausen, 1700–1870* (Cambridge, 1990).

4. For a recent attempt to view the history of kinship in Europe, see David Warren Sabean, Simon Teuscher, and Jon Mathieu, eds., *Kinship in Europe: Approaches to Long-Term Development (1300–1900)* (New York, 2007).
5. M. Frédéric Le Play, *L'organisation de la famille selon le vrai modèle signalé par l'histoire de toutes les races et tous les temps* (Paris, 1871); Wilhelm Riehl, *Die Famille*, vol. 3 of *Die Naturgeschichte des Volks als Grundlage einer deutschen Social-Politik*, 3rd ed. (Stuttgart, 1855).
6. Otto Brunner, "Das 'ganze Haus' und alteuropäische 'Oekonomik'," in Otto Brunner, *Neue Wege der Verfassungs- und Socialgeschichte*, 2nd ed. (Göttingen, 1968), 103–27.
7. Werner Trossbach, "Das 'Ganze Haus'—Basiskategorie für das Verständnis ländlicher Gesellschaften in der Frühen Neuzeit," in *Blätter für deutsche Landesgeschichte* 129 (1993), 277–314; Valentin Groebner, "Ausser Haus. Otto Brunner und die 'Alteuropäische Ökonomik'," in *Geschichte in Wissenschaft und Unterricht* 2 (1995): 69–80; Claudia Opitz, "Neue Wege Der Sozialgeschichte? Ein Kritischer Blick Auf Otto Brunners Konzept des 'Ganzen Hauses'," in *Geschichte und Gesellschaft* 20 (1994): 88–98.
8. Pierre Bourdieu, "Marriage Strategies as Strategies of Social Reproduction," in Robert Forster and Orest Ranum, eds., *Family and Society: Selections from the Annales*, trans. Elborg Forster (Baltimore, 1976): 117–44.
9. Ibid., 135.
10. See for example the discussion throughout the collection of essays in Ina Baghdiantz McCabe, Gelina Harlaftis, and Ioanna Pepelasis Minoglou, eds., *Disapora Entrepreneurial Networks: Four Centuries of History* (Oxford, 2005).
11. Gelina Harlaftis, "Mapping the Greek Maritime Diaspora from the Early Eighteenth to the Late Twentieth Centuries," in McCabe, Harlaftis, and Minoglou, eds., *Disapora Entrepreneurial Networks*, 147–71. Talking about the Black Sea trade in the nineteenth century: "The main strength of Greek shipowners … were the networks of Greek diaspora merchant communities" (155). "The Chiot [from the Island of Chios] network was formed by members of about sixty Greek families." On p. 156, she discusses one of the large family networks, the Rallis, the largest and most influential family in the Chiot network with sixty-six members—siblings, first and second cousins married within twenty-four families. A prime characteristic of the multinational network was family control: "Kinship and common place of origin implied trust and facilitated entrance into the 'club'." But their power derived from the "discipline dictated by the hierarchy and cohesion of the family." "Intermarriage was extensive as each family sought to mix with equals. … Intermarriage made the family even more powerful" (164). "Intermarriage was used as an important strategy in keeping business together and the heirs were selected and educated carefully among this international family business elite, at the heart of which lay personal contacts and trust."
12. Jonathan Israel, "Diaspora Jewish and Non-Jewish and the World Maritime Empires," in McCabe, Harlaftis, and Minoglu, eds., *Diaspora Entrepreneurial Networks*, 3–26. Armenian success was built "on a system of trust supplemented by informal methods of enforcing family, religious and business discipline" (7).
13. Deborah Bryceson and Ulla Vuorela, "Transnational Families in the Twenty-First Century," in Deborah Bryceson and Ulla Vuorela, ed., *The Transnational Family: New European Frontiers and Global Networks* (Oxford, 2002), 3–30. "Transnational families have to mediate inequality amongst their members" (7).

14. Ina Baghdiantz McCabe, "Global Trading Ambitions in Diaspora: The Armenians and Their Eurasian Silk Trade, 1530–1750," in McCabe, Harlaftis, and Minoglu, eds., *Diaspora Entrepreneurial Networks*, 27–48. Dealing with Armenians in the Safavid Empire, she points out that one has to understand the household system of government—the same as with Ottomans (33).
15. See also the discussion of migration and paternalism in Akram Fouad Khater, *Inventing Home: Emigration, Gender, and the Middle Class in Lebanon, 1870–1920* (Berkeley, 2001), 5: the new patriarchal order (upon remigration) subjected women to "new forms of control and discipline."
16. Bryceson and Vuorela, "Transnational Families in the Twenty-First Century," 7.
17. Ibid., 25.
18. Jürgen Osterhammel, "Transnationale Gesellschaftsgeschichte: Erweiterung oder Alternative?," in *Geschichte und Gesellschaft* 27 (2001): 464–79.
19. Hilde Bras and Theo van Tilburg, "Kinship and Social Networks: A Regional Analysis of Sibling Relations in Twentieth-Century Netherlands," in *Journal of Family History* 35 (2007): 296–322.
20. Bernard Derouet, "Pratiques successorales et rapport à la terre: Les sociétés paysannes d'ancien régime," in *Annales ESC* (1989): 173–206; "Territoire et parenté: Pour une mise en perspective de la communauté rurale et des formes de reproduction familiale," in *Annales HSS* (1995): 645–86; "La transmission égalitaire du patrimoine dans la France rurale (XVIe–XIXe siècles): Nouvelles perspectives de recherche," in Francisco Chacón Jiménez and Llorenc Ferrer Alós, eds., *Familia, casa y trabajo*, vol. 3: *Historia de la Familia* (Murcia, 1997), 73–92; "Les pratiques familiales, le droit et la construction des différences (XVe–XIXe siècles)," in *Annales HSS* (1997): 369–91; "Pratiques de l'alliance en milieu de communautés familiales (Bourbonnais, 1600–1750)," in Guy Brunet, Antoinette Fauve-Chamoux, and Michel Oris, eds., *Le choix du conjoint* (Lyon, 1998), 227–51; "Parenté et marché foncier à l'époque moderne: une réinterprétation," in *Annales HSS* (2001): 337–68; "La terre, la personne et le contrat: exploitation et associations familiales en Bourbonnais (XVIIe–XVIIIe siècles), in *Revue d'histoire moderne et contemporaine* (2003): 27–51.
21. Leonard Kasdan, "Family Structure, Migration and the Entrepreneur," in *Comparative Studies in Society and History* 7 (1965): 345–57.
22. Sigrid Khera, "An Austrian Peasant Village under Rural Industrialization," in *Behavior Science Notes* 7 (1972): 29–36.
23. Markovits, *Global World of Indian Merchants*.
24. Anne K. Bang, *Sufis and Scholars of the Sea: Family Networks in East Africa, 1860–1925* (London, 2003), 12, discusses the importance of genealogy and descent. She develops an interesting discussion of the culture of migration (23). Going overseas became a natural option. At each stop on the migration route, families were crucial for support (61). "In the pre-national world of the Indian Ocean, a ramī *sāda* identity remained stable through several mechanisms. One was the rules applied to marriage, another was the status ascribed to them by other Islamic peoples. This identity was genealogical in origin, and was maintained as a tight-knit, trans-oceanic network of individuals linked together by blood and common experiences" (198).
25. See the articles in Bryceson and Vuorela, eds., *Transnational Family*.
26. Markovits, *Global World of Indian Merchants*, 25.
27. Huibert Schiff, "Jewish Bankers 1850–1914: Internationalization along Ethnic Lines," in McCabe, Harlaftis, and Minoglu, eds., *Diaspora Entrepreneurial Networks*, 191–216, here 194. He emphasizes bankers as members of extended families with far-reaching international contacts. Trust was based most powerfully on kinship re-

lations (196). Starting up a banking house abroad began with extensive kinship network (202). Intermarriage was an important strategy to create trust.

28. The pioneering work has been done by Gérard Delille in two important studies: *Famille et propriété dans le royaume de Naples (XVe–XIXe siècle)* (Rome, 1985); *Maire et le prieur: pouvoir central et pouvoir local en Méditerranée occidentale, XVe–XVIIIe siècle* (Paris, 2003).
29. The argument here is taken from Sabean, *Kinship in Neckarhausen*, 451.
30. Lynn Hunt, *The Family Romance of the French Revolution* (London, 1992).
31. Donna R. Gabaccia and Fraser M. Ottanelli, "Introduction," in Donna R. Gabaccia and Fraser M. Ottanelli, eds., *Italian Workers of the World Labor Migration and the Formation of Multiethnic States* (Urbana, IL, 2001), 1–17. They discuss the thesis of transnational migrants being "harbingers of nation-states in decline" but point to the central importance of migration as nationalism was being constructed (4).
32. Ulla Vuorela, "Transnational Families: Imagined and Real Communities," in Bryceson and Vuorala, eds., *Transnational Family*, 63–82. "While some might see transnational family loyalties over-riding the individual's sense of loyalty to the nation, in fact it is national loyalties that may get in the way of family loyalties." Mary Chamberlain, *Narratives of Exile and Return* (New Brunswick, NJ, 1997), 29: "International migrants are by definition international people with allegiances and loyalties which transcend the nation-state."
33. The issue of the powerful central woman who keeps kin in contact with each other and who manages relationships is dealt with in Deborah Bryceson, "Europe's Transnational Families and Migration: Past and Present," in Bryceson and Vuorela, eds., *Transnational Family*, 31–57. She discusses a Moroccan family in the Netherlands. A central figure to the extended family is Fatima, whose "determination and force of personality have made her a focal point for extended family network activity." She also points to family gatherings and feasts.
34. She also raises the issue of whether the international family is inimical to the nation. On this see also Bryceson and Vuorela, "Transnational Families," 9. They pose the question of whether transnational families are contradictory to national feeling, a subversive threat to coherence of national state.
35. Chamberlain, *Narratives*.
36. Chamberlain, *Narratives*; Khater, *Inventing Home*.
37. See, for example, the recent study by Francesca Trivellato, *The Familiarity of Strangers: The Sephardic Diaspora, Livorno, and Cross-Cultural Trade in the Early Modern Period* (New Haven, CT, 2009).

Chapter 1

The Historical Emergence and Massification of International Families in Europe and Its Diaspora

Jose C. Moya

Today international families can be easily defined as those with members in more than one of the 192 nation-states that presently claim every inch of land on the planet.[1] But despite their present omnipresence, nation-states are a relatively recent phenomenon. Few scholars would date it farther than five centuries ago. Some argue that even in Western Europe, nations—as social, economic, and cultural units rather than simply administrative ones—emerged only within the last two centuries.[2]

In the rest of the world, nation-states appeared, even as administrative units, after 1800. No single decade since then has failed to witness the birth of at least one of these polities. But the creation of these peculiarly modern forms of organizing and delimiting physical space has concentrated in four temporal booms that coincided with the end of more expansive imperial entities. The first rose from the ashes of the Iberian dominions in the Americas between 1810 and 1824; the second from the ruins of the Austro-Hungarian, Russian, and Ottoman empires after World War I; the third followed the disintegration of European overseas empires after World War II; and the fourth sprung in the 1990s from the Communist carcass of what few now remember used to be the "Second World."

By present definition, then, transnational families have existed at most for the last five centuries. Those five centuries account for merely the last tenth of human history, if we use the traditional narrow definition of the term as the period since the invention of writing and the appearance of cities, or for the last one-third of 1 percent if we define human history broadly as the human past.

This definition of transnational families, however, centers on the political component: nation-states and transnationality. The family in and of itself, as a social unit if not a cultural concept, is actually older than humans insofar as it predates *Homo sapiens.* And so is migration, the other element that makes transterritorial families possible. After all, early hominids, *Homo erectus* among them, had migrated out of their African homeland to places as far apart as Georgia and China more than a million years before the appearance of anatomically modern humans or *Homo sapiens* about 150,000 years ago.

Early *Homo sapiens* families seem also to have had already the three basic traits that characterize families today: pair-bonding or semimonogamous unions (the result in part of our altricial nature); alloparenting (the participation of individuals other than the biological parents in the raising of children); and the most complex kinship webs in the animal kingdom. This triptych has continued to form the basic family organization for the vast mass of humanity. From the perspective of the species, any other arrangement, from nannies to harems, have been—and can only be—costly, unsustainable extravagances for the few.

The Paleolithic: Cross-communality as Biological Necessity

Early *Homo sapiens* may have also had what could be considered the fourth peculiar trait of human families: cross-communality, the earliest version of transnationality. Historian Patrick Manning has identified cross-community movements as unique to *Homo sapiens* and dated the practice to our species earliest migrations 100,000 years ago.[3] Cross-community movement, however, is not really exclusive to humans. Many other animals leave their natal group and join others. But they do not keep contact with their old group. This is what is uniquely human: cross-community families as opposed to simply cross-community migration. The latter may not have been intense in the Paleolithic, when groups had comparable resources and technological levels, which provided few incentives for individual or families to move from one to the other.

Significant cross-community movement, however, had to exist during the Paleolithic out of biological necessity. The size of hunter-gatherer bands varied between 25 and 500 depending on the carrying capacity of the land, and the minimum size for a self-sustaining population has been estimated at 475.[4] This means that all but the largest needed to interact with other bands for breeding purposes. Theoretically, cross-community mobility alone could have accomplished the task. But it is unlikely that all movers cut relations with their groups of origin. Mere chances made this an unlikely outcome. A band at the smaller end of the spectrum had to interact with nineteen others to form a sustainable mating network. It would have been difficult for "foreigners" in all twenty bands to have been isolated from their natal groups. Ethnographies of nomadic hunter-gatherer groups in the first half of the twentieth century before they had any contact with modern society can illuminate this aspect of the Paleolithic past. These studies have shown average extratribal marriage rates of 15 percent, the rarity of abduction as most unions were based on exchange and consensus, and the prevalence of some connection between in-migrants and their original family.[5]

The Neolithic: Cross-communality as Response to Sociogeographic Inequality

The advent of agriculture provided the first impetus to cross-community movement beyond reproductive sustainability. Agriculture, animal husbandry, sedentariness, and a division of labor developed at uneven temporal rates in different places. This change generated the sine qua non condition for significant cross-community movement: inequality between regions or sociospatial entities. These inequalities created (1) incentives for individuals and families to move from less to more endowed regions, what social scientists would call *push and pull factors;* and (2) the possibility of conquest and slavery.

Evidence for cross-community movement during the Neolithic was, until recently, indirect. It came mainly from archeological findings of similar practices and materials (such as agriculture itself, seeds, burial types, and artifacts) in different sites. These similarities, however, could have originated from independent innovation rather than diffusion or from sporadic contact rather than cross-community movements.

A recent methodological breakthrough in paleontology based on strontium isotope analysis of human skeletal remains is now providing increasing direct physical evidence not only of the existence but also of the level of Neolithic cross-community movement in Europe.[6] A study of a 7,000-year-old mass grave in southern Germany found that a quarter of the individuals were born outside the zone and likely outside the Linearbandkeramik cultural area, a striking level of mobility for the Early Neolithic.[7] A similar study of various 4,500-year-old sites in Central Europe during the Bell Beaker period that marks the transition between the Neolithic and Bronze Age indicates an even higher level of mobility. Fifty-one of the eighty-one individuals analyzed had moved during their lifetime.[8] Another study of the same period in the Corded Ware region of Northeastern Europe added an analysis of autosomal, mitochondrial, and Y-chromosomal markers, providing not only the oldest molecular genetic evidence of a nuclear family but also establishing that males and children came from different regions from females.[9] This evidence indicates that exogamy, and in this case patrilocality, acted as a mechanism for early cross-community mobility.

Strontium and DNA analysis cannot determine, so far, if outsiders in a particular community kept contact with their families in their birthplaces or elsewhere. But the prevalence of significant levels of transcommunal migration and examples from modern agricultural populations indicate the existence of transcommunal families not simply in the sense of geographically dispersed people who are related by blood but also in terms of their continuing connection.

Metals, Empires, and the Birth of Transregional Families

Direct evidence in historical annals for the existence of transregional—as opposed to just transcommunal—families first appears for the era of metal technology and empires. Extratribal marriages in the Stone Age took place with individuals from adjacent or nearby groups. This type of mobility has continued into the twentieth-first century. But a new type appeared with the dramatic increase in group inequality at the turn of the second millennium BCE: families that were both dispersed beyond nearby communities and connected.

Some of the earliest written evidence for this new phenomenon can be found in the Torah. One case is the story of Joseph, who is sold into slavery by his jealous brothers, taken to Egypt where he becomes powerful by interpreting the dreams of the pharaoh, later encounters his poor brothers in Egypt, forgives them, and helps the rest of the family settle there (Genesis 37–50). The story, usually dated to the Hyksos occupation of Egypt (1674–1567 BCE), can be interpreted as one of the first in what would become a genre: the tale about the successful pioneer in the migration chain, who makes good (not necessarily by interpreting dreams) and brings some of the rest of the family over. An ancient Egyptian fresco at the Bijbels Museum in Amsterdam showing Hebrews as free migrants rather than slaves supports the notion that the story of Joseph, although it was later turned into a tale of group oppression and liberation, was originally about a "transnational" family. The fact that Joseph and his father Jacob were embalmed (in the Egyptian usage) rather than buried (as Hebrews would do) further suggests a process of volitional assimilation. Archeological evidence supports this interpretation. More than half a century ago, D. E. Derry's statistical analysis of skulls and anatomical remains showed a significant presence of foreigners (probably from Mesopotamia) in Pre- and Early Dynastic Egypt. The timing and temporal dispersion of the findings suggested not an abrupt invasion but a gradually increasing influx of itinerant merchants and craftsmen, precisely the type of migrants likely to form and maintain transcommunal families.[10]

The story of the Tower of Babel (Genesis 11:9), in which God punishes human arrogance by confounding the tongues of the people in Babylonia and dispersing them throughout the world, is purely mythical in some respects but telling in others. As an account of the emergence of linguistic diversity and global migration, it does not hold any water. Both processes obviously did not appear suddenly three thousand years ago, fifty miles south of Baghdad, but slowly some sixty thousand to seventy thousand years before. The tale, however, supports the archeological, linguistic, and historical evidence on the existence of multiethnic and multilingual immigrant labor forces in Mesopotamian cities. And it would have been unlikely if all of these multilingual immigrants kept no relation with the families they left behind.

Mediterranean Maritime Migration and the Extension of Transregionality

Maritime transportation in the Mediterranean during the first millennium BCE lengthened the average distance of migrations and added a new form of transregional family: those that transcended territorial contiguity. Movement between adjacent communities continued and so did exogamy as a mating mechanism, since most population centers continued to be too small to be reproductively sustainable. But we also find now transterritorial families loci that are not contiguous or even reachable by land. These could be described as the antecedent of the international, transoceanic families of the early modern period.

To what degree transregional families characterized the movements of classical antiquity is not clear. Greek diasporic settlements were not colonies in the commonly understood sense of the term. They were not really organized migrations orchestrated by a particular state but movements of disposed groups seeking land elsewhere.[11] One could say the same about Roman private colonization, which—despite the greater visibility of official colonization in the historiography—was the most widespread form of settlement. Group migration was common in all these movements.[12] This means that clans were more likely to either stay or depart rather than split, diminishing the occurrence of transregional families. Since colonization involved the wholesale transplanting of the group's culture, it is also difficult to speak of transnational families at least in the early generations. Were the Spanish-born Seneca, Hadrian, and Trajan part of transnational families or Roman provincials moving to the capital? When around 50 CE Seneca observed that *ubicunque vicit, Romanus habitat* (wherever he conquers, the Roman lives) he clearly included himself among these omnipresent Romans.

It is likely, however, that eventually the cultural difference between the colonies and the metropole became wide enough to create something akin to transnational families, as it would happen later between, say, Great Britain and Australia. Moreover, an important impetus for Greek colonization was the lack of primogeniture rights.[13] This means that colonization could not have taken only the form of entire group or clan transplantation. Particularly in the islands and other areas with limited agricultural land, at least some migration had to involve sons who were either dissatisfied with the size of their inherited parcels, were bought out by other siblings, or left as part of a family strategy to preserve larger estates. Those individuals would form, by definition, transterritorial families. And the copious evidence about the persistence of contact between colonies and metropoles suggests that these were transregional families not only in the sense of dispersion but also in the more meaningful criterion of connection. Similarly, a recent textual and archeological study of archaic Greeks in the Levantine coast argues that the early arrivals were mercenaries driven out of their homeland, a group that was not likely to keep in touch with their families back home.[14] But the same study also suggests that some eventually returned and that Greek merchants arrived in the ensuing decades. So although the original Greek presence may not have been favorable for the formation of transregional families, it eventually created more propitious conditions for this process. (This pattern in which official recruitment eventually leads to kinship-based migration would later surface in countless cases from East Indian coolies in the British West Indies to Turkish *Gastarbeiter* in Germany).

In the Roman case, the metropole, rather than the colonies of settlement, offers a different example of transnational families. We do not usually think of classical Rome as a city of immigrants, but it was.[15] Greeks were so numerous that they became a stereotype, the *Graeculi* or "little Greeks" who would do anything for a buck and became a familiar site on Roman streets and popular humor. Some fifty thousand Jews accounted for about 5 percent of the city's population circa 100 CE. Egyptians and Mesopotamians, from the lands of "ancient wisdom," provided a disproportionate number of the city's physicians, astrologers, and soothsayers. Many of its bookmakers and binders came from Alexandria and its street musicians from Syria. The immigrant presence may have been even greater in the maritime cities of the empire. At least, Cicero complained that the corrupting influx of foreign tongues and morals was greater there.[16] It is true that probably the majority arrived there as slaves. But many others did not. And manumission was so common that even among those who did, connections with their families back home were likely to emerge eventually. So although we have limited direct evidence, most immigrants in Rome and the maritime cities of the empire probably formed part of transregional families that kept some contact, rather than living in total isolation from their homelands. This also seems to have been the case for Norse maritime migration towards the end of the first millennium.[17]

European Overseas Expansion and the Global Spread of International Families

European overseas expansion after 1400 amplified the phenomenon of international families and spread it geographically to an unprecedented degree. The settlements and trading stations of the pioneering Portuguese may have had relatively few settlers, but they spread along Atlantic islands, the Western and Eastern coast of Africa, the coasts of Arabia, India, Southeast Asia, Indonesia, and Brazil. Recruitment of new merchant-adventurers took place, to a large degree, through family connections.[18] The same was true of the posterior mercantile empire of the Dutch, including its Sephardic community. The latter formed, as Jonathan Israel aptly put it, a series of diasporas within the diasporas of European maritime empires and kinship-linked mercantile networks that stretched from the Netherlands and the Ottoman Near East, through the Mediterranean and the Maghreb, to the Antilles, South America, and North America.[19] The 200,000 or so Huguenots who left France for England, British North America, Switzerland, the Netherlands, Brandenburg-Prussia, Ireland, Scandinavia, Quebec, and South Africa provide the other extreme example of international families during the early modern period.[20] The fact that, despite the entrenched image of a sudden exodus from persecution, these people actually moved over a period stretching more than a century increased the importance of kinship-based migration.

Family migration to the Americas during the colonial period became a common mode only in a few regions such as New England, Pennsylvania, Cuba, Southern Brazil (in the case of Azoreans), and Puebla—a particularly Spanish area in Mexico. But family migration and the internationalization of families are not synonymous. Indeed, the former can diminish the latter. If too many entire families migrate from a given microregion or religious group, it will weaken connections with the area of origin. For example, linkages between Massachusetts Puritans and their English hometowns—and thus the phenomenon of international families—were probably weaker after the "Great Migration" of the 1630s than those between the conquistadors of Peru and their Extremaduran hometowns had been a century earlier.[21] Neither did these international families require a relatively even migration sex ratio.

To begin with, the female-to-male ratio of settled immigrant communities is normally higher than that of the migration inflow itself because women are less likely to return than men. Equally significant, what appear in statistics as single men are actually sons, brothers, husbands—that is, members of international families. Their connection with their families back home did not break by simply crossing the ocean. On the contrary, it was precisely those transatlantic family connections that brought them across the "pond." Only about one-fourth of the million or so English migrants who came to the New World during the colonial period were women.[22] For the similar number of Spaniards who came to the Indies, the equivalent proportion was one-fifth; and for the Portuguese it was less than 15 percent.[23] But that was high enough for biological and cultural reproduction. Ida Altman and David Studnicki-Gizbert have shown how Spaniards in the New World and the Portuguese in the Americas and Seville tended to marry the locally born daughters of previous arrivals from the same hometown.[24] The recruitment of Iberian "nephews"—more often than not the sons of a sister but also more distantly related younger kin—by Spanish and Portuguese merchants in the American colonies (and in the imperial entrepôts of Seville and later Cadiz) became such a common mode of migration that it turned into a stereotype and a theater stock character.[25] Many of these "nephews" would marry their American-born "cousins."

The Nineteenth-Century Massification of International Families

Two apparently contradictory processes accelerated the internationalization of families during the long nineteenth century: a dramatic increase in nation-states and political boundaries, on the one hand, and the fast growth of globalization and long-distance migrations and connections in general, on the other. The first process was a Euro-American phenomenon. Of the forty-eight countries founded between the late eighteenth century and the end of World War I, twenty-one came to life in Europe and an equal number in the Americas, with only four surfacing in Asia and Australasia and two in Africa. At times this process created international families by simply delineating new international borders. Many families in, say, Southern California and Baja California or Central European Galicia became international not because any of its members crossed a national border but because newly drawn national borders crossed or recrossed the territories where they were living. But moving, crossing borders and oceans became a much more important mass producer of international families.

Moving was not as Euro-American a phenomenon as nation-state creation. Between the middle of the nineteenth century and the world depression of 1930, five million Japanese, sixteen million southern Chinese, and twenty-six million Indians left their birthplaces.[26] Asian emigration, however, was not only somewhat smaller than the transatlantic exodus out of Europe but it was also much less distant, and less transcontinental, transoceanic, and international. Less than one-tenth of Asian emigration crossed the Pacific or Indian Oceans. Almost the entire Indian outflow headed to other English colonies, and over nine-tenths moved to nearby Burma, Ceylon, and Malaysia. A similar proportion of southern Chinese headed for nearby Southeast Asia. Even more relevant for the formation of international families, Asian emigration was overwhelmingly (95 percent plus) male while European emigration was more even in its sex ratio (about 60 percent male).

These global waves, and particularly the one across the Atlantic, were unprecedented in human history in their volume, average distance, and temporal concentration. During three centuries of colonial rule, between 1500 and 1800, less than three million Europeans had arrived in the New World. More people had forcibly come to the Americas from Africa (ten million) than from Europe before 1850. Over the next eight decades, some fifty million Europeans arrived. Indeed, more entered the New World in just the three years preceding World War I than had done so in the three centuries preceding 1800.

Those unprecedented movements created an unprecedented situation: international families as a mass phenomenon. The closest thing to mass long-distance migration before 1850 had been the Sub-Saharan African slave trade to the New World and to North Africa and the Middle East. But those movements had created actual rather than functional international families insofar as transplanted African slaves could not keep in touch with their families in Africa or with enslaved kin in other destinations. International families had thus been limited to the aristocracy, mercantile classes, imperial bureaucrats, and colonial settlers. The nineteenth century democratized the experience. By the early twentieth century, international families around the world numbered not in the thousands or even millions but in the scores of millions, and the vast majority were peasants and proletarians.

Using evidence from my own work on European immigration to Argentina and from the secondary literature, I will outline now some of the key aspects of this unprecedented phenomenon.[27] To begin with, international families were not only the outcome of mass international migrations but they also provided the basic mechanisms that made those migrations possible. It is true that broader elements such as demographic growth, global trade, and transportation fueled the movement. Indeed, mass migration formed part of other processes of massification (of human reproduction, production, transportation and communication, trade and financial flows, consumption and aspirations) that forged the modern world. It is also true that many people migrated through nonprimary mechanisms of recruitment—such as military drafts, imperial bureaucracies, churches, political parties or groups, *padroni* (employment agents), and labor recruiters for local governments, plantations, and businesses. But the vast majority moved through the sponsorship and assistance of family members even in cases in which the flow had originated in more formal or bureaucratic recruitments.

Internal, shorter-distance migrations and the transcommunal family connections they created promoted the diffusion of information in the regions of origin that made overseas migration possible. The practice of international migration normally appeared first in specific spots along channels of communication and trade, such as ports and railroad connections, and spread to hinterlands in a manner resembling an ink spot on a paper. The spot, however, would often leap to farther regions rather than spreading evenly on the map because people residing there had learned of opportunities overseas from relatives who lived in zones of emigration. This process would form new, and seemingly isolated, foci of overseas emigration from which the behavior would then spread, speeding this way the geographical diffusion of the behavior.

This kinship-based diffusion of information and behaviors carried through family letters and photographs, local tales, and word of mouth had a multiplying effect. So-called chain migration in reality resembled more webs or unending branches than a chain: links not simply attached sequentially to one another but joined in every direction. Forward, they connected to younger relatives and new generations, something that enhanced the process's temporal dimension. Laterally, they branched out to increasingly distant relatives, to "cousins of cousins of cousins," who would in turn become "trunks" and ramify even further. And as mentioned above, the fact that emigrants overseas often had relatives in villages or towns other than their native ones meant that forward and lateral branching also served to disseminate emigration geographically in the country—or continent for that matter—of origin. This tendency of network-based emigration to branch out allowed the process to spread and multiply with self-generating force. Emigration developed an autonomous, self-perpetuating dynamic, which explains why people kept on arriving during the host country's worst economic depressions or after wages had actually dropped lower than in the home country. This pattern also explains the recurrent appearance of the metaphor "emigration fever" anywhere from Scotland to Hungary and Finland to Spain. The habit of migrating overseas not only spread geographically in the country of origin in a form resembling that of communicable diseases, but it also possessed the psychological contagiousness that the term *fever* implies.

Links between international families could also survive during long periods when direct contact through immigration or return was not possible due to external limitations such as wars, disruption of transportation, or exit and entry restrictive policies, and then renovate the migration flow when the external limitations disappear. The renovation of Spanish emigration to the Americas half a century after the wars of independence in the colonies, or of post–World War II European migration to the United States after a two- to three-decade hiatus, offer some examples of this "dormant chain" phenomenon. How long these international family connections could survive without direct contact, however, was strongly correlated to the economic success of the immigrant members of the family.

Socioeconomic inequality relates to emigration in various other ways. Unlike short-distance internal movements, which require few resources and draw people from families who are on average poorer than those who do not move, long-distance international migration is an expensive enterprise that requires various sorts of capital (information, connections, money) and draws people from families who are better off and more educated than those who stay behind. This is particularly true during the early stages of the flow when money for the passage can only come from family savings or loans (which normally require property to mortgage). Remittances and prepaid passages from relatives overseas eventually make it affordable for larger numbers of people to leave. But even at its most inclusive, the flow is not representative of the population of origin. Those who leave continue to be of higher socioeconomic background than those who stay. Other mechanisms reproduced social inequalities through kinship-based migration.

One such mechanism is that the success of emigrants in their destination was strongly related to the sociocultural (as opposed to just economic) capital of their families back home. Data that I collected to link immigrants residing in Buenos Aires during the early 1900s and their parents in seven Spanish localities illuminate the workings of this transatlantic and intergenerational persistence. To begin with, family property back home had no effect on the economic success of the immigrants at destination because it did not represent transferable capital. The descendants of peasant-proprietors in Spain actually appeared more concentrated in low-skilled occupations in Buenos Aires than the descendants of landless rural laborers. Parental occupational skills, on the other hand, were highly transferable. If at the time of the immigrant's birth his or her father had worked in a white-collar occupation in Spain, the immigrant's chances of doing the same in Buenos Aires came close to a sure bet (95 percent); if the father had worked in a manual occupation, they merely surpassed a coin's toss (56 percent).[28] The children of professionals accounted for only 5 percent of the total sample of Spanish immigrants and for 55 percent of the professionals in the sample.

Urban or semiurban ancestry, as a proxy for transferable cultural capital, had a strong impact on the socioeconomic status of the immigrants in their host city. The progeny of low-skilled laborers from towns or cities were only one-fourth as likely to work in low-skilled jobs as the progeny of the peasantry. Matrilineal urbanism appeared particularly relevant. The odds of being stuck in a menial job in Buenos Aires were 1 in 10 if the immigrant's mother had been born in a city of over 20,000 inhabitants; 1 in 5 if a town of 2,000 to 20,000 inhabitants was her birthplace; and 1 in 3 if she was born in the countryside. Even among immigrants of otherwise similar conditions, say of urban birth themselves and working-class origins, those with city-born mothers continued to be significantly less likely to cluster on the lower end of the occupational spectrum. Paternal literacy played a similar role. Among immigrants of urban birth, 8 of the 47 whose fathers signed their birth certificates became business owners in Buenos Aires; none of the 21 whose fathers scratched an *X* did.

These continuities indicate that we find at a lower socioeconomic level the same ability of upper-middle-class parents to transfer habits to their children that go beyond formal education and that reproduce inequalities, as Pierre Bourdieu noticed, even in relatively meritocratic settings and even in the putative classless societies of Communist Eastern Europe.[29] The advantages these mechanisms provide are particularly powerful precisely because they are neither formal nor evident. They relate to familiarity and comfort with implicit codes, naturalized habits and expectations, manners and mannerism.

These imperceptible forms of cultural capital were reinforced by an equally indiscernible form of social capital. Immigrants whose extended families in Buenos Aires were more prosperous fared better than those who belonged to less successful immigrant networks even if their level of skills, ages, gender, and length of residence in the new country were identical. Their "invisible skill" lay in who, rather than what, they knew.

These mechanisms created a self-reproducing cycle. Because emigrating required significant resources, those who left belonged to better-off families than those who stayed behind. Remittances from those overseas would further enrich those families. Even if remittances democratized the flow by making it possible for a larger number of people to leave, the trickle-down effect tended to be restricted to poorer members of better-off families. Moreover, because among the emigrants those with higher family cultural capital back home and the resulting higher social capital at destination were more successful economically, they could also send more money to their families, strengthening the gap.

Emigration, however, did not simply preserve preexisting inequalities. Immigrants may have seemed to be following in their parents' footsteps despite crossing an ocean. But heredity—as stored environment—was far from an iron law and surely less binding in the relatively fluid social structures of the Americas than in the European countries of origin. Many children of humble peasants and workers became magnates on the other side of the pond. The Atlantic's waves no doubt eroded ancestral shackles. Even in the more common cases of social persistence, the exodus provided an opportunity for middling families with little property but some cultural capital to narrow the gap between them and local landowning elites, who rarely emigrated. The children of school teachers, printers, petty merchants, store clerks, literate tailors, and similar folk used their visible and less-visible skills to prosper overseas and made their families prosper back home. In many of the less developed regions of Europe, local middle classes had their origins in overseas emigration.

The international, long-distance outflow then did not simply reproduce preexisting structures. It produced new ones based not on the traditional inequality between the few and the many but on the modern inequality between the many and the many, between the top third and the bottom third of the population—the type of disparities that still mark developed societies in the twenty-first century. Inequalities between places had fueled cross-community migration since the Neolithic. Millennia later, transnational families ended up restructuring inequality within groups.

Mass international migration also exhibits patterns in terms of who within the family leaves. In terms of land tenure and inheritance systems, those areas with some form of primogeniture and midsized farms tended to send younger sons and, later, daughters. Areas with partible inheritance and *minifundia* sent large numbers of fathers. These material conditions, however, eventually forged cultural norms, such as ideals of domesticity, which seem to have become semi-independent variables. This seems to be the only explanation for why propertied fathers from zones of partible inheritance were more likely to emigrate than landless fathers from areas of primogeniture. Rural areas with widespread land ownership, such as Galicia and the Basque country in Spain, Ireland, and south-central Sweden not only sent higher proportions of young, single women overseas at an earlier stage of the emigration stream, but these women were also more prone to work in domestic service than women from areas of latifundia (such as southern Spain and the Italian *mezzogiorno*) or nonpeasants (such as Ashkenazi Jews, and Sephardic, Armenian, Greek, and Lebanese middlemen minorities in the Ottoman empire).[30]

The sex ratio of migratory currents was, and continues to be, conditioned by three other principal and locally specific factors besides inheritance and land-tenure patterns. Government policies—such as asylum laws, family-reunification preferences in the issuing of visas, and guest-worker programs—are rarely gender neutral. The first two examples tend to favor women and the third, men. The second factor relates to labor demand and the sexual division of work at destination. In some of these cases, like mining or cutting sugar cane, the division was actually sexual in that it was based on physical considerations. In most cases, from general agricultural and factory work to nursing and the domestic service, it reflected gendered definitions that shifted temporally and geographically.[31] The third factor relates to family structures at origin.

Patrilocality, polygyny, early and high rates of marriage, and extended families promote short-distance female mobility but tend to curb women's participation in long-distance migration. Matrilocality, late and low rates of marriage, and high rates of informal unions, separation, divorce, widowhood, and female-headed households have the opposite effect on long-distance mobility.

The most consistent factor affecting sex ratios in migration, however, relates not to local specificities but to intrinsic aspects of the process itself. Countless psychological and anthropological studies have shown that, cross-culturally, men are on average more prone to undertake risky endeavors than women. This includes behaviors ranging from crime and war to investing and sports. It also applies to migrating. Women's presence at the start of migrations to places considered remote and dangerous is only significant in cases—such as the Mormon westward journey in the United States or the Boer "Great Trek" in South Africa—where the risk is lowered by moving in large family groups. Women's participation is also high in cases, such as refugee flows, where the risk of staying surpasses that of leaving.

In most other cases, however, the female proportion increases as the migration flow from a specific area or social network becomes denser and older, and it reaches a peak during the declining phase of the migration growth curve, that is, towards the temporal end of the stream, when women often outnumber men. This upward trend is accomplished through two principal mechanisms, and both are grounded on the ties of international families. The first is the movement of married and older women (such as mothers or mothers- and sisters-in-law) and children coming to join their husbands and immediate families. The other is the migration of single young women coming to join a wider spectrum of kin and friends. The first process usually precedes the second, particularly before the last wave of post-1960s global migration, and in the case of remote destinations. These destinations become "safer" mainly through the familiarity and sense of security that international family networks provide rather than due to any structural changes in the host society itself. Indeed, women's participation in many migratory flows has increased precisely at a time when the destinations (as measured by crime and homicide rates) were becoming more dangerous.

Conclusion

Ritual gripes against teleologies have tended to obscure antecedents, directionality, and pattern in historical processes. International families—and for that matter, nations—did not leap into the world stage two or five (or even thirty) centuries ago out of nowhere. They are rooted in the history of our species, and that history is much longer than nations or "civilization." International families have a genealogy. They have antecedents in the cross-communal movements and families of the Paleolithic, when such arrangements were a reproductive necessity. This type of short-distance movement through exogamy continues—even across national boundaries—among many within the half of the world's population that live in rural areas.[32] Transregional families as a response to geographical inequalities in resources and opportunities began, at least, in the Neolithic and developed their basic strategies of assistance and moving in the metal age. The next three thousand years witnessed the appearance of the noncontiguous transregionality, globalization, and massification (in that order) of international families. The specific local stories may have been endless. But they do fit in a general historical pattern, one with no known design, purpose, or goal, but a pattern nevertheless.

Notes

1. *Inter-* and *transnational* are used here in an interchangeable or transposable manner since the connections of families residing in more than one country could be both "between or among" and "beyond and above" the national. The latter end of the spectrum will likely characterize situations where national boundaries are mainly nominal, e.g., ethnically homogenous regions that transverse the borders of countries with weak national identities and weak or disinterested states. The stronger that national identities and the state's presence and control are, the less able dispersed families would be to transcend the national realm and the closer the situation would be to other end of the spectrum.
2. The classic example is Eugene Weber, *Peasants into Frenchmen: The Modernization of Rural France, 1870–1914* (Stanford, CA, 1976) for what was supposed to be the prototypically precocious nation-state. Those who challenge Weber's chronology date the emergence of the French nation to no earlier than the late seventeenth century. See David A. Bell, *The Cult of the Nation in France: Inventing Nationalism, 1680–1800* (Cambridge, MA, 2001).
3. Patrick Manning, *Migration in World History* (New York, 2005), 6–10.
4. H. Martin Wobst, "Boundary Conditions for Paleolithic Social Systems: A Sociological Approach," *American Antiquity* 39 (1974): 147–78.
5. Norman B. Tindale, "Tribal and Intertribal Marriage Among the Australian Aborigines," *Human Biology* 25 (1953): 169–90.
6. The method analyzes a series of connected facts. The amount of elemental strontium and its isotopic ratios vary by rock types and thus identify local ecologies. These atoms move through diet and the food chain (groundwater, plants, and herbivores) from the bedrock into skeletal tissue, where humans and other animals deposit 99 percent of digested strontium. While bone changes continually through life, teeth

form in childhood and do not change. Thus a comparison of the strontium in bones and in tooth enamel can tell if an individual has moved between different geological areas or not. And a comparison of the strontium in the tooth enamel and that of the burial site can tell if the individual was not born in the geological area where he or she died.

7. T. Douglas Price, Joachim Wahl, and R. Alexander Bentley, "Isotopic Evidence for Mobility and Group Organization among Neolithic Farmers at Talheim, Germany, 5000 BC," *European Journal of Archaeology* 9 (2006): 259–84.
8. T. Douglas Price et al., "Strontium Isotopes and Prehistoric Human Migration: The Bell Beaker Period in Central Europe," *European Journal of Archaeology* 7 (2004): 9–40.
9. Wolfgang Haak et al., "Ancient DNA, Strontium Isotopes, and Osteological Analyses Shed Light on Social and Kinship Organization of the Later Stone Age," *Proceedings of the National Academy of Science of the United States of America* 105, no. 47 (2008): 18226–31.
10. D. E. Derry, "The Dynastic Race in Egypt," *Journal of Egyptian Archaeology* 42 (1956): 80–85.
11. Mary E. White, "Greek Colonization," *Journal of Economic History* 21 (1961): 443–54.
12. A. J. N. Wilson, *Emigration from Italy in the Republican Age of Rome* (Manchester, UK, 1966).
13. White, "Greek Colonization," 444–45.
14. Wolf-Dietrich Niemeier, "Archaic Greeks in the Orient: Textual and Archaeological Evidence," *Bulletin of the American Schools of Oriental Research* 322 (2001): 11–32.
15. David Noy, *Foreigners at Rome: Citizens and Strangers* (London, 2000) and George La Piana's classic *Foreign Groups in Rome during the First Centuries of the Empire* (Cambridge, MA, 1927).
16. Emily Gowers, "The Anatomy of Rome from Capitol to Cloaca," *Journal of Roman Studies* 85 (1995): 30.
17. Jenny Jochens, *Old Norse Images of Women* (Philadelphia, 1996), describes Norse migration as involving "entire tribes composed of men, women, children, animals and other possessions" (209). But other studies have questioned this traditional view, showing continuing contact between settlements and the areas of origin and the movement of individuals and families, not only entire tribes. See Jared Diamond, *Collapse: How Societies Choose to Fail or Succeed* (New York, 2005), chapters 6–8 for a summary of these studies.
18. Malyn Newitt, *A History of Portuguese Overseas Expansion, 1400–1668* (New York, 2005), 66–67, 151, 175, 194–96.
19. Jonathan I. Israel, *Diasporas Within a Diaspora: Jews, Crypto-Jews, and the World of Maritime Empires, 1540–1740* (Leiden, 2002).
20. Susanne Lachenicht, "Huguenot Immigrants and the Formation of National Identities, 1548–1787," *Historical Journal* 50 (2007): 309–31.
21. Ida Altman, *Emigrants and Society: Extremadura and Spanish America in the Sixteenth Century* (Berkeley, CA, 1989).
22. David Eltis and Stanley L. Engerman, "Was the Slave Trade Dominated by Men?," *Journal of Interdisciplinary History* 23 (1992): 237–57, give the following women-to-men ratios in the flows to the Americas (243): women represented 23 percent of indentured servants departing from England in the period 1654–99 and 10 percent in the period 1700–75; they counted 24 percent of indentured servants leaving Ireland between 1745 and 1773 and 33 percent of those leaving Germany between

1745 and 1831; finally, women were 37 percent of the nonindentured migrants from Britain in the years from 1773 to 1776.

23. Peter Boyd-Bowman, "Patterns of Spanish Emigration to the Indies until 1600," *Hispanic American Historical Review* 56 (1976): 580–604.
24. Altman, *Emigrants and Society*; and her *Transatlantic Ties in the Spanish Empire: Brihuega, Spain, and Puebla, Mexico, 1560–1620* (Stanford, CA, 2000). David Studnicki-Gizbert, *A Nation Upon the Ocean Sea: Portugal's Atlantic Diaspora and the Crisis of the Spanish Empire, 1492–1640* (New York, 2007).
25. Jose C. Moya, *Cousins and Strangers: Spanish Immigrants in Buenos Aires, 1850–1930* (Berkeley, CA, 1998), 258.
26. Adam McKeown, "Global Migrations, 1846–1940," *Journal of World History* 15 (2004): 156.
27. The following section draws mainly from Moya, *Cousins and Strangers,* chapters 1, 2, and 5; and "A Continent of Immigrants: Postcolonial Shifts in the Western Hemisphere," *Hispanic American Historical Review*, 86 (2006): 1–28.
28. The average odds were probably lower, since the sample is drawn from members of voluntary associations, that is, people who tended to be more concentrated in white-collar occupations than the overall immigrant population.
29. For one of Pierre Bourdieu's early discussion of the various forms of capital see "Avenir de classe et causalité du probable," *Revue française de sociologie* 15 (1974): 3–42.
30. Jose C. Moya, "Domestic Service in a Global Perspective: Gender, Migration, and Ethnic Niches," *Journal of Ethnic and Migration Studies* 33 (2007): 569, 571–72.
31. See ibid. for an example of a job that was feminized at very different rates in Europe, the Western Hemisphere, Africa, Australia, India, and Japan from the seventeenth to the twentieth century.
32. For an overview of the literature on short-distance exogamy and transcommunal families, see Rajni Palriwala and Patricia Uberoi, "Marriage and Migration in Asia: Gender Issues," *Indian Journal of Gender Studies* 12 (2005): v–xxix.

Part I

The Medieval and Early Modern Experience

Chapter 2

Mamluk and Ottoman Political Households

An Alternative Model of "Kinship" and "Family"

Gabriel Piterberg

The risk any generalization contains notwithstanding, it can be suggested that one of the most conspicuous features in the space stretching from the Indian subcontinent to Egypt in the period from 1100 to 1800 was the prevalence of the military patronage states, which were ruled by Turkic-speaking or Mongol-speaking elites and dynasties. One of the most consistent features of these states was the perpetual attempt to rule via a one-generation elite and thus to limit the scope of elites that have consequential roots in the ruled societies. This political organization gave birth to what is generally called the elite political household, which was the most basic structural unit of the military-administrative rulers of these states. This chapter will propose that within certain temporal and spatial confines, the elite political household can be seen as an alternative model to kinship in terms of social relations and as an alternative to the family in terms of sociopolitical structures. By *alternative,* I of course do not mean that the family and kinship as conventionally understood disappeared, but rather that the household became a conspicuous and consequential addition. This chapter is concerned with the

Mamluk Sultanate and the Ottoman Empire. The method of analysis will combine a structural characterization of the household with an examination of the role it played in politics. To avoid confusion, it should be clearly stated that the use of "household" in this chapter always refers to the elite political structures in the societies in question, not to households in the quotidian sense.

The Turco-Mongol origins of the political household is not certain, and the inextricable connection between modern scholarship and nationalism as well as Marc Bloch's pertinent warning against the risk of fetishizing origins make one wary of the theme of origins. With this cautionary note in mind, it might be said that in Eurasian nomadic societies, the power of the tribal elites was counterbalanced by the khan through the institution of *nöker*ship (*nöker* meaning a retainer or client). The *nökers* were free individuals recruited from nomadic groups, often defeated tribes, who were trained and sustained by the ruler. Serving as their master's bodyguards, the *nökers* were absolutely loyal to him. When such a leader was defeated and retreated deeply into the steppe to recuperate, he was not deserted by his *nökers,* who followed him in a well-rehearsed procedure. The steppe institution of *nöker*ship was implemented in both the Aqqoyunlu state in Persia and eastern Anatolia in the fourteenth and fifteenth centuries and the Tatar Khanate in the Crimea. In both cases, the *nökers* of the ruler's household constituted a pivotal element in the palace and central administration, and each of the prominent beys had his own group of *nökers.*[1]

It is not implausible that the underlying principle of *nöker*ship passed to the Mamluk Sultanate in Egypt and geographical Syria (1250–1517) and later to what Marshall Hodgson called the three gunpowder empires (which he deemed the perfection of the wider category of the military patronage state): the Ottoman, the Safavid in Iran, and the Mughal in Afghanistan and northern India.[2] The recruitment to servitude in the ruling household or the grandees' households also became the basic socioeconomic divide between members of households and state office-holders, on the one hand, and the surplus-producing, tax-paying strata, on the other. Let me now zoom in on the two entities with which this chapter is concerned, the Mamluks and the Ottomans, and begin by explaining the basic terminology. The terms used in these two states for household were *bayt* (Arabic) and *kapı* (Ottoman Turkish). *Bayt* in Arabic (and in Hebrew as well) means "house" or "home," while kapı in Turkish denotes "gate" (thus the literal meaning of the famous Ottoman palace, Topkapı, is "the canon's gate").

Although neither the Mamluk Sultanate nor the Ottoman Empire invented it or was the sole user of it, they nonetheless perfected the attempt to create a slave elite at the core of the household system of the military patronage state. The two central terms here were *mamluk* and *kapı kulları*. Despite the fact that the ruler and the elite of the Mamluk Sultanate came from Turkish-speaking peoples, its historical record was almost exclusively written in Arabic. The word *mamluk* is derived from the Semitic radical *mlk*. One group of words derived from this radical in Aramaic, Hebrew, and Arabic creates meanings associated with kingship and kingdom. In Arabic, however, there is another group of words that is associated with property. The word *mamluk* belongs in the latter group; it is a passive participle declined from *mlk*, and it literally means "one who is the property of [someone else]" or "one who is owned [by someone else]." *Kapı kulları* literally means in Ottoman Turkish "slaves of the gate," but contextually it should be rendered as "the sultan's servants." The Ottomans often used the shorthand *kul*, which is convenient for us too for the sake of brevity.

The political households were inextricably and, as I shall show in my conclusion, dialectically intertwined with the formation and later development of the state. Let me furnish two Ottoman examples to illustrate this point, one from the early formative period and the other from a period of adjustment to the sixteenth-century price revolution and its consequences in Eurasia (1550–1650).[3]

In his masterful study on early Ottoman historical writing and the formation of the Ottoman state in the fourteenth and fifteenth centuries, Cemal Kafadar draws attention to the crucial decades of the 1360s and 1370s. This was the period in which, during the reign of Murad I (1362–1389), the Ottoman household began to distinguish itself from the groups and clusters of other important frontier warlords (*gazis* in Ottoman Turkish); from the status of primus inter pares in relation to the other important *gazi* groupings, the Ottoman household slowly emerged as an autocratic source of authority and the locus of the state.[4]

In the late 1360s, the budding Ottoman entity lost control of Gallipoli, the point of passage between Asia Minor and southeast Europe, to Amedeo of Savoy. The chief *gazis* in Thrace sought to use this to enhance their autonomy from the Ottoman household. When Murad I regained Gallipoli in 1376, the status quo ante was altered at the advice of his chief ministers. First, the sultan was for the first time able to appoint powerful *gazis* as provincial governors of important frontier areas. In retrospect, this made the Ottoman household a locus from which authority emanated in the shape of appointments that were a source of income for their holders; at the same time, the frontier gradually ceased being a site for spoils to be had without acceptance of Ottoman suzerainty. Second, Murad I was able to impose a tax called *pencik*, or the fifth.

Levied at Gallipoli as the nexus between Ottoman Anatolia and Ottoman Thrace and overseen by an official from the sultan's household, the *pencik* stipulated that the first fifth, and perforce most qualitative, of the human booty belonged to the Ottoman household, and the rest could be divided among other powerful *gazis* and dignitaries. Again in retrospect, this can be seen as the starting point for the regularization of the Ottoman standing army and the Janissary corps in particular. More generally, it would make the Ottoman household irrevocably more powerful than the rest and, until mid-seventeenth century, coterminous with the state.

The link between the history of the political household and the state is demonstrated in a different way by Metin Kunt, in his study of the changes in the upper echelon of the Ottoman provincial administration in the period 1550–1650. What Kunt shows is the increasingly prevalent and favorable position among the ranks of the provincial governors of appointees coming from the central government, at the expense of those emerging from the ranks of the provincial administration, and especially among those appointed to the provincial governorships directly from the inner service (*enderun*) of the sultan's household. Of particular significance for the point I am trying to make is the way Kunt's research unfolded. He states at the outset of his book:

> This study developed as a by-product of my general research on the importance of households in the Ottoman polity. In Ottoman historiography there have been studies on the imperial palace—the sultan's household—and on the relationship between the palace and the government. However, not only the sultan but also the leading officials of the empire supported households, made up of their "inner" and "outer" retinues, needed to fulfill their official functions. The make-up of such households, their inter-relations, and their relations with the imperial palace and also with government offices have hitherto been neglected.[5]

To clarify this observation for the non-Ottomanist reader, since his study was based on the official documentation of the state, which acknowledged the political household but did not deem it an official institution, Kunt was led by his source material away from the household to a formal institution like the upper crust of the provincial administration; and yet, because of his initial interest, the household remained throughout his study an ever-present and irreducible unit of analysis.

Pertinent to the theme of this volume is the fact that political households were in their own way international, recruiting people (both females and males) from a wide variety of locales in Eurasia such as Venice, the Balkans, the Black Sea region, the Caucasus, Ukraine, and Russia. This geographical diversity created one of the main conflictual fault-lines within the Ottoman political class in the seventeenth century. Throughout that period there developed a cleavage along ethnic-regional (*cins* in Ottoman Turkish) lines between "westerners" and "easterners." Westerners in this context were those recruited to serve in households (the sultan's first and foremost, but by no means exclusively) from Albania and Bosnia, whereas the easterners were originally Abkhasians, Circassians, and Georgians. As the seventeenth century wore on, the westerners gained the upper hand, and a sort of Albanian-Bosnian alliance dominated the Ottoman establishment. The clearest manifestation of the westerners' ascendancy was the rise to power of the "dynasty" of Albanian grand vezirs, the Köprülüs, who monopolized that position in the second half of the seventeenth century.[6]

The Mamluk Household

Mamluks had been in the military service of rulers and warlords in the medieval Middle East well before the sultanate came into being. They were certainly conspicuous, indeed indispensable, in the short-lived entity that Saladin created in Egypt in the latter part of the twelfth century, namely, the Ayyubid state. The conjunction of the collapse of Ayyubid order, the ensuing interregnum in the 1250s, and the impending Mongol invasion of Syria (after Baghdad was sacked in 1258, though the sack was not as destructive as the one that occurred seven and a half centuries later) gave birth to the Mamluk Sultanate. This was a state in which the Mamluks not only constituted the ruling military elite, but also produced the ruler (the sultan) from among their ranks. The founding sultan was Baybars, the general who had defeated the Mongols in northern Palestine in 1260. Like almost all rulers of the Turco-Mongol polities before and after, the Mamluk sultans too prudently refrained from claiming the title of caliph, which was suffused with a religious pedigree for which their arrival in Islam was too recent. Most mamluks, including the sultans, were ethnically Kipchak Turks, from the northern Caucasus, until roughly 1400. Thereafter and until the sultanate's demise in 1517, they were mostly Circassians from the western Caucasus. With Cairo as its capital, the core territory of the sultanate comprised Egypt and geographical Syria.

An ideal-type sketch of a mamluk household would be the following. It consisted of two kinds of relations: vertical, between master and his mamluk slaves, as in private patron-client relations; and horizontal, among mamluks of the same cohort, that is, mamluks recruited and trained more or less at the same time. The collective noun that expressed the horizontal fraternity was *khushdashiyya*. Newly arrived mamluks were Islamized, acculturated, and, most importantly, trained as warriors on horseback through the system that produced apparently the finest cavalry in the Eurasian world. At the end of the training process, the mamluks were legally manumitted and became free Muslims. This rite of passage was done in pomp and ceremony, and the main features were the permission granted to the manumitted mamluks to grow a beard, to marry and have a family, and potentially to establish their own mamluk household in the future.

It is most interesting to point out the spillover in the sources of both the Mamluk and later the Ottoman period in Egypt of a kinship terminology to convey mamluk relations. Vertically, for instance, the master could not only be referred to as the "father" of his own mamluks, but also as the "grandfather" of the mamluks of his manumitted mamluks, if and when they established their households. Horizontally, mamluks of the same cohort could not only be "brothers," but also the one could be addressed as the "uncle" of his "brother's" mamluks. After manumission, what the master tried to do was to install his men in good positions in the state apparatus, most obviously the army, and through it in such functions as governors of provinces and subprovinces, and commanders of the pilgrimage to Mecca, since the two holy cities were under Mamluk sovereignty. Conflicts notwithstanding, the norm and custom dictated that mamluks should remain deferent and loyal to their master after manumission.[7]

The households, and certainly the big and powerful ones about which we know more, resided in palatial homes in the big cities, Cairo first and foremost. It was there that the mamluks were trained. In addition to mamluks and their barracks, however, the household residence also included the master's family quarters, in which dwelt his wife or consort (or wives and consorts), and their offspring. This cohabitation of mamluk and kinship relations within the household is most interesting. According to the logic that inheres in the concept of the military patronage state, especially after the state had grown out of its frontier stage and became sedentary, the expectation was to perpetuate a one-generation elite recruited from outside the ruled society in order to avoid the emergence of an aristocracy with long-standing vested interests in the ruled society and to refrain from creating consequential ties with the ruled society. Accordingly, the offspring of Mamluk elite's members were labeled *Awlād al-Nās*, literally "Children of the People." What the label signified was that a master's offspring through kinship were not eligible to join the elite, which ought to have included only a master's "offspring" through mamluk relations.

There is scholarly disagreement on the extent to which the concept and its articulation in reality were congruous.[8] There are certainly cases when wives or consorts were successful in having their sons inserted into the Mamluk elite by securing for them state positions that, in theory, were reserved for mamluks alone. The preponderance of mamluk relations, however, has its own evidence, the most compelling of which is, I think, the eventually unsuccessful attempts by sultans to create a dynasty, that is, a sultanate in which succession would be from father to son rather than from master to another manumitted mamluk. There were relatively few sultans who tried, and their attempts were never successful for more than a couple of generations at best. It should be noted that as conflict-ridden as these attempts were (and conflict was a staple of mamluk politics in general), the sultanate lasted stably for two and a half centuries. The failure to create a dynasty is indicative of the prevalence of mamluk relations. When a prominent individual ascended to the throne, his household automatically became the royal household and his mamluks became known as the royal mamluks, *al-mamalik al-sultaniyya* in Arabic. These royal mamluks formed the ruler's entourage and were his close confidants. They did not, however, feel obliged or emotionally attached to their master's sons. More often than not, the succession by an offspring meant that the royal mamluks withdrew their support, and the more ambitious among them considered themselves no less—indeed more—entitled to become a sultan than the son of their deceased master, the previous sultan.

To illustrate the prevalence of kinship within Mamluk society, I would like to employ a piece of evidence furnished by the most notable scholar of Egypt's military elite in the Ottoman period, Jane Hathaway. In recent research she has studied the cultural history of the two factions out of which emerged all the households in Ottoman Egypt in the seventeenth and eighteenth centuries. One of the main origin myths of these two factions identified by Hathaway goes back to the Ottoman conquest of Egypt and demise of the sultanate in 1517. The split into the two rival factions began, says the origin myth, when the two sons of a defeated high-ranking Mamluk officer named Sudun had a deadly quarrel before the examining eyes of the Ottoman sultan, Selim I.[9] The point is of course not the origin myth itself, but rather the fact that the two jousting individuals were biological brothers, not comrade-mamluks, as well as the biological sons of Sudun, not his mamluks. That such an apocryphal story could make sense and gain currency within the society in which it was disseminated strongly suggests that the sight of kinship relations within the military Mamluk elite was not inconceivable. It is very telling, in other words, that in a myth of origin, which goes back to a high-ranking Mamluk official and which is supposed to account for the foundation of political households based on patron-client (i.e., mamluk-like) relations, kinship in the shape of biological sons plays such a pivotal role. In terms of vertical relations, those vying for the right to succeed the Mamluk Sudun were not his own mamluks but his own sons, and horizontally, the sons were fighting each other, not two mamluks of the same cohort.

The Ottoman Household

After two decisive battles, one in northern Syria in 1516 and the other east of Cairo in 1517, the Ottoman sultan, Selim I, entered the Mamluk capital victoriously. Traditional Orientalist scholarship held that the appearance of elite political households in Ottoman Egypt as the basis for the province's military society was a revival of Mamluk institutions and traditions, a neo-Mamlukism of sorts. The proponents of this interpretation were not only ill inclined toward the Ottoman Empire, but also their excellent Arabic was not for the most part accompanied by knowledge of Ottoman Turkish. Moreover, their readiness to write studies of Ottoman Egypt that were simultaneously provincial and imperial was nonexistent. That view has been put to rest. It is now clear that from the mid-seventeenth century onward, the network of political households—or in Rifaat Abou-El-Haj's apt term, the *vezir/pasha* households—became the most basic unit in Ottoman politics and that they were ubiquitous in all the empire's big cities beginning with Istanbul itself.[10] This socio-political structure—the vezir/pasha or elite household—emerged as a major locus of power that recruited, trained, and socialized manpower into the Ottoman state. The networks of patronage extended by these households became the sine qua non for participating in state politics and for attaining a successful career within it. Though gaining power at its expense, the vezir/pasha households coexisted with, rather than challenged, the sultan's. The vast and variegated territory ruled by the Ottomans meant that each province or region had its institutional memory and cultural lore. There is no question that Mamluk heritage was most vivid in Egypt, but the political households that underlay its military society were part of a pivotal Ottoman phenomenon, albeit with its own local twist.

In the Mamluk case, the elite household preceded the sultan's household, which was a larger and more powerful replica of the existing structure. In the Ottoman Empire, the order seems to have been reversed, and the prototype for the elite household was that of the sultan himself, which reached its full development during the reign of Süleyman I

(1520–1566), whom the Europeans called the Magnificent, whereas the Ottomans called him the Law-giver or *Kanuni*. Also, unlike its Mamluk predecessor, the Ottoman sultanate established a dynasty that operated on the principle of kinship succession and did so with unequalled success. The imperial household resided at the Topkapı Palace and combined the domestic and the military within the same compound. The residence included such domestic components as kitchens, gardens, and women's quarters guarded by eunuchs. Together with them were the military-administrative training schools for palace pages and guards, as well as the pages, valets, and guards themselves, who served and protected the sultan and his household in both the domestic and public aspects of their life. Some of these units, such as the Gardeners and the Axe-men, played a role that was both domestic and military.

The reproductive facet of the sultan's household is interesting for the present discussion in that it combined the logic of the military patronage state with kinship politics in a way that managed to avoid the undermining of the former by the latter. Consistent with the logic of the military patronage state, the Ottoman dynasty forbade its male members from marrying into the free society it ruled. In the early stage of the frontier state, Ottoman sultans tended to marry into the dynasties around them, the Byzantine most importantly but also other Turco-Muslim and Christian ruling houses in Asia Minor and southeast Europe. These marriage alliances helped them gain legitimacy and a stake in the diplomacy of the region that was becoming the core of their budding empire. With the marginalization of the frontier ethos and the ascendancy of the imperial project after the mid-sixteenth century, the dynasty reproduced itself through the consort-denizens of the women's quarters in the royal household, namely, the imperial harem. At the same time, queen mothers were busy marrying off Ottoman princesses to promising or already-powerful state officials. This was one of the ways in which the queen mother became one of the most powerful figures at the imperial center together with the chief black eunuch, who was in charge of the imperial harem. The men who thus gained proximity to the ruling house through real kinship ties were known in Ottoman political culture as *damad*s (sons-in-law). The point is that, on the one hand, kinship became significant, and numerous *damad*s even became grand vezirs; on the other hand, the logic of the military patronage state was not disrupted because, even though married into the ruling Ottoman household, a princess-*damad* couple never challenged the sultan's sovereignty nor did it ever lay claim to the sultanate for its offspring.

Because the Ottoman Empire surpassed its predecessor and contemporary states in longevity and power, it yielded a greater variety of elite households. The first type of Ottoman elite households was the sultan's, which was also the model for emulation on a smaller scale. The second type was the household of the very high-ranking officials in the imperial center and of the governors of the main provinces. The third type is the trickiest for the historian to identify in the sources: the Janissary barracks households, which really treaded the fine line between political households and barracks gangs. These structures were created in the seventeenth century and led by the chief barracks commanders of the Janissaries in Istanbul and Cairo, that is, by middle- to low-ranking officers. Unlike the previous two types of households, this third type did not have a mansion or palatial residence. Some of them did become full-fledged elite households with an identifiable physical location, but only when their heads became sufficiently powerful and prominent. The networks of the Ottoman elite households in both the capital and provincial cities were nearly infinite and therefore constituted a nexus between the provinces and the center. At least at the elite level, these networks made for a tightly knitted imperial structure.

Conclusion: The Elite Households and the State

Since modern European thought is steeped in the Hegelian dialectical evolutionary narrative in which the family and the state figure prominently, it seems appropriate to end with a comment on the elite household—rather than the family—and the Ottoman state. The comment picks up observations made earlier and is concerned with how the early modern Ottoman state relates to the Weberian continuum of patrimonial-to-bureaucratic state. During the first half of the seventeenth century, two major households left the sultan's household, physically and politically. The first was the household of the empire's chief finance minister (*başdefterdar*), and the second was the grand vezir's. They took with them their domestic and professional entourage—the latter was virtually the backbone of the Ottoman imperial bureaucracy—and relocated to palatial mansions in Istanbul, not too far from Topkapı Palace. Of the two, the grand vezir's residence would become famous in Europe. The mansion was called Bab-i Ali, the Sublime Porte, and it became a metonymy in European parlance for the Ottoman government.

This separation was the top echelon of a more general process engendered by the elite household: the emergence of a state less and less coterminous with the ruler's household. These elite households, and not only those of the chief finance minister and the grand vezir, kept recruiting manpower that became at the same time a reservoir for the military and administration of the state. The sultan's household continued to recruit members and remained the largest and the sole formal source of sovereignty, but it lost its monopolistic grip over the abstraction we call—and sometimes reify as—the state. To use Weberian language, we have here an interesting paradox whereby the Ottoman state was being increasingly bureaucratized through the spread of structures—the elite households—that were quintessentially patrimonial.

Notes

1. The bey was a military-administrative office holder. For these early origins see David Ayalon, "The European-Asiatic Steppe: A Major Reservoir of Power for the Islamic World," in Ayalon, *The Mamluk Military Society* (London, 1979), 47–52; Halil Inalcık, "Ghulām," *Encyclopaedia of Islam*, 2nd ed. (Leiden, 1960), and "The Khan and the Tribal Aristocracy," in Inalcık, *Studies in Ottoman Social and Economic History* (London, 1985), 49–52; John E. Woods, *The Aqquyunlu* (Minneapolis, 1976), 8–12.
2. Marshall Hodgson, *The Venture of Islam*, vol. 3, *The Gunpowder Empires and Modern Times* (Chicago, 1974), esp. 1–16. See also James L. Gelvin, *The Modern Middle East: A History*, 2nd ed. (New York, 2008), 27–35.
3. For a thorough discussion on the connection between the Ottoman political household and the state, see Gabriel Piterberg, *An Ottoman Tragedy: History and Historiography at Play* (Berkeley, CA, 2003), part III.
4. Cemal Kafadar, *Between Two Worlds: The Construction of the Ottoman State* (Berkeley, CA, 1995), 138–54.
5. I. Metin Kunt, *The Sultan's Servants: The Transformation of Ottoman Provincial Government, 1550–1650* (New York, 1983), xiii.
6. I. Metin Kunt, "Ethnic-Regional (*Cins*) Solidarity in the Seventeenth-Century Ottoman Establishment," *International Journal of Middle East Studies* 5 (1974): 233–39.
7. See especially David Ayalon, "Studies in al-Jabarti: Notes on the Transformation of Mamluk Society in Egypt under the Ottomans," *Journal of Economic and Social History of the Orient* 3 (1960): 285–93.
8. The main locus of disagreement is between the two central scholars of Mamluk institutions and the Mamluk Sultanate: David Ayalon, for whom the ideal-type concept and historical reality converged (hence, no offspring permitted into the Mamluk caste), and P. M. Holt, who deemed historical reality messier than its conceptual portrayal. See especially Ayalon's "Mamluk," and, following directly on it, Holt's "Mamluks," both in *Encyclopaedia of Islam*, 2nd ed. (Leiden, 1960).
9. Jane Hathaway, *A Tale of Two Factions: Myth, Memory, and Identity in Ottoman Egypt and Yemen* (Albany, NY, 2003), see index under "Sudun, father of Qasim and Dhu'l-Faqar."
10. Rifaat Ali Abou-El-Haj, "The Vezir and Paşa Households, 1683–1703: A Preliminary Report," *Journal of the American Oriental Society* 94 (1974): 438–47.

Chapter 3

From Local *Signori* to European High Nobility

The Gonzaga Family Networks in the Fifteenth Century

Christina Antenhofer

In the course of the fifteenth century, the Gonzaga managed to rise from local *signori* to become members of the European high nobility. Before then, they had to solve severe internal family problems, culminating in fratricide and patricide in the fourteenth century. Their rise was accompanied by a reorganization of the family from a horizontal and competitive structure to one characterized by both hierarchy and collaboration.[1] In the process of becoming members of the European high nobility, the Gonzaga gave ever-greater influence to the main line, while reducing the influence of the collateral lines and cadets, leaving their local sphere of action behind to establish themselves as a transregional and transnational family. This reconfiguration was achieved in three major ways: through marriage alliance, military service, and ecclesiastical political activity. Both Gonzaga men and women were actively involved in the construction of networks among the political forces in northern Italy: the Italian *signorie*, the Holy Roman Empire, France, and the papacy.

In this chapter, I study the Gonzaga as an example of the transnational and transregional character of Renaissance Italian princely families. Choosing this family for analysis can be justified from three main points of view: first of all, they are emblematic of the rise of a small local family into the highest Italian aristocracy. Second, their successful transregional and transnational networks played an important part in their ascent, which makes them an interesting example for this book. Finally, the Gonzaga family of the fifteenth century has been studied quite closely already in a dissertation by Ebba Severidt. This anthropological study of three Gonzaga generations provides ample data still lacking for other similar Renaissance families.[2]

Systematic approaches to Italian dynasties—let alone studies with anthropological questions—have not been central in Italian historiography, as scholarly interest has focused primarily on the history of political institutions. Only in the past several years has a new approach to political culture developed that takes on activities of women and the interactions of family members as a central feature. The best comparative study at the moment is provided by Angelantonio Spagnoletti, who focuses on Italian dynasties between 1530 and the beginning of the eighteenth century.[3] Comparable studies for the earlier centuries, when the system of Italian princes slowly evolved, remain however to be written.

Considering the Gonzaga as a "transnational" family seems anachronistic, since their marriage networks and political choices developed in a period well before the establishment of the nation-state.[4] But they offer an interesting case, nonetheless, in the way—like other medieval noble kinship groups—they used attachment to particular geographic areas to build networks across quite considerable spaces. The Italian *signori* had substantially different origins from the old nobles of the Empire (*Reichsadel*). Most of them rose out of rapidly changing political circumstances in northern Italy, which had seen the emancipation of cities from the emperor in the course of the eleventh century. The cities, which formerly had been ruled by bishops as representatives of the emperor, developed communal structures, where citizens ruled.[5] In most cities of northern Italy in the course of the thirteenth and fourteenth centuries, one family took over power establishing a so-called *signoria*, the monocratic regime of a *signore*. The typical *signore* had usurped power using either his (previously temporarily restricted) position as leader of the citizens (*capitano del popolo*) or as administrator of the city (*podestà*). As *signore* he held rule over the city for his lifetime, but needed to be legitimized as administrator by the emperor (or the pope if the city was part of the Papal States) and stabilize his power in the city in order to make sure his sons could inherit his position. Italian *signori* originally came from among the local patricians or nobility, but for them to raise their status and solidify their rule, they needed among other things to obtain princely titles—margrave, duke, or even king—of the Holy Roman Empire bestowed by the emperor. Once achieved—usually through a suitable payment—the *signoria* became a princedom and the former *signore* a member of the European high nobility. This process was often complemented with political alliances through marriages with Imperial princely families.

Against the background of these general political developments, we can understand the rise of the Gonzaga, quickly summarized as follows.[6] The Gonzaga of Mantova initially came from a rural background and began their ascent as vassals of the monastery of San Benedetto in Polirone. During the course of the thirteenth century, the Buonacolsi, as *capitani del popolo,* established themselves as *signori* of Mantova, with the Gonzaga becoming their devoted vassals. As the latter gained more and more wealth during the twelfth and thirteenth centuries, they solidified their position in the city, and in 1328, they unexpectedly seized power and made themselves the new *signori* of Mantova. They managed to legitimize their usurped status in 1432, when the emperor recognized the state of affairs and appointed Gianfrancesco Gonzaga margrave of Mantova.[7] The next step in the successful story of the family was their Imperial appointment as dukes in 1530. From 1432 until 1627, the main line of the Gonzaga remained princes of Mantova until it died out in the male line, succeeded after a dynastic war by the collateral Gonzaga-Nevers line. They, in turn, were deposed in 1708 during political conflicts with the Holy Roman Emperor.

In what follows, I will first draw attention to the evolution of the Gonzaga family during the fourteenth and fifteenth centuries, dealing with questions of succession, hierarchy, inheritance, and property. Subsequently, I will focus on their transregional and transnational networking strategies. Finally, I will offer a view of Gonzaga family politics through a reading of Andrea Mantegna's famous frescoes of the *Camera Picta.*

Authority, Hierarchy, and Succession in the Gonzaga Family

On 16 August 1328, Luigi I Gonzaga (1328–1360) assassinated Passerino Buonacolsi and secured power in the city by obtaining two offices: *capitano del popolo,* conferred by the city in a formal act, and *imperial vicar,* the imperial administrator, obtained from the emperor.[8] This first period of Gonzaga dominion over Mantova saw a remarkable collaboration between the father Luigi and the three sons of his first marriage, Guido, Filippino, and Feltrino. In fact, while the office of the *capitano del popolo* belonged only to Luigi—later passed on to his eldest son Guido—the Gonzaga received a collective investiture from Karl IV in 1349 of the father and all three sons as imperial vicars.[9]

This collective government soon crumbled: Filippino died early, Feltrino tried to establish his own *signoria* in Reggio, and in 1362 two of Guido's sons killed their brother Ugolino.[10] When in 1368–69 Guido and his second son Francesco died under unclear conditions, Ludovico (1369–1382) remained the sole *signore* in the city.[11] From this period onward, there was a clear end to the strategy of collective dominion, and only one Gonzaga at a time held the positions of *capitano del popolo* and vicar of the city.

From 1328, when they assumed power, until 1432, the Gonzaga continued to hold the position in Mantova as *signori* and stayed in power as rulers, with son succeeding to father.[12] To secure their position and solidify their claims, their ambition led them to seek Imperial princely status and elevation into the European high nobility. This step was achieved in the generation of the son of Francesco (1382–1407) and grandson of the Ludovico who had usurped power within his own family. In 1432, Gianfrancesco (1407–1444) was elevated to margrave by Emperor Sigismund of Luxemburg; at the same time, Gianfrancesco's son Ludovico II (1444–1478) was engaged to a princess of the Holy Roman Empire, which resulted in the first significant transnational marriage of the Gonzaga family. In 1433, he married Barbara von Hohenzollern, margravine of Brandenburg and kin to the emperor.[13] With this marriage, the Gonzaga reached beyond the local and transregional spheres

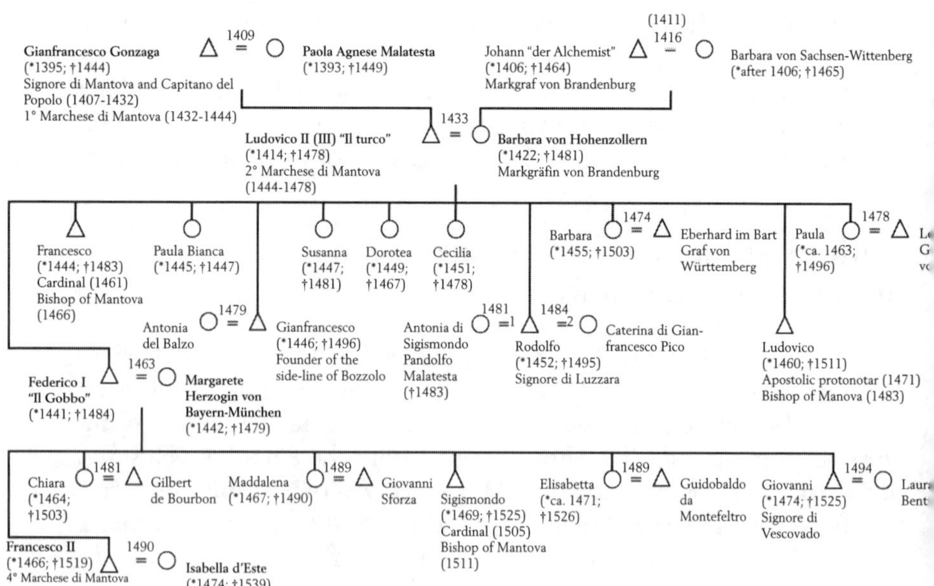

Figure 3.1. The Gonzaga of the fifteenth century.

to enter into a much broader arena of political and social activity. This opening up to new possibilities was reflected in the growing threads of extensive networks through a regular policy of transnational marriages and stationing of younger sons at European courts. They also began to extend their connections through high position in the church: with Barbara's influence, her son Francesco became the first Gonzaga cardinal.

Despite the reorganization of the dynasty, conflicts still arose, but now they resulted from the practices of succession within the single main line, rather than from competition among different, equal lines. Above all the problem lay in the succession of a single son to titles and offices. In fact, during the fifteenth century, precisely this problem led to a defining moment inside the Gonzaga main line. In 1436, Ludovico II and his father Gianfrancesco chose to fight on opposite sides in one of the many political clashes between Milan and Venice.[14] Gianfrancesco, fighting as a condottiere for Venice, expelled Ludovico from Mantova, disinherited him, and installed his second son Carlo as successor. Two years later, however, Gianfrancesco himself switched sides, leaving Venice to fight for Milan, yet father and son only reconciled in 1440. In a ritualized encounter, Ludovico had to ask for forgiveness, throwing himself on the ground before his father to show submission.[15] All through the conflict, Ludovico's wife Barbara—eighteen at the time of the reconciliation—had stayed in Mantova supported by her mother-in law Paola Malatesta.[16] Even though their husbands were enemies, the women shared solidarity, an early sign of independent spheres of action of Gonzaga women, which will be discussed more in detail later in this chapter. Moreover, Paola's support of Barbara was certainly due to the fact that treating Barbara in a bad way or sending her back home would have resulted in the breaking of the newly established ties to the Empire.

Traditionally, historians have seen two main results of this conflict: First, they have argued that the resolution of this conflict led to designating the second son to an ecclesiastical career from the next Gonzaga generation onward. However, as recent studies have shown, assigning cadets to careers in the Church was part of a general trend that accompanied the slow rise of primogeniture among the European nobility.[17] Primogeniture itself was not introduced at once, but along a slowly evolving process. The Gonzaga by this time had established a rule of succession by the eldest son, which, however, could be altered or come into question in conflict situations as has been shown above. As a second result of the conflict, historians mention the division of Gonzaga territory among all the sons of the next generation. After the intestate death of Ludovico II in 1478, the Gonzaga holdings were divided among all the sons, secular and ecclesiastic, on the word of their mother, Barbara, who declared that the division had been her husband's will.[18] Even with tendencies to concentrating power, noble sons could not yet be simply excluded from the process of devolution, and mothers played an important role in determining how the sons would be treated.[19]

It is important to understand, however, that "succession" and "inheritance" were not the same thing. Only one son, Federico (1478–1484), the oldest, was able to succeed to the title and prerogatives of margrave, which formed the core element of descent around which the family came to be organized. A good example of how this could play out came with the early death in 1484 of Federico, who was succeeded as margrave by his son Francesco II (1484–1519). One of Francesco's uncles (Francesco) had earlier been elevated to a cardinalship and become bishop of Mantova. Upon the cardinal's death, his younger ecclesiastic brother succeeded him as bishop and aspired for the cardinalship as well. Yet Margrave Francesco, his nephew, determined to have his own son, Sigismondo, attain the cardinal's hat, which is exactly what happened.[20] Whatever rights and properties were distributed in each generation, the dynastic succession to high office of margrave became the central point around which power and authority were organized.

Inheritance and Property

The Gonzaga of the first generations had attained their income mainly from military service—the so-called *condotte.*[21] Wars in late medieval Italy were not fought by a standing army, which did not yet exist, but by soldiers, led by a *condottiere* (man of war), who could be hired for a certain period of time to fight for one or the other Italian political instances (the pope, the cities, *signorie,* the emperor). As soon as the Gonzaga became *signori* of Mantova, they profited from the communal mint and became involved in commercial ventures, especially with trading with grain and salt. Profits went immediately into buying ventures in the city (the beginning of the Gonzaga palazzo) and in properties and estates in the territory surrounding Mantova.[22] Inheritance in Mantova followed Langobardian law, which accorded property rights—however small—to all sons.[23] But this form of devolution could conflict with the emerging system of primogeniture. In the case of Ludovico II and his brothers, the latter received only small territories to support them during periods when they did not have a *condotta*. The primacy of his position, however, was demonstrated in 1451 when he withdrew inherited territories from his brother Carlo after yet another conflict.[24] As late as 1478—another generation down the road—all the sons inherited equal portions of the family's Mantovan lands.[25] In this case, small independent *signorie* were created that never again were integrated in the main line: Gianfrancesco founded the two collateral lines of the Gonzaga di Sabbioneta and the Gonzaga di Bozzolo, and Rodolfo founded the line of the Gonzaga di Castiglione delle Stiviere.[26] That was the last time that cadets of the main line received parts of the territory; from that time onward, they either were designated to ecclesiastical careers or earned their living with military and diplomatic services for various courts, remaining in the shadow of the oldest brother.[27]

One of the ways that the Gonzaga dealt with dividing family property was to exclude married daughters from the inheritance and pay them off with a dowry and trousseau (*Brautschatz*).Whatever was paid out, according to the marriage contracts, had to be returned should the daughter die without heirs.[28] In the sixteenth century, this led to an interesting lawsuit for the Gonzaga family. Two daughters of Ludovico II and Barbara von Brandenburg—Barbara (Barbarina), married to the count of Württemberg, and Paula, married to the count of Görz—died without children. Paula had never received the whole amount of her dowry by the time she died in 1496, her husband following in 1500.[29] In 1502, shortly before Barbara died as well, Antonia del Balzo, the widow of Paula and Barbara's brother Gianfrancesco, opened a lawsuit with Margrave Francesco first concerning the rest of Paula's dowry and then the belongings of both Paula and Barbara. Antonia argued that the inheritance of both sisters as well as the amount of Paula's dowry that still had not been paid belonged to all of Paula's brothers and their heirs and not only to the leading margrave. The amount of the outstanding dowry should have been divided among the brothers and their heirs, as it was part of the patrimony of the whole house and not just of Francesco as leading margrave. Francesco sought legal advice from the jurists of Padova, who wrote long experts' reports. In the end he had to give in to "save peace in the family," as he explains in a document of 5 February 1504 where he agreed that Paula's and Barbara's heritage including dowry (*Brautschatz* and *Mitgift*) and *Morgengabe* was to be divided among all the brothers and their heirs.[30]

The Gonzaga as Transnational and Transregional Family

Along with the elevation of the Gonzaga to princes of the empire went their establishment as a transregional and transnational family. Because the distinction between *transregional* and *transnational* is to some extent anachronistic, with every princedom in Italy being a state of its own, the terms can be used but with due caution. In the context of this book, it makes sense to distinguish between contacts with other Italian courts (transregional) and contacts with European courts and the Papal States (transnational). Which one of the networks dominated depended on the political situation at any one time and on the status of the nobles and courts that the Gonzaga dealt with. At various times, the family operated on one or the other level in four different spheres of activity: marriage, military employment, diplomatic service, and ecclesiastical careers.

The first Gonzaga generations who had seized power in Mantova mostly sought marriage alliances with important Italian families such as the della Mirandola, d'Este, Visconti, and Malatesta. However, already in the fourteenth century, a Habsburg-Gonzaga marriage took place, following the confirmation of the investiture of all Gonzaga brothers as vicars by Emperor Charles IV in 1354. The second brother, Filippino Gonzaga, married Verena, countess of Habsburg-Laufenburg, while her uncle Rudolf IV married Filippino's second daughter, Elisabetta. This double marriage, however, remained exceptional in this early period.[31] The next transnational marriage took place almost a century later in combination with the elevation of the Gonzaga to margraves by the emperor in 1432.

From the beginning of their rule, the Gonzaga obviously arranged transnational marriages in close contact with the emperor. The marriages to German houses were thus motivated by the Gonzaga's orientation towards the emperor's politics and interests. With Barbara von Brandenburg, the Gonzaga married a princess of the Empire, granddaughter of an elector. How important this marriage was for the Gonzaga is underlined by the fact that the Brandenburg were able to get the Gonzaga to pay the dowry of their daughter-in-law.[32]

Barbara came to Mantova at the very early age of eleven, and she was educated together with the other Gonzaga children in the humanist school Casa Giocosa.[33] She was allowed to have very few German servants, as the Gonzaga wanted her to integrate as soon as possible. This alliance with German princes provided a context for their political activities: in 1459, they hosted a diet Pope Pius II organized to discuss measures against the Turks, upon which occasion, the second son, Francesco, was designated to become cardinal.

The next steps in dynastic imperial politics were the German-Italian marriages arranged for three of the children of Ludovico II and Barbara: Federico married Margarete von Bayern-München in 1463; Barbarina married Eberhard im Bart von Württemberg in 1474; and Paula married Leonhard, count of Görz, in 1478. The last two of these marriages were not the Gonzaga's first choices, however. In fact, they had been looking for marriage alliances with the Sforza, who refused the first two of the Gonzaga daughters (Susanna and Dorotea), apparently because they were subject to hereditary deformity.[34] It also became difficult to arrange marriages for the two "healthy" daughters, Barbarina and Paula. Finally, it was their sister-in-law Margarete von Bayern-München who arranged a series of marriages during a visit to her court of origin, Munich, in 1473.[35] In the next generation, German marriages ceased in the main line with interest directed to France: Federico's daughter Chiara married Gilbert de Bourbon in 1481. The French had long been engaged in Italy, above all in the kingdom of Naples, where the Anjou fought against Aragon for dominion, and in the northwest, where the crown had close contacts with Savoy and Milan (moreover, the Valois possessed Asti since the end of the fourteenth century and Genova had been temporarily under French dominion).[36]

It is obvious that the women in these marriages were designated to play political roles, keeping contact with their families of origin.[37] The Gonzaga expected a close collaboration between husband and wife, illustrated by such prominent couples as Gianfrancesco Gonzaga and Paola Malatesta, Ludovico II and Barbara von Brandenburg, and Francesco II and Isabella d'Este. The margravines shared administration and governance with their husbands, staying in Mantova when their husbands were engaged in *condotte*, or looking after their other belongings in the princedom.[38] The margravine received ambassadors, and she also received and answered diplomatic letters, discussing all the correspondence and the ambassadors' reports with the margrave. Wives not only supported their husbands, but also developed individual spheres of influence, which could culminate in husband and wife supporting different political sides as in the example of Isabella d'Este and Francesco Gonzaga.[39]

It was moreover the wife's duty to look after the children and to arrange marriages. For this purpose, Margarete, Federico's wife, traveled home to the court of Munich in 1473 to arrange a series of marriages not only for her own children but also for her unmarried sisters-in-law, as well as for the children of Ludovico's brother, Carlo. In the sixteenth and seventeenth centuries, Gonzaga and Habsburg wives played important roles, arranging marriage exchanges linking the two houses in a series of cross-marriages.[40] It was typical for the Gonzaga wives that they were allowed to make long visits to their families of origin—stays they always used to undertake political negotiations, arrange marriages, and deal with dowries.[41]

The situation of the Gonzaga daughters who married German princes in the fifteenth century appears to have been less fortunate than those of the German princesses who married Gonzaga sons. Neither Barbarina nor Paula had very happy marriages, probably because neither had surviving children. Both complained about the harsh and unfamiliar customs in their new countries and had great difficulties integrating into their new houses.[42] The situation of the women could be quite difficult when they did not speak the new language—which, however, seems to have been the normal case in such transnational marriages.[43] Taking their own servants along with them allowed for companionship, of course, but foreign courts often could not easily integrate them, and husbands frequently forbade their wives to bring their own servants in order to avoid conflicts at the new court. Such was the case for Anna Caterina Gonzaga, married to Ferdinand, archduke of Austria.[44] Barbara von Brandenburg was allowed very few servants, too. New servants arriving at a court always created conflicts with the established servants, above all if they spoke different languages. This is documented for Paula Gonzaga's servants, who continuously provoked the count's complaints, and most of them were sent back to Mantova.[45] Whether wives were allowed to visit their families depended on their husbands' will: Paula came back to Mantova on several occasions, while Barbarina was not allowed by her husband to visit at all.[46]

None of these marriages were the result of romantic sentiments.[47] Both the emotional tenor of marriage and the satisfactions a woman could find in her new familial situation depended on three central factors: the political relevance of her family of origin, the size of her dowry as well as other claims to property and status, and her physical capacity for bearing children. Positive emotional feelings between husband and wife depended on these aspects; problems rarely seem to have arisen from mere personal dislike but rather from the fact that women had no children or a promptly paid dowry.[48] A large dowry alone, however, did not compensate for the inability to give birth to children.[49] On the other hand, as the case of Barbara von Brandenburg shows, if the bride's family guaranteed social ascent, the exchange of property or cash played a small role. In the following generation, as well, the Gonzaga paid more to get their daughters married to German princes (each with a dowry of 20,000 florins), than they received from the family of Margarete von Bayern-München (half as much).[50]

In general, the only Gonzaga men to enter into international alliances were the title-holding margraves themselves, reflecting their elevated status. The only exception is to be found in the sixteenth century, when one of the cadets went abroad and founded a new transnational branch of the family. Ludovico (1539–1595), the fourth son of Federico II (*1519–†1540) and Margherita Paleologa, in 1549 at the age of ten years left Mantova for France where his maternal grandmother, Anna d'Alençon, had left him her property.[51] In 1565, he married Henriette de Cleves to become the duke of Nevers and found the collateral line Gonzaga-Nevers. It was this branch that took over Mantova's territory after the main line died out in 1627.[52]

Transregional alliances, that is, marriages with other Italian families, clearly reflected the relative status of a spouse. But it also should be clear that marriages with important Italian princes could be on a level with those with European princes. Between the German and French marriages of the fifteenth century and the Habsburg marriages of the sixteenth, the Gonzaga concluded only Italian marriages, among which were the distinguished ones of Francesco II with Isabella d'Este and of Federico II with Margherita Paleologa (the latter brought to the Gonzaga Monferrato and its territory).[53] While the daughters and the oldest brother concluded marriages on the highest level with European and Italian princely families, the cadets married daughters from less-important princes or even patricians.[54] This practice went along with the establishment of one main line and primogeniture—a phenomenon that is confirmed by recent studies for German houses as well.[55] The marriages of the Gonzaga cadets with Italian nobles and patricians were important to keep alive the network of clientage and of alliance with Italian families.[56] This complex situation led to the coexistence around 1500 of about two hundred Gonzaga living at the same time with close consanguineal ties to the local nobles.[57] The collateral lines founded by the cadets served as a biological pool for the main line in case it produced no heirs. Ecclesiastical brothers could play the same role, too—leave the Church, marry, and provide heirs.[58]

The cadets, moreover, played an important role in contracting transregional and transnational networks through military service. Their careers could start with visits to other courts in the course of their education. This practice began with the generation of the children of Barbara and Ludovico II (1444–1478). Two of their sons went abroad. The first and longer stay was the one of Gianfrancesco Gonzaga, who at the age of nine went to the courts of his grandfather and granduncle, Johann and Albrecht Achilles of Brandenburg, for four years.[59] The youngest of the secular sons, Rodolfo, spent some time at the court of Burgundy.[60] While they both came back to Mantova, received a portion of territory, and founded their own collateral lines, cadets of the next generations, when territory was no longer partitioned, constantly moved around European and Italian courts and gained their livings with military and diplomatic services.[61] With these activities, they also became important sources of information for their brother, the margrave in charge.[62]

The fourth sphere of transregional and transnational activity by Gonzaga sons and daughters was the Church. A common strategy adopted among European nobility was to place younger sons and daughters in ecclesiastical offices, since, on the one hand, marriages were expensive, and on the other, ecclesiastical children did not compete for power within the dynasty.[63] In the case of the Gonzaga, placing children in ecclesiastical offices played an important role in the political strategies of the dynasty. At the beginning of Mantova's rise, the bishop and monasteries had ruled the city, and they remained centers of considerable political power. From the first generations of Gonzaga activity in the city onward, relatives and clients of the Gonzaga tried to occupy all the important local ecclesiastic offices in the territory, and above all, they had their eye on the episcopate. In the fifteenth century, starting with Francesco, the cardinal, the Mantovan episcopate was always occupied by a Gonzaga son of the main line.[64] Gonzaga daughters and wives entered the local monasteries—sometimes forced, because they were physically deformed, and sometimes out of piety, something for which they achieved a considerable reputation in the sixteenth century.[65]

With the diet in Mantova of 1459 and the creation of Francesco as first Gonzaga cardinal, dynastic ecclesiastical politics began to reach beyond the local sphere. As Chambers has shown in his many works, Francesco became the first of the so-called *cardinali-príncipi*, cardinals who were at the same time princes.[66] Every princely family in Italy tried to have at least one son who would become cardinal.[67] The aim was to influence politics in the Papal States, which culminated in the conclave, where cardinals elected a new pope or could even become pope themselves. The cardinals represented the interests of their families and friends, who had supported their creation. Francesco thus was created a "German" cardinal with the help of the emperor and his mother's connections in the Empire. In fact, Barbara had argued, he could be looked upon as German because: "ipse quidam caredinalis meus, quamquam pater italicus sit, a teutonico sanguine non degenerat."[68]

Holding high ecclesiastical office within the dynasty could be ambivalent, and bishops and cardinals did not always put the interests of the family above the interests of the Church.[69] Still, they always kept close contacts with their families, sustained their brothers and sisters, and took over political responsibilities as regents when a margrave died prematurely.[70] Spagnoletti suggests that cardinals and cadets offered a sort of alter ego for the head of the family. The cardinal represented his religious soul while the cadets, especially the *condottieri*, represented the aspect of the *capitano*, the warrior, a career that from the sixteenth century most leading princes abandoned, leaving it to younger brothers.[71]

Family and Kinship and the Formation of Family Networks: The Camera Picta

The vision of the family and kin as the basis for Gonzaga dominion is celebrated in the famous *Camera Picta* in Castello San Giorgio. It is one of the earliest examples of family representations showing the intersection of private and public spheres as the foundation of political dominion.[72] From 1465 to 1474 Ludovico II Gonzaga had Andrea Mantegna paint a series of frescoes in his sleeping and audience room in Castello San Giorgio. On the northern wall, Ludovico celebrated himself as paterfamilias surrounded by all of his children, his wife, his deceased parents, and people of his court. This panel can be looked at as the commemoration of Ludovico's inner familiar circle and his family line, with him as the first Gonzaga patriarch. On the western wall he celebrated his success on a more political level. Here we find the elevation of his son Francesco to cardinal, depicting the moment when the latter met his father and two generations of Gonzaga cadets who had been destined to ecclesiastical career.[73] However, the Gonzaga are joined by two more people, whom Ludovico portrayed as his most distinguished kin from

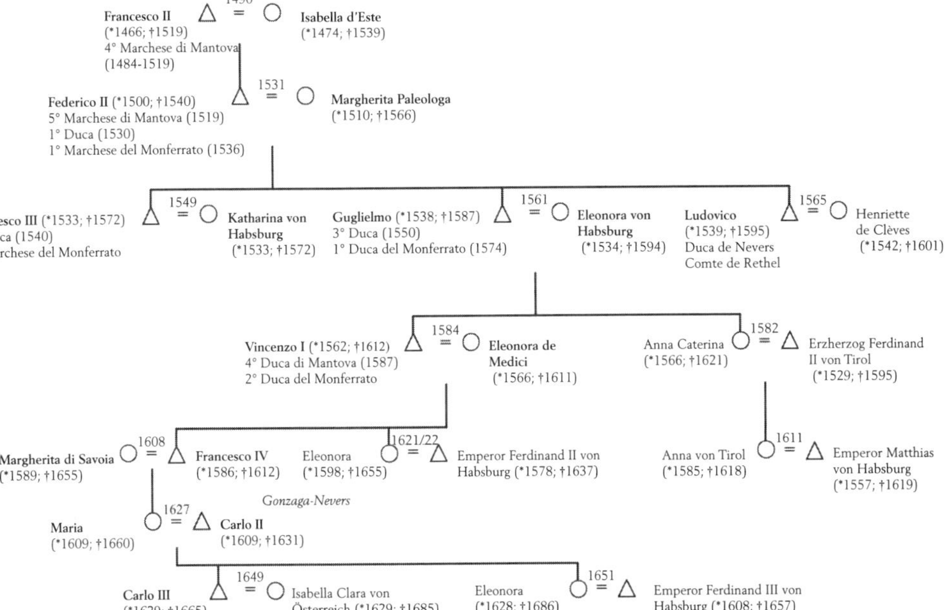

Figure 3.2. The transnational marriages of the Gonzaga in the sixteenth and seventeenth centuries.

Figure 3.3. *Castello San Giorgio, Camera degli Sposi,* fresco by Andrea Mantegna, La Corte, North Wall (Archivio di Stato di Mantova, Archivio Giovetti, Fotocolor n 51). Used with permission of the Ministero per i Beni e le Attività Culturali.

north of the Alps: his brother-in-law Christian of Denmark and emperor Friedrich III of Habsburg, related to Ludovico through his daughter-in-law Margarete von Bayern-München, wife of Federico Gonzaga.

The series of frescoes tells the story of the reception of two letters that may have communicated the happy event of Francesco's elevation. In this staging of the scene, Ludovico celebrated both friendship and kinship and their capacity to build and maintain networks as fundamental pillars of the Gonzaga politics. How successful Ludovico had been in the building of networks was to become obvious in the rise of the next Gonzaga generations, culminating in their Habsburg marriages of the sixteenth and seventeenth centuries. However, the foundation for this "golden age" of the Gonzaga family had been built in the fifteenth century. The small size of Mantova's territory, mainly consisting of one city and its *contado,* makes it obvious that political power in early modern Europe did not just depend on the size of a territory, but it also mirrored the success of various strategies involving the skillful deployment of family resources through marriage alliances, diplomacy, and courtly, military, and ecclesiastical service. The Gonzaga were by no means unique in this regard, but they offer a particularly good example of the patient construction from generation to generation of networks of kin and friends, with dense, overlapping, interwoven threads of connections throughout the region of their local power base, on the one hand, and strategically constructed ties to some of the great players on the European stage, on the other.

Notes

Sources for the genealogical trees: Severidt, *Familie,* p. 319; *DBI, vol.* 57; Annibaletti, "Niedergang"; http://genealogy.euweb.cz/gonzaga/; Cordula Nolte, *Familie, Hof und Herrschaft. Das verwandtschaftliche Beziehungs- und Kommunikationsnetz der Reichsfürsten am Beispiel der Markgrafen von Brandenburg-Ansbach (1440–1530)* (Ostfildern, 2005); Pompeio conte di Litta-Biumi, *Famiglie celebri d'Italia* (Milano, 1834), table IV.

1. This process characterizes German noble dynasties of that time as well, see Karl-Heinz Spiess, "Lordship, Kinship, and Inheritance among the German High Nobility in the Middle Ages and Early Modern Period," in *Kinship in Europe: Approaches to Long-Term Development (1300–1900),* ed. David Warren Sabean, Simon Teuscher, and Jon Mathieu (New York, 2007), 57–75.
2. Ebba Severidt, *Familie, Verwandtschaft und Karriere bei den Gonzaga: Struktur und Funktion von Familie und Verwandtschaft bei den Gonzaga und ihren deutschen Verwandten (1444–1519)* (Leinfelden, 2002).
3. Angelantonio Spagnoletti, *Le dinastie italiane nella prima età moderna* (Bologna, 2003). Besides Spagnoletti's work, two important collections of essays are: Letizia Arcangeli and Susanna Peyronel, eds., *Donne di potere nel Rinascimento* (Rome, 2008), which deals with the role of women in ruling families, and a comparative study based on the Habsburg, Marco Bellabarba and Jan Paul Niederkorn, eds., *Le corti come luogo di comunicazione: Gli Asburgo e l'Italia (secoli XVI–XIX) / Höfe als Orte der Kommunikation: Die Habsburger und Italien (16.–19. Jh.)* (Berlin and Bologna, 2009).
4. However, even contemporaries noticed that having to marry into a distant country provided greater problems for the young brides. Erasmus of Rotterdam compared the women who had to leave for distant countries to people who were condemned to exile. See Anthony F. D'Elia, *The Renaissance of Marriage in Fifteenth-Century Italy* (Cambridge, MA, and London, 2004), 87.
5. For an overview, see Giancarlo Andenna et al., eds., *Storia d'Italia,* vol. 6, *Comuni e signorie nell'Italia settentrionale: La Lombardia* (Torino, 1998); Luisa Chiappa Mauri, ed., *Contado e città in dialogo: Comuni urbani e comunità rurali nella Lombardia medievale* (Milan, 2003); Gerhard Dilcher, *Die Entstehung der lombardischen Stadtkommune: Eine rechtsgeschichtliche Untersuchung* (Aalen, 1967); Werner Goez, *Geschichte Italiens in Mittelalter und Renaissance,* 3rd ed. (Darmstadt, 1988).
6. The exhaustive literature on the Gonzaga is listed in the following bibliography: Raffaele Tamalio, *La memoria dei Gonzaga: Repertorio bibliografico Gonzaghesco 1473–1999* (Florence, 1999).
7. They had, however, been officially recognized as vicars of Mantova in 1329, as vicars of Mantova and Reggio Emilia in 1349, and the renewal of this investiture was

accompanied by the first Gonzaga-Habsburg marriage in 1354; Isabella Lazzarini, "Gonzaga, Filippino," in *Dizionario Biografico degli Italiani* (henceforth *DBI*) (Roma, 2001), 57: 749–51.

8. See Mario Vaini, *Ricerche Gonzaghesche (1189–inizi sec. XV)* (Florence, 1994), 8–33. Unlike the Buonacolsi, Luigi I at once stipulated total monocratic rights of the *capitano* over the commune, wiping out the power of communal offices and the council.
9. See Isabella Lazzarini, "Gonzaga, Feltrino," in *DBI*, 57: 729–32. First, only Luigi had been invested as vicar in 1329. Vaini, *Ricerche,* 11–12.
10. However, Feltrino failed in the end and sold Reggio to the Visconti. See Lazzarini "Feltrino."
11. Vaini, *Ricerche,* 45–51; Roberta Monica Ridolfi, "Gonzaga, Guido," in *DBI*, 57: 791–94.
12. Only in 1383 did the emperor declare that the vicariat could be inherited by the Gonzaga. Vaini, *Ricerche,* 11–12.
13. Barbara was not a niece of the emperor, as some historians claim. Her grandfather, elector Friedrich I of Brandenburg, was a close friend to the emperor, and his brother Johann was married to the emperor's youngest sister, Margarete von Luxemburg. See Severidt, *Familie,* 200.
14. Some historians mention as further reason for the conflict between father and son that Barbara did not get pregnant at once. In fact, she was only eleven years old when the couple was married and only in 1441, eight years after their marriage, did she give birth to her first son. Gianfrancesco should have feared that the couple might not have an heir, and therefore he should have made Carlo his successor. However, this argument sounds weak given the very young age of the bride. Moreover, two historians of the nineteenth century mention another "Federico," who had been born as eldest son—obviously before the next Federico—and who should also have been portrayed in the *Camera Picta*. See Giovanni Pasetti and Gianna Pinotti, "La camera in luce: La Camera degli Sposi di Andrea Mantegna in Palazzo Ducale a Mantova—redazione 1999," http://xoomer.alice.it/gpasett/luce.htm (accessed 10 July 2008).
15. See Elisabeth Ward Swain, "My Most Excellent and Most Singular Lord: Marriage in a Noble Family of Fifteenth-Century Italy," *Journal of Medieval and Renaissance Studies* 16/2 (1986): 171–95.
16. This results from a letter in which the Brandenburgs thanked Paola Malatesta for her support. See Severidt, *Familie,* 208. As Paola was not related to Barbara and both Carlo and Ludovico were her sons (in fact Gianfrancesco only married once), there seems to have been no political reason for her help; perhaps it was motivated by her deeply humanist ideas. (She founded the humanist school Casa Giocosa in Mantova and after her husband's death became a nun.) Kate Simon, *A Renaissance Tapestry: The Gonzaga of Mantua* (New York, 1988), 32–37, and Severidt, *Familie,* 103.
17. See Spiess, "Lordship," 62. Spagnoletti points out that this strategy had been adopted by other leading families as well, and yet the Gonzaga were among the most successful "cardinal making" families. Spagnoletti, *Dinastie,* 271–94.
18. A Mantovan chronicler of that time, Andrea Schivenoglia, refers to secret negotiations among the mother and the sons. Isabella Lazzarini, "Gonzaga, Gianfrancesco," in *DBI*, 57: 771–73.
19. On the part women played in familial architectures see Michaela Hohkamp, "Sisters, Aunts, and Cousins: Familial Architectures and the Political Field in Early Modern Europe," in Sabean, Teuscher, and Mathieu, *Kinship in Europe,* 91–104.
20. Severidt, *Familie,* 131–33.

21. Maria-Jose Rodríguez-Salgado, "Terracotta and Iron: Mantuan Politics (ca. 1450—ca. 1550)," in *La corte di Mantova nell'età di Andrea Mantenga, 1450–1550 / The Court of the Gonzaga in the Age of Mantenga, 1450–1550: Atti del convegno (Londra, 6–8 marzo 1992; Mantova, 28 marzo 1992)*, ed. Cesare Mozzarelli, Robert Oresko, and Leandro Ventura (Roma, 1997), 15–59.
22. As in the political field, the Gonzaga also controlled the finances together, see Vaini, *Ricerche*, 20–45; Marina Romani, *Una città in forma di Palazzo: Potere signorile e forma urbana nella Mantova medievale e moderna* (Brescia, 1995), 73–88.
23. Isabella Lazzarini, "Gonzaga, Carlo," in *DBI*, 57: 693–96.
24. Lazzarini, "Carlo," 695.
25. One ecclesiastic and one secular brother formed a couple that possessed the territory together, yet after the death of the ecclesiastic brother, his rights would pass on to the heirs of the secular brother.
26. Isabella Lazzarini, "Gonzaga, Rodolfo," in *DBI*, 57: 838–40; Lazzarini, "Gianfrancesco."
27. Hohkamp also notices a substantial loss of status for younger brothers going along with unigeniture. Hohkamp, "Sisters," 93.
28. Christina Antenhofer, *Briefe zwischen Süd und Nord: Die Hochzeit und Ehe von Paula de Gonzaga und Leonhard von Görz im Spiegel der fürstlichen Kommunikation (1473–1500)* (Innsbruck, 2007), 145–72.
29. Shortly before her wedding in 1478, her father died, and her brother Federico as well as his heir Francesco never paid the full amount of the dowry. It was always a problem for the daughter if the father died before she married; the brother was more interested in supplying his own daughters rather than his sisters. This is a result that is also confirmed by the analysis of Karl-Heinz Spiess regarding the counts and lords of the empire. See Karl-Heinz Spiess, *Familie und Verwandtschaft im deutschen Hochadel des Spätmittelalters, 13. bis Anfang des 16. Jahrhunderts* (Stuttgart, 1993), 168.
30. Antenhofer, *Briefe*, 197–211.
31. See Christina Antenhofer, "Briefe, Besuche, Hochzeiten: Die Gonzaga im Kontakt mit deutschen Fürstenhäusern," in Bellabarba and Niederkorn, eds., *Le corti come luogo di comunicazione*. For the marriage, see Detlev Schwennicke, ed., *Europäische Stammtafeln: Neue Folge* (Frankfurt a.M., 1998), vol. 1.I, table 39; Lazzarini, "Filippino."
32. In her later years, however, Barbara sued her native family to pay the dowry as she argued that this was part of her heritage. Barbara finally obtained the money, which is, however, also a sign for the importance the Gonzaga and Barbara herself had reached in the meantime. See Severidt, *Familie*, 293–94; Ward-Swain, "Lord," 171–95.
33. The school had been founded by Barbara's mother-in-law, Paola Malatesta, and its leader was Vittorino da Feltre. Simon, *Renaissance*, 32–37; Severidt, *Familie*, 59, 275.
34. Stefano Davari, "Il matrimonio di Dorotea Gonzaga con Galeazzo Maria Sforza," *Giornale Ligustico* 17 (1890): 3–43; Luca Beltrami, "L'annullamento del contratto di matrimonio fra Galeazzo Maria Sforza e Dorotea Gonzaga (1463)," *Archivio storico lombardo* 6 (1889): 126–32.
35. Severidt, *Familie*, 193; Antenhofer, *Briefe*, 50–54. For the role women played in the marriage-making process see Hohkamp, "Sisters," 97–101.
36. Goez, *Geschichte*, 265–70.
37. For the political role of the women see Arcangeli and Peyronel, *Donne*. See also Spagnoletti, *Dinastie*, 252–71.
38. Severidt points out that even if both margrave and margravine were in Mantova, they not always lived in the same place. Generally the Gonzaga did not all live to-

gether in the same place but scattered around the regional state, each in a different rural palazzo. See Severidt, *Familie,* 5. On this idea of husband and wife forming a "professional" team, see Heide Wunder, *"Er ist die Sonn' sie ist der Mond": Frauen in der Frühen Neuzeit* (München 1992), 137–38, with examples of couples sharing offices.

39. In fact Isabella supported France while Francesco supported the Empire—which might however have been a strategy of the two to maintain the famous Gonzaga politics of balance between the forces of the time. On the female spheres of power in Renaissance Italy, see Arcangeli and Peyronel, *Donne.* On these collaborations see Severidt, *Familie,* 214–21. Some historians even speak of "friendship" between husband and wife citing the humanist concept of marriage; if friendship is looked at as political bond of collaboration and expectation among kin and not in the romantic sense, I agree with this point of view. For the concept of friendship between husband and wife see Carolyn James, "Friendship and Dynastic Marriage in Renaissance Italy," *Literature and History* 17 (2008): 4–18; D'Elia, *Renaissance.*
40. See Paula Sutter Fichtner, "Dynastic Marriage in Sixteenth-Century Habsburg Diplomacy and Statecraft: An Interdisciplinary Approach," *American Historical Review* 81 (1976): 243–65; Giuliano Annibaletti, "Ein irreversibler Niedergang? Die Beziehungen zwischen Mantua und dem Reich nach 1627," *Zeitenblicke* 6 (2007), http://www.zeitenblicke.de/2007/1/Annibaletti/ (accessed 30 June 2008); Antenhofer, "Briefe, Besuche, Hochzeiten."
41. Severidt, *Familie,* 191–4.
42. Antenhofer, *Briefe,* 81–120; Karl-Heinz Spiess, "Unterwegs zu einem fremden Ehemann: Brautfahrt und Ehe in europäischen Fürstenhäusern des Spätmittelalters," in *Fremdheit und Reisen im Mittelalter,* ed. Irene Erfen and Karl-Heinz Spiess (Stuttgart, 1997), 17–36; Karl-Heinz Spiess, "Fremdheit und Integration der ausländischen Ehefrau und ihres Gefolges bei internationalen Fürstenheiraten," in *Fürstenhöfe und ihre Außenwelt: Aspekte gesellschaftlicher und kultureller Identität im deutschen Spätmittelalter,* ed. Thomas Zotz (Würzburg, 2004), 267–90.
43. See Spiess, *Fremdheit,* 276.
44. Elena Taddei, "Anna Caterina Gonzaga und ihre Zeit. Der italienische Einfluss am Innsbrucker Hof," in *Der Innsbrucker Hof: Residenz und höfische Gesellschaft in Tirol vom 15. bis 19. Jahrhundert,* ed. Heinz Noflatscher and Jan Paul Niederkorn (Vienna, 2005), 217–18.
45. Marriages led to an exchange of "personnel" in the widest sense. Some servants went to live at the other courts, and there is also the phenomenon of the "clientage." People from different backgrounds used these new contacts to work "abroad"; they asked the princes to accept their children as servants or to help them in their demands. Very famous are examples of illegitimate siblings, such as Friedrich of Brandenburg, Barbara's illegitimate half-brother, who became one of the most important members of her entourage. He married an Italian woman, Caterina de Torelli, who later accompanied Paula to her new home. Antenhofer, *Briefe,* 184–96.
46. Severidt, *Familie,* 191–92.
47. See on this theme Christina Antenhofer, "Letters Across the Borders: Strategies of Communication in an Italian-German Renaissance Correspondence," in *Women's Letters Across Europe, 1400–1700: Form and Persuasion,* eds. Jane Couchman and Ann Crabb (Aldershot and Burlington, 2005), 103–22; Gerhard Vowinckel, *Verwandtschaft, Freundschaft und die Gesellschaft der Fremden: Grundlagen menschlichen Zusammenlebens* (Darmstadt, 1995); Hans Medick and David Warren Sabean, eds., *Interest and Emotion: Essays on the Study of Family and Kinship* (Cambridge, 1984).

48. This parallels the results Sablonier presented in his study on the Aragonese royal family. Roger Sablonier, "The Aragonese Royal Family Around 1300," in Medick and Sabean, *Interest and Emotion*, 210–39. See also Antenhofer, *Briefe*, 145–50, 301–5.
49. In fact this is the case for Barbarina Gonzaga, whose marriage started very positively and cooled down when she lost her only child and never got pregnant again; Severidt, *Familie*, 221–22. With Paula the situation was even worse, as she lost her only child and never received the whole amount of her dowry; these may have been the two basic reasons for her "unhappy" marriage, see Antenhofer, *Briefe*, 301–5.
50. Severidt, *Familie*, 200–201.
51. Obviously because he was her favored grandson; see Gino Benzoni, "Gonzaga, Ludovico," in *DBI*, 57: 803.
52. Ibid.
53. In the sixteenth century, three Gonzaga-Habsburg marriages took place: Francesco III and Katherina von Habsburg in 1549; Guglielmo and Eleonora von Habsburg in 1561; Anna Caterina and Archduke Ferdinand II von Tirol in 1582; for all the Habsburg-Gonzaga marriages, see the genealogical tree.
54. In his study on the Italian dynasties in the sixteenth and seventeenth centuries, Spagnoletti identifies three groups of princes characterized by three different marriage circles. The Gonzaga along with the Savoia, Medici, Este, and Farnese belong to the highest group that could marry women of the same status or even a higher one, that is, daughters of kings and emperors. The second group disposed over small territories and married women from the cadet lines of the five leading families or "natural" daughters of the great princes. The last group includes princes who were not sovereign; they mostly intermarried in their own group, although sometimes princes of the first and second group would marry the daughters of this last group. Between the second and the third group are the papal families; their daughters were requested by the princes of the second group, when a pope of the family was actually in power; as soon as a new pope was elected, the family lost its status and daughters were sought only by princes of the third group. Spagnoletti, *Dinastie*, 168–76.
55. See Hohkamp, "Sisters," 97. Severidt sees the beginning of this process in the generation of Carlo and Ludovico II. Severidt, *Familie*, 89–90.
56. The cadets and the collateral lines they founded are slowly attracting the interest of historians, yet comparative studies or just profound studies on the single collateral lines are still to be written. Information on the Gonzaga cadet lines so far can be deduced from the *Dizionario Biografico degli Italiani* (Rome, 1960ff). On the Gonzaga of Gazzuolo see Carlo Togliani, ed., *Gazzuolo, Belforte: Storia, arte, e cultura* (Mantua, 2007).
57. See Vaini, *Ricerche*, 88–89. He refers to Ercolano Marani, "Osservazioni sopra l'albero genealogico di una grande casata: i Gonzaga," in *Gazzetta di Mantova*, 17 March 1964. For insights in the complex genealogy see http://genealogy.euweb.cz/gonzaga/ (accessed on 4 September 2008).
58. See Spagnoletti, *Dinastie*, 291–94.
59. Jürgen Herold, "Der Aufenthalt des Markgrafen Gianfrancesco Gonzaga zur Erziehung an den Höfen der fränkischen Markgrafen von Brandenburg 1455–1459: Zur Funktionsweise und zu den Medien der Kommunikation zwischen Mantua und Franken im Spätmittelalter," in *Principes: Dynastien und Höfe im späten Mittelalter; Interdisziplinäre Tagung des Lehrstuhls für Allgemeine Geschichte des Mittelalters und Historische Hilfswissenschaften in Greifswald in Verbindung mit der Residenzen-Kommission der Akademie der Wissenschaften zu Göttingen vom 15.-18. Juni 2000*, ed. Cordula Nolte, Karl-Heinz Spiess, and Ralf-Gunnar Werlich (Stuttgart, 2002), 199–234.

60. Lazzarini, "Rodolfo."
61. See, for example, Giampiero Brunelli, "Gonzaga, Ferrante," in *DBI*, 57: 734–44 and Gino Benzoni, "Gonzaga, Giovanni," in *DBI*, 57: 775–83.
62. Severidt, *Familie*, 134–35. On this role of siblings as informants see also Sophie Ruppel, "Geschwisterbeziehungen im Adel und Norbert Elias' Figurationssoziologie: ein Anwendungsversuch," in *Höfische Gesellschaft und Zivilisationsprozeß: Norbert Elias' Werk in kulturwissenschaftlicher Perspektive*, ed. Claudia Opitz (Cologne, 2005), 220.
63. See also Spiess, "Lordship."
64. See Isabella Lazzarini, *Fra un principe e altri stati: Relazioni di potere e forme di servizio a Mantova nell'età di Ludovico Gonzaga* (Rome, 1996), xi–xiii; Isabella Lazzarini, "Gonzaga, Francesco," in *DBI*, 57: 756–60. This practice continued into the sixteenth century; see http://genealogy.euweb.cz/gonzaga/ (accessed 4 September 2008).
65. This surpassing piety may have begun with Eleonora von Habsburg; see Sonia Pellizzer, "Eleonora d'Asburgo," in *DBI*, 42: 419–22. On the Gonzaga nuns, see Severidt, *Familie*, 91.
66. David Sanderson Chambers, *Renaissance Cardinals and Their Worldly Problems* (Aldershot, UK, 1997).
67. See Spagnoletti, *Dinastie*, 271–94.
68. Severidt, *Familie*, 41.
69. See Lazzarini, "Gonzaga, Francesco," 757–58. See also Severidt, *Familie*, 104–6. Conflicts mainly arose between Ludovico II and his son Francesco, the first cardinal and bishop of Mantova. When Francesco tried to pursue his own politics, his father answered with the famous saying, that he brought him his cardinal's hat, yet Francesco had not brought him the margrave's cap: "non deliberamo finché vivemo comportare che ne esso cardinale ne alcun altro sia signore de Mantua. … havemo cussiícara la beretta nostra com'el cardinale el suo capello, perchè la beretta nostra ha dato il capello a lui, ma non il suo capello ha dato la beretta a nui" (Archivio Gonzaga, libro 2891, folio 65); quoted in Severidt, *Familie*, 106.
70. See the famous example of Cardinal Ercole; Giampiero Brunelli, "Gonzaga, Ercole," in *DBI*, 57: 711–22.
71. See Spagnoletti, *Dinastie*, 239–40.
72. On the *Camera Picta*, see Rodolfo Signorini, *Opus hoc tenue: La camera dipinta di Andrea Mantegna; Lettura storica iconografica iconologica* (Parma, 1985).
73. There is still some debate among art historians about the exact historical event that is celebrated and the identification of the people portrayed in the frescoes. However, it is certain that Francesco is celebrated as cardinal representing the Gonzaga ecclesiastical politics; moreover, the presence of Emperor Friedrich III and of Christian as well as of the daughters Paula and Barbarina is proved by contemporary sources. See Rodolfo Signorini, *La più bella camera del mondo: La camera dipinta di Andrea Mantegna detta "degli Sposi,"* 2nd ed. (Mantua, 2002).

Chapter 4

Property Regimes and Migration of Patrician Families in Western Europe around 1500

Simon Teuscher

We tend to think of premodern patrician families as strongly attached to their cities. Many city councils at the end of the eighteenth century were still dominated by the same families that had acquired a leading position before 1500. Moreover, we find, among patricians probably more frequently than in any other social group of early modern Europe, property that remained over centuries in the possession of the same family and tied the latter to a particular city: family palaces and representative townhouses, pieces of land and manors in the city's vicinity, venal offices, and trade monopolies. While members of the higher nobility both had to relocate in the service of princes and could relocate without losing their status, the social position of a patrician could not be easily transferred beyond his city.[1]

This chapter will not call patricians' sedentariness into question. On the contrary, there is a lot to indicate that these families' attachment to their cities grew even firmer at the end of the Middle Ages, when elites closed off and relied more and more on monopolizing civic offices and commercial privileges.[2] I will argue, however, that precisely this remarkable rootedness of entire families would not have been possible without a considerable mobility on the part of some individual family members. A great deal of patrician migration in the period was directly linked to group-specific property regimes and patterns of property devolution that exposed individual family members to considerable financial stress. Despite their attempts to tie their fate to one particular place, patrician families were in fact often scattered over several cities, and often created kin connections with the elites of the new cities where they settled. I will argue that the particular patterns of such transregional kin connections are in part the outcome of a characteristically patrician situation, in which a desire to stay collided with economic incitements to leave.

In order to demonstrate the interdependence of property regimes and the transregional dispersion of families, this chapter will relate the life course of some individuals to the ways in which property circulated within their families of origin. Among the few sources that explicitly address such connections are the so-called family chronicles, which began to emerge in different cities of German-speaking Europe in the fifteenth and sixteenth centuries.[3] These texts can in many ways be compared to the better-known *ricordanze* that were kept in parts of Italy already more than a hundred years earlier. Whether these texts grew out of business records is subject to controversy.[4] In any case, the authors of family chronicles gave accounts of their own and their families' histories that openly and frequently addressed questions of business and property.

The argument that follows is based primarily on the close reading of two well-known family chronicles, but I will also draw from additional material more selectively. The first of the two chronicles was written by Burkhard Zink in Augsburg in the mid-fifteenth century, the second by Ludwig von Diesbach of Bern in the early sixteenth century. Both authors are fairly representative of the upper strata of the urban patriciates of Western Europe.[5] Families of this class were almost constantly represented in the high offices of their cities' governments and had at least a few members who were very wealthy. The Diesbach family in particular combined urban activities with an aristocratic lifestyle. The Diesbachs acquired castles and small noble seigneuries in the countryside. Members of both families were frequently called on by their cities to serve as ambassadors to kings, princes, and other cities. They can generally be said to have participated, although as rather peripheral figures, in contemporary court life.[6] Although families of this kind engaged in trade, among other things, they cannot be characterized as international merchants, and even less as representatives of the vanguard of a new capitalist era. Rather, they embody the values of traditional, premodern elites and on several counts resembled lesser nobilities with whom they occasionally intermarried.[7] Much like lesser noblemen, these patricians had some property of their own, which could include even minor lordly rights in a village outside their city, while deriving most of their income from serving as municipal officers.[8] While lesser nobles primarily served princes, patricians served cities.

Geographical mobility among urban patricians and other elite groups of the period around 1500 is far too conspicuous a phenomenon to have gone completely unnoticed by historians. My point is that the travel and dislocation of medieval urban elites have to be reexamined in light of the kinship structure and the inheritance patterns they favored. I will begin with some historiographical remarks. I will then move to examine family chronicles with two purposes. First, I will attempt to relate moments of dislocation to particular stages in the cycle of intergenerational property devolution. Second, I will discuss how families with members scattered over wide geographical areas operated, to what extent patrician mobility was the outcome of collective strategies, and how it contributed to the formation of transregional networks of kin.

A Historiography Built on Patricians' Own Ideals

My attempt to relate mobility to family organization goes up against three broad trends in recent historiography on patriciates, which to a considerable extent reflects patricians' own ideals and self-perceptions. The first trend is to conceive of mobility as characteristic of exceptional individual patricians, rather than of the entire social group. Historians have long been fascinated with individual high-ranking citizens who set out for great travels. Many scholars, for example, focus on the authors of reports of pilgrimages to Jerusalem that are extant from almost every major city in Europe.[9] As a broader social phenomenon, mobility into and between cities has been investigated with regard to the lower and middle classes, but not the patriciate.[10] Asking about mobility among the latter seems to run counter to what has been a main concern of the social history of patriciates in the last few decades, namely, to explain how in almost every European city around 1500 a few families succeeded in monopolizing most of the political and economic power.[11] On one level, the processes of closing off patriciates had everything to do with families' attachment to one particular place. Towards the end of the fifteenth century at the very latest, wealthy merchants in most cities began to invest more of their capital into real estate, including minor noble rights in the villages around their city. At the same time there emerged strategies of marrying within narrow circles of few interrelated families, which allowed for keeping real estate and offices within closed circuits.[12] In politics it seems that belonging to a family that had long been well established locally became an increasingly important prerequisite of eligibility to city councils.[13]

An exceptional degree of stability and continuity undoubtedly characterized urban elites in early modern Europe. These features, however, have been exaggerated by investigations that took it for granted that families—understood to be patrilines of people bearing the same name—were the basic building blocks of society, while losing sight of the individuals contained in such families. Men with the family names von Diesbach and von Erlach, for example, occupied leading offices in the city of Bern with almost no interruption from the late fifteenth to the late eighteenth century. But this does not mean that all descendants of these two families held leading offices or even stayed put in Bern. In fact, if one begins to take into consideration how patrician families distributed social rank and wealth internally, it becomes clear that a family's stable position in power went hand in hand with the emigration of some of its members.

The tendency to conceive of patrilines as the bearers of continuity and basic units of society perpetuates the image that premodern patricians liked to offer of themselves. In seals, coats of arms, genealogical trees, ancestral portraits, and family chronicles, prominent patricians presented themselves as scions of patrilines with a long ancestry. In addition, representative buildings in the city as well as pieces of land and lordly rights in its surroundings were known to be property that had been firmly attached to such patrilines for many generations and should belong to them also in the future.[14] Some family chronicles refer to the origins of a family in a remote or even mythical past and most stress the length of that family's rootedness in a city.[15] If such representations of a family's past were not outright fiction, they were very selective. Publicly displayed family memories usually only included one or two male family members for each generation and essentially consisted in lists of successive proprietors of a few pieces of property.[16] Such representations almost never included references to property that had been lost by the family or to branches of the family that had descended into the lower classes or entirely disappeared from the city. If the patrician family as it was put on public display appears to be stable and sedentary, this was to a large extent the outcome of specific strategies of self-representation.

A second trend in historiography has been to discuss patrician mobility—if at all—in terms of cultural experience rather than of economic necessities. In the last few years, scholars have paid more attention to the fact that mobility, in particular in the form of travels, was more than incidental in the lives of many members of late medieval and early modern elites. From the late fourteenth century onward, members of the landed nobility in particular, and to some extent patricians as well, went on pilgrimages to Santiago, Rome, and Jerusalem; they traveled to participate in the so-called crusades in Iberia and the Baltic provinces; they enrolled as mercenaries, served at the courts of foreign princes, and studied at universities in towns different from their own.[17] Moreover, the politics of prenational Europe constrained even minor cities to develop their own diplomatic activities, often without the mediation of major territorial governments. Thus, each of the cities belonging to the Swiss Confederation relied at any given period on a number of its patrician citizens who were traveling in order to conduct diplomatic negotiations with nearby cities as well as with city-states and noble rulers across Germany and Italy, the king of France, the Holy Roman Emperor, and the Pope.[18] Patricians themselves immortalized their journeys in travelogues, pilgrimage reports, and family chronicles, all of which have come down to us in considerable numbers. Many collected souvenirs they had brought from far away or letters of recommendation that kings, dukes, and cities had granted them to facilitate their travel.[19] In sum, historians have increasingly recognized that the elites of prenational Europe moved about with a surprising ease considering how underdeveloped systems of transportation were at the time. Being on the road could be such an essential part of life in the later Middle Ages that some scholars recently elevated itinerancy to the status of a central concept of the period's elite culture.[20]

Recent research has become interested in the multiple forms of elite mobility as a kind of prehistory of tourism or of the emergence of perceptions of "the other" that could be related to a genealogy of colonialism and slavery.[21] Werner Paravicini, who has pioneered this approach in a brilliant article, established continuities—and some significant ruptures—between crusades, pilgrimage, young noblemen's travels to courts, and the early forms of tourism arising from the Grand Tour of English aristocrats.[22] In order to draw such lines of continuity and to prevent other related topics, such as craftsmen's travels, from interfering, Paravicini confined his investigation to travels that were pursued "for the sake of traveling," by which he understood everything but travels originating out of economic necessity.[23] Methodologically, this approach has proven very productive, because it allows us to examine elite travels in the context of piety, self-affirmation, adventurousness, education, escapism, conspicuous consumption, class consciousness, and self-representation. But just because historians have chosen to leave economic factors aside, it does not mean that they were absent from the motivations that led patricians to travel and migrate. An entirely different picture emerges when geographical mobility is analyzed from the point of view of family organization and property regimes—and thus from an angle that would ultimately permit us to relate mobility not only to leisurely travel, but also to the more sensitive topic of past and present mass migration.

The inclination to disregard economic aspects of patricians' dislocation, too, has its roots in premodern patricians' own self-image. Patricians developed their own lofty conceptions of what traveling was all about. While modern historians have chosen to look at premodern travel with regard to multiculturalism, cultural transfers, and transnationalism, contemporaries themselves associated travel to adventure, glory, and honor. These values abound in the fictional travel literature that patricians cherished. Money and property are largely absent from late medieval literature about knights-errant, dating back to the *Histoire de Guillaume le Maréchal* (1220), through the *Frauenlob* of Ulrich von Lichtenstein, and on to the numerous chronicles of the fourteenth and fifteenth centuries about noble and patrician travelers memorialized by heralds and the travelers themselves.[24] In the seventeenth century, Miguel Cervantes would finally ridicule this medieval literary tradition denying the economic dimensions of elite traveling. When an innkeeper asks Don Quixote whether he has money, the knight replies that he has never read in stories of knights-errant that they filled their pockets with money before heading off.[25]

The third trend in recent historiography that needs to be addressed briefly is the tendency to treat family cohesion and geographical mobility as incompatible. This conception can be traced back to modernization narratives that attribute the mobility of Western societies to a weakening of traditional bonds to families and local communities. A variation of this argument has recently been restated by the historian Michael Mitterauer in his book on the medieval preconditions for what he celebrates as the West's uniqueness.[26] Mitterauer believes that the so-called European marriage pattern, i.e., the fact that Europeans, at least since the early modern period, on average married late, providing them with a particularly long youth, that is, the period after adolescence and before marriage, the establishment of a new household, or the takeover of a parental farm or enterprise. This prolonged adolescence provided Western Europeans with unique opportunities to be geographically mobile, and thus, to sever ties to their families of origin and to affiliate with others, to find employers on the market, to develop friendships, and to join voluntary associations, corporative bodies and—ultimately—modern states.[27] A similar connection between an extended period of youth and motivations to leave had already been pointed out by George Duby in his work on the nobility in Western Europe during the high Middle

Ages—a phenomenon that can be easily corroborated with examples from patricians' family chronicles from around 1500.[28] However, there is less evidence to support the equation of geographical mobility with a disengagement from the family of origin. On the contrary, to a large extent, contemporary chronicles deal with how migration was not only triggered by family cycles but also organized along kinship relations.

Family Cycles

The mere complexity of many patrician property arrangements called for the kind of extended narration that we find in early modern family chronicles.[29] In principle, families maintained inheritance systems in which each son and each daughter had a claim to an equal share of the parents' inheritance. However, the bulk of these families' fortunes often consisted of assets that for legal or practical reasons could not be divided: rural castles and seigneuries, representative townhouses, venal political offices, or monopolies, such as the exclusive right to import salt to a city. As a rule, the child (not necessarily a son) who succeeded to such an estate had to compensate his siblings in cash. Moreover, widows and widowers frequently remarried, and, in theory, were thus required to give their children their share of the late parent's estate. In fact, those who succeeded to the estate often did not possess enough liquid assets to pay fair compensations to their co-heirs. Instead, they resorted to a number of other agreements: they delayed the distribution of an estate as long as possible, gave some relatives the role of silent partners, promised others annual rents, paid a dowry to their daughters only on condition that they renounce their legitimate share, accumulated obligations, and passed these on to the next generation.[30] Advancing claims on family assets often made it necessary to tell exactly the kind of stories our family chronicles contain. Most authors give detailed accounts of how they acquired property, how they divided inherited goods with other family members, how they provided their children with advances, and how these agreements were related to alliances and conflicts within the family.

Family chronicles show that geographic mobility in the concerned families was often directly related to problems of succession to family estates. Both Burkhard Zink and Ludwig von Diesbach begin the chronicles of their lives not with their births, but with the death of one of their parents.[31] For both chroniclers the loss of a parent while they still were children was the beginning of long years of homelessness. Burkhard Zink's father almost immediately remarried with "a young, proud wife, who did not like us children, was hard against us, and acted against us, but"—Zink continues—"our father loved her as many old men love young women."[32] Given this situation, Zink left his native city of Memmingen in Upper Swabia, and at the age of eleven walked several hundred kilometers to Ribnica at the border between today's Slovenia and Croatia. There, he went to school and was taken care of by his father's brother, a priest who had arrived there in the service of a Swabian noblewoman married to a local count.[33]

After seven years in Slovenia, Zink returned to Memmingen. In the meantime, his father had separated from his new wife, and the son had reason to hope that he could now stay with his father and thus, as he writes, live as a *jungkher,* a squire.[34] But Zink's hopes were immediately shattered. His family, assuming that he would never return, had given the entire estate of Zink's late mother to his only sister, in order to allow her to marry a wealthy husband. Everybody, Zink relates, was of the opinion that it was too late for him to get anything, "and no one was happy to have me around."[35] He thus returned to Slovenia, only to find that his uncle had died. The latter had promised to install Zink as his heir, but by the time Zink arrived, the uncle's four illegitimate children had already divided the estate among themselves. Successively, Zink spent several years studying in different cities, always in great poverty. At times, he wrote, he had to beg for bread in the streets. He got married in Augsburg, not far from his native Memmingen, and ultimately acquired considerable wealth and prestige as merchant and city councilman.[36] Toward the end of the chronicle, the reader begins to recognize an agenda behind Zink's graphic descriptions of his poverty-stricken youth. By the time Zink wrote, he was in his third marriage and was probably confronted with claims from his son from his first marriage who wished to get his share of his late mother's inheritance. The father tried to fend off this demand, arguing that neither his wife nor he had had money at the time of his first marriage, so that children issued from the latter had nothing to claim. As if he wanted to prove the contrary, Zink ended his chronicle with a list of expenses he had made for his son.[37] In other words, the chronicle itself was probably an instrument of defending an estate against the claims of a competing heir.

The family of our second chronicler, Ludwig von Diesbach, was originally from Bern in Switzerland. But at the point when Ludwig's chronicle begins, that is, at the moment of his father's death, the family lived about five hundred kilometers north of Bern, in the castle Godesberg near Cologne. Ludwig's father held the castle and seigneurie of Godesberg as collateral for his loans to the bishop of Cologne.[38] After the death of Ludwig's father, the Diesbach family took upon themselves the difficult task of recovering the credits from the bishop on condition that the Diesbach children would be the only beneficiaries of these efforts, while the widow was given an indemnity amount and had to leave her children to their paternal kin. Ludwig's older brother and his sister were brought to their cousin in Bern. Ludwig, who was still a baby, was given to a wet nurse in a shoemaker's home in Cologne.[39] Only at the age of eight was little Ludwig brought to Bern. And a few years later, the Diesbach family finally succeeded in recovering their money from the bishop of Cologne. As a result, Ludwig's brother was able to establish his own household and get married. Now Ludwig became a possible rival to his siblings—and had to leave town. He was to spend the next twelve years abroad. First he served a Burgundian nobleman. As soon as the city of Bern shifted allegiance in the 1470s conflict between Burgundy and France, he went on to serve at the court of the king of France.[40] Only when his brother's wife died did the Diesbach family call him back to the city and urge him to find a wife, after having done everything to keep him out of Bern for several years. Now, it was his turn to succeed as head of the family's principal household.[41]

These stories both point to the same structural problem. The estates that patrician families passed on from one generation to the next could hardly ever sustain the aristocratic lifestyle of more than one or two adult men and their respective households. Additional male offspring had either to commit to an ecclesiastic career or find ways of bridging the time gap until it was their turn to run the estate. Patrician sons apparently tended to leave, or were made to leave by their families, before they reached the age of marriage. This pattern marks an important difference between patrician and princely families: among the latter, a great share of geographical mobility concerned young women who got married.[42] Patrician men, in contrast, left in order to delay marriage. Ideally, they neither returned nor married before they could reasonably take up the position as head of the family's main household. In many cases, this circumstance would never materialize, and the émigrés' best alternative was to gain enough to establish their own households in a location different from their place of birth.

Many, however, seem to have kept returning and leaving. Thus did, for example, Conrad von Scharnachthal, a patrician from Bern with roots in the lesser nobility. He left no family chronicle or travel account, properly speaking, but an amazing collection of letters of recommendation and certifications of his stay in different places, which he solicited from princes and city councils from all over Europe.[43] Scharnachthal repeatedly went on major travels across Europe, staying away from home for several years each time. He remained a bachelor and seems to have waited almost his entire life to succeed to a leading position in his family. However, his cousins occupied major political offices in Bern for decades, and only two years before his death, when he was over fifty, did Conrad's father leave him a first share of his inheritance, the castle of Oberhofen.[44]

Burkhard Zink and Ludwig von Diesbach were not the only ones who had to leave while waiting to succeed. Their sons, we learn from the family chronicles, followed the same destiny. Ludwig's chronicle mentions explicitly that he sent all his sons except for one to Paris for long periods of time.[45] Moreover, we know what our authors' sons were doing at the time their fathers were writing the chronicles.[46] Diesbach had one married son who still—or again—lived in his hometown, began a career in the city offices, and seemed ready to take over after his death. Diesbach mentions explicitly that he had decided to give this one son "a wife and a rural estate"—one of the family's main assets.[47] Both Diesbach and Zink also had sons who obviously were almost constantly absent from their hometowns. Only in passing does Zink mention that he had been without any news of one of his sons for nine years. The latter had meanwhile been a mercenary in the Italian wars; another son died while he was serving a nobleman in France.[48] Ludwig von Diesbach's youngest son was also a notorious mercenary and recruiter of mercenaries.[49] We find the same pattern in the family chronicle of Niklaus Muffel. Muffel never left his hometown of Nuremberg but stepped right into his father's footsteps. Nevertheless one of his sons traveled, in Muffel's words, to twelve different kingdoms serving the brother of the queen of Bohemia (a position that suggests that he was a professional mercenary).[50] Much like some of their fathers, these sons seem to have been among the ones whose contribution to preserving the family's estates was to leave.

Mobility as a Collective Endeavor

Being gone was not a position outside, but inside the family. This point needs to be further substantiated since it runs counter to widely held ideas about direct connections between geographical mobility, the rise of individualism, and the weakness of family structures. The chronicles make it clear that family members played a role in several aspects of migration: making some leave a place of origin, assisting each other on arrival in a new place, and providing role models and know-how about migration. Patrician migration, in sum, was often part of families' collective strategies.

For one thing, young men did not simply go away on their own and empty handed. The first stages of the journeys, if not more, were planned by their families, who also provided financial support. When Ludwig von Diesbach's brother took possession of their paternal inheritance, it was the family at large who placed Ludwig with a Burgundian nobleman.[51] As the political constellation changed, family members also told him when it was time to leave Burgundy and to move on to the king of France—and when to return back to Bern.[52] Both the Burgundian nobleman and the French king welcomed Ludwig as a member of the Diesbach family, who they knew well and had long been in touch with. Conversely, Ludwig expresses pride over having furthered the Diesbach's reputation with the king and to have been able to provide his family in Bern with important information from the inner circles of French politics.[53] In one way or the other, the family was constantly present on Ludwig's mind and in his everyday life during his extended leave from home.

The departure of some family members could be an integral part of the agreements on how estates were passed from one generation to the next. This becomes apparent in the memoirs of Georg von Ehingen (1428–1508). Although not a patrician, Georg belonged to a closely related group that faced very similar challenges, namely, the lesser Swabian nobility. Among lesser noblemen, families also often based their social status on no more than one major royal office and one main estate that they needed to pass down undivided to the next generation.[54] Georg describes how he discussed his plans for traveling to various European courts as an itinerant knight and how the father praised his resolution, stressing that Georg was exceptionally well suited for such a career, and promised to remunerate him with an important amount of cash.[55] In a different passage Georg explains—maybe as a defense against his siblings' competing claims—that his brothers, too, had agreed that the father should give him this amount to support his travels and that this simply represented his share of their father's estate.[56] In Georg's account, it appears to be a conscious family strategy to let one son who was supposed to be particularly well suited for the task try his luck in an itinerant existence with an uncertain destination.

In the case of Burkhard Zink, his sister and her husband—the ones who had seized his late mother's estate—helped him pay for his relocations. They had sent him on his second, very frustrating journey to Slovenia, where he learned that his uncle's inheritance had been squandered. When Zink returned empty handed, his sister and her husband provided him with cash amounts, first, so that he could start an apprenticeship, and then, so that he could study—and leave town again.[57] When after nine years of silence, Zink, now a wealthy citizen of Augsburg, heard that his son was a war captive in Italy, he rode to Venice, ready to spend a considerable though not unlimited amount to buy his son free.[58] It seems that the sons who had to go away could make some limited claims to being supported by the ones who held the estate. Such claims helped to soften the rather harsh conditions that the excluded sons had to face—but also kept them tied to their family of origin and its estate.

Moreover, men who had to get away from their immediate family often found refuge with their remote kin. Burkhard Zink left his father and traveled several hundred kilometers in order to move in with his father's brother.[59] And Ludwig von Diesbach, who had left because his brother married, was welcomed at the French court by a cousin of his brother's wife.[60] When a patrician son arrived in a city abroad, he was likely to find kin who had come before him and could help him getting started.

Some families seem to have been particularly efficient in passing on migration experience and migration skills and thus in facilitating the mobility of their members. Such families could, in the first place, develop a habit of frequent travels. Ludwig von Diesbach from Bern describes in his chronicle how he participated in a war in Italy on the French side and accidentally ran into his brother and his uncle, who were on their way to Jerusalem.[61] Similarly, Sebaldt Rieter senior from Nuremberg describes how he and his uncle on their way to Rome happened to meet his father and mother on their way home from Italy.[62] Indeed several generations of the Rieter had set out for major travels, mainly, but not only, for the sake of pilgrimage. Peter Rieter had been to Bruges, Italy, Spain, Jerusalem, and Rome in 1450; his son, Sebald senior, went to Santiago (1450) and Jerusalem (1464); and Sebald junior went again to Jerusalem (1479).[63]

Such families also left outstanding collections of documents related to their travels: not only specimens of the well-known pilgrimage descriptions, but also more practical texts such as travel guides with annotations, slips of paper containing descriptions of fast itineraries, tables of distances between major European cities, and collections of rules for safe traveling, all of which could be used to pass on know-how about traveling to future generations.[64] As far as a family's "culture of travel" is concerned, there was no sharp divide between leisurely and forced travels. Even what appear to be "travels for the sake of traveling" and celebratory accounts thereof could contribute to building experience, something a family's members could consult when they needed to dislocate for less sublime reasons. Even the chronicles analyzed here may have aimed at advising future generations on how to succeed away from home. Thus, Ludwig von Diesbach, who explicitly states that he wrote his chronicle for his children and grandchildren, reports numerous stories about how he failed and succeeded in difficult situations abroad.[65] What we find in extant documents is probably no more than a slim selection of the know-how about travel and migration that was passed down orally within particular families.

In general, then, patrician dislocations often make the most sense when seen as the outcome of the collective strategies not of individuals, but of entire families—with all the impositions this could entail for some of their members. From the point of view of the individuals who left, there appeared to be two different and similarly probable outcomes. On the one hand, they had reason to hope that they could return some day and step into the place of a previous possessor of the family's main estate. On the other hand, they pursued opportunities in order to acquire wealth elsewhere and some, including Zink, to build a patrician estate of their own in a new place. Why did people not pursue these two strategies while staying in their native towns? It is not easy to offer a fully satisfactory answer to this question. But there is a great deal to indicate that an individual's decision to leave was seldom fully voluntary. In the cases analyzed here, the families exerted considerable pressure on members they wanted to leave, often in order to keep conflicts over the control of a family estate from escalating. While it often was easy for a male family member to bring such an estate under his control, to consolidate such claims and to legalize them in a system of equal inheritance was much more complicated. When patricians took precedence over their siblings and half-siblings, this was usually not by virtue of a legal and definitive settlement of an estate, but the result of their ability to assert themselves de facto through provisional or silent agreements. Moreover, both the family as a whole and its excluded members, for reasons of reputation, probably preferred an honorable absence to an overt social descent in the city where the family competed for a leading position.

Conclusion

To conclude, I would like to put these examples into a wider perspective and relate the practices discussed here to patterns of transregional kin connections that have been established on the basis of prosopographic and more structure-oriented research. I am thinking in particular of the so-called interurban kindreds (*zwischenstädtische Versippung*) in the late Middle Ages and of Gérard Delille's sophisticated description of a spatial structure of social inequality among early modern patrician families.[66] Analyzing genealogies from the kingdom of Naples from the sixteenth to the eighteenth century, Delille found that the major noble lineages, most of which resided in the kingdom's major cities, tended to have cadet lines belonging to the patriciates of minor cities. These cadet lines had in turn even poorer cadet lines of their own that were attached to yet smaller towns. Between the different lines there evolved clientage relationships, and whenever a major line of a family failed to produce its own successors, someone from a cadet line would step in. As a result, there emerged a regular structure in the spatial distribution of intra-familial inequality.

The pattern Delille describes is highly regular. It seems to have resulted from centuries of rule-bound behavior: cadets were regularly pushed out of town in a movement that consistently went from centers to peripheries, and yet main and cadet lines remained in touch over generations. Among the German patricians in the late Middle Ages, things were less regular. Both first-borns and cadets emigrated; they could move to bigger or smaller cities; they could return or break ties with their families of origin. But around 1500, a pattern resembling the one that Delille found in the south of Italy emerged—a pattern that consolidated as social hierarchies became less permeable and family regimes more rigid. The temporary dislocations of "surplus sons" may also have prepared the ground for the modern urban elites' inclination to send their sons for shorter or longer periods in the service of territorial and national states, be it in the military, in the central administration in the capital, or as colonial officers. On a less speculative note, we can maintain with some assurance that attempts to tie a family to a stably located estate kept causing migration. Thus, the patrician property regime brought about its own unique pattern of migration and of geographically spread but interdependent family members.

Family chronicles provide only anecdotal evidence of the connection between geographical mobility and families' property regimes—enough to raise new questions, but not enough to offer full answers. To follow these suggestions further would require systematic archival research and attempts to juxtapose individuals' biographical data with the aggregate dynamics of how families made arrangements on the distribution and devolution of property. But even family chronicles give clear enough indicators to dispute the image of the geographical rootedness that patrician families propagated about themselves. A closer look at the organization of patrician families reveals that geographical mobility was part of many individual life courses—including those that eventually contributed to the acclaimed lasting attachment of the family to one place. The underlying tension between representation and practice is of particular interest to an archaeology of contemporary Western perceptions: it generated—long before the beginning of modern mass migration—a positive valuation of settledness and a certain disdain for mobility.

Notes

1. Ernst Schubert, *Einführung in die Grundprobleme der deutschen Geschichte im Spätmittelalter* (Darmstadt, 1992), 114.
2. David Warren Sabean and Simon Teuscher, "Kinship in Europe: A New Approach to Long-Term Development," in *Kinship in Europe: Approaches to the Long-Term Development (1300–1900)*, ed. David Warren Sabean, Simon Teuscher, and Jon Mathieu (New York, 2007), 1–32.
3. Simon Teuscher, "Parenté, politique et comptabilité: Chroniques familiales du Sud de l'Allemagne et de la Suisse autour de 1500," in *Annales: Histoire, Sciences Sociales* 59 (2003) : 847–58.
4. See the classic, Christiane Klapisch-Zuber, "L'invention du passé familial," in Christiane Klapisch-Zuber, ed., *La maison et le nom: Stratégies et rituels dans l'Italie de la renaissance* (Paris, 1990), 19–35; Raul Mordenti, *I libri di famiglia in Italia*, vol. 2, *Geografia e storia* (Rome, 2001); and, more recently, the monographic issue of *Annales: Histoire, Sciences Sociales* 59 (2004) : 785–858 and Birgit Studt, ed., *Haus- und Familienbücher in der städtischen Gesellschaft des Spätmittelalters und der frühen Neuzeit* (Cologne, 2007).
5. Urs Martin Zahnd, "Ludwig von Diesbach," in *Historisches Lexikon der Schweiz* (Basel, 2004), 3:714; Urs Martin Zahnd, *Die autobiographischen Aufzeichnungen Ludwig von Diesbachs: Studien zur spätmittelalterlichen Selbstdarstellung im oberdeutschen und schweizerischen Raume* (Bern, 1986).
6. Zahnd, *Aufzeichnungen*, 151f; Franz Moser, *Ritter Wilhelm von Diesbach, Schultheiss von Bern 1442–1517* (Bern, 1930); Karl Stettler, *Ritter Niklaus von Diesbach 1430–1475* (Bern, 1924).
7. On the complex interrelation between urban patricians and the minor nobility, see Joseph Morsel, *L'aristocratie médiévale Ve–XVe siècle* (Paris, 2006), 253–60; Schubert, *Einführung*, 114–16.
8. Schubert, *Einführung*, 108–24; François De Capitani, *Adel, Bürger und Zünfte im Bern des 15. Jahrhunderts* (Bern, 1982).
9. For an overview: Werner Paravicini, *Europäische Reiseberichte des späten Mittelalters: Eine analytische Bibliographie*, 3 vols. (Frankfurt am Main, 1994–2001).
10. Rainer Christoph Schwinges, ed., *Neubürger im späten Mittelalter: Migration und Austausch in der Städtelandschaft des alten Reiches (1250–1550)* (Berlin, 2002); Hans-Jörg Gilomen and Martina Stercken, eds., *Zentren: Ausstrahlung, Einzugsbereich und Anziehungskraft von Städten und Siedlungen zwischen Rheinlauf und Alpen* (Zürich, 2001).
11. Schubert, *Einführung*; Eberhard Isenmann, *Die deutsche Stadt im Spätmittelalter, 1250–1500: Stadtgestalt, Recht, Stadtregiment, Kirche, Gesellschaft, Wirtschaft* (Stuttgart, 1988); Hans Conrad Peyer, "Die Anfänge der Schweizerischen Aristokratien," in *Luzerner Patriziat: Sozial- und Wirtschaftsgeschichtliche Studien zur Entwicklung im 16. und 17. Jahrhundert; Mit einer Einführung von Hans Conrad Peyer*, ed. Kurt Messmer and Peter Hoppe (Lucerne, 1976), 1–28; Martin Alioth, *Gruppen an der Macht: Zünfte und Patriziat in Strassburg im 14. und 15. Jahrhundert; Untersuchungen zu*

Verfassung, Wirtschaftsgefüge und Sozialstruktur, 2 vols. (Basel, 1988). For additional literature, see Isenmann, *Stadt,* 269–90.

12. De Capitani, *Adel;* Isenmann, *Stadt,* 297f; Gérard Delille, *Le maire et le prieur: Pouvoir central et pouvoir local en Méditerranée occidentale (XVe–XVIIIe siècle)* (Paris, 2003), 221–34.
13. Simon Teuscher, "Politics of Kinship in the City of Bern at the End of the Middle Ages," in Sabean, Teuscher, and Mathieu, *Kinship in Europe,* 76–90.
14. Zahnd, *Aufzeichnungen,* 189–202.
15. See the Familienbuch des Werner Overstolz discussed in Marc von der Höh, "Zwischen religiöser Memoria und Familiengeschichte: Das Familienbuch des Werner Overstolz," in *Haus- und Familienbücher in der städtischen Gesellschaft des Spätmittelalters und der frühen Neuzeit,* ed. Birgit Studt (Cologne, 2007), 55–57.
16. Anita Guerreau-Jalabert has coined the very telling term *topologinée* for such lines of possessors of landed property that we tend to mistake for genealogies. Anita Guerreau-Jalabert, "Sur les structures de parenté dans l'Europe médiévale (Note Critique)," *Annales: Economies, Société et Civilisation* 36 (1981): 1028–49.
17. Ludwig Schmugge, "Kollektive und individuelle Motivstrukturen im mittelalterlichen Pilgerwesen," in *Migration in der Feudalgesellschaft,* ed. Gerhard Jaritz and Albert Müller (Frankfurt, 1988), 263–89; Werner Paravicini, "Von der Heidenfahrt zur Kavalierstour: Über Motive und Formen adligen Reisens im späten Mittelalter," in *Wissensliteratur im späten Mittelalter* (Wiesbaden, 1993), 13:91–130; Rainer Babel and Werner Paravicini, eds., *Grand Tour: Adeliges Reisen und europäische Kultur vom 14. bis zum 18. Jahrhundert* (Stuttgart, 2005); Stephan Selzer, *Deutsche Söldner im Italien des Trecento* (Tübingen, 2001); Stephan Selzer, "Die Iberische Halbinsel als Ziel bewaffneter Mobilität deutschsprachiger Edelleute im 14. Jahrhundert: Eine Skizze," in *'Das kommt mir spanisch vor': Eigenes und Fremdes in den deutsch-spanischen Beziehungen des späten Mittelalters,* ed. Klaus Herbers and Nikolas Jaspert (Münster, 2004), 185–216; Philippe Contamine, "Le problème des migrations des gens de guerre en Occident durant les derniers siècles du Moyen Âge," in *Le migrazioni in Europa secc. XIII–XVIII,* ed. Simonetta Cavaciocchi (Florence, 1994), 459–76. See also William Caferro, *John Hawkwood, English Mercenary in Fourteenth-Century Italy* (Baltimore, 2006).
18. Andreas Würgler, "Boten und Gesandte an der eidgenössischen Tagsatzung. Diplomatische Praxis im Spätmittelalter," in *Gesandtschafts- und Botenwesen im spätmittelaterlichen Europa,* ed. Rainer Christoph Schwinges and Klaus Wriedt (Ostfildern, 2003), 287f.
19. Werner Paravicini, "Seigneur par itinérance? Le cas du patricien bernois Conrad de Scharnachtal," in *L'itinérance des seigneurs (XIVe-XVIe siècles),* ed. Agostino Paravicini Bagliani, Eva Pibiri, and Denis Reynard (Lausanne, 2003), 27–71; Karl Schib, ed., *Hans Stockars Jerusalemfahrt 1519 und Chronik 1520–1529* (Basel, 1949), 14–15.
20. Paravicini Bagliani, Pibiri, and Reynard, *L'itinérance des seigneurs,* 27–71. See also Paravicini, "Heidenfahrt."
21. See Michael Harbsmeier, *Wilde Völkerkunde: Andere Welten in deutschen Reiseberichten der Frühen Neuzeit* (Frankfurt, 1994); Dorothea Nolde, "Die Assimilation des Fremden: Nahrung und Kulturkontakt in de Brys 'America'," *Historische Anthropologie* 3 (2004): 355–72.
22. Paravicini, "Heidenfahrt."
23. Ibid., 92.
24. Werner Paravicini, „Fahrende Ritter: Literarisches Bild und gelebte Wirklichkeit im Spätmittelalter," in *Mittelalterliche Menschenbilder,* ed. Martina Neumeyer (Regens-

burg, 2000), 205–54; Paul Meyer, ed., *L'histoire de Guillaume le Maréchal comte de Striguil et de Pembroke régent d'Angleterre de 1216 à 1219*, 3 vols. (Paris, 1891–1901); Theodor Nolte, *'Lauda post mortem': Die deutschen und niederländischen Ehrenreden des Mittelalters* (Bern, 1983); Arnold Esch, "Gemeinsames Erlebnis: Individueller Bericht," *Zeitschrift für historische Forschung* 25 (1984): 385–416.

25. Cervantes, *Don Quixote*, I, 3; this passage was first pointed out by Paravicini, "Ritter," 207.
26. Michael Mitterauer, *Warum Europa? Mittelalterliche Grundlagen eines Sonderwegs* (Munich, 2003).
27. Ibid., 104–8.
28. See the classic account in Georges Duby, "Au XIIe siècle: Les 'jeunes' dans la société aristocratique," *Annales: Economies, Société et Civilisation* 19 (1965): 835–46.
29. Simon Teuscher, "Parenté," 847–58; Gerhard Köbler, "Das Familienrecht in der spätmittelalterlichen Stadt," in *Haus und Familie in der spätmittelalterlichen Stadt*, ed. Alfred Haverkamp (Cologne, 1984), 136–60; Martha C. Howell, *The Marriage Exchange: Property, Social Place, and Gender in Cities of the Low Countries 1300–1550* (Chicago, 1998).
30. Eugen Huber, *System und Geschichte des Schweizerischen Privatrechts*, 4 vols. (Basel, 1886–93); Thomas Weibel, *Erbrecht und Familie: Fortbildung und Aufzeichnung des Erbrechts in der Stadt Zürich, vom Richterbrief zum Stadterbrecht von 1716* (Zürich, 1986); Gerhard Köbler, "Familienrecht," 136–60.
31. Ludwig von Diesbach, "Herr Ludwigs von Diesbach Chronick," in Urs Martin Zahnd, *Die autobiographischen Aufzeichnungen Ludwig von Diesbachs: Studien zur spätmittelalterlichen Selbstdarstellung im oberdeutschen und schweizerischen Raume* (Bern, 1986), 30.
32. Burkhart Zink, "Chronik 1368–1468," in *Die Chroniken der schwäbischen Städte: Augsburg*, ed. Ferdinand Frensdorff and Matthias Lexer (Leipzig, 1866), 2:122 (my translation): "die was ein junge stoltze frau, die was uns kinden nit günstig und hett uns hert und tet uns übel, aber sie was unserm vater lieb und geviel im wol, als noch oft und dick alten mannen junge weib wol gevallen."
33. Ibid., 123.
34. Ibid., 124.
35. Ibid.: "und was mein niemant fro."
36. Ibid., 134ff.
37. Ibid., 140–42.
38. Diesbach, "Chronick," 28–30.
39. Ibid., 32–34.
40. Ibid., 36–66.
41. Ibid., 66.
42. Cordula Nolte, "'Ir seyt ein frembs weib, das solt ir pleiben, dieweil ihr lebt'. Beziehungsgeflechte in fürstlichen Familien des Spätmittelalters," in *Geschlechterstudien im interdisziplinären Gespräch: Kolloquium des Interdisziplinären Zentrums für Frauen- und Geschlechterstudien an der Ernst-Moritz-Arndt Universität Greifswald*, ed. Doris Ruhe (Würzburg, 1998), 11–41; Karl-Heinz Spiess, "Unterwegs zu einem fremden Ehemann. Brautfahrt und Ehe in europäischen Fürstenhäusern des Spätmittelalters," in *Fremdheit und Reisen im Mittelalter*, ed. Irene Erfen and Karl-Heinz Spiess (Stuttgart, 1997), 17–36; Karl-Heinz Spiess, "Europa heiratet: Kommunikation und Kulturtransfer im Kontext europäischer Königsheiraten des Spätmittelalters," in *Europa im späten Mittelalter: Politik, Gesellschaft, Kultur*, ed. Rainer Christoph Schwinges, Christian Hesse, and Peter Moraw (Munich, 2006), 435–64; Roger Sablonier, "Die

Aragonesische Königsfamilie um 1300," in *Emotionen und materielle Interessen: Sozialanthropologische und historische Beiträge zur Familienforschung,* ed. Hans Medick and David Warren Sabean (Göttingen, 1984), 282–317.

43. Paravicini, "Seigneur."
44. Karl Ludwig von Sinner, "Versuch einer diplomatischen Geschichte der Edlen von Scharnachthal," in *Der Schweizer Geschichtforscher* 3 (1820): 157f.
45. Diesbach, "Chronick," 100f.
46. For Diesbach see Simon Teuscher, *Bekannte, Klienten, Verwandte: Soziabilität und Politik in der Stadt Bern um 1500* (Cologne, 1998), 48–54. For Zink, see "Chronik des Burkard Zink," 142f.
47. Diesbach, "Chronick," 108.
48. Zink, "Chronik," 139, 142.
49. Teuscher, *Bekannte,* 52.
50. Gedenkbuch von Niclaus Muffel in *Die Chroniken der deutschen Städte vom 14. bis ins 16. Jahrhundert,* ed. Carl Hegel (Leipzig, 1874), 11:749.
51. Diesbach, "Chronick," 36f.
52. Ibid., 40f, 64–66.
53. Ibid., 48, 60.
54. For similar problems among the lower German nobility, see Joseph Morsel, "Geschlecht als Repräsentation: Beobachtungen zur Verwandtschaftskonstruktion im fränkischen Adel des späten Mittelalters," in *Die Repräsentation der Gruppen: Texte, Bilder, Objekte,* ed. Otto Gerhard Oexle and Andrea von Hülsen-Esch (Göttingen, 1998), 259–325.
55. Gabriele Ehrmann, ed., *Georg von Ehingen: Reisen nach der Ritterschaft. Edition, Untersuchung, Kommentar* (Göppingen, 1979), 25f, 28.
56. Ibid., 15.
57. Zink, "Chronik," 125.
58. Ibid., 142f.
59. Ibid., 123.
60. Diesbach, "Chronick," 42, 46–48, 62.
61. Ibid., 41.
62. Reinhold Röhricht and Heinrich Meisner, eds., *Das Reisebuch der Familie Rieter* (Tübingen, 1884), 10.
63. Ibid., 2–3.
64. Edited in ibid.
65. For explicit advice to his children, see Diesbach, "Chronick," 26, 51.
66. Isenmann, *Stadt,* 298f; Delille, *Le maire,* 171–84.

Chapter 5

Transdynasticism at the Dawn of the Modern Era

Kinship Dynamics among Ruling Families

Michaela Hohkamp

Modern nations have long been regarded in European historical research as the result of long-term and successful territorialization and nation-building processes. On the basis of the implicit assumption that undisputed territorial ownership is the foundation of stable political power, "land" is considered to be the material substructure of power. Following this premise, the emergence of modern statehood is usually described as a linear process, which begins with the so-called *Personenverbandstaat* (personal union of ruling princes) and ends with the modern, territorially defined and democratically legitimated nation-state. During this process, the redrawing of territorial boundaries and the emergence of bureaucratically managed and run territorial states are thought to play a prominent role. At the center of this development, according to traditional political historiography, are the princely houses of early modern Europe. As the prevailing argument goes, their evolution is the result of *Fortschritt* in *Hausdenken* (building noble houses).[1] This progress, it is said, can be seen primarily in the fact that, in the course of early modern European history, female relations—usually meaning daughters and sisters of possessors of power—were less and less frequently involved in inheritance directly, but rather were more likely to play an indirect role in the transfer and circulation of property, such as with the exchange of a dowry. This gender-specific practice, which was in evidence in princely society (not only) of the Holy Roman Empire beginning in the late Middle Ages, is widely considered to be the basis for the establishment of a dynasty and hence for the origin of modern European statehood.[2] As has recently been argued, this approach favors a view of society in which the political and societal functions of kinship are continuously undervalued, while state institutions are given more and more significance and kinship "is the functional predecessor of almost everything, but never a constructive factor of the emergence of anything."[3]

Now, this perspective on modern state and nation building has been neither historically nor historiographically limited to purely political and social aspects of power. Rather, it has been accompanied by very diverse discourses in which the so-called *primogenitus*, the first-born son, was designed and designated as the sole legal successor to power and preferred heir. This historical production process of the "one and only," which can be traced in historiographical, genealogical, and juridical writings up to the turn of the late eighteenth or early nineteenth century, has been transported into historical and politico-historical writings of the late nineteenth and twentieth centuries, and to some extent even of the early twenty-first century.[4] The talk of *Aussterben eines Geschlechtes* (extinction of a dynasty), prevalent in the traditional historical auxiliary sciences (for example, in genealogy) refers in historical texts about the early modern noble and ruling houses to the failure of a male heir and characterizes this extinction as a break in the (male) blood-related, traditional lineage. This view forms the general, gender-specific frame of reference for an exclusive discourse, which seems to privilege a single male heir over his brothers and sisters in the context of authority and property transfer in the early modern period. But if the gaze is shifted away from the male ego at the center of kinship events, then it becomes possible to detect horizontal kinship networks whose nodes are frequently formed by female relations, such as daughters, sisters, and aunts. In this context, special attention needs to be given to the sisters of a ruling prince.[5]

The significance of this phenomenon should not be underestimated, because these sisters were also often wives and are therefore regarded by researchers as agents between two families or houses. This function, as is typically argued, could be fulfilled by married princesses, because they left their ancestral families behind to become members of new families. Historically, this move is visibly represented by the fact that brides usually were sent to reside at the court of future husbands—and not the other way around. It is not easy to say how difficult this change was for the people involved, especially when it was bound not only to a shift in geographical location, but also to changes in language and customs. Indeed, one repeatedly finds in the contemporary writings comments in which the princess's malaise and illness were related to the unfamiliarity of her new residence and the distance from her birth family and place of origin. Yet such evidence, especially between the fifteenth and the eighteenth century, should be handled with caution because this time of global expansion framed a period in which special local and territorial identities were developed.[6] For this reason, the conception of a bride moving into a "foreign" territory should be examined critically.[7] In the contemporary understanding (documented in dictionaries all the way through the eighteenth century), a "sister" in the full sense of the word was always a female sibling who was married. In that culture the term *sister* was not used to designate a daughter among brothers except in the context of her as an actual, or, perhaps, a potential wife.[8] This practical and lexical understanding of the term shows that kinship relations were not seen simply as natural facts, but as culturally defined ties making up networks of relationships. Such webs allowed for the creation of overlapping, translocal spaces of exchange and communication for the accumulation and extension of power.

The idea that marriages within aristocratic society were among the most important instruments for early modern princely politics is not exactly new. The establishment of dynasties through the politics of marital exchange among the European ruling nobility and its meaning for the political history of the early modern period are topics as old as both historiography and historical scholarship.[9] What is new here is the idea that in the eyes of contemporaries, married sisters kept families and houses in touch with each other and that marriages both played a role for constructing vertically structured lineages and dynasties and served as instruments for creating horizontal transfamilial and transdynastic networks. Quite central to any understanding of the parallel—or perhaps better, *interlocking*—working of both principles is to track the way the culture of exchange, reciprocity, and intercommunication intersected with the ever greater emphasis on primogeniture. For one thing, in the dynamics of this kind of political culture, bitter conflicts of all kinds about the transfer of property constantly arose. To understand the internal complexity of these conflicts, an interesting line of research about the degree of consanguinity between princely spouses needs to be reconceptualized. In traditional historical research, such questions were often raised in the context of suggested or actual "inbreeding." Indeed the proximity of kinship between spouses has sometimes been called upon as an explanation for the mental and physical weaknesses of ruling princes and princesses—and not only in German literature.[10] Other disciplines have asked if members of the European nobility followed the marriage prohibitions established in Catholic canon law or Protestant ecclesiastical law. Since the 1960s, the development of interest within historical research for socioanthropological methods and questions has also brought about a reconsideration of the topic of "incest."[11] And there have been some studies directed towards the phenomenon of marriage between close relatives within the context of complex strategies for securing authority and expanding property, wealth, and territory.[12] Recent scholarship suggests that there were two large shifts in the configuration of kinship during the early modern period in Europe. The first shift that leads from the late Middle Ages into the early modern period can be described as an ever growing stress on familial coherence and the construction of lineages and descent groups with vertically organized relationships. The second shift, characterized by a strengthening of alliance and affinity and a refocusing on the web of horizontal relationships, initiated changes around the middle of the eighteenth century.[13] In this context, marriages between various types of cousins became especially significant.

In the following analysis, I want to examine and comment upon the potential for developing familial and political networks on the basis of a sample of 218 marriage settlements among ruling families in early modern Europe between 1480 and 1800. The sample comes from a database containing demographic data on the most powerful princely houses (Wettin, Wittelsbach, Brandenburg-Hohenzollern, Welf, Habsburg, margraves and landgraves of Baden and Hessen as well as the earls and dukes of Württemberg). On the basis of a historically defined "Urperson" for each dynasty in the fourteenth century, the database contains information on all male and female descendants with a date of birth after 1499 and before 1801 (i.e., between 1500 and 1800), or after 1449 and before 1829 (i.e., between 1450 and 1830), including their respective husbands or wives, as well as the brothers and sisters and parents of the in-marrying spouses.[14]

Over a period of three hundred years, we can see that marriages between near relatives and marriages outside the family were common options (Figure 5.1).

With respect to marriages between relatives, it may be said that the proportion of marriages between cousins is just as high as that between sister-brother pairs, or brother-brother and sister-sister pairs. All together, marriages between uncles and their nieces, or between a brother-sister

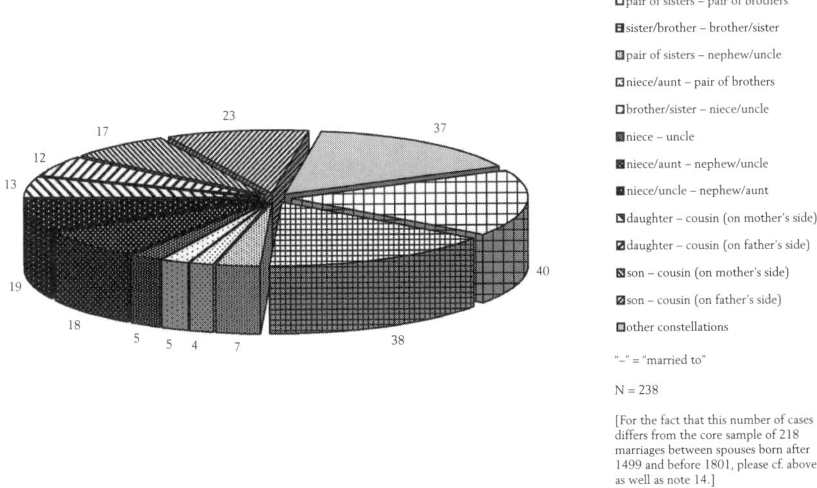

Figure 5.1. Marriages between close relatives in the sixteenth to eighteenth centuries.

pair and an aunt-nephew or an uncle-niece pair, made up a smaller share of the marriages between relatives between the sixteenth and the eighteenth century. When the sixteenth century is compared to the seventeenth century in terms of the frequency and types of marriage between relatives, the picture emerges (Figure 5.2).

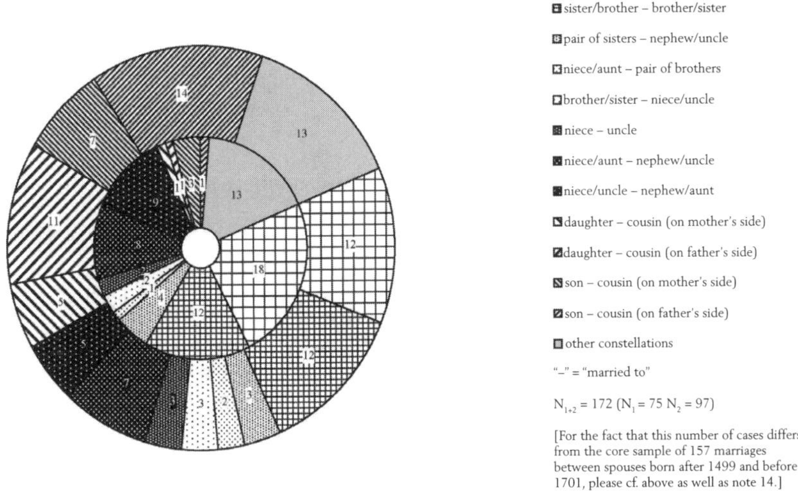

Figure 5.2. Marriages between close relatives in the sixteenth (inner circle) and seventeenth centuries.

Seen against the three hundred years spanning 1500 to 1800, two remarkable changes can be observed in kinship politics from the sixteenth to the seventeenth century. In relation to the total number of all determinable marriages between relatives, the number of marriages between cousins rose in the seventeenth century over the previous century, while the number of marriages between brother-brother and sister-sister pairs fell markedly. The rate of marriages between brother-sister pairs did not change, however. The proportion of marriages whose partners belonged to different generations and were first-degree relatives—marriages between uncles and nieces or between brother-sister and aunt-nephew or uncle-niece—remained relatively constant. Comparing the formation and maintenance of noble relations in the seventeenth century with that of the eighteenth century in terms of types of marriage and their frequency, we find the picture in Figure 5.3.

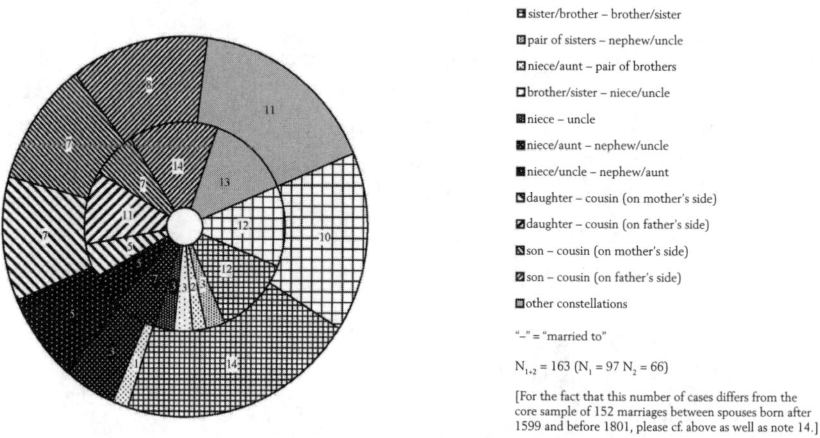

Figure 5.3. Marriages between close relatives in the seventeenth (inner circle) and eighteenth centuries.

What is remarkable is the complete disappearance of marriage between cousins where the son of the brother or sister of a princess's husband marries her daughter; this type of marriage enjoyed relative popularity just a century earlier. At the same time, the trend that emerged in the seventeenth century of fewer marriages between sister-sister and brother-brother pairs continued, while the proportion of marriages between brother-sister pairs rose steadily.

In summary, marriage between cousins, in which the daughter of a brother or sister of a princess married one of her own sons, occurred 17 times in the period under study. The case where the son of the brother or sister of a princess married one of her daughters happened 13 times. The type of marriage in which the daughter of a brother or sister of a prince married one of his sons occurred 23 times, and the case where the son of a prince's brother or sister married one of his daughters happened 12 times. The study sample consisted of 218 marriages settled after 1499 and before 1801. Between the sixteenth and the eighteenth century, there were 29.81 percent (65 out of 218) marriages between cousins, of which 6 took place in the sixteenth century, 37 in the seventeenth century, and 22 in the eighteenth century. Thus marriages between cousins, in absolute terms, were highest in the seventeenth century. Yet, because the marriage rate in our sample decreased by nearly half between the sixteenth/ seventeenth century and the eighteenth century, then, relatively speaking, the eighteenth century—the time of consolidation of power—was the heyday of marriages between cousins.[15]

With respect to marriages between sister-sister and brother-brother pairs, there was a decrease in absolute terms, but this also needs to be viewed in relation to the falling marriage rate in the eighteenth century. The absolute number of brother-sister pairs marriages increased slightly over the three centuries under investigation. As this finding has to be viewed in relation to the overall marriage rate, it can be said that there was a slight rise in the eighteenth century of cross-marriages of brother-sister pairs. Marriages between aunt-niece pairs and brother pairs or those between a sister pair and an uncle-nephew pair occurred very rarely over the three hundred years under study. While they need to be considered in the "big picture" for the constellations they formed in the overall kinship configuration, they occurred too infrequently to warrant a separate analysis in a short overview such as this. The same applies to marriages between nieces and their uncles, as well as marriages between niece-uncle pairs with brother-sister pairs. Even though these types of marriages between relatives were of marginal significance in statistical terms, they do help to complete the picture of the complex kinship network that unfolded around the figure of the married princely sister, whose high networking potential resulted primarily from her position as consanguineal aunt or by marriage. Marriage between consanguineal nephews and nieces or between nieces and nephews of a married couple, that is, marriages between the offspring of brothers and sisters of a married princess and the offspring of consanguineal brothers and sisters of her husband, were not that infrequent. They occurred 37 times and thus account for 16.97 percent of all marriages, while there were only 21 instances of uncle-nephew-niece-aunt-brother-sister marriages over three hundred years, accounting for less than 10 percent of all marriages. Thus marriage between cousins, as compared to other types of marriage between close relatives among European princes and princesses in the second half of the eighteenth century, was demonstrated to be a valid tool for consolidating power.

To deepen the argument and from a perspective that considers kinship as relationally determined, these marriages between cousins can be described as part of a relational network that extends between aunts and nieces, aunts and nephews, uncles and nieces, etc., since each of the marrying cousins was also for their part the daughter or son of brothers and sisters. Or, in other words, the future parents-in-law of each of two married cousins counted one consanguineal and one affinal aunt and uncle. This kind of perspective affords the opportunity to turn attention away from one single type of kin marriage. By shifting and decentralizing one's viewpoint, a multirelational kinship network based on mutuality is revealed, which allows the identification of complex kinship architectures from a gender-historical perspective as well. In order to illustrate the network potential from the perspective of a married princess, I have taken the total group of women in the sample who had nephews and nieces in order to map their complex set of kin relations. The set is composed of both consanguineal and affinal aunts, whose wedding date was after 1499 and before 1801.[16] A further criterion for selection is the condition that the father of the aunt's husband (her father-in-law) was a ruling prince. The group of aunts by marriage is restricted by the similar condition that their husbands were ruling princes. The total sample includes 581 female "aunt-egos," who, in turn, had 1,890 corresponding "niece-egos." The network of these sets of aunt- and niece-egos totaled a potential kinship network of 7,140 relations.[17] Taking the 1,984 consanguineal nephews together with their (581) aunts and tracing out the circle of possible relations, we find a formidable net built by 14,435 relations (between aunts, nieces, and nephews).[18] This purely mathematical reckoning demonstrates the exceptional networking *potential* that the aunt figure offers, being positioned at the crossroads of generations, families, houses, and dynasties. Such an enormous networking opportunity warrants a reexamination of central historiographic figures such as *Haus* and *Dynastie* and a rethinking of the emergence of modern nations and statehood not so much in terms of centralization around a vertical line of succeeding princes as through the cohesive web of relations-constructed translocalities, regions, and nascent states through the dynamics of kinship.

That the sister of a ruling prince was at the center of a kinship network can be deduced in part from her position on the marriage market. Married sisters—who in turn were daughters, mothers, grandmothers, aunts, nieces, and not least cousins—were apparently of value based on the endeavor of princes to marry their sisters to other ruling princes and thus to keep the kinship ties intact. In viewing the quantitative analysis of the group under study, it comes as a surprise that, over the entire study period, sisters were not significantly behind their brothers in terms of the rank and frequency of their marriages, although a shift in the marriage pattern is discernable in the seventeenth century.[19] But it must be noted that aristocratic society, especially in the period between the late seventeenth and the late eighteenth century, generally tried to marry sons before their sisters, even when the latter were older than the sons. Overall, the nobility reacted to the lower birth rate among elites in the eighteenth century by allowing their daughters and sons to marry within their own ranks. In other words: though in absolute terms there were fewer marriages and fewer offspring, relatively speaking there were a greater number of daughters and sons on the marriage market. Apparently, the nobility expected their daughters and sons to expand and stabilize the kinship network, thus it helped both brothers *and* sisters to attain powerful positions.

Together, the group under study created quite a homogeneous group of princes and princesses in which there was very little upward or downward mobility in the sixteenth and seventeenth centuries.[20] Only in the eighteenth century—as the ruling elite was multiplying in number and power struggles among them were becoming more acute—do we see an increase of marriages between sisters of ruling princes and lower-ranking noblemen. This downgrading of the status of the princely sisters coincided with a concentration of power among the ruling elite evidenced from the middle of the eighteenth century, which resulted from higher life expectancy, longer-lasting marriages, fewer children, and fewer new marriages, especially at the end of the eighteenth century. In comparison with the sixteenth and seventeenth centuries, this trend was accompanied by a reduction in the number of aunts per nephew and per niece as well as a decrease in the number of nephews and nieces per aunt. As a consequence, there was a concentration of vertically and linearly aligned kinship formations among full relatives. But this vertical concentration was compensated by a rise in the number of brothers- and sisters-in-law. As the data-based analysis shows, during the process of power consolidation among the ruling elite in the eighteenth century, the number of new marriages fell in absolute terms. However, the rate of new marriages per family unit rose at the same time, meaning the number of aunts by marriage per nephew and per niece was subject to the opposite trend as that of consanguineal aunts. As the number of such aunts decreased, the number of aunts by marriage per nephew and per niece grew during this study period.[21] This visible increase in the number of aunts-by-marriage meant that the in-laws—the sisters and brothers of the wives or the wives and husbands of brothers and sisters—had greater power in shaping the horizontal network of relatives and relations. This shift in in-law relations may have been politically significant. If the princesses seen here as *angeheiratete Tanten* (in-law-aunts) had a brother or father who was a ruling prince, and if he died before his daughter or sister and without leaving any heir, this would make the married princely sister a central figure in the process of transferring property and power.[22] The numerous European wars waged over succession to a throne in the late seventeenth and eighteenth centuries can be seen as one of the results of these kinship dynamics, reflecting an absolute decrease in consanguineal relatives, on the one hand, and the expansion of the horizontally organized in-law network, on the other.

Conclusion

This essay has examined the kinship network of the European nobility in the period between the late fifteenth and the early nineteenth century. One central figure in this network has been identified—that of the married princely sister, who has allowed insights into aristocratic society of early modern Europe across dynasties, families, and territories. By taking the sister as the point of departure for our study, it has been possible to expand the prevalent view of kinship relations among European nobility to include the consanguineal relatives and their families as well as in-laws and their families. This focus on horizontal kinship networks has been informed by the conception of kinship relations that are not only mutual, but are also multirelational and demand investigation. In other words: a married sister of a prince could be an aunt, a niece, a sister-in-law, and a cousin all at the same time. It is this multirelational nature that has allowed us to understand marriages between cousins, for example, also as relationships between aunts, nieces, nephews, and uncles, and furthermore to describe a kinship network that is not only potentially existent but is far reaching in Europe. The sheer breadth of kinship relations has not been represented here due to limitations of space. One illustrative example for the European networking that is usually described as an particular case of a relation between one aunt and one niece is Sophie of the Palatinate (1630–1714), daughter of the elector of the Palatinate, Frederick V (1596–1632), sister of Charles I Louis of the

Palatinate (1617–1680), as well as wife (the marriage dating from 1658) of the later elector of Hanover, Ernest Augustus of Brunswick-Lüneburg (1629–1698). Although Sophie had a total of thirty-three consanguineal and in-law nieces and nephews, generally most attention is paid to her relationship with one niece, the daughter of Sophie's brother Charles I Louis, the famous and infamous Elizabeth Charlotte of the Palatinate, who was married to the brother of the French king Louis XIV. But her wider (usually unknown) relational network that encompasses all the nieces and nephews connected to her through her marriage (as well as those sons and daughters stemming from her brother's morganatic marriage to Louise of Degenfeld) brings us into a huge geographical space, one that reaches also to England, Ireland, and Denmark in the north and northwest, extends south of the Alps into the northern Italian realms of the dukes of Este, and also encompasses the territory of the German Empire. The proximity of this princess to the Northern Italian dukes of Mantova-Gonzaga, who were related not only to the earls and dukes of Württemberg but also to the Wittelsbach princes and princesses, will only be mentioned here in passing.[23]

The systematic analysis of our sample of 218 princely marriages concluded across Europe between the late fifteenth and the early nineteenth century has shown that certain types of marriages between relatives may be attributed to various time periods. Most noticeable are the marriages between cousins, which became more and more relevant beginning in the second half of the eighteenth century in the phase of power consolidation, without, however, completely supplanting other models. But despite the different varieties of marriage that coexisted in the eighteenth century, a strong trend towards ever more collateral and in-law relations may be observed. This is a process that coincided with secular genealogical, theological, juridical, and increasingly medical and emotionally charged discourses on the legitimacy of male progeny that had appeared for instance in historiographical works since at least the middle of the eighteenth century and was used to legitimate political power by pointing to a long line of male agnates. The overlapping of these scientific and practical arenas sufficed to produce an intersectional political space of kinship networking that gave rise to armed conflicts from time to time in early modern Europe.

Notes

1. Karl-Heinz Spiess, *Familie und Verwandtschaft im deutschen Hochadel des Spätmittelalters, 13. bis Anfang des 16. Jahrhunderts* (Stuttgart, 1993), 337.
2. Johannes Kunisch, ed., *Der dynastische Fürstenstaat: Zur Bedeutung von Sukzessionsordnungen für die Entstehung des frühmodernen Staates* (Berlin, 1982).

3. David Warren Sabean and Simon Teuscher, "Kinship in Europe: A New Approach to Long-Term Development," in *Kinship in Europe: Approaches to Long-Term Development (1300–1900)*, ed. David Warren Sabean, Simon Teuscher, and Jon Mathieu (New York, 2007), 1. See also Carola Lipp, "Verwandtschaft—ein negiertes Element in der politischen Kultur des 19. Jahrhunderts," *Historische Zeitschrift* 283 (2006): 31–77.
4. Beate Kellner, "Genealogien," in *Höfe und Residenzen im spätmittelalterlichen Reich: Hof und Schrift*, ed. Werner Paravicini (Ostfildern, 2007), 347–60. Johann Daniel Schöpflin, for example, constructed a long line of male agnates of the noble house of Baden back to the eleventh century in his *Historia Zaringo Badensis*, 7 vols. (Karlsruhe, 1763–1766).
5. Sophie Ruppel, *Verbündtete Rivalen: Geschwisterbeziehungen im Hochadel des 17. Jahrhunderts* (Cologne, 2006). See also Michaela Hohkamp, "Tanten: vom Nutzen einer verwandtschaftlichen Figur für die Erforschung familiärer Ökonomien in der Frühen Neuzeit," *WerkstattGeschichte* 46 (2007): 5–12, and "Sisters, Aunts, and Cousins: Familial Architectures and the Political Field in Early Modern Europe," in Sabean, Teuscher, and Mathieu, *Kinship*, 128–45.
6. Klaus Graf, "Geschichtsschreibung und Landesdiskurs im Umkreis Graf Eberhards im Bart von Württemberg (1449–1496)," *Blätter für deutsche Landesgeschichte* 129 (1993): 165–93.
7. Cordula Nolte, "'Ir seyt ein fremds weib, das solt ihr pleiben, dieweil ihr lebt': Beziehungsgeflechte in fürstlichen Familien des Spätmittelalters," in *Geschlechterdifferenz im interdisziplinären Gespräch: Kolloquium des interdisziplinären Zentrums für Frauen- und Geschlechterstudien an der Ernst-Moritz-Arndt-Universität Greifswald*, ed. Doris Ruhe (Würzburg, 1998), 11–41.
8. Michaela Hohkamp, "Do Sisters have Brothers? Or the Search for the 'rechte Schwester:' Brothers and Sisters in Aristocratic Society at the Turn of the Sixteenth Century," in *Sibling Relations and the Transformations of European Kinship, 1300–1900*, ed. Christopher H. Johnson and David Warren Sabean (New York, 2011).
9. Tobias Weller, *Die Heiratspolitik des deutschen Hochadels im 12. Jahrhundert* (Vienna, 2004); Peter Moraw, "Das Heiratsverhalten im hessischen Landgrafenhaus ca. 1300–1500: auch vergleichend betrachtet," in *Hundert Jahre Historische Kommission für Hessen 1897–1997*, ed. Walter Heinemeyer (Marburg, 1997), 115–40; Alfred Kohler, "'Tu Felix Austria Nube …': Vom Klischee zur Neubewertung dynastischer Politik in der neueren Geschichte Europas," *Zeitschrift für historische Forschung* 21 (1994): 461–82; Heinz Reif, *Westfälischer Adel 1770–1860: Vom Herrschaftsstand zur regionalen Elite* (Göttingen, 1979).
10. H. C. Erik Midelfort, *Mad Princes of Renaissance Germany* (Charlottesville, VA, 1994).
11. David Warren Sabean, "Inzestdiskurse vom Barock bis zur Romantik," *L'Homme: Zeitschrift für feministische Geschichtswissenschaft* 13 (2002): 7–28.
12. David Warren Sabean, *Kinship in Neckarhausen, 1700–1870* (Cambridge, 1998).
13. Sabean and Teuscher, "Kinship in Europe," 2–3.
14. In order not to limit our options with respect to aunt-niece and aunt-nephew relations, we extended our study to accommodate aunts and uncles and a generation of marriages. The database was thus expanded to include siblings who entered into their first marriage between 1480 and 1500. Accordingly, the condition based on the birthdates of the persons under study has been extended for this segment. This means that those aunts and uncles are included in the study who were born after 1449. In this way it was possible to include those nephews and nieces in our investi-

gation whose dates of marriage fell within the beginning (1500) of our study period. The end point of our study was set to 1800. Data on rulers and their relatives are available until the birth year of 1830. See Michaela Hohkamp, "Transmission von Herrschaft und Verwandtschaft in der reichsfürstlichen Gesellschaft vom 15. bis zum 18. Jahrhundert" (Habilitation thesis, Freie Universität Berlin, 2007), 455ff.

15. Ibid., chapter 5.
16. They belong to this group of persons whose date of birth was after 1449.
17. I want to emphasize that the "network" described here is simply a mathematical model of relationships and not a description of relations that were actually used nor ones that could be completely empirically researched.
18. Michaela Hohkamp, "Eine Tante für alle Fälle: Tanten-Nichten-Beziehungen und ihre politische Bedeutung für die reichsfürstliche Gesellschaft der Frühen Neuzeit (16. bis 18. Jahrhundert)," in *Politiken der Verwandtschaft*, ed. Margareth Lanzinger and Edith Saurer (Vienna, 2007), 149–71.
19. Michaela Hohkamp, "Transmssion," chapter 5.
20. The group examined here includes 218 marriages dating between 1480 and 1800, and 205 marriages dating between 1500 and 1800.
21. Hohkamp, "Eine Tante."
22. Elisabeth Koch, "Die Frau im Recht der Frühen Neuzeit: Juristische Lehren und Begründungen," in Ute Gerhard, ed., *Frauen in der Geschichte des Rechts: Von der Frühen Neuzeit bis zur Gegenwart* (Munich, 1997), 73–93.
23. See chapter 3 in this volume. For information on the Gonzaga in the late medieval and early modern period, see Ebba Severidt, *Familie, Verwandtschaft und Karriere bei den Gonzaga* (Leinfelden-Echterdingen, 2002).

Chapter 6

Marriage, Commercial Capital, and Business Agency

Transregional Sephardic (and Armenian) Families in the Seventeenth- and Eighteenth-Century Mediterranean

Francesca Trivellato

Historical studies of trading diasporas have grown in number and sophistication in the last two decades, especially with regard to the early modern period.[1] Almost without fail, this literature refers to the importance of transregional family ties. Typically, such ties are seen as a key factor for the commercial success enjoyed by small but proactive ethnoreligious communities of merchants scattered across space. Yet these studies rarely examine how specific kinship structures, inheritance practices, and dowry systems influenced the business organization of trading diasporas. This omission leaves us without a description of the specific social and economic mechanisms that allowed family firms to operate effectively in the increasingly competitive and militarized arena of long-distance trade during the seventeenth and eighteenth centuries. It also has the paradoxical—if unintended—consequence of undermining a primary goal of most studies of early modern trading diasporas, which implicitly or explicitly stress the continued significance of stateless commercial formations and their impact on European commercial expansion. Without a detailed, even microanalytical examination of the ways in which family members raised, managed, and transmitted capital across a diaspora, we risk reinforcing the characterization of merchant communities as weak and archaic business organizations rather than developing a nuanced understanding of them.

This chapter begins to redress such a lacuna by looking closely at the marriage, dowry, and inheritance customs prevalent among Sephardic Jews in Livorno and Venice during the seventeenth and eighteenth centuries. In so doing, it moves beyond generic invocations of the transregional family's importance in the commercial and financial activities of Sephardic merchants. It also offers a brief but, I hope, revealing comparison between Sephardic and Armenian family firms with the aim of showing how transregional kinship systems varied from one trading diaspora to the next and how these differences affected the working of business networks.[2]

The relationship between family and European capitalism has long been subject to a thorny debate among historians and social scientists, and has generated too large a literature to review here. Suffice it to say that among the issues at stake are the chronology of the demise of family firms and the rise of new forms of contractual agreements that allowed for more impersonal business associations. More precisely, economic historians since Max Weber debate whether family firms ceased to be the prevailing practitioners of long-distance commerce in the late Middle Ages or in the seventeenth century, although some concede that the influence of family businesses over Western capitalism may extend even further in time. The date of this transition toward more impersonal business forms, however, should not be our sole concern. As generations of anthropologists have taught us, "family" means different things not only across time and space, but also among different communities who live side by side. My interest here is less in tracing transformations of family firms over time than in examining how particular kinship structures and devolutionary practices help us explain the different ways in which transregional Sephardic and Armenian families operated in Europe and the Mediterranean during the seventeenth and eighteenth centuries. I thus suggest some potential advantages of comparing trading diasporas rather than studying them in isolation, as is most commonly done.

European Commercial Partnerships in the Early Modern Mediterranean

The commodities exchanged between Europe and the Ottoman Empire were highly heterogeneous. As a result, Mediterranean trade required great flexibility in adjusting to supply and demand, favored the role of intermediaries, and demanded that individual merchants had access to credit. After all, no European state or trading company in the Mediterranean ever came close to exerting the control over the production process, price setting, or the transport system that the Dutch did in parts of Southeast Asia or that various European powers did in the New World. With the exception of the English Levant Company (1581–1825), few European chartered and monopolistic companies operated in the Mediterranean until the French Compagnie Royale d'Afrique was created (1741–93); and even then, the Compagnie only controlled exchanges with North Africa.[3] The European commercial presence in the early modern Mediterranean, in sum, involved only a minimal development of large, state-chartered joint-stock companies of the kind that was launched in the Indian Ocean, notably the English and the Dutch East Indian Companies (established in 1600 and 1602, respectively), and their less-effective counterparts in the Atlantic.

Countless private partnerships plied the Mediterranean. Most, though not all, were formed by merchants of the same religious or national group. The early modern Mediterranean is thus an ideal place and time in which to compare the roles of different family firms in transregional commerce. However, it would be wrong to portray the Mediterranean as simply lagging behind in the path toward modern European commercial structures. In spite of the rise of new financial institutions, including the first European stock markets, kinship ties in fact continued to play an important role in the management of long-distance trade and other large, private investments in Amsterdam and London as well.[4] A focus on the Mediterranean may therefore disclose structural comparisons that can also prove useful in the study of other regions.

Among the ethnoreligious communities that were engaged in long-distance commerce in the early modern Mediterranean, Sephardic merchants, and especially those based in Livorno, were particularly influential from the mid-seventeenth to the third quarter of the eighteenth century. There was a significant difference between the private partnerships of Christian and Sephardic merchants in the Mediterranean. Both frequently selected their associates and overseas agents from among relatives, but Venetian, English, French, and Dutch merchants also sealed medium-term, limited-liability agreements with non-kin in order to raise additional capital and sometimes hired salaried employees ("factors") to serve overseas.[5] In contrast, Sephardic merchants based in Livorno and Venice routinely used the most traditional model of family firm: the general partnership. Unlike limited liability partnerships, general partnerships had no expiration date, and all their members shared mutual agency with full liability.

Max Weber famously lamented the backward nature of general partnerships. For him, capitalism in its *uniquely Occidental* form was born when distinctions between business employees and household members and between the company's and household's debts emerged in the limited liability partnerships of late medieval Tuscany.[6] In what follows, I will show that as late as the eighteenth century, the use of a traditional business model such as the general partnership should not be immediately associated with a precapitalist mentality or a closed, inward-looking "coalition" of merchants.[7] In fact, Sephardic merchants were able to expand their market niches by working in general partnerships with their overseas relatives while also hiring commission agents from among Jews and non-Jews alike.

General partnerships came with concrete advantages (reciprocal agency) and considerable risks (unlimited liability). I argue that positive incentives (the strong informal commitments generated by marriage) and external conditions (social discrimination) rather than a passive adherence to custom and tradition led Sephardim to adopt such partnerships. In Livorno, where records of limited liability partnerships are preserved more systematically than in Venice, we find that Sephardic merchants did not enter into long- or even medium-term partnerships with non-Jews until the late eighteenth century. Even then, they did so sporadically. Social and cultural barriers rather than legal impediments explain the infrequency of joint Jewish-Christian commercial ventures. A purely institutional recapitulation of the available business contracts would therefore overlook the impact that social and cultural norms had on the Sephardim's choice of types of commercial association. I thus turn to the specific kinship structures prevalent among Sephardim and their differences from those emerging as dominant in southern Europe at the time in order to account for the preference for general partnerships among most Sephardim.

Marriage, Dowry, and Inheritance among the Sephardim of Livorno and Venice

Whereas canon law and Protestant ecclesiastical law in continental Europe prohibited marriages within third and second cousins, respectively, and rarely granted dispensations, Sephardim encouraged marriages among close kin.[8] Marriages between uncles and nieces as well as among parallel first cousins were so frequent in the Sephardic communities of Venice and Livorno that those who wished to avoid them had to leave special instructions for their progeny. For reasons that he did not disclose, in

1640 one Sephardic patriarch, Abraham Camis, alias Lopo de Fonseca, threatened to disinherit his son if he married a cousin.[9] Nevertheless, Jewish endogamy was the norm and, in the absence of geographical limitations, it favored the formation of transregional families.

Moreover, while primogeniture became widespread among the elites of southern Europe after the sixteenth century, including in Venice and Tuscany, Jewish families customarily divided their estates equally among all sons and required them to live on and manage their father's estate together.[10] The latter provision curbed the risk that partible inheritance would parcel family assets into smaller and smaller fractions in each successive generation. In 1752, for example, Salomon Aghib reminded his three sons that the family patrimony would be ruined if they parted ways and implored them to remain united at the very least until the youngest of them reached the age of thirty.[11] However, testaments allowed for occasional corrections of this prevalent norm when tradition threatened to supersede economic efficiency. We thus encounter instances in which one brother was favored over the other when commercial talent was unevenly distributed among siblings. We also find a few Sephardic merchants who bound part of their assets to an entail.[12] But overall, brothers inherited and administered the estate, and especially commercial capital, jointly, which explains their preference for general partnerships.

With differences in marriage and devolution practices also came a unique dotal system. After the late Middle Ages, the groom's contribution, or dower, increasingly disappeared from Christian marriages in southern Europe.[13] Daughters were excluded from any claims on their family's estate in addition to the dowry that the bride's family paid to the groom and received back at the husband's death or in the event of his insolvency. With the exponential inflation of women's dowries in early modern Italy and the progressive retreat of the upper classes from active commerce, moreover, fathers and brothers increasingly paid their daughters' and sisters' dowries in real estate rather than movable assets—a phenomenon that was far less pronounced among Sephardic families, although Jews in Livorno were entitled to own real estate.

According to Jewish law and custom, marriage contracts comprised two main payments—a dowry (*nedynya*) and a dower (*tosefet*)—and an additional small sum (*mohar*) that varied with the bride's status as a virgin, on the one hand, or a divorcee or widow, on the other. Among the Sephardim in Venice and Livorno, the *tosefet* normally amounted to 50 percent of the *nedynya*. The two sums merged to form a totality of assets managed by the husband. If the wife died before the husband, both the dowry and the dower passed to him. At the husband's death or insolvency, a widow was entitled to the restitution of the dowry paid by her family as well as the entire dower (or at least half of it if she was childless). The fact that dower and dowry were generally indivisible after the marriage generated an added advantage to the preservation of commercial capital in the Tuscan context because both Jewish law and local statutes shielded dotal assets (in this case both dower and dowry) from creditors' claims when a partnership went bankrupt.[14] The same norm applied both to Jewish and Christian merchants. But intergenerational endogamy assured Jewish families that commercial capital in the form of dowries and dowers rarely threatened the patriarchal line. Christian merchants, in contrast, conceived dowries as eroding the family patrimony.

An additional custom, levirate marriage, helped Sephardim contain the risk that large dowries jeopardized the integrity of the groom's family patrimony. In principle, in the seventeenth and eighteenth centuries, Sephardim continued to abide by the halakhic prescription of levirate marriage (*yibbum*), according to which a childless widow had to marry the oldest brother of her deceased husband and a widower had to marry his late brother's widow. In practice, however, many among the wealthiest Sephardim sought to contain levirate unions and avoid bigamy in order to conform to the precepts and moral conventions of Catholic society. Some well-to-do Sephardic women stipulated in their dowry contracts that their husbands would not be allowed to take a second wife. Thus, when Sarah Baruch Carvaglio moved from Venice to Livorno to marry Moses Attias in 1667, the marriage contract included a provision against her future husband's right to take a second wife. The provision was particularly important considering that Sarah brought with her the unparalleled dowry of 17,000 Venetian ducats.[15] In 1721 Rebecca Francia added a similar clause to her marriage contract, prohibiting her groom, Moses Alvares Vega, from marrying a second wife. When seven years into the marriage Moses violated this clause, the Jewish tribunal forced him to divorce Rebecca in partial fulfillment of the nuptial agreement, and a belated *halizah* ceremony was performed.[16]

Available sources do not allow us to assess the frequency of levirate marriages in Livorno and Venice, but Jewish authorities in Livorno were sufficiently concerned about Catholic disapproval of bigamy that they actively discouraged such unions in the 1660s and 1670s.[17] Nevertheless, levirate marriages did not disappear. In fact, they even spread among those who married into a Sephardic family. When Salomon Gallico, an Italian Jew of lesser means, married Miriam Pegna (a Sephardic woman) as his second wife in 1753, two arbiters determined that his first wife, Sarah Vigevano (an Italian Jewess), was required to live with them.[18]

The two traditional ways of avoiding levirate marriages included performing a ceremony (*halizah*) or drafting a document (*setar halizah*) that freed the brother-in-law from this duty or issuing a divorce. The obligation to perform *halizah* was a serious injunction and not taken lightly. In 1754, a widow traveled from Amsterdam all the way across the Atlantic to meet her brother-in-law, risking her very life in the harsh journey in order to fulfill this precept.[19] Levirate marriage was not required if the deceased husband had previously divorced his wife. This is why in November 1746, on the brink of death, Moses Ergas divorced his wife Rachel in Livorno.[20]

These specific devolution and marriage practices—large dowries resulting from the 50 percent supplement combined with consanguineal marriages and occasional levirate unions—helped Sephardim keep commercial capital circulating within an interlocking group of endogamic families and ensured its intergenerational transfer. As a result, Sephardim rarely availed themselves of the contracts (including limited liability partnerships) that would have allowed them to raise liquid capital for their commercial enterprises from non-kin. This choice, however, did not prevent them from remaining competitive in several commercial niches.

General and Limited Liability Partnerships

After the sixteenth century, general partnerships became increasingly less frequent in Europe and the Mediterranean.[21] In Tuscany, already in the fifteenth century, we observe the rise of two types of contracts, *accomandita* (known in French as *société en accomandite*) and *compagnia*, which limited the risks of full mutual liability. The former was a more sophisticated version of the medieval bilateral *commenda* by which a sedentary partner contributed his capital to a traveling merchant. *Accomandite* always included a clause limiting the responsibility of each investor and normally established that profits be shared in proportion to the monetary and work contributions. They usually had an initial duration of three or four years, although they could be renewed. These contracts became tools through which Tuscan merchants raised capital among noblemen as well as a broader spectrum of investors who shunned direct involvement in distasteful commercial ventures in hopes of advancing their aristocratic pretensions.[22]

In Tuscany, Jews were not forbidden from adopting these types of associations in Livorno.[23] However, the minority who did, mostly Jews of Italian origin, used *accomandite* to run shops or small trades in Florence, Pisa, and other Tuscan towns. Jewish merchants based in Livorno who were involved in long-distance trade rarely resorted to these stipulations. The few who did sign *accomandite* were normally not related by kinship ties and only invested small amounts in these ventures. Note that the frequency with which Jews sealed these contracts in Livorno intensified in the second half of the eighteenth century, when the Sephardic hegemony in the Jewish community of the Tuscan port city was waning and marriage alliances likely became less endogamic because of the need to build ties to new North African and Italian Jewish families. Eventually, *accomandite* between Jews and Christians began to appear in the 1770s, but remained rare. Further research is necessary to determine how frequent associations between Jews and non-Jews were in Amsterdam and London and what types of contracts sealed them. The situation in Livorno, however, suggests that social rather than legal discrimination worked against Sephardim using *accomandite.*[24]

In Venice, too, most Sephardic merchants ran general partnerships rather than limited liability partnerships. There, they could draw up a local type of contract, called *fraterna,* which provided for joint liability among brothers. After resettling in Venice from Portugal, brothers Isaac and Moses Baruch Carvaglio established such a general partnership (*fraterna e compagnia*) that yielded high profits from the 1650s to the 1690s.[25] Special arrangements were only stipulated when brothers wanted to split unevenly the burden of running a family partnership. Thus at their father's death in 1642, Salomon and Joseph Franco de Almeida (alias Antonio and Simon Mendes) agreed before a notary to run a *fraterna* to which they contributed 60 and 40 percent, respectively. Their business fared well, and in 1672 Salomon made bequests to his sons for 30,000 ducats that were deposited in the public debt.[26]

Less common among the business agreements of the Livornese and Venetian Jews was a contract known in Italian as *compagnia.* This was a more stable type of association than the *accomandita*; it appeared in the fourteenth century and could be more or less centralized.[27] After a series of failures of Florentine international banks in the 1340s, the *compagnia* emerged as a new business form that linked together multiple autonomous entities under the guidance of one person (as in the case of Francesco Datini, c. 1335–1410) or one family (as in the case of the Medici bank, 1397–1494). This organization has been compared to the modern holding company because it subsumed a network of interconnected branches (some directed by salaried employees and others by junior partners, with varying degrees of independence) under the main house's control. Even this modular organization, however, did not eliminate the risks stemming from unreliable or inept representatives. Fraudulent and incompetent branch managers eventually weakened the Medici bank, for example.[28] Yet the *compagnia* struck a balance between centralization and limited liability, and was adopted by many influential sixteenth-century European merchants, including the Ruiz of Medina del Campo in Spain, the Flemish della Faille, and the Fugger and Welser in southern Germany.[29]

Why did most Sephardim in Livorno and Venice choose to run general partnerships when more secure and centralized business forms were readily available to them? Institutional and cultural inertia may have played a role, but more positive incentives did too. The marriage, dowry, and inheritance customs that we just reviewed allowed Sephardim to diminish several weaknesses of general partnerships and exploit the latter's advantages. For instance, *accomandite* helped merchants raise capital, but unlike family firms, they did not count on extraeconomic motivations for renewing investments. They certainly protected investors from imprudent or poor decisions made by partners, but *accomandite* were ill suited to finance activities that required a long-term turn over and the ability to make fast and independent decisions in face of slow communication.[30] *Compagnie* also had benefits and drawbacks, although they were perhaps the most effective of the three types of association for large-scale overseas trade.

Because they entailed full mutual liability, general partnerships had considerable advantages that could potentially outweigh their inherent risks. Their duration was unlimited and they provided for the ability to delegate decisions to an overseas partner—two unbeatable advantages if the partner was capable and trustworthy. Of course, anyone involved in long-distance trade had to weigh the pros and cons of these contracts and determine whether they could gain from general partnerships while also keeping such dangers in check.

Rarely did Sephardic partnerships include a contract that defined the partners' rights and obligations. Rather, marriage contracts substituted for partnership contracts: dowries and dower merged together and were registered in the partnership's account books.[31] Nor did Sephardic general partnerships include a separate fund to which partners and external investors contributed to the partnership's capital assets in return for a fixed interest rate.[32] In other European port cities as well, Sephardic merchants and financiers operated on the basis of implicit contracts with relatives and kin. The successful New Christian banker Gabriel de Silva (c. 1683–1763) in Bordeaux, for example, never drew up a formal contract with which to establish his family business.[33] Further research is necessary, but it appears that Dutch Sephardim also avoided notaries when stipulating partnership contracts with their own kin, although they constantly drafted a whole variety of notary deeds (for freight contracts, maritime insurance, powers of attorney, short-term credit agreements, certifications to be used in future litigation, purchases and sales, and other types of transactions) when dealing with both Jews and non-Jews.[34]

Chains of endogamic marriage alliances ensured the effectiveness of the implicit agreements that governed general partnerships. Additionally, the absence of a notarized contract did not make a general partnership any less real or liable toward third parties. Roman law, commercial customs, and the *lex mercatoria* jurisprudence recognized the use of a corporate name, such as "Ergas & Silvera" or "Moses Franco and Company," in business letters, bills of lading, and other such records, as evidence of a partnership's liability toward its creditors. Any one partner in a general partnership could thus sign a business letter or have a notary draft a deed in the name of the company at large. In the terminology of the time, all members of a general partnership were *socii in solidum* and *ad infinitum*, that is to say, they were all liable for the total amount of any debts incurred by another associate or contracted in the company's name until the dissolution of their association.[35] After they established a branch of their general partnership in Aleppo in 1704, the Ergas and Silvera families in Livorno promised a Christian merchant in Venice that he could count on the punctual and satisfactory business of their partners in the Syrian city.[36] Bound *in solidum* to their relatives in Aleppo, the Livorno branch of Ergas & Silvera could even commit to third parties on their behalf.[37]

Of course, mutual liability had its risks because family members were not always competent and could even become intentionally harmful. As we have already mentioned, the dowry, inheritance, and marriage patterns prevalent among Sephardim helped contain these risks. Such practices also allowed Sephardic merchants to enjoy the advantages of mutual agency in a world in which slow transportation and communication continued to hamper merchants' decision-making abilities. The autonomy of each branch of Sephardic general partnerships operating in, say, Livorno and Aleppo meant that they could act more swiftly than their European competitors. While it is true that the representatives of English limited partnerships in the Levant could count on the influx of broadcloth, an item that was in high demand there, they faced a major limitation that Sephardim did not. As the correspondence of the Radcliffe company of London from the 1730s to the 1760s testifies, the agent of the subsidiary branch had to receive written permission from London in order to make his purchase and was thus constrained in his ability to seize short-term opportunities.[38] Most French partnerships in the Mediterranean also depended on the orders issued by their principals (*régisseurs*) in Marseille, although they sometimes took some leeway for themselves.[39]

Here it is crucial to emphasize that the ample recourse to general partnerships among Sephardic merchants did not inhibit them from building opportunistic alliances with non-Jews, sometimes even for extended periods of time. In fact, Sephardim combined a very traditional form of partnership at the core of their business model with a very flexible type of contract: commission agency. A commission agent was paid a percentage of the value of goods and services that he negotiated on behalf of a third party (percentages varied usually between 1 and 7 percent, depending on the agent and the type of service and goods that were negotiated). He also assumed full legal responsibility for his services. A combination of legal and reputation mechanisms monitored the good behavior of commission agents. The commission agents of Ergas & Silvera included Christians in European and Mediterranean ports and Hindus in Goa, the capital of Portuguese India.[40] Thus, while trans-regional families were glued by traditional marriage and partnership arrangements, they were nevertheless able to expand their commercial networks in spite of their infrequent engagement with limited-liability types of partnerships.

Armenian Family Firms and *Commenda* Agents

A comparison between Sephardic and Armenian mercantile organizations in the seventeenth and eighteenth centuries highlights how family firms could generate very different types of commercial networks. This comparison is relevant because Armenians dominated the export of raw silk from Persia to Europe from about 1620 and 1720 and were active in the gem trade. Thus, Armenians were occupied in some of the same regions and commodity specializations as Sephardim. Overall, however, Sephardim appear to have been more prone than Armenians to hire commission agents from outside of their own communities—a tendency that likely gave them a competitive advantage over Armenians.

Shah Abbas I forcibly resettled a large Armenian population living near the Iranian border with the Ottoman Empire to the neighborhood of New Julfa in the Safavid capital, Isfahan, in 1604–05. After violently uprooting this population, however, the shah gave it commercial and administrative advantages that allowed the wealthiest Armenian families to acquire a near monopoly in the export of Iranian silk. They sustained their commercial and financial activities until political events led to the destruction of New Julfa between 1722 and 1747.[41]

The family firm was at the heart of the commercial organization of this successful segment of the Armenian diaspora. Armenian and Sephardic family firms shared many similarities. Whether the family patrimony was divided equally among all male and female siblings (as prescribed by customary laws) or inherited by the oldest surviving son, the wealthy commercial clans of New Julfa were pressured into living under the same roof. In these extended patriarchal families, brothers (and sometimes brothers-in-law) worked together with complete mutual responsibility after their father's death. Thus they could trade on their own account or take up obligations on behalf of the family partnership at large. These customs often ensured the preservation of a family firm over generations.[42]

Unlike Sephardim, however, Julfa Armenians relied more on traveling agents than on commissioned ones.[43] Traveling agents were normally selected from a pool of young men who lacked their own capital and undertook long voyages sponsored by the commercial elite in New Julfa. A *commenda* contract stipulated the terms according to which the sedentary partner financed the goods transported and part of the expenses incurred by the traveling agent, who received a proportion of any profit in return for his services. A recent study has found that Iranian Armenian traveling agents were invariably chosen from a closed "coalition" of Julfa families, most belonging to the Armenian Church but some to the Catholic Church as well.[44]

Several reasons account for Iranian Armenians' more insular business organization—some reasons were specific to their respective kinship organization, while others depended on the general political, economic, and religious conditions in the regions of migration. One factor played an especially critical role in the different commercial organization of Armenians and Sephardim: the gender balance in the diaspora. While many Sephardic women traveled from one port to the other in order to marry, most Armenian merchants returned to New Julfa in order to set up their own family after having spent their youth on the road. Alternatively, they remained abroad and sometimes married local women outside of their ethnic group. This pattern is visible among those Armenians who converted to Catholicism and settled in Livorno and Venice, but can also be observed in India and the Ottoman Empire.[45]

Numerically, Armenians and Sephardim were roughly comparable. Sephardic men and women in Europe, the Mediterranean, and the New World numbered a total of about 15,000, although only a fraction was active in commerce and finance. The Spanish and Portuguese Jewish synagogue of Amsterdam may have enlisted as many as 4,500 members in the 1680s, and possibly more around 1735.[46] The ghetto of Venice reached its zenith of 3,000 before the plague of 1630–31, and then declined steadily.[47] The Jews of Livorno, most though not all of Iberian origin, grew steadily from just 134 in 1601 to 4,327 in 1784.[48] A recent estimate puts the overall number of Iranian Armenians involved in long-distance trade at about 1,000–1,500.[49] While this figure may have been analogous to the total number of active Sephardic merchants during this time, Armenian settlements in western Europe and the Mediterranean were numerically smaller and were comprised essentially of men. In seventeenth-century Amsterdam, Armenian men never exceeded a hundred at a time.[50] In Venice, it is unlikely that they ever reached that figure.[51] Even though the rise of Livorno attracted growing numbers of Armenian merchants, only a handful settled there on more than a temporary basis.[52] Armenian colonies were much larger in the Levant. An Armenian traveler passing by Aleppo in 1613 counted three hundred households of his people, and a hundred in Smyrna.[53] However, we should note that Ottoman Armenians were not as commercially active as were Julfa Armenians, just as European Sephardim were more involved in long-distance trade than Ottoman Jews.

Armenian networks, in sum, were more centralized (with a nodal point in New Julfa) and their settlements in Europe smaller. This migratory structure explains why in order to oversee *commenda* and other contracts sealed with relatives, couriers, and traveling merchants, Iranian Armenians formed a corporate governance body called the Assembly of Merchants, which was based in New Julfa and functioned as their central clearing house. The Assembly of Merchants acted with ample administrative and jurisdictional power conferred upon them by the Safavid rulers to deter malfeasance, although punishment came mostly in the form of reputational sanctions. To members of the Julfa "coalition," the Assembly of Merchants and its representatives in the diaspora (who worked as judges of "portable courts") offered an effective, well-coordinated, semiformal arbitration institution. In addition, when necessary or convenient, Armenian merchants brought their lawsuits against fellow Armenians before the British court in India and perhaps before other local courts as well.[54] Surviving documentation, however, indicates that the Assembly of Merchants did not monitor dealings between Julfans and Ottoman Armenians, or any other strangers for that matter. Indeed, business letters by Julfa Armenians do not include grants of powers of attorney or commission agency to outsiders of their "coalition."[55]

In truth, little is known about business relations between Armenians and non-Armenians. Scattered evidence indicates that time and again Armenians entered into agreements with Hindus, Muslims, and other Christians but usually on a temporary basis and only for the collection of short-term credit.[56] Ergas and Silvera bought and sold a few commodities with Armenians in Livorno and traded on their behalf overseas several times, but all told, they had limited interactions with the Armenians.[57] Abraham and Jacob Franco in London shipped coral and diamonds to and from Madras on account of David Sceriman, likely the richest Armenian in Livorno, in the 1740s.[58] Still more, the Amsterdam notary archives contain numerous deeds showing that Armenians sold Persian silk to Dutch merchants and bought local textiles from them. Some even used bottomry loans (a mixture of bills of exchange and insurance policies) to transfer goods and credit between Moscow and the Netherlands.[59] Nevertheless, it remains unclear whether and how often commission agency developed between Armenians and non-Armenians, and if it did, how the parties involved protected themselves from opportunism.

While the global reach of Iranian Armenians is impressive if we consider that they relied almost exclusively on traveling merchants, their spotty presence in European and Atlantic ports compared to that of the Sephardim likely undermined their ability to engage in prolonged commission agency with strangers.

Conclusion

Historians and social scientists interested in the cultural and institutional bases of capitalism have drawn attention to a variety of past and contemporary groups sometimes referred to as "middleman minorities." Geographical dispersion, with transregional family ties in particular, is a strategic feature of such groups. Consistently tending toward abstraction and generalizations, however, the sociological literature has done little to illuminate the variations in kinship organization across different middleman minorities.[60] Historians, on the other hand, generally prone to detail and particularities, have proven surprisingly ready to assume the importance of family ties in the working of trading diasporas but show little patience for description and comparison.[61] Partly for this reason, the scholarship on early modern trading diasporas has also offered a feeble response to the prevailing tendency among economic historians to emphasize long-term changes rather than synchronic heterogeneity in forms of business organization. This is particularly so in the transition from family firms to limited liability partnerships, to joint-stock chartered companies, and eventually to modern corporations. By comparing the family structures of Sephardim and Armenians, we can do more than reassert the centrality of the family in long-distance trade. We can begin to explain the plurality of business forms that coexisted in the early modern period and the particular strengths and weaknesses of each trading diaspora.

No legal prohibition existed in Venice and Livorno against the formation of partnerships between Jews and non-Jews, but the absence of Jewish-Christian intermarriage and the social distance between the two groups made such partnerships nearly inconceivable. Most Sephardim in Livorno and Venice worked on the basis of implicit contracts with kin and in-laws to form general partnerships. Social incentives and deterrents both influenced this choice. *Accomandite* shielded investors from reckless partners but were not ideal to sustain long-term and complex investments.[62] At the same time, the matrimonial practices prevalent among Sephardim offset large portions of the risk that a general partnership entailed. Consanguineal marriages, the merging of dowry and dower, and levirate unions facilitated the circulation of commercial capital within small endogamic circles. Mutual agency permitted family partnerships to act promptly in a world where slow communication could be lethal to striking a good bargain. Furthermore, the greater longevity that family partnerships enjoyed over *commenda* agreements allowed them to overcome short-term crises and strengthen their credit and reputation over time. All in all, these advantages seem to have been sufficiently attractive to compensate for the perennial risk that one dishonest or inexpert partner would bring down all the others.

The modern theory of the business firm assumes that a firm's boundaries are chosen in order to provide the optimal allocation with respect to the parties involved in a transaction; it may, for example, be more convenient to subcontract in some areas and work in partnership in others.[63] Sephardic merchants did not have this freedom to choose. Social conditions discouraged them from forming even limited liability partnerships with non-Jews, and strongly encouraged them to rely on blood relatives and in-laws. Sephardic patriarchs were no innovators when it came to family firms. They reproduced social norms that happened to serve them well, for they could use their daughters to expand their networks as well as secure their commercial capital. The persistence of kinship structures that we readily label as traditional, however, did not automatically restrict the undertakings of Sephardic merchants to a small pool of kin and coreligionists. Many Sephardim, it turns out, did hire non-Jews as commission agents, even if they would not seal partnerships with them. In so doing, they expanded their activities to locales where coreligionists did not reside or did not hold a strong position in the market.

The same conclusion does not seem to hold for Armenians. Overall, both Sephardim and Armenians relied amply on extended patriarchal families to operate general partnerships. But Julfa Armenians preferred to hire traveling agents from their immediate circles by means of *commenda* contracts and did not seem to have relied consistently on commission agents selected from among other groups. The migratory patterns of the two trading diasporas as well as their legal and religious status in Europe help explain the different governance institutions that each used to monitor their respective agents. Armenians relied heavily on the Assembly of Merchants in Isfahan because the Safavid rulers granted it considerable autonomy and because many Armenian merchants maintained their basis in New Julfa. In contrast, in Christian Europe, where suspicion against Jews extended to the most acculturated Sephardim, no government would have allowed the creation of even a semiformal Sephardic tribunal with jurisdiction over the entire diaspora. Sephardim lived in different sovereign territories, and each community negotiated the terms and reach of its own jurisdictional autonomy with local political authorities, whether in Livorno, Venice, Hamburg, Amsterdam, London, or elsewhere. At same time, the larger population of each Sephardic community, the constant movement of people and information from one community to the other, and the circulation of women across the diaspora ensured the emergence of distinctive transregional networks. These networks, in turn, enacted multilateral channels of reputational control that worked both within and beyond the Sephardic diaspora.

If the comparison that I offered is correct, it shows that the Sephardim were the less formalized and less centralized of the two diasporas, and yet relied on non-kin and strangers more than the Armenians, who had a centralized, semiformal adjudication system. That Julfa Armenians were more insular than Sephardim in their business dealings is also at odds with the fact that as Christians they enjoyed several advantages in Europe unavailable to Sephardim. This apparent paradox may reflect the absence of secondary literature on the effect of intermarriage between Armenians and non-Armenians on this trading diaspora's business strategies in the seventeenth and eighteenth centuries. At any rate, a comparison with the Sephardim suggests that the limited circulation of women across the Armenian diaspora contributed to its greater business insularity because it reinforced the centrality of New Julfa, on the one hand, and accelerated the assimilation of Armenian men of the diaspora, on the other. Most settlements of Armenian merchants were too spotty and too small to enforce efficient informal oversight over non-Armenian commercial partners. In order to understand the business organization of Sephardim and Armenians, in sum, we need to consider not only the types of legal contracts that they used, but also the subtle differences in their kinship systems and how transregional families adapted to internal and external conditions, including geographical location, demographic consistency, and religious identity. Transregional families could take many forms and generate different models of business organization with which to contend in the competitive arena of long-distance trade.

Notes

1. This chapter draws from my *The Familiarity of Strangers: The Sephardic Diaspora, Livorno, and Cross-Cultural Trade in the Early Modern Period* (New Haven, CT, 2009).
2. By "Sephardim," I mean the descendents of those Jews expelled from Spain in 1492 or forced to convert to Catholicism in Portugal in 1497 who later formed stable communities in Europe (with principal settlements in Venice, Livorno, Amsterdam, Hamburg, and London) and the Caribbean. By the seventeenth century, this segment of the Sephardic diaspora was collectively distinct from Ottoman Sephardim, that is, those descendents of Iberian Jews who settled in the Ottoman Empire. After 1630, Livorno was the largest Sephardic settlement in Europe after Amsterdam, and it surpassed Venice in population and economic influence. In this chapter, I will only discuss Iranian Armenians, who were the branch of the Armenian diaspora most involved in long-distance trade in the seventeenth and early eighteenth centuries.
3. The Dutch Levant Company (1625–1826) was an organization of private merchants that did not receive a patent from the state. For a comparison between the Dutch and the English presence in the eastern Mediterranean, as well as on their cooperation and rivalry, see Alastair Hamilston, Alexander H. de Groot, and Mauritius H. van den Boogert, eds., *Friends and Rivals in the East: Studies in Anglo-Dutch Relations in the Levant from the Seventeenth to the Early Nineteenth Century* (Leiden, 2000).
4. On seventeenth-century Amsterdam, see W. Klein, *De Trippen in de 17e eeuw* (Assen, 1965); W. Klein and J. W. Veluwenkamp, "The Role of the Entrepreneur in the Economic Expansion of the Dutch Republic," in *The Dutch Economy in the Golden Age: Nine Studies*, ed. Karel Davids and Leo Noordegraaf (Amsterdam, 1993), 27–53; Clé Lesger and Leo Noordegraaf, eds., *Entrepreneurs and Entrepreneurship in Early Modern Times: Merchant and Industrialists within the Orbit of the Dutch Staple Market* (Den Haag, 1995); Julia Adams, *The Familial State: Ruling Families and Merchant Capitalism in Early Modern Europe* (Ithaca, NY, 2005). On the importance of family partnerships in the eighteenth-century British Atlantic, see Jacob M. Price, "The Great Quaker Business Families of Eighteenth-Century London: The Rise and Fall of a Sectarian Patriciate," in *The World of William Penn*, ed. Richard S. Dunn and Mary Maples Dunn (Philadelphia, 1986), 363–99; Jacob M. Price, "Transaction Costs: A Note on Merchant Credit and the Organization of Private Trade," in *The Political Economy of Merchants Empires*, ed. James Tracy (Cambridge, 1991), 276–97; Jacob M. Price, *Perry of London: A Family and a Firm on the Seaborne Frontier, 1615–1753* (Cambridge, 1992); David Hancock, *Citizens of the World: London Merchants and the Integration of the British Atlantic Community, 1735–1785* (Cambridge, 1995), 105–6; David Hancock, *Oceans of Wine: Madeira and the Organization of the Atlantic Market, 1640–1815* (New Haven, CT, 2009), 141–50, 188–90. Admittedly, Jacob Price, Kenneth Morgan, and others also found that after 1685—and particularly

after the mid-eighteenth century—specialization and trade in partnerships increased significantly in British Atlantic commerce; Jacob Price and Paul G. E. Clemens, "A Revolution of Scale in Overseas Trade: British Firms in the Chesapeake Trade, 1675–1775," *Journal of Economic History* 47 (1987): 1–43, and Kenneth Morgan, "Business Networks in the British Export Trade to North America, 1750–1800," in *The Early Modern Atlantic Economy*, ed. John J. McCusker and Kenneth Morgan (Cambridge, 2000), 36–62.

5. Ralph Davis, *Aleppo and the Devonshire Square: English Traders in the Levant in the Eighteenth Century* (London, 1967); Charles Carrière, *Négociants marseillais au XVIIIe siècle: Contribution à l'étude des économies maritimes* (Marseilles, 1973); Richard Grassby, *The English Gentleman in Trade: The Life and Works of Sir Dudley North, 1641–1691* (Oxford, 1994).
6. Max Weber, *Economy and Society: An Outline of Interpretative Sociology*, ed. Guenther Roth and Claus Wittich (Berkeley, CA, 1978), 378–79 (emphasis in the original). See also Max Weber, *The History of Commercial Partnerships in the Middle Ages*, ed. Lutz Kaelber (Lanham, MD, 2003). Note that Sylvia Yanagisako points out that Weber mistook the legal and accounting separation of household and commercial capital, which was born out of the desire to limit the financial liability of family members, for evidence of actual separation between family and business relations; Sylvia J. Yanagisako, "Bringing it All Back Home: Kinship Theory in Anthropology," in *Kinship in Europe: Approaches to Long-Term Developments (1300–1900)*, ed. David Warren Sabean, Simon Teuscher, and Jon Mathieu (New York, 2007), 42.
7. Here and throughout this essay I refer to the definition of "coalition" given by Avner Greif, *Institutions and the Path to the Modern Economy: Lessons from Medieval Trade* (Cambridge, 2006), 58–59.
8. On the rules of exogamy in Christian Europe during the early modern period, see David Warren Sabean, *Kinship in Neckarhausen, 1700–1870* (Cambridge, 1998), 63–89. Wherever Jews were permitted to reside in early modern Italy, including in Venice and Livorno, Jewish law prevailed in matters of marriage; Vittorio Colorni, *Legge ebraica e leggi locali: Ricerche sull'ambito d'applicazione del diritto ebraico in Italia dall'epoca romana al secolo XIX* (Milan, 1945), 185–87.
9. Archivio di Stato, Venice (henceforth ASV), *Notarile testamenti* (henceforth *NT*), Giovanni Piccini, 756.21. Two generations later, in 1702, Samuel Camis reiterated the injunction to his nieces; ASV, *NT*, Luca Calzavara, 247.115.
10. Primogeniture is often linked, among other things, to the rise of entail and declining investments in liquid assets in both Venice and Florence. On Venice, see James C. Davis, *The Decline of the Venetian Nobility as a Ruling Class* (Baltimore, 1962), 68–72; Jutta Gisela Sperling, *Convents and the Body Politic in Late Renaissance Venice* (Chicago, 1999), 42–50; Jean-François Chauvard, *La circulation des biens à Venise: Stratégies patrimoniales et marché immobilier (1600–1750)* (Rome, 2005), 323–31. On Florence, see R. Burr Litchfield, "Demographic Characteristics of Florentine Patrician Families from the Sixteenth to the Nineteenth Centuries," in *Journal of Economic History* 29 (1969): 191–205; Stefano Calonaci, *Dietro lo scudo crociato: I fedecommessi di famiglia e il trionfo della borghesia fiorentina (1400 ca-1750)* (Florence, 2005).
11. The age of thirty was likely chosen as it marked the moment when a merchant had established his autonomy (whether successfully or not). Archivio di Stato, Florence (henceforth ASF), *Notarile Moderno: Protocolli, Testamenti* (henceforth *NMT*), Giovanni Battista Gargani, 26286, fols. 19r–22r, no.12. In Venice in 1701, Moses Baruch Carvaglio left special instructions in the undesirable event that his sons decided to part ways (ASV, *NT*, Carlo Gabrieli, 518, fols. 234v–240v).

12. Abraham Attais was probably the first Jew in Livorno to stipulate an entail (*fideicommissum*) in 1694; Lucia Frattarelli Fischer, "Proprietà e insediamento ebraici a Livorno dalla fine del Cinquecento alla seconda metà del Settecento," *Quaderni storici* 54 (1983): 884. Moses Ergas also established "a sort of fideicommissum" in 1747 (ASF, *Magistrato Supremo*, 4045, letter E, no. 2). Examples from Venice are in ASV, *NT*, Giuseppe Uccelli, 1123.74; ASV, *NT*, Carlo Gabrieli, 516.166 (note that when Grazia Baruch Carvaglio created a *fidei commissum* for her 6,000 ducats invested in the Venetian public debt, she bequeathed it equally to all four sons).
13. Diane Owen Hughes, "From Brideprice to Dowry in Mediterranean Europe," *Journal of Family History* 3 (1978): 262–96.
14. Lorenzo Cantini, *Legislazione toscana raccolta e illustrate* (Florence, 1800–32), 2:178–79, 22:131–36; Umberto Santarelli, *Per la storia del fallimento nelle legislazioni italiane dell'età intermedia* (Padua, 1964), 147–52, 245–47, 284.
15. Archivio di Stato, Livorno, *Captiano poi Governatore poi Auditore: Atti civili*, 429, no. 203.
16. ASF, *Notarile Moderno Protocolli* (henceforth *NMP*), Giovanni Giuseppe Mazzanti, 23703, fols. 170r–175v, no. 36. The dowry of five thousand pieces and a 50 percent dower exchanged between Moses and Rebecca indicate a union between a man and a woman from the middle-upper stratum of Sephardic society.
17. Renzo Toaff, *La nazione ebrea a Livorno e Pisa (1591–1700)* (Florence, 1990), 574, 586, 612. On bigamy among the Livorno Jews in the seventeenth century, see Cristina Galasso, *Alle origini di una comunità: Ebree ed ebrei a Livorno nel Seicento* (Florence, 2002), 27–41.
18. ASF, *NMP*, Nicolò Mazzinghi, 27112, fols. 70v–71v, no. 129.
19. Evelyne Oliel-Grausz, "Networks and Communication in the Sephardi Diaspora: An Added Dimension to the Concept of Port Jews and Port Jewries," in *Jews and Port Cities, 1590–1990: Commerce, Community and Cosmopolitanism*, ed. David Cesarani and Gemma Romain (London, 2006), 63.
20. ASF, *NMP*, Roberto Micheli, 27236, fols. 177v–179r.
21. Henri Lévy-Bruhl, *Histoire juridique des sociétés de commerce en France aux XVIIe et XVIIIe siècles* (Paris, 1938), 30; Henri Lapeyre, *Une famille des marchands: Les Ruiz* (Paris, 1955), 145–52; Wilfrid Brulez, *De Firma della Faille en de internationale handel van Vlaamse firma's in de 16e eeuw* (Brussels, 1959), 35–123; Klein, *De Trippen*, 224–25, 379–88, 418–21.
22. Maurice Carmona, "Aspects du capitalisme toscan aux XVIe et XVIIe siècles: Les sociétés en commandite à Florence et à Lucques," *Revue d'histoire moderne et contemporaine* 11 (1964): 81–108; R. Burr Litchfield, "Les investissements commerciaux des patriciens florentins au XVIIIe siècle," in *Annales ESC* 24 (1969): 685–721; Jordan Goodman, "Financing Pre-Modern Industry: An Example from Florence, 1580–1660," *Journal of European Economic History* 10 (1981): 415–35; Franco Bertini, "Le società di accomandita a Firenze e Livorno tra Ferdinando III e il regno d'Etruria," in *Istituzioni e società in Toscana nell'età moderna (Atti delle giornate di studio dedicate a Giuseppe Pansini)* (Rome, 1994), 538–63; Paolo Malanima, "I commerci del mondo del 1674 visti da Amsterdam e da Livorno," in *Ricerche di storia moderna in onore di Mario Mirri*, ed. Giuliana Biagioli (Pisa, 1995), 153–80.
23. What follows is based on the examination of the copies of Tuscan *accomandite* registered in the merchant court of Florence from 1632 to 1777; ASF, *Mercanzia*, 10841–59.
24. Partnership between Jews and non-Jews among merchants involved in the Anglo-Indian diamond trade in the eighteenth century are mentioned in Gedalia Yogev,

Diamonds and Coral: Anglo-Dutch Jews and Eighteenth-Century Trade (Leicester, UK, 1978), 146–48, although with no reference to the specific terms of these agreements.

25. ASV, *NT*, Cristoforo Brambilla, 167.281. On the Baruch Carvaglios, see Federica Ruspio, *La Nazione Portoghese: Ebrei ponentini e nuovi cristiani a Venezia* (Torino, 2007), 180–85. On the Venetian *fraterne*, see Frederic C. Lane, "Family Partnerships and Joint Ventures in the Venetian Republic," *Journal of Economic History* 4 (1944): 178–96.
26. ASV, *NA*, Angelo Maria Piccini, 11062, fols. 27r–29r; ASV, *NT*, Andrea Calzavara, 260.830.
27. One of the difficulties of identifying these types of agreement among the papers of Jewish merchants is that the term *compagnia* had both a specific meaning and a generic one. In the latter case, it could refer to any type of commercial partnership, as did the expressions *compagnia di negozio* or the even more common *società* (from the Latin *societas*). Note, for example, that the Baruch Carvaglio called their business based in Venice a *fraterna e compagnia* (see above in the text). The agreement signed by Solomon Enriques and Joseph Franchetti in 1782 seems to establish a *compagnia* in the strict sense of term to operate in Tunis, Livorno, and Smyrna. For a transcription of the contract, see Jean-Pierre Filippini, "Gli ebrei e le attività economiche nell'area nord africana (XVII–XVIII secolo)," *Nuovi studi livornesi* 7 (1999): 143–44.
28. Raymond de Roover, *Money, Banking and Credit in Medieval Bruges: Italian Merchant-Bankers, Lombards and Money-Changers; A Study in the Origins of Banking* (Cambridge, MA, 1948), 31–34; Raymond de Roover, *The Rise and Decline of the Medici Bank, 1397–1494* (Cambridge, MA, 1963); Raymond de Roover, "The Organization of Trade," in *The Cambridge Economic History of Europe*, vol. 3, *Economic Organization and Policies in the Middle Ages*, ed. M. M. Postan, E. E. Rich and Edward Miller (Cambridge, 1963), 42–118; John F. Padgett and Paul D. McLean, "Organizational Invention and Elite Transformation: The Birth of Partnership Systems in Renaissance Florence," *American Journal of Sociology* 111 (2006): 1463–568.
29. Lapeyre, *Une famille des marchands*; Wilfrid, *De Firma della Faille*; Pierre Jeannin, *Les marchands au XVI*[e] *siècle* (Paris, 1967).
30. In modern legal scholarship, this point is emphasized by Henry Hansmann, Reinier Kraakman, and Richard Squire, "Law and the Rise of the Firm," *Harvard Law Review* 119 (2006): 1372–74.
31. As the two brothers Jacob and Daniel Navarro stated when they dissolved their partnership in Venice in 1661, they had to "purify their accounts of the dowries" before they could divide the remaining assets among themselves; ASV, *NA*, Angelo Maria Piccini, 11068, fol. 162v. When Lazzaro Racanati married his cousin in 1750, it was established that both the dowry and the dower would be registered in the account books of his partnership, although the capital was only transferred there nine years later (ASF, *NMP*, Giovanni Battista Gamerra, 25273, fols. 80r–81r, no. 80, and 25277, fols. 162r–163r, no. 416). The same provision had been recorded in 1718 at the marriage of Salvatore Recanati (ASF, *NMP*, Giovanni Battista Gamerra, 25271, fols. 3r–4v, no. 3). Other examples from the account books of Ergas & Silvera are in ASF, *Libri di commercio e di famiglia* (henceforth *LCF*), 1933 (11 September 1730; 22 October 1730); ASF, *LCF*, 1946 (22 August 1735); ASF, *LCF*, 1954 (21 March 1741).
32. Medieval Italian family firms had long introduced the use of such a fund (called *sovraccorpo*): Weber, *History of Commercial Partnerships*, 162–66; de Roover, "Organization of Trade," 77.

33. José do Nascimento Raposo, "Don Gabriel de Silva: A Portuguese-Jewish Banker in Eighteenth-Century Bordeaux" (PhD diss., York University, Toronto, 1989), 172. Gabriel de Silva lived his life as a New Christian, but in 1763 was buried in the Jewish cemetery in Bordeaux (290).
34. See the documents published in the section called "Notarial Records Relating to the Portuguese Jews in Amsterdam up to 1639," which appears in most issues of the journal *Studia Rosenthaliana* beginning in 1967. More evidence surfaces in Cátia Antunes's current work ("Atlantic Entrepreneurship: Cross-cultural Business Networks, 1580–1776," paper presented at the European Social Science History Conference, Ghent, Belgium, 13 April 2010).
35. On the general partnership as an institution of Roman law, see Reinhard Zimmermann, *The Law of Obligations: Roman Foundations of the Civil Traditions* (Oxford, 1996), 466–72.
36. ASF, *LCF*, 1931, letter to Stefano Ceccato in Venice (20 January 1708).
37. Examples in ASF, *LCF*, 1931, letter to Zuanelli and Iolotta in Venice (15 March 1705); ASF, *LCF*, 1935, letter to Lazzaro Sacerdoti in Genoa (15 February 1715).
38. Davis, *Aleppo*, 147–48. On the obsolete information that English principals dispatched to Aleppo, see also Grassby, *English Gentleman*, 45, 47.
39. Edhem Eldem, *French Trade in Istanbul in the Eighteenth Century* (Leiden, 1999), 208–9. In eighteenth-century Marseille, merchants had the habit of drafting detailed contracts to stipulate their individual and family obligations; Carrière, *Négociants marseillais*, 879–81.
40. For a full illustration of the range of commission agents used in Europe and Portuguese India by the Ergas & Silvera of Livorno, and the systems through which these agents were monitored, see my *Familiarity of Strangers*, chapters 7, 8, 9.
41. Edmund Herzig, "The Iranian Silk Trade and European Manufacture in the XVIIth and XVIIIth Centuries," *Journal of European Economic History* 19 (1990): 73–89; Edmund Herzig, "The Volume of Iranian Raw Silk Exports in the Safavid Period," *Iranian Studies* 25 (1992): 61–79; Rudolph Matthee, *The Politics of Trade in Safavid Iran: Silk for Silver 1600–1730* (Cambridge, 1999); Sebouh Aslanian, *From the Indian Ocean to the Mediterranean: The Global Trade Networks of Armenian Merchants from New Julfa* (Berkeley, CA, 2011).
42. Edmund Herzig, "The Armenian Merchants of New Julfa, Isfahan: A Study in Premodern Trade" (PhD diss., Oxford University, 1991), 160–73, 223–30; Edmund Herzig, "The Family Firm in the Commercial Organization of the Julfa Armenians," in *Études Safavides*, ed. Jean Calmard (Paris-Louvain, 1993), 287–304; Aslanian, *From the Indian Ocean*, 147–48; Sebouh Aslanian, "The Circulation of Men and Credit: The Role of the Commenda and the Family Firm in Julfan Society," *Journal of the Economic and Social History of the Orient* 5 (2007): 149–50.
43. Herzig, *Armenian Merchants of New Julfa*, 231.
44. Aslanian, *From the Indian Ocean*, 157–58; Aslanian, "Circulation of Men and Credit," 237–52, 280–83. For the accounts kept by a *commenda* agent traveling to Central Asia, see Levon Khachikian, "The Ledger of the Merchant Hovhannes Joughayetsi," *Journal of the Asiatic Society* 8 (1966): 153–86. Bhaswati Bhattacharya shows that in practice some traveling agents gained autonomy by working away from home for long periods of time and sometimes accumulated capital of their own; see her "The 'Book of Will' of Petrus Woskan (1680–1751): Some Insights into the Global Commercial Networks of the Armenians in the Indian Ocean," *Journal of the Economic and Social History of the Orient* 51 (2008): 76.

45. Already in 1629 a prosperous merchant from Isfahan married a woman from Livorno following the prescription of the Council of Trent; Frattarelli Fischer, "Insediamento degli Armeni," 29. On the marriage alliances between the business elite of Livorno and Armenians, see also Lucia Frattarelli Fischer, "'Pro Armenis Unitis cum conditionibus': La costruzione della Chiesa degli Armeni a Livorno: un *iter* lungo e accidentato," in *Gli Armeni a Livorno: L'intercultura di una diaspora (Interventi nel Convegno "Memoria e cultura armena fra Livorno e l'oriente)*, ed. Giangiacomo Panessa and Massimo Sanacore (Livorno, 2006), 29. The Sceriman, the richest Catholic Armenian family of the diaspora, married into Venetian patrician families; Donald Maxwell White, *Zaccaria Seriman (1709–1784) and the Viaggi di Enrico Wanton: A Contribution to the Study of the Enlightenment in Italy* (Manchester, UK, 1961), 19, note 3. For Armenian women who married officers of the Dutch East India Company in Surat in the late seventeenth century, see Bhaswati Bhattacharya, "Armenian European Relationship in India, 1500–1800: No Armenian Foundation for European Empire?," *Journal of the Economic and Social History of the Orient* 48 (2005): 306. In Smyrna, Persian Armenians married among themselves, while only a few built kinship ties to resident French merchants; see Kéram Kévonian, "Marchands Arméniens au XVIIe siècle: À propos d'un livre arménien à Amsterdam en 1699," *Cahiers du monde russe et soviétique* 16 (1975): 210; Marie-Carmen Smyrnelis, "Les arméniens catholiques de Smyrne aux XVIIIe et XIXe siècle," *Revue du monde arménien moderne et contemporaine* 2 (1995) : 38–39.
46. H. P. H. Nusteling, "The Jews in the Republic of the United Provinces: Origins, Numbers and Dispersion," in *Dutch Jewry: History and Secular Culture (1500–2000)*, ed. Jonathan Israel and Reinier Salverda (Leiden, 2002), 51–53. More conservative figures set the number of Sephardim at 2,800 in 1683, with a peak of 3,000 in the mid-eighteenth century (Miriam Bodian, *Hebrews of Portuguese Nation: Conversos and Community in Early Modern Amsterdam* [Bloomington, IN, 1997], 156, 158) or, on the basis of marriage data, to 3,275–3,475 individuals in the 1680s (Daniel M. Swetschinski, *Reluctant Cosmopolitans: The Portuguese Jews of Seventeenth-century Amsterdam* [Oxford, 2000], 91).
47. Giovanni Favero and Francesca Trivellato, "Gli abitanti del ghetto di Venezia in età moderna: dati e ipotesi," *Zakhor: Rivista della storia degli ebrei in Italia* 7 (2004): 9–50.
48. Elena Fasano Guarini, "La popolazione," in *Livorno e Pisa: due città e un territorio nella politica dei Medici: Livorno, progetto e storia di una città tra il 1500 e il 1600* (Pisa, 1980), 199–215; Toaff, *La nazione ebrea*, 121–23.
49. Aslanian, *From the Indian Ocean*, 179. For a drastically lower figure of 300 to 400, see Bhaswati Bhattacharya, "Making Money at the Blessed Place of Manila: Armenians in the Madras-Manila Trade in the Eighteenth Century," *Journal of Global History* 3 (2008): 18. The same author also emphasizes the growth of Armenian mercantile settlements in India and their autonomy from New Julfa in the eighteenth century.
50. Silvio Van Rooy, "Armenian Habits as Mirrored in 17–18th Century Amsterdam Documents," *Revue des études arméniennes* 3 (1966): 347. The number of Armenians identified through Amsterdam notary records peaked at an average of 41 per year in 1701–20; René Bekius, "A Global Enterprise: Armenian Merchants in the Textile Trade in the 17th and 18th Centuries," in *Carpets and Textiles in the Iranian World, 1400–1700*, ed. Jon Thompson, Daniel Shaffer, Pirjetta Mildh (Oxford, 2010), 226. See also Edmund Herzig, "Venice and the Julfa Armenian Merchants," in *Gli armeni e Venezia: Dagli Sceriman a Mechitar: Il momento culminante di una consuetudine millenaria*, ed. Boghos Levon Zekiyan and Aldo Ferrari (Venice, 2004), 159–61.

51. In 1653, 73 adult men elected the new priest of the Armenian Church in Venice. In 1710, 36 Armenians were counted as being in transit through Venice and 27 as permanent residents. Some forty years later, there were 70 lay Armenians and 17 clergymen there; Giorgio Nubar Gianighian, "Segni di una presenza," in Zekiyan and Ferrari, *Gli armeni e Venezia*, 62.
52. Armenians began to appear in Tuscany in the mid-sixteenth century. Their presence grew slowly, to peak in the mid-seventeenth century when there were at least 47 Armenian merchants in Livorno. In 1763, there were a mere 14 Armenian heads of household. See Paolo Castignoli, *Studi di Storia: Livorno dagli archivi alla città* (Livorno, 2001), 117; Lucia Frattarelli Fischer, "Per la storia dell'insediamento degli Armeni a Livorno nel Seicento," in *Gli Armeni lungo le strade d'Italia: Atti del convegno internazionale (Torino, Genova, Livorno, 8–11 marzo 1997); Giornata di studi a Livorno* (Pisa, 1998), 23, 26–30, 35. Claims that there were 120 Armenians in Livorno in the early seventeenth century and from one to two hundred in the eighteenth century seem inflated; Boghos Levon Zekiyan, "Le colonie armene del Medio Evo in Italia e le relazioni culutrali italo-armene," in *Atti del primo simposio internazionale di arte armena (Bergamo, 28–30 giugno 1975)* (Venice, 1978), 856; and Herzig, "Venice and Julfa Merchants," 156. Also unreliable is the report sent by the Papal Nuncio to the *Propaganda Fide* in 1669, which mentioned 300 resident Armenian merchants in Livorno; Aslanian, "Circulation of Men and Credit," 160–61, and his *From the Indian Ocean*, 73.
53. Herzig, "Venice and the Julfa," 153.
54. For India, see Bhattacharya, "The 'Book of Will'," 79–81.
55. Sebouh Aslanian, "Social Capital, 'Trust' and the Role of Networks in Julfan Trade: Informal and Semi-Formal Institutions at Work," *Journal of Global History* 1 (2006): 393–99, and his *From the Indian Ocean*, 164, 196–97, 199. The Assembly of Merchants was formed by a Julfan appointed representative (*kalantar*), who acted as delegate of, and intermediary with, the shah and twenty other officials. It is possible that the correspondence and other business records examined by Aslanian underestimate business cooperation between Julfa Armenians and all others because they are, for the most part, kept in a dialect that was only comprehensible to Julfa Armenians.
56. Edmund Herzig, "Borrowed Terminology and Techniques of the New Julfa Armenian Merchants: A Study in Cultural Transmission," Paper presented at the *Sixth Biennial Conference on Iranian Studies* (London, 3–5 August 2006). Sparse examples in Bhattacharya, "Armenian European Relationship," 291, 293–300; Bhattacharya, "The 'Book of Will'," 83; Bhattacharya, "Making Money," 7, 10, 14, 16. The Sceriman family possibly relied on a Hindu agent to acquire diamonds in Goa; Aslanian, *From the Indian Ocean*, 158, and "Circulation of Men and Credit," 156.
57. In 1732, they bought about 556 pieces of eight of indigo from "David di Jacoppo Armenio"; ASF, *LCF*, 1942, fol. 17 (Debts, 19 March 1732). The following year, they sold cacao to "Giovani di Gaspari Armenio"; ASF, *LCF*, 1942, fol. 4 (Credits, 24 April 1733). In 1731, Ergas & Silvera had a credit of 70 pieces of eight with "Gregorio de Pietro Armenio" to whom Touche and Jauna of Cyprus had remitted a bill of exchange; ASF, *LCF*, 1942, fol. 11 (Credits, 17 December 1731). Purchases made by Ergas & Silvera on account of Armenians in Livorno are mentioned in ASF, *LCF*, 1945, letters to Ergas & Silvera in Aleppo (6 May 1738) and Medici and Niccolini in Lisbon (3 August 1739).
58. Bhaswati Bhattacharya, e-mail communication.
59. Bekius, "A Global Enterprise."

60. Edna Bonacich, "A Theory of Middleman Minorities," *American Sociological Review* 38 (1973): 583–94; Walter Zenner, *Minorities in the Middle: A Cross-Cultural Analysis* (Albany, NY, 1991).
61. An important, if partial, exception is Claude Markovits's study of the Sindhi trading diaspora, although women played a minimal role in this commercial diaspora; *The Global World of Indian Merchants, 1750–1947: Traders of Sind from Bukhara to Panama* (Cambridge, 2000).
62. While there is compelling evidence that the *commenda* was "the single most important source of the dramatic expansion of Julfan commerce in the seventeenth and eighteenth centuries," when compared to commission agency, it is not clear that it was always "the ideal means for the circulation of merchants, goods, and credit across vast distances," as maintained by Aslanian, "Circulation of Men and Credit," 125.
63. In his analysis of the internal organization, ownership, and boundaries of firms, Oliver D. Hart, unlike most economists, considers power as exogenous to the market but does not define exactly what he means by "power," nor does he contextualize its forms. See his *Firms, Contracts, and Financial Structure* (Oxford, 1995).

Chapter 7

Those in Between

Princely Families on the Margins of the Great Powers—The Franco-German Frontier, 1477–1830

Jonathan Spangler

To a gentleman, any country is a homeland.
— Cardinal Jules Mazarin (Giulio Mazzarino)[1]

We are looked upon as the last of the Gauls or as the first of the Germans. We are neither Gauls nor Germans; we belong at once to both of them.
— from an eleventh-century necrology, Saint-Lambert de Liège[2]

Strasbourg, 1827. After having resided peaceably in this city since his Alsatian estates were restored to him by the Congress of Vienna in 1815, the Prince of Salm-Salm was required to leave France by the new Conservative Catholic Royalist government. His crime? He had declared his intention to convert to Protestantism. The issue at stake, however, was whether the formerly sovereign prince was to be considered an alien or a citizen and thus subject to French law. In his defense, the prince produced example after example of his ancestors' and his own service to the French crown in the preceding centuries. His uncle was a French field marshal who had raised troops from Alsace for Louis XV at his own expense, and his younger brother had worked to keep the northeast frontier loyal to Louis XVI as bishop of Tournai.[3] But examples could be provided in equal numbers of his ancestors' service to the Holy Roman Empire. His own father, the French field marshal's brother, had been an Austrian field marshal and governor of Luxembourg.[4] Two brothers, two careers; one French, one Austrian. For a princely family hailing from the borderlands between France and the empire, this scenario was entirely commonplace, a standard family practice for survival between larger powers.

An interesting cap to this story is the identity of the man who tried the hardest to prevent the prince's conversion: the former bishop of Strasbourg, Cardinal-Prince de Croÿ.[5] His family had been princes in the Southern Netherlands since the sixteenth century and readily displayed the same pattern of military service. The cardinal himself had five brothers: two French field marshals, a Spanish brigadier, a Bavarian general, and an Austrian colonel.[6]

At the beginning of the era of nationalism and citizenship, where would these formerly pan-European families fit in? Their kinship networks were almost exclusively with one another, across linguistic, geographical, and political frontiers, rather than with one particular national nobility or another. Cardinal de Croÿ was the most natural person for King Charles X to send to the Prince of Salm-Salm. He was his cousin, and he understood his family values. This chapter will analyze the issues affecting the positions of such semisovereign families in the borderlands between France and the Holy Roman Empire and their impact on the development of national loyalty or identity and early modern state building, particularly in the Southern Netherlands (modern Belgium) and Alsace.

Large multilineal princely dynasties such as the Salm or the Croÿ were part of a wider European order of transregional families, who appear with great regularity in political and cultural histories of most European nation-states but have never been systematically studied as a whole. The task of course is daunting, requiring reading knowledge of every major European language (with the exception perhaps of English) and an understanding of the politicocultural workings of most European states. This chapter will attempt only to identify some common features, based on general prosopographical and genealogical sampling and some specific archival material, with an aim to define characteristics for a set of aristocrats with similar geographical origins and a similar modus vivendi. Their number can be set at about thirty distinct yet thoroughly interconnected dynasties, defined by a loose understanding of the concept of sovereignty and the title of prince. Aside from the difficulty of fitting these princely transregional families into strictly national studies, this group has also been overlooked as neither typically noble nor strictly speaking royal. They can be described as the bottom of the top of the European hierarchical system and, in following a recent trend to rehabilitate and recognize the relevance of dynasticism in the political culture of the early modern world, are worth our attention, particularly in our understanding of the shift in conceptualizations of the state from a feudalist perspective as merely those estates and individuals loyal to an individual sovereign to the view of a physical territory occupied by a distinct population, "imagined as an egalitarian horizontal comradeship."[7]

Since the splitting of the Frankish dominions into eastern and western kingdoms in the ninth century, sovereignty over the middle portion was rarely formalized and often contested. The descendants of this Middle Kingdom—the future Belgium, Alsace, Lorraine, western Switzerland, Dauphiné, Provence, Savoy, and Piedmont—formed a patchwork of conflicting feudal loyalties to the king of France or to the German emperor, to both or indeed to neither. In the era before nationalism, these regions thrived not as a frontier, but as a meeting place for economic and cultural exchange.[8] As Strasbourg once again becomes a center of European political and economic activity for the twenty-first century, it is important to recognize that this region was once the center of imperial power, not the periphery. The nobles who established themselves in this middle corridor cultivated links with both east and west, and retained dual identities, as revealed in something as simple as their names: Ribeaupierre and Rappoltstein, Montjoye and Frohberg, Petit-Pierre and Lützelstein, Deux-Ponts and Zweibrücken, Lorraine and Lothringen. Exact borders mattered little, and families on the margins easily shifted alliances and loyalties across the generations. But the early sixteenth-century consolidation of government across Europe brought a need to define effective jurisdictions in the larger states and the need for smaller territories to define their status more precisely. Duke Antoine of Lorraine, for example, signed the Treaty of Nuremberg with Emperor Charles V in 1542, which clarified that only Antoine's imperial fiefs (principally to the north and east of Lorraine) were directly accountable to the emperor, while Lorraine itself was sovereign, "*liber et non incorporatus*," under the *protection* of the empire.[9]

Several basic characteristics are shared by the transregional princely dynasties. The first is privilege generated from rank at birth. As princes, these men (and women) had the closest daily access to European monarchs, not because of their offices or military achievements, but because of their birth. The kinship network as a whole profited from individual success, whether in Paris or Vienna—the location did not matter. But a particular strategy appears in the genealogical record again and again, the strategy of "two sons, two armies," placing sons on both sides of a political divide. This not only provided employment for younger sons, but "hedged the bets" for the survival of a dynasty between the rivalries of its larger neighbors. The system also maintained a regular flow of information between these neighbors, useful to the families and the monarchs they served alike.[10] The second is privilege generated by location. These families were courted by monarchs and statesmen on both sides of the borders in ways that more "central" nobles were not. In particular, provinces with an absentee ruler, like the Southern Netherlands, Alsace, Naples, or Scotland, saw the elevation to the highest ranks in greater number than in locations closer to the sovereign, both to keep the local elites loyal and to create a surrogate court with enough sparkle and mystique to reinforce the loyalty of the rest of the population. In the processes of early modern nation building, border families were courted in newly annexed provinces to stimulate or maintain the loyalty of the entire province. The great powers competed with each other in awarding their highest titles and chivalric honors, to the obvious benefit of these nobles and their families. It is important to consider, however, that many of these families can be considered as transregional not because they moved but because the frontiers moved across them. The characteristics shared by this elite subset of European nobility represented both a centripetal and a centrifugal force in state formation: maintaining a separateness of regional identities in the midst of centralization and at the same time a more general sense of Europeanness, forged and supported by networks of kinship.

The existence of small sovereignties between larger sovereignties was problematic. They were ignored at the Great Powers' peril. Protestant dissenters found haven in Navarre and principalities in the Vosges like Salm and the county of Saarbrücken.[11] Debased coinage from small states blessed with mineral wealth like Lorraine or the Ardennes principalities of Château-Regnault or Sedan upset French and imperial markets.[12] But larger states could make use of these factors as well, as seen in the Jewish creditors of Metz, theoretically under the jurisdiction of the king of France from 1552 (de facto; de jure from 1648), but exempted from French law banning Jews, as Metz continued to be a foreign territory, not fully integrated into France until 1789.[13] Kings and capitalists could thus obtain funds in ways restricted in the capital, not unlike modern tax havens in today's surviving sovereign border principalities of Monaco and Liechtenstein. As a force counter to modern state building, aristocratic internationalism, in tandem with the Republic of Letters of the Enlightenment, took the place of the Catholic church as the main unifier of a single European consciousness after the splits of the Reformation. From this perspective, the transregional princely families can be represented as a conservative force in early modern Europe, which, from a nineteenth-century *étatist*, centralist point of view is undoubtedly negative, but with a nod to recent reappraisals of decentralized, fragmented polities like the Holy Roman Empire, can be seen as defenders of an alternative system of governance that defied the absolutist tendencies of kings and middle-class bureaucrats.[14] Even as the appeal of federalism in Europe weakened in the nineteenth century, border princes continued to play formal and informal roles, particularly in diplomacy, before becoming obsolete in the aftermath of World War I. Yet it is worth noting that as late as 1943, Hitler purged members of the high aristocracy from sensitive positions in the Third Reich, mistrusting their loyalties due to their cosmopolitan families.[15] This chapter will focus on these two aspects of transregional princely families: their relationships with monarchy and their roles in the integration of border provinces and state building.

Historians have regularly highlighted the leading roles played by the high nobility of the Low Countries at the courts of the Burgundian dukes and their immediate Habsburg successors.[16] Yet attempts to locate these great nobles in subsequent periods becomes more difficult. Any collection of essays on the nobility will undoubtedly contain a chapter on the Dutch Republic, on France, or on the Holy Roman Empire, but where can one look to find out what has happened to those in between? After playing such a large part in the struggle between rebellion and loyalty in the 1570s, did the great Southern Netherlandish houses simply disappear? Were they completely impotent under Spanish rule as has been suggested?[17] In the words of Dutch historian Pieter Geyl, they were "glittering with honors, but with sadly restricted power."[18] If this was so, why were these nobles courted so intensely by the major powers of western Europe well into the seventeenth century?

Part of the answer to these questions can be found in prosopographical surveys of families who gained princely rank in the Southern Netherlands and other border regions between France and Germany in the period 1500 to 1800. Ever since the advent of detailed studies using the models of anthropology and sociology to identify and define trends in history emerged in the Annales School and the followers of Lewis Namier, prosopography has become an integral part of in-depth research into institutions of many western European states.[19] But most of these have focused on families and networks within one particular state. There have been studies of a more "European" nobility in general and some that continue to divide the nobles into national groups.[20] But these too tend to avoid elites from regions in between the larger states such as

Alsace or the Southern Netherlands.[21] There has been no published systematic analysis of the princely border families as a type. Difficulties to overcome for such a study include the wide variety of languages and the geographical dispersal of archival materials. Sources for the Salm and the Croÿ, for example, must be sought in Paris, Brussels, Vienna, and Madrid.[22] Late medievalists have embraced the idea of a transregional prosopographical study with greater gusto than modern historians, mostly in the context of Burgundy and its neighbors.[23] Not sharing any land borders with continental Europe, British historians have been involved only infrequently in such transregional studies, again, with the exception of medievalists, who have focused prosopographical studies on the Anglo-Norman barons or the Angevin empire.[24] Two recent collections of essays, however, have made linkages with these ideas for the early modern period, analyzing the relationships of William III of Orange and of the House of Hanover with the rest of Europe.[25] It is within this comparative context that the present research must be situated.

Two Trajectories: Salm and Croÿ

Let us therefore return to the princes of Salm and Croÿ, one essentially Alsatian and one Belgian. Of all the border families in my survey of princely families, these two stand out as the ultimate success stories in playing up the rivalries between east and west to their own advantage. The Salm claimed descent from an ancient ruling dynasty of the German Empire and had established their mountaintop principality in the Vosges as early as the twelfth century.[26] They did not need to be encouraged in their princely pretensions, but in order to secure their loyalty to him personally, Emperor Ferdinand II elevated them to the rank of *Reichsfürst* in 1623. They were given a vote in the Imperial Diet, thereby equating them with the ancient princes like Bavaria and Saxony, but without the significant territorial base to make them a threat to imperial authority. These were among the first of the new princes who would multiply across the remaining two centuries of the Holy Roman Empire, adequately fulfilling their function of increasing the emperor's control of the diet.[27] The Salm princes of the seventeenth century served primarily in the imperial armies and at the imperial court. One of them rose to become leader of the Privy Council (and indeed uncle by marriage) of Joseph I. But because of their immediate proximity to the Duchy of Lorraine, several of the family members served at the ducal court or in ducal armies, until Lorraine itself became part of France in 1737. In fact, the first *fürst* (who incidentally had married a Croÿ) served in succession as a French lieutenant general, an imperial field marshal, then governor of Nancy for the Duke of Lorraine.[28] After 1737, as international treaties guaranteed the sovereignty of their enclave between Lorraine and Alsace, Salm princes built large palaces in both Paris and Vienna, and occupied positions at both courts. They became grandees of the Austrian Netherlands as well, with the addition of the dukedom of Hoogstraten to their patrimony in 1740.[29] But the survival of what was now considered a feudal anachronism in the Vosges was anathema to the French revolutionary government, which called for annexation in 1792, thus serving as the casus belli for the invasion of imperial armies and the start of the Revolutionary Wars.

The Croÿ, in contrast, originated as fairly ordinary nobles in Picardy, but during the time that Picardy was under the influence of the dukes of Burgundy, they drifted across the frontier to become the most important landowners in Hainaut and amassed great wealth through the Burgundian patronage machine.[30] They nevertheless continued to play a balancing game between France and the Netherlands, acquiring the rich and fertile county of Porcean in Champagne and the semisovereign lordship of Aerschot on the frontiers of Brabant, a territory with genuine regalian rights over its small patch of territory (coinage, justice, etc.).[31] The man who elevated the family to grandee status was Guillaume de Croÿ, seigneur de Chièvres—governor, tutor, then premier minister of Emperor Charles V in the Low Countries and Germany. He organized the imperial elections of 1519 and was rewarded with titles and almost endless amounts of wealth in Spain and Southern Italy for himself and his family, a champion of what John Elliott has termed the "rapacity" of the Flemings.[32] Chièvres was succeeded by his nephews, who, as was perfectly natural at the time, divided their attentions between French and imperial service. The elder was created Duke of Aerschot in the Netherlands by the emperor, while the younger retained the family loyalty to the king of France. In the next generation, both branches were raised to princely rank, the elder as Prince of Chimay by Philip II of Spain and the younger as Prince of Porcean by Henri II of France. Over the following century, the Croÿ would outstrip all other families of the Low Countries in the number of knights of the Golden Fleece awarded by the kings of Spain—twenty-seven, in contrast to an average of five or six.[33] The reason? The desirability of Hainaut as a border province and the need to secure its leading family by the contending powers. This is made evident from the late seventeenth century, when, after the annexation of southern Hainaut by France, the degree of Croÿ military, ecclesiastic, and court service in France rose as with other border families previously in Habsburg service who suddenly found their lands located primarily in France. In the sixteenth century, the Croÿ remained loyal to Spain; in the eighteenth century, they maintained their rank as princes of the empire but were nevertheless more firmly situated in the ranks of French service.

These two families, Salm and Croÿ, share several points of similarity, notably as representatives of the forces of national or supranational identity. Both were involved in the attempt of the Burgundian dukes and their successors to form a centralized state by pulling together nobles from all over their dominions and were rewarded for remaining committed to the idea after the collapse of 1477 and after the revolt of 1568.[34] The Croÿ in particular maintained a strong presence in the Low Countries as regional governors and senior counselors.[35] At the same time, the two dynasties helped to maintain a degree of separateness in their respective regions of Hainaut and Alsace. Alsatian nobles clung to the idea of belonging to the Holy Roman Empire only when their separate identity was threatened, as with the threat of Burgundian expansion in the 1470s.[36] Salm princes governed Alsace during its occupation by Swedish forces in the Thirty Years' War as relatives and coreligionists of the Swedish king and as local leaders with previously established clout. They were completely excluded from French administration of the province after 1648 for precisely the same reasons. Hainaut was increasingly divided between France and the Spanish (later Austrian) Netherlands from the mid-seventeenth century, but its magnates remained a constant presence in the province as a whole. The Croÿ retained direct control over their seigniorial lands in French Hainaut and dominated the local estates, despite the more centralized administration imposed from Paris after the annexation.[37]

The Links between Transregional Princely Families and Monarchy

In analyzing border families as groups rather than individuals, we can discern patterns of distribution of honors like ducal and princely titles and chivalric orders with increasing frequency across the seventeenth century, sometimes in startling degrees in terms of overall number or concentration within single families. Having learned from the Dutch Revolt that a contented nobility was a loyal nobility, the kings of Spain created titles in ever-increasing numbers in Naples and Sicily, rising from seventeen in the middle of the sixteenth century to over four hundred in 1675.[38] This rise was greatest among the princes, multiplying by 5.6 between 1590 and 1675, to 118 in total.[39] Numbers were not so high in the Southern Netherlands, but individual families could gather together great prizes by playing off rivalries. When one branch of the Croÿ was created prince and hereditary marshal of the Holy Roman Empire in 1594, the king of France countered with the creation of a duchy of Croÿ in 1598 in an (unsuccessful) attempt to create a rival branch based in France.[40] A family that is usually considered to be quintessentially French, the Montmorency, demonstrates a similar scenario, with one branch based at the French court, and the other, the princes de Robecque, prominently placed in the Spanish administration of the Southern Netherlands, until their lands (located primarily around Lille) were annexed by France following the treaty of Rijswijk in 1697.[41]

Families benefited from these territorial rivalries but also manipulated confessional differences. Although the early seventeenth-century threat of a great northern Protestant dynastic alliance had abated, nevertheless, there remained several princely families split by confessional divides, notably the Catholic dukes of Neuburg, cadets of the Calvinist Electors Palatine; or the Catholic branches of the House of Nassau (Siegen and Hadamar), which were created *Reichsfürsten* to counterbalance the Protestant Orange and Dillenberg-Dietz branches. The Catholic margraves of Baden-Baden kept their distance from their Protestant Baden-Durlach kin. But religion could be changed to follow the needs of politics. A key ally of William of Orange during the Dutch Revolt was his brother-in-law Van den Berghe, but the latter's son followed the change in the wind and became a prominent leader of Spanish troops *against* the separatists in the 1620s.[42]

The Spanish monarchy in particular attempted to keep its disparate parts together through grants of titles and respect of local privileges and traditional grandee dominance. Although they usually relied on governors and viceroys from other parts of the monarchy—a notable progression of foreign ministers in Brussels included Gattinara and the Granvelles (father and son), Alba, Parma, and so on—they mostly left in place the system of self-rule for each individual province inherited from the Burgundian regime.[43] And like the Burgundian dukes, the Habsburgs used the Order of the Golden Fleece to bind together Flemings, Walloons, Sicilians, and Castilians into one transnational aristocratic elite, though there was no impulse towards the creation of anything like a common enterprise for the various parts of the Spanish monarchy. Philip II encouraged intermarriage but no merging of institutions.[44] The award of the Golden Fleece helped maintain these elites in a position of exclusiveness and authority within their own localities and generated a new elite group in Europe, to whom borders continued to have little meaning at a time when "national" nobilities were increasingly narrowing in scope. At times of heightened crisis in the Spanish monarchy, there is a correlation between the highest rates of intermarriage between Belgians, Spaniards, and Italians in the later years of the reign of Carlos II with the fastest growth of princely and ducal titles in all three regions.[45]

The business of these families remained for the most part war and peace. They continued to dominate military positions across Europe, and they served as regional governors in their base locale (especially in the Southern Netherlands) or as viceroys or governors-general in a different locale. None of the Middle Kingdom families served as viceroy in Spanish America, but they did act occasionally as viceroys closer to home in the late seventeenth century: Egmont in Sardinia, and Chimay, Bournonville, and Hesse-Darmstadt in Catalonia.[46] Princes continued to serve as statesmen in the fragmented Holy Roman Empire, but were mostly promoted to this rank for this purpose, such as Dietrichstein in the seventeenth century, Kaunitz in the eighteenth, or Bismarck in the nineteenth. Official political roles declined sharply in France, where fifteenth-century grandees were succeeded in the sixteenth century by cardinals (princes of the church), then by nobility of the robe at the end of the seventeenth.

Habsburg attempts at keeping the multinational Spanish monarchy together through the kinship of its elites instead generated something else, a counterforce to the emergence of nationalism: aristocratic internationalism. When the Austrian Habsburgs took over in Brussels in 1715, Charles VI actively discouraged intermarriage of princely clans in the Southern Netherlands, fearing further defections into Bourbon service.[47] Nevertheless, their kinship networks remained a cornerstone of the Habsburg multinational state, typified by aristocrats like the prince de Ligne, the so-called Prince of Europe, at home in Paris, Vienna, or St. Petersburg.[48]

The Role of Transregional Families in State Formation: Internal and External

The second general theme of this chapter concerns the usefulness of dynastic structures to the early modern state, both in its efforts towards centralization and integration of new territories and in the evolving mechanisms of international diplomacy. Border families of princely rank were useful to early modern governments not only for the links they maintained between the royal capital and frontier provinces but also for their kin relationships that crossed these same frontiers, potentially serving as convenient conduits for informal diplomacy from one capital to another.

The first of these key roles was in assisting the transferal of loyalties from one sovereign (or state) to another. Magnates in provinces far from the centers of power were appointed to regional administrative posts primarily because monarchs recognized that patronage needed to be regulated by locals who knew the territory and its people.[49] Such magnates owned large numbers of fiefs (both real estate and seigneurial property like tolls and fees) and retained the loyalties of hundreds of tenants, agents, lawyers, merchants, and creditors. These loyalties could thus be transferred en masse when a province was passed from one power to another. Key examples for French expansion can be seen in the princes of Epinoy and Bournonville in Artois and Flanders in the 1660s, the princes of Bauffremont in the Franche-Comté in the 1680s, or the princes of Lorraine itself in Lorraine in the 1740s.[50] Monarchs thus obtained ready-assembled patronage networks in newly acquired provinces. These families in turn looked to their new sovereigns for protection.[51]

Using the princes of Epinoy as an example, we can see how they attempted to gain the favor of the French monarch soon after the annexation of their lands in Artois and Flanders by the Treaty of the Pyrenees, 1659, by marrying into two of the leading princely families at the French court, Rohan-Soubise and Lorraine-Guise. The Melun-Epinoy family's mixed loyalties derived from the fact that their main hereditary fiefs in Artois had been joined together to form a county (a real juridical term as much as an honorific) by Louis XII when Artois was under French suzerainty, but was then elevated to the status of a principality by Emperor Charles V in 1545 once it was within imperial territory.[52] Prince Pierre was deposed for his role in the Dutch Revolt in the 1580s, but his son realigned himself with the Spanish government and served as constable of Flanders. The constable's son in turn abandoned his post as governor of Tournai to join the service of France after the Peace of the Pyrenees in 1659, for which he was rewarded with the Order of the Saint Esprit, the highest chivalric order in France. A younger brother, however, stuck to the pattern of splitting bets, serving as Spanish governor of Valenciennes and Gelderland and was awarded the Golden Fleece; his sons were in turn viceroys of Galicia and grandees of Spain.[53] The neighboring family of Bournonville was similarly doubly courted: members were created both princes of the empire and dukes of France (both circa 1600). They too continued to play both sides of the political divide even after the annexation of Artois. One son served as governor of Paris in the 1660s, while another was viceroy of Catalonia in the 1680s.[54] Epinoy efforts to gain favor at the French court were done in part to counter the support their rivals enjoyed at the Spanish court in a struggle to reclaim the bulk of the Epinoy patrimony. These properties, sequestered during the Dutch Revolt, had been given to a sister of the prince and her heirs, the princes de Ligne from neighboring Hainaut.[55] But the Epinoy were not reliant on the French king alone and continued to cultivate their transregional status, as shown in a letter from 1714 written by the princesse d'Epinoy (a Lorraine-Guise) to her own distant cousin, the Emperor Charles VI, asking for his support as new ruler of the Southern Netherlands.[56] The Epinoy and Ligne families continued to pursue each other in French and imperial courts throughout the eighteenth century for lands on both sides of the frontier.

Croÿ and Salm princes were also involved in lawsuits that serve to illustrate border families playing off state rivalries. The heirs of the Lorraine-Guise pursued the Croÿ for a sizeable debt assigned for repayment on the principality of Chimay in Hainaut, but had to contend with shifting frontiers—gaining satisfaction from the Parlement of Paris in 1706 when Chimay was occupied by France, but having to pursue this debt further in the high courts of the Austrian Netherlands once the borders had again been rearranged.[57] The Salm and other princes from Alsace similarly looked to preserve their independence by playing off rivalries between France and Germany. Alsatian nobles had looked to the king of France to defend them from aggressive Habsburg centralizing policies in the 1640s, only to find themselves aggressively centralized by France after 1648. In contrast to Flanders and Artois, more of the magnates of Alsace like Salm, whose lands were specifically excluded from French jurisdiction by the terms of the Treaty of Münster, migrated to the imperial court in Vienna, and many of the large feudal estates remained in the hands of essentially foreign dynasties in the last century of the Old Regime. There was no great presence at the eighteenth-century French court of the princes of Leiningen, Hanau-Lichtenberg, Hohenlohe-Bartenstein, Württemberg-Montbéliard, or Nassau-Saarbrücken.[58] French influence and authority was instead brought to the region by outsiders, but by outsiders with transregional qualifications, first through the Fürstenbergs in the 1680s, then the Rohans who held the position of prince-bishop of Strasbourg throughout the eighteenth century.[59]

Two Fürstenberg brothers in particular were courted by Louis XIV for their diplomatic skill and given key ecclesiastical posts (notably the bishoprics of Metz and Strasbourg), while the emperor countered by raising the entire family to princely rank.[60] But like the Epinoy, the Fürstenbergs knew they had to solidify this hold on princely status, which brought with it tangible privileges at the French court, notably proximity to the royal family—the most lucrative source of patronage, crucial for the survival of any aristocratic family.[61] They did this by marrying into powerful French court families and other transregional princely families with similar aims. Contemporaries at Versailles commented on the marriage patterns of the Fürstenbergs in the 1680s and noted that while Louis XIV was content to grant them individual privileges, he also made it clear that French daughters were *not* to be married off to them for the sole purpose of obtaining the *honneurs du Louvre* (the visible recognition of the foreign princes) for the family as a whole.[62] The ambassador from Brandenburg, in particular, was watching the Fürstenbergs closely, as they were at that time potential claimants to the vast inheritance of the House of Orange in the Franche-Comté and the sovereign county of Neuchâtel, properties that were also claimed by his master in Berlin.[63]

At the same time that the transregional princely families were working in partnership with early modern statesmen in the centralization process, they were also continuing to act as useful middlemen between European capitals. They were not normally employed as formal ambassadors, because such a person had to represent (or "be") his prince, so being oneself a prince complicated issues of representational sovereignty.[64] There were, however, informal roles adequately suited to these princely families based in large part on kinship ties. Financial networks, for example, like that of the Grimaldi, whose *albergo* or clan included sovereign princes at Monaco but also bankers in Genoa and Brussels, were crucial in funding Spanish military enterprise across Europe.[65] Such transregional financial networks worked alongside transregional confessional networks to drive politics and diplomacy. International Protestantism connected regions via kinship between the Stuarts, Orange-Nassau, Hesse, and the Palatinate, and with French Huguenot grandees like the Rohan and La Trémoïlle.[66] Once again, relationships in the borderlands were significant, as seen in the marriage of the count of Zweibrücken (Deux-Ponts), a leader of Calvinist troops, and the sister of the duc de Rohan, general of the French Huguenots, in 1604. The French genealogist Père Anselme commented that this marriage made Rohan an effective leader on the international stage because it enabled him to understand the interests of the German princes.[67] Similarly, the Prince of Orange's advantage as leader of the Dutch Revolt was said to be his Europeanness, which gave him the vantage point, status, and connections to make good decisions, and to make them heard.[68] The contrasting concept of "international Catholicism" is a tautology, but it is certainly worth considering continuous links among princely dynasties that remained loyal to Rome. These family links could be used for political ends: James VI was raised a Protestant but on more than one occasion allowed rumors to circulate that he was sympathetic to the cause of his Catholic Guise cousins, unbalancing his advisors and those in England who feared that Elizabeth I would be succeeded by a Catholic.[69] Indeed it was a Guise who represented James's son Charles in a proxy wedding to Henriette-Marie of France in 1625.[70] This was a formal role apt for transregional princes: performing proxy services for royal marriages or acting as escorts for royal brides across frontiers.[71]

In these ways, princes acted as informal conduits of information between courts, due to the particular nature of their rank: a prince could "let his hair down" in front of another prince, even if one was a powerful king and the other merely sovereign of a few small villages. An example of a friendship network that spanned Europe in the 1680s can be seen in the links of the prince de Vaudémont, whose ambiguous status as illegitimate son of the sovereign duke of Lorraine both forced and allowed him to meander across Europe's borders in the course of his career. He was at one point ally of William III of Orange in his anti–Louis XIV coalitions and Spanish governor of Milan. He maintained ties with his cousin the prince of Salm, governor and confidant of Archduke Joseph, and with another cousin, Duke Charles V of Lorraine, governor of the Tirol and commander of imperial troops. At the same time, Vaudémont cultivated connections with the French court via his sister, a favorite of the Dauphin, and via another Lorraine cousin, the comte d'Armagnac, a favorite of Louis XIV.[72] Transregional kinship connections like this were watched by the meticulous memoirists of the French court: Dangeau and Saint-Simon both commented on the brief dispute and reconciliation in 1707 between Salm and (now Emperor) Joseph I, carefully noting that Salm was uncle of the empress and brother-in-law of both the princesse de Condé and the Duchess of Hanover.[73] It has been suggested that this same Paris to Vienna via Hanover network had been instrumental in the secret negotiations for the granting of the electoral dignity to Hanover in 1692.[74]

Monarchs continued, therefore, to monitor and cultivate loyalties of the transregional princes. One of the primary defining characteristics of a prince was the *potential*, actualized or not, to rule as a sovereign. The succession of the duc de Nevers (Charles de Gonzagues, who was also sovereign prince of Arches-Charleville in the Ardennes) to the sovereign duchy of Mantova in 1627 sparked one of the early phases of conflict in the Thirty Years' War between France and the Empire.[75] A century later, Prince Friedrich Michael, younger brother of the Duke of Zweibrücken, caught the attention of the Great Powers for a similar reason, though at the time of his birth, he was the most junior of all the princes of the house of Wittelsbach. He was an imperial field marshal during the Seven Years' War but not particularly reckoned as a leading military figure.

He was nevertheless a potential power to be watched by the emperor, Prussia, and France as the *only* Wittelsbach with legitimate sons. In anticipation of his dynastic rise, he became a Catholic in 1741 but died before he could rise further in the princely hierarchy.[76] Instead, it was his second son, known for much of his career as Prince Maximilien-Joseph de Deux-Ponts, French lieutenant-general and colonel of the Régiment d'Alsace, who rapidly succeeded his distant patrilineal cousins as Duke of Zweibrücken in 1795, then Elector Palatine and Elector of Bavaria in 1799, and was finally elevated to the rank of king by Napoleon in 1805.

Finale

With the coming of the French Revolution, the golden era for transregional princely dynasties came to an end. Though they continued to serve as ambassadors and continued to marry across national lines, members of these families were required to choose one state and one citizenship. As the early modern shifted into the modern, the demands of government shifted, and transregional princely families were no longer needed. A widening electoral franchise and improved bureaucracies allowed monarchs and their governments to communicate directly with their subjects, eliminating the need for strong regional families to act as middlemen. The role of princes as ministers had long been given over to men of education rather than birth, but diplomacy remained an essential sphere of activity well into the modern period.[77] Although elite groups in border regions continued to express their loyalties to dynasties rather than nation-states in the revolutionary period, by the early nineteenth century, the forces of nationalism forced the transregional princely families to choose sides.[78]

In the centuries that preceded this change, we have examined periods of growth, consolidation, and decline in the prominence of such families in two areas: in their relationships with individual monarchs and in their roles in the processes of state formation. They made use of their rank and connections to gain political, honorific, and fiscal privileges for their families from monarchs across Europe. In return, they aided these monarchs by contributing to national centralization, both in royal capitals and in the provinces in which they maintained large and powerful clientage networks. This task continued into the eighteenth century, especially in regions along the linguistic-cultural frontier such as Alsace or the Austrian Netherlands. But transregional families also worked to consolidate existing monopolies on power in these regions and at court by regulating dynasticism and through increasingly exclusive endogamous marriage practices.

Further research is required to uncover the details of efforts made by these families to regulate dynasticism, optimally for the betterment of the dynasty rather than the individual. Families like the Salm and the Croÿ maintained several sub-branches, each with high rank and sociopolitical profile. But how regular and regulatory was communication between these branches? And did they adhere purely to patrilineal loyalties or function more loosely across both male and female relations? By the eighteenth century some transregional dynasties, notably the Croÿ, had evolved into what might be called "superclusters." Rather than one single family, these were multiple families who descended from mixed paternal and maternal successions, keeping sizeable properties tightly locked inside their kinship circle. Properties like the principality of Chimay thus were guarded within the Belgian supercluster of Arenberg, Ligne, Croÿ, and Hénin-Liétard for several centuries. Following the inheritance pathways of properties held by foreign princes like the Lorraine, Rohan, and Epinoy in France in the eighteenth century reveals a more tightly knit group, the "matriclan," who all descended from one woman. This group accumulated a geographically spread collection of estates from Brabant to Languedoc, in an effort to minimize damages in one region with sustainability in another. These were then passed back and forth from one branch to the other, ensuring dowries and dowager pensions for several generations, but maintaining patronage networks as well.[79]

In the eighteenth century, both the dynasties of Croÿ and Salm included several branches active on the wider European stage. Preliminary assessment using genealogical data can track an increasing pattern of clan endogamy. A pattern emerges of both steady rates of intermarriage between the same elite regional families and *also* an increase in marriage with princely families from other regions. The Croÿ spent most of the sixteenth century marrying other Netherlandish grandee families, while in the eighteenth century, increased the percentage of cosmopolitan marital alliances and at the same time continued to marry within their own patrilineage. The Salm display a more varied pattern much earlier, marrying across linguistic frontiers from the late fifteenth century. By the eighteenth century, Salm marriages were cosmopolitan and almost exclusively of princely rank.

The professional activities of the Croÿ and Salm in the last decades of the ancien régime demonstrate the continued flourishing of the transregional princely order and its decline following revolutionary upheaval and the development of truly "national" identities. The Croÿ moved more conspicuously into French service, as their main estate (Solre) was now on the French side of the border. These included a prominent marshal of France and the last governess of the children of Louis XVI.[80] They were officially recognized by treaty in 1767 as both dukes of France and princes of the empire. But with the loss of sovereign territory they held west of the Rhine to France (notably Fénétrange), they emigrated and were rewarded with the sovereign duchy of Dülmen in Westphalia in 1803. Dülmen had formerly been a possession of their cousins the Salm, and though it did not survive the mediatization of the small princely houses in 1806, it remained the seat of the family into the nineteenth century.

The Salm princes also operated in the French sphere but maintained a more foreign identity overall. Prince Friedrich III of Salm-Kyrburg, or Frédéric-Jean, began his military career in imperial service but by the 1770s had firmly settled on a French career and, like the duke of Deux-Ponts, was colonel of the Régiment d'Alsace. In the 1780s, he built a grand palace on the banks of the Seine (today's Palais de la Légion d'Honneur) and joined the liberal opposition led by the duc d'Orléans and the marquis de Lafayette.[81] He maintained his ties with the empire, of course, marrying a princess of Hohenzollern-Sigmaringen, while his sister married his bride's brother. In late 1789 he was named by Lafayette as commandant of a battalion of the National Guard, and in 1792 he went so far as to abolish feudal rights and to introduce a French-style constitution in his principality. Nevertheless, providing us with an exemplar of the dangers of transregional princely identity, on his return to Paris he was confused with his cousin, the more reactionary prince of Salm-Salm, and was arrested during the Terror and executed on 5 Thermidor, Year II (23 July 1794). The prince who escaped was none other than Constantine, prince of Salm-Salm, with whom this chapter began. He had been condemned somewhat contradictorily by the Republic as both a threatening foreigner *and* a treasonous citizen but had survived, only to court controversy again when he converted to Protestantism in 1827.

Notes

1. Quoted in Geoffrey Parker, *Europe in Crisis, 1598–1648* (London, 1979), 270.
2. Herman Van der Linden, *Belgium: The Making of a Nation*, trans. Sybil Jane (Oxford, 1920), 43.
3. *Précis historique des faits qui ont eu lieu lors de la conversion de Son Altesse le prince de Salm-Salm de la religion catholique-romaine au culte chrétien évangélique de la confession d'Augsbourg, le 17 mai 1826; suivi des motifs de ce changement de communion* (Paris, 1826); the event was deemed significant enough to warrant publication of

the pamphlet in English as well: *Historical summary of facts attending the conversion of His Highness the Prince of Salm-Salm, from the Roman Catholic religion to the Christian evangelical worship of the confession of Augsbourg, on May 17, 1826*, trans. Evanson (London, 1827).

4. Wilhelm Karl, Prinz zu Isenburg, *Stammtafeln zur Geschichte der europäischen Staaten* (Marburg, 1961–1978), vol. 4, tables 99–100. Other genealogical data is derived from the later editions of this monumental work: Detlev Schwennicke, ed., *Europaische Stammtafeln, neue Folge* (Frankfurt am Main, 1998–2009).
5. Bishop of Strasbourg until 1823, then archbishop of Rouen and grand almoner of France.
6. Jean-Baptiste de Courcelles, *Histoire généalogique et heraldique des pairs de France… et maisons princières de l'Europe* (Paris, 1822–33), vol. 6, 229–38.
7. Benedict Anderson, *Imagined Communities: Reflections on the Origin and Spread of Nationalism* (London, 1983; revised 1991), 6. See also Jeremy Black, *Kings, Nobles and Commoners: States and Societies in Early Modern Europe; A Revisionist History* (London, 2004).
8. See Daniel Nordman, *Frontières de France, de l'espace au territoire XVIe–XIXe siècle* (Paris, 1998); Samuel Clark, *State and Status: The Rise of the State and Aristocratic Power in Western Europe* (Cardiff, UK, 1995).
9. Jean-Daniel Pariset, "La Lorraine dans les relations internationales au XVIe siècle," in *Les Habsbourg et la Lorraine: Actes du colloque international organisé par les Universités de Nancy II et Strasbourg III dans le cadre de l'UA 703 (Nancy II-CNRS), 22, 23, 24 mai 1987*, ed. Jean-Paul Bled, Eugène Faucher, and René Taveneaux (Nancy, 1988), 50–51; Emile Duvernoy, "Recherches sur le Traité de Nuremberg de 1542," *Annales de l'Est*, series 4, vol. 1 (1933): 153–70. The original text of this treaty can be seen in Dom Augustin Calmet, *Histoire écclésiastique et civile de Lorraine* (Nancy, 1728), 5:537. The duke agreed to pay the taxes required by the Imperial Diet (at two-thirds the amount paid by the other territorial princes) but would not contribute to levies for the emperor's wars. The right of final appeal was vested in the duke, removing Lorraine from the jurisdiction of the highest Imperial courts of appeal.
10. On secret diplomacy between Vienna and Versailles, Heinrich, Ritter von Srbik, *Wien und Versailles, 1692–1697: Zur geschichte von Strassburg, Elsass und Lothringen* (Munich, 1944), 45–83.
11. Guy Cabourdin, *Encyclopédie illustrée de la Lorraine: Les temps modernes*, vol. 1, *De la Renaissance à la guerre de trente ans* (Nancy, 1991), 105–7. The fortified town of Pfalzburg was established in 1568 by Count Palatine Georg-Johann of Veldenz, comte de la Petite-Pierre (Lützelstein). He gave it a judicial officer, set up a mint, and settled refugees from both German Lutheran and French Calvinist confessions. The foundation was approved by Emperor Maximilian II in 1570, but by 1584, the count was in financial trouble and mortgaged the territory to the Duke of Lorraine, and was never able to redeem it. It remained, however, the only town officially not Catholic in the Duchy as late as 1600, and was created a principality for the duke's sister in 1624 (160). Saarwerden was contested between Catholic Lorraine and Protestant Nassau from the beginning of the sixteenth century until the Treaty of Rijswijk, 1697, and was then held by Nassau until it was incorporated into France in 1798 (185).
12. Debased coinage from Lorraine and the bishopric of Metz was a constant problem for France, and one of the reasons behind the invasion of 1552. Cabourdin, *Encyclopédie illustrée*, 21. Cabourdin also notes the reputation of Louise-Marguerite de Guise as a "billoneur" (a maker of debased coins) in her tiny principality of Châ-

teau-Regnault deep in the Meuse valley (176). Her "state" was forcibly exchanged for *rentes* with Louis XIII in 1629 (Bibliothèque Nationale de France [BN], Factum 10065). See also Simon Hodson, "Politics of the Frontier: Henri IV, the Maréchal-Duc de Bouillon and the Sovereignty of Sedan," *French History* 19 (2005): 413–39.

13. Gilbert Cahen, "La Région Lorraine," in Bernhard Blumenkranz, ed., *Histoire des Juifs en France* (Toulouse, 1972), 77–136. Jews were also protected in the neighboring sovereign Alsatian county of Hanau-Lichtenberg. André-Marc Haarscher, *Les Juifs du Comté de Hanau-Lichtenberg entre le XIVe siècle et la fin de l'Ancien Régime* (Strasbourg, 1997).
14. Peter H. Wilson, *From Reich to Revolution: German History, 1558–1806* (Basingstoke, UK, 2004), 11–17, following (with caution) the path laid down first by authors lauding diversity and federalism such as Francis Ludwig Carsten, *Princes and Parliaments in Germany from the Fifteenth to the Eighteenth Century* (Oxford, 1959) and Gerhard Benecke, *Society and Politics in Germany, 1500–1750* (London, 1974). See also Maiken Umbach, ed., *German Federalism: Past, Present and Future* (Basingstoke, UK, 2002).
15. Indeed, it was acknowledged that until the 1940s the lingua franca of princely families across northern Europe was English, attributed to the singular dominance (some quipped "political power") of the English nanny before 1918. Jonathan Petropoulous, *Royals and the Reich: The Princes von Hessen in Nazi Germany* (Oxford, 2006), 6–7, 35–36.
16. Werner Paravicini, "The Court of the Dukes of Burgundy. A Model for Europe?," in *Princes, Patronage and the Nobility: The Court at the Beginning of the Modern Age, c.1450–1650*, ed. Ronald G. Asch and Adolf M. Birke (Oxford, 1991); and Georges Bischoff, "Une enquête: la noblesse austro-bouguignonne sous le règne de Maximilien I," in *Les Pays de l'entre-deux au moyen-age: Questions d'histoire des territories d'empire entre Meuse, Rhône et Rhin* (Paris, 1990). More recently, see contributions in D'Arcy J. D. Boulton and Jan R. Veenstra, eds., *The Ideology of Burgundy: The Promotion of National Consciousness, 1364–1565* (Leiden, 2006).
17. See, for example, Van der Linden, *Belgium*, 153–55.
18. Geyl, *History of the Dutch-Speaking Peoples, 1555–1648* (London, 2001 [originally 1932]), 71. This view is being revised in more recent historiography, notably in Paul Janssens, ed., *La Belgique au XVIIe siècle* (Brussels, 2006).
19. See essays in Françoise Autrand, ed., *Prosopographie et genèse de l'état moderne* (Paris, 1986). Models were set in the 1960s by French historians like François Bluche, *Les magistrats du Parlement de Paris au XVIIIe siècle, 1715–1771* (Paris, 1960), and Jean Meyer, *La noblesse bretonne au XVIIIe siècle*, 2 vols. (Paris, 1966).
20. Recent examples include Jonathan Dewald, *The European Nobility, 1400–1800* (Cambridge, 1996); George Lukowski, *The Eighteenth-Century European Nobility* (Basingstoke, UK, 2003); Ronald G. Asch, *Nobilities in Transition, 1550–1700: Courtiers and Rebels in Britain and Europe* (London, 2003).
21. The collection of essays edited by Hamish Scott, *The European Nobilities*, 2 vols. (London, 1995), for example, has been reworked but again without any inclusion of nobles of the Southern Netherlands. Transregional elites are briefly examined by Tom Scott, *Regional Identity and Economic Change: The Upper Rhine, 1450–1600* (Oxford, 1997); and by Georges Bischof, *Gouvernés et gouvernants en Haute Alsace à l'époque autrichienne* (Strasbourg, 1996). My own book on the Lorraine-Guise analyzes a princely family that continued to be considered "foreign" at the French court long after they had permanently settled in France: *The Society of Princes: The Lorraine-Guise and the Conservation of Power and Wealth in Seventeenth-Century*

France (Aldershot, UK, 2009). Similar cross-cultural work on elite dynasticism has been done by Robert Oresko, for example, "The Marriages of the Nieces of Cardinal Mazarin: Public Policy and Private Strategy in Seventeenth-Century Europe," in *Frankreich im Europäischen Staatensystem der Frühen Neuzeit*, ed. Rainer Babel (Sigmaringen, 1995), 109–51.

22. Both have cartons in the Archives Générales du Royaume in Brussels and at the Haus- Hof- und Staatsarchiv in Vienna, in the Reichskanzlei Kleinere Reichsstände, the Imperial Chancellery for small states of the Holy Roman Empire. The Croÿ also have documents in the Archives de l'État in Mons as well as a private archive at the Château de Rumillies in Tournai and at their formerly sovereign town of Dülmen in Westphalia. The Salm archive is similarly split between their castle at Anholt in the Rhineland and the Archives Départementales (henceforth AD) des Vosges in Epinal (series 3C), with additional papers in Nancy (AD, Meurthe-et-Moselle, series B, 889–893, and 9026–9128). See Gabriel Wymans, *Inventaire des archives des ducs de Croÿ* (Brussels, 1977), and Michel Parisse, "La Lorraine, la maison de Salm et les archives d'Anholt," *Annales de l'Est* 26 (1975) : 148–57.
23. Gerard Nijsten, *In the Shadow of Burgundy: The Court of Guelders in the Late Middle Ages,* trans. Tania Guest (Cambridge, 2004); Robert Stein, ed., *Powerbrokers in the Late Middle Ages: The Burgundian Low Countries in a European Context,* Burgundica IV (Turnhout, Belgium, 2001), part of a wider project, "Prosopographia Burgundica." Older examples include the previously cited *Les Pays de l'entre-deux au moyen-age,* and H. Hardenberg, "Les divisions politiques des Ardennes et des Pays d'Outremeuse avant 1200," in *Études sur l'Histoire du Pays Mosan au Moyen Age: Mélanges Félix Rousseau* (Brussels, 1958).
24. C. Warren Hollister, ed., *Anglo-Norman Political Culture and the Twelfth-Century Renaissance: Proceedings of the Borchard Conference on Anglo-Norman History, 1995* (Woodbridge, UK, 1997); Jean M. Bell, *Anglo-Norman Talbots: 11th-13th Centuries* (n.p., 2000); *L'état angevin: pouvoir, culture et société entre XIII*[e] *et XIV*[e] *siècle; Actes du colloque international organisé par l'American Academy in Rome, l'École française de Rome, l'Istituto storico italiano per il Medio Evo (Rome-Naples, 7–11 novembre 1995)* (Rome, 1998).
25. Esther Mijers and David Onnekink, eds., *Redefining William III: The Impact of the King-Stadholder in International Context* (Aldershot, UK, 2007); Brendan Simms and Torsten Riotte, eds., *The Hanoverian Dimension in British History, 1714–1837* (Cambridge, 2007).
26. Pierre de La Condamine, *Salm en Vosges: Une principauté de conte de fées* (Paris, 1974); Michel Parisse, "Les comtes de Salm et l'évêché de Metz, XIème–XIIème siècles," in *Histoire des terres de Salm* (Saint Dié-des-Vosges, 1994), 23–35.
27. Wilson, *From Reich to Revolution,* 45; Peter Moraw, "Conseils princiers en Allemagne au XIVème et au XVème siècle," in Stein, *Powerbrokers in the Late Middle Ages,* 175.
28. Jean-Charles Fulaine, *Le Duc Charles IV de Lorraine et son armée, 1624–1675* (Metz, 1997), 47; La Condamine, *Salm,* 65–69.
29. My thanks to Luc Duerloo of the University of Antwerp for highlighting this point.
30. Père Anselme de Sainte-Marie (Pierre de Guibors), *Histoire généalogique et chronologique de la Maison Royale de France, des Pairs, des Grands Officiers de la Couronne & de la Maison du Roy,...* (Paris, 1726–33), s.v. "Croÿ", 5:631ff, with supplements for the later eighteenth century from vol. 9-b. Croÿ is spelled with a dieresis on the *y* to indicate its full pronunciation, rather than as a diphthong.
31. Piet de Fraine, "Gouvernés et gouvernants au Pays et Duché d'Aerschot," *Anciens pays et assemblées d'états* 33 (1965): 181–94.

32. John Elliott, *Imperial Spain, 1469–1716* (London, 1963; 1990 reprint), 145.
33. R. De Smedt, ed., *Les chevaliers de l'Ordre de la Toison d'or au XVe siècle: Notices bio-bibliographiques* (Frankfurt, 1994).
34. Georges Bischoff notes in particular the prominence of the bilingual Alsatian nobles in the politics of Emperor Maximilian ("La Noblesse austro-bourguignonne"). His later successor in the Low Countries, Margaret of Austria, pursued a similar policy with her administration staffed largely with nobles from the Franche-Comté. Hugo de Schepper, "Le voyage difficile de Marguerite de Parme en Franche-Comté et en Flandre, 1580–1583," in *Margherita d'Austria (1522–1586): Costruzioni politiche e diplomazia, tra corte Farnese e Monarchia spagnola*, ed. Silvia Mantini (Rome, 2003), 127–40.
35. The Croÿ appear at the head of the list of seven families that dominated the provincial governorships in the Low Countries throughout the sixteenth century, and were cited as particular threats to Habsburg centralization attempts. Paul Rosenfeld, "The Provincial Governors from the Minority of Charles V to the Revolt," *Anciens pays et assemblées d'états* 17 (1959): 3–63.
36. Scott, *Regional Identity and Economic Change*, 8, citing Claudius Sieber-Lehmann, *Spätmittelalterlicher Nationalismus: Die Burgunderkriege am Oberrhein und in der Eidgenossenschaft* (Göttingen, 1995).
37. Louis Trenard, "Provinces et départements des Pays-Bas français aux départements du Nord et du Pas-de-Calais," in *Régions et régionalisme en France du XVIIIe siècle à nos jours*, ed. Christian Gras and Georges Livet (Paris, 1977), 66, 68.
38. Claudio Donati, "The Italian Nobilities in the Seventeenth and Eighteenth Centuries," in Scott, *European Nobilities*, 1:249.
39. Rosario Villari, *The Revolt of Naples* (Cambridge, 1993), 118–21.
40. Anselme, *Histoire généalogique*, s.v. "Croÿ," 5:631.
41. Ibid., s.v. "Montmorency," 3:551ff.
42. Geyl, *History of the Dutch-Speaking Peoples*, 119–20, 376–78. The Van den Berghe or Bergues were elevated to princely rank by the king of Spain in 1686.
43. This would change with the regime in the early eighteenth century. Piet Lenders, "Trois façons de gouverner dans les Pays-Bas autrichiens," in *Unité et diversité de l'Empire des Habsbourg à la fin du XVIIIe siècle*, ed. Roland Mortier and Hervé Hasquin (Brussels, 1988), 41–86.
44. Elliott, *Imperial Spain*, 167, 256–57.
45. Julio de Atienza, baron de Cobos de Belchite, *Nobiliario Español* (Madrid, 1954); Paul Janssens and Luc Duerloo, *Armorial de la noblesse belge du XVe au XXe siècle* (Brussels, 1992).
46. It is probably too much of a stretch to include in the category of transregional princely families two viceroys in South America from the noble family of Croix, from Lille, and one O'Higgins, from an ancient Celtic "princely" house in Sligo, Ireland.
47. Arnout Mertens, "Noble Independence, Monarchical Power and Early Modern State Building. Pedigreed Nobles from Brabant in the Age of Absolutism," unpublished conference paper (Antwerp, 2008).
48. Philip Mansel, *Prince of Europe: The Life of Charles Joseph de Ligne, 1735–1814* (London, 2003).
49. Elliott, *Imperial Spain*, 180.
50. This process was in part hindered in Lorraine, however, by the fact that many of the local grandees such as the prince de Beauvau-Craon and the comte de Mercy departed with the ducal family when they transferred first to Tuscany, then to Vienna. It was a Mercy-Argenteuil who, as Austrian foreign minister, was largely responsible

for the great reversal of alliances of 1756 … a perfectly logical choice, as he was a relative and neighbor in Lorraine of the French foreign minister, Choiseul. See Alain Petiot, *Au service des Habsbourg: Officiers, ingénieurs, savants et artistes lorrains en Autriche* (Paris, 2000); and Jean Peltre and Maurice Noël, "Les Mercy en Europe aux XVIIe et XVIIIe siècles: De la Lorraine au Banat," *Le Pays Lorrain* 77, no. 3 (1996): 185–98.

51. Early work on this topic was done by Roger Mettam for the province of Boulonnois (next to Artois) and the ducs d'Aumont in his "The Role of the Higher Aristocracy in France under Louis XIV, with Special Reference to the Faction of the Duke of Burgundy and Provincial Governors" (DPhil thesis, Cambridge University, 1967).
52. It was not sovereign as principalities would be considered in the later, post-Westphalia, Holy Roman Empire, but it was held directly (or "immediately") from the sovereign, not requiring homage to the count of Artois (who was in fact the same person), and obtained juridical rights and fiscal privileges not shared by other ordinary lordships. Archives Nationales [AN], 273 AP 76, papers of the Melun-Epinoy Succession.
53. Anselme, *Histoire généalogique*, s.v. "Melun," 5:221.
54. Ibid., s.v. "Bournonville," 5:806.
55. For this case, see BN, Factums 5661 to 5677.
56. AD, Meurthe-et-Moselle, 3F 317, no. 62: "Madame la Princesse d'Espinoy estant de la maison de Lorraine a lieu d'esperer que la Cour de Vienne voudra bien luy estre favorable." She had written to the Duke of Marlborough as well, in 1708, when he was still in charge of the region. British Library, Ms. Add. 61366, Blenheim Papers, fol. 112.
57. BN, Factums 11618, 12140–45. It is worth noting that the principal Guisard heir was none other than the duc d'Orléans who was from 1715 regent of France.
58. Louis Batiffol, *Les Anciennes Républiques alsaciennes* (Paris, 1918), 233. These princes were known during the French Revolution as the *princes possessionnés*. The termination of their sovereignty is an understudied aspect of the Revolution, with few works appearing between Theodor Ludwig's *Die deutschen Reichstände im Elsass und der Ausbruch der Revolutionskriege* (Strasbourg, 1898), and Daniel Fischer, "La France révolutionnaire face à l'affaire des princes d'Empire possessionnés en Basse Alsace, 1789–1801," *Chantiers historiques en Alsace: Jeunes Chercheurs en Histoire de l'Université Marc Bloch de Strasbourg et de l'Université de Haute-Alsace* 8 (2005): 123–34.
59. The princes de Rohan, whose princely rank and transregional kinship links were forged in the early seventeenth century as prominent leaders of the Protestant movement in northern Europe, belong in this study through their (partially recognized) claims as "foreign princes" at the French court. Their province of origin is not, however, from the ancient Middle Kingdom, but the formerly independent duchy of Brittany. Alain Boulaire, *Les Rohan, 'Roi ne puis, duc ne daigne, Rohan suis!'* (Paris, 2001).
60. Scott, *Regional Identity and Economic Change*, 59, 242. Much of the relationship between France, the Holy Roman Empire, and the Fürstenbergs can be gleaned usefully from two older works: Claude Badalo-Dulong, *Trente ans de diplomatie française en Allemagne. Louis XIV et l'electeur de Mayence, 1648–78* (Paris, 1956); and Geneviève Moisse-Daxhelet, "La Principauté de Stavelot-Malmédy sous le règne du Cardinal Guillaume-Egon de Fürstenberg. Problèmes politiques et institutionnels, 1682–1704," *Anciens pays et assemblées d'Etats* 29 (1963): 1–224.
61. This subject forms one of the main themes in my *Society of Princes*.

62. Marquis de Sourches, *Mémoires sur le règne de Louis XIV*, ed. Gabriel-Jules de Cosnac and Arthur Bertrand (Paris, 1882), 1:179; Primi Visconti, conte di San Maiolo, *Mémoires sur la Cour de Louis XIV, 1673–1681*, ed. Jean-François Solnon (Paris, 1988), 107.
63. Baron Spanheim, *Relation de la Cour de France en 1690*, ed. E. Bourgeois (Paris, 1973), 125.
64. Ellen McClure, *Sunspots and the Sun King: Sovereignty and Mediation in Seventeenth-Century France* (Urbana, IL, 2006), 10.
65. Paul Coles, "The Crisis of Renaissance Society Genoa, 1488–1507," *Past and Present* 11 (1957): 17–47.
66. Simon Hodson, "The Power of Female Dynastic Networks: A Brief Study of Louise de Coligny, Princess of Orange, and Her Stepdaughters," *Women's History Review* 16 (2007): 335–51; Sonja Kmec, "'A Stranger Born': Female Usage of International Networks in Times of War," in *The Contending Kingdoms: France and England, 1420–1700*, ed. Glenn Richardson (Aldershot, UK, 2008), 147–60.
67. Anselme, *Histoire généalogique*, s. v. "Rohan", 4:73.
68. Geyl, *History of the Dutch-Speaking Peoples*, 105.
69. Albert J. Loomie, "Philip III and the Stuart Succession in England, 1600–1603," in *Spain and the Early Stuarts, 1585–1655*, ed. Albert J. Loomie (Aldershot, UK, 1996), 501–2.
70. Archives Nationales de France (AN), K 539, no. 42.
71. Spangler, *Society of Princes*, ch. 1.
72. There is no modern biography of the fascinating Vaudémont, though his papers can be found in AN, AP 273 74; AD, Meurthe-et-Moselle, 3F 317; BN, Collection de Lorraine, no. 566; and in collections of correspondence with William III at the British Library, Ms. Eg. 1172 and Ms. Add. 21493. Correspondence with Salm apparently once existed at the Kriegsarchiv in Vienna but has been lost.
73. Marquis de Dangeau, *Journal*, ed. E. Soulié, L. Dussieux et al., *Additions inédites du duc de Saint-Simon* (Paris, 1854–60), vol. 11, 482 (7 October 1707); vol. 12, 21 (30 November 1707).
74. John Spielman, *Leopold I of Austria* (London, 1977), 155.
75. David Parrott, "The Mantuan Succession, 1627–1631: A Sovereignty Dispute in Early Modern Europe," *English Historical Review* 112 (1997): 20–65.
76. *1758, Zweybrücken in Command: A journal of the speedy army of execution of the Empire under the orders of His Most Serene Highness the Prince von Pfalz-Zweybrücken in 1758*, ed. Neil Cogswell (Guisborough, 1998).
77. For example, Stefan Lippert, *Felix Fürst Schwarzenberg: Eine politische Biographie* (Kiel, 1995).
78. Gilbert Trausch, "Les Habsbourg, incarnation de l'Empire au Luxembourg à la fin du XVIIIe siècle: fidélité dynastique et manque de conscience impériale," in Mortier and Hasquin, *Unité et diversité*, 138–48. The same can be said for Franche-Comté: Maurice Gresset, "Les Franc-Comtois entre la France et l'Empire," in Gras and Livet, *Régions et régionalisme*, 87–101.
79. See the marriage contract of Marie-Louise de Rohan-Guéméné and the prince de Rohan-Rochefort in 1780 (AN, 273 AP 373), in which the bride's dowry was in large part made up by her aunt, a Rohan-Soubise, who had married a Lorraine-Guise. These estates had been given to her by her grandmother, the princesse d'Epinoy, Anne de Lorraine. The duchy of Joyeuse in Languedoc, passed from the last of the Guise in 1688 to the princesse de Lillebonne, who donated it to her Epinoy grandson in 1714; on his death it passed to his Rohan nephews, who continued to pay, for

example, the wages of nuns in a school there as late as 1788. AD, Ardèche, B125, fol. 6 (donation of duchy); 1 E 1060 (wages).

80. André Delcourt, *Le duc de Croÿ, maréchal de France, 1718–1784: Un grand seigneur au siècle des lumières* (Saint-Amand-les-Eaux, 1984); Marie-Pierre Dion, *Emmanuel de Croÿ, 1718–1784: Itinéraire intellectuel et réussite nobiliaire au siècle des Lumières* (Brussels, 1987); *Mémoires de la duchesse de Tourzel, gouvernante des enfants de France de 1789 à 1795*, ed. J. Chalon (Paris, 1969).

81. AN, R^3 211, sale of property on the quay d'Orsay by the prince de Conti to the prince de Salm-Kyrbourg, 1759. The prince made an unfortunate appearance in a well-known scandal of the period, detailed by Jeffrey S. Ravel, "The Coachman's Bare Rump: An Eighteenth-Century French Cover-Up," *Eighteenth-Century Studies* 40 (2007): 279–308.

Chapter 8

Spiritual Kinship

The Moravians as an International Fellowship of Brothers and Sisters (1730s–1830s)

Gisela Mettele

The subject of this chapter is not a family in the conventional sense of the word but a chosen spiritual kinship. From this specific angle, the chapter will address issues that may be significant for an understanding of any transregional or transnational kinship system, such as the power of organization and central coordination, the creation of an imaginary order of belonging, networks of mutual aid and solidarity, and observance of common rituals and remembrance days. In what cultural forms do transnational families stabilize their collective memory? What are the media of family tradition? How does information about family events in different locations circulate? How is knowledge about family history transmitted through generations? How significant is the existence of a common language? How do nationally dispersed families deal with conflicting loyalties in times of war?

The Moravians originated from a group of Moravian and Bohemian refugees, who traced their heritage back to the Hussite movement of the early fifteenth century. Fleeing from religious persecution in the Bohemian borderlands, they were granted permission to settle on the Saxon estate Herrnhut of the pietistic Count Nikolaus Ludwig von Zinzendorf in 1722. Under the count's guidance, in 1727 they created a pietistic community named "Unitas Fratrum" or "Brüdergemeine." The name "Moravian Brethren" came into use as the group spread within the English-speaking world.

From the very beginning, the Moravians were an extremely mobile community. Within a few years of their founding, they traveled extensively and engaged intensively in missionary work. Their central goal was the furthering of the kingdom of God (*Reich Gottes-Arbeit*) through the gathering in of the "hidden community of the Spirit," which was separated by national and religious borders, as well as the progressive expansion of the universal mission to the "heathen," and thus preparation for the return of Christ.[1]

Moravian preachers traveled all over Europe in order to create a network of contacts with friends and like-minded people. Beginning in 1732, new settlements were founded in Denmark, the Netherlands, England, and North America.[2] Numerous mission stations were established, for example, in Greenland, Labrador, Suriname, and the West Indies. During the eighteenth and nineteenth centuries, missionary activities led the Moravians all the way to Russia and South America, to the Nicobar Islands and into the Himalayas, although their activities always centered on the Atlantic world.

By the middle of the eighteenth century, the significance of the Moravians went far beyond a local or national framework. The founding town Herrnhut remained the spiritual home and administrative center, the central point of reference, to which members repeatedly returned, for example, in old age. However, in principle, life was conceived as a journey, both metaphorically and literally.

The Moravian Brethren remained a relatively small group whose membership did not grow to more than twenty thousand. They were not oriented toward mass growth, as were, for example, the Methodists; rather, their community was based on a certain elite religious consciousness.[3] Though much value was placed on converting the "heathen," the converts in the countries of their mission stations were rarely accepted as members, but rather stood in a paternalistic relationship with the missionaries.[4] Intermarriage between Moravian missionaries and converts remained a rare exception.[5]

The geographical and national origins of the members were very heterogeneous; and when one joined the group, he or she was required to cast off "the way of thinking of father, mother, nation, state, and town."[6] Instead of feeling attached to a family, city, or nation, they were supposed to place "increasing value on the honor of being citizens of God's Kingdom."[7] Moravians did not understand themselves as a community tied to a region or land, but—oriented on the ideal of the wandering apostles—as a "purely pilgrim society," to which "all witnesses to Christ in the entire world belong."[8]

Characteristic for Moravians were very diverse "pilgrimages," which frequently crossed several continents. During her life as a missionary wife, for example, Benigna Sophia Cunow, who was born in Herrnhut in 1765 and who died in 1836 only twenty kilometers away in Niesky, had "made the trip over the Atlantic Ocean, from Germany to North America and back, no less than six times … and, on such occasions, also visited England several times."[9] Office-holders were, as a rule, relocated every ten years, for example—to take an arbitrary, though also typical, example—Johann Christian Bechler, born in 1784 in the Baltic States, whose stations in life included the American settlements of Salem and Hope, Sarepta in Russia, Zeist in Holland, and Rixdorf in Prussia, before he died in 1857 in Herrnhut in Saxony.[10]

In the eighteenth century, not only the Moravian preachers and missionaries but also many common members changed their residencies sometimes multiple times in their lives as for instance the inhabitants of the German settlement Herrnhaag who migrated to the American settlements after Herrnhaags's dissolution in the period between 1750 and 1753. Many of them had arrived in Herrnhaag only some years earlier from the Danish settlement Pilgerruh that the Moravians had to give up after the Danish king had withdrawn his support from the Moravian cause.[11]

Members were sent regularly as colonists to newly created settlements.[12] Before their departure in 1759, the future settlers in North Carolina were reminded that this move was not necessarily a permanent one: they belonged, so they were told, to a "pilgrim society" and were not permitted to permanently establish themselves in one place "damit sich der Heiland ihrer bedienen kann, wenn er sie braucht" (so that the Savior could use them when He needed them).[13]

Travel activities never included all members. No statistics are available, but it can be generally stated that in the nineteenth century, the number of traveling preachers and missionaries increased while the mobility of the common members decreased. But whether the individual members traveled around the world or spent their lives more or less constantly at one of the European or North American settlements, in songs, stories, and commemoration ceremonies their own restless tradition was celebrated again and again and the idea of pilgrimage remained central for the identity of the whole community.[14]

The expulsion of the Brethren's founder, Zinzendorf, from Saxony in 1736 on ecclesiastical and political grounds reinforced the conception of the Moravians as a "pilgrim community." The center of the group was always the place where Zinzendorf and his following of some fifty to sixty women and men—the so-called Pilgerhaus (Pilgrims' House)—were residing at the moment.[15] At first, this was the new settlement of Herrnhaag in the Wetterau; in 1738, the Pilgerhaus traveled over the Atlantic and settled initially in the Caribbean, then beginning in 1741 and 1743, in North America. Following sojourns in the communities of various European countries, the members of the Pilgerhaus primarily resided in London from 1749 to 1755. Additional trips throughout Europe followed. It was not until 1759, following the lifting of Zinzendorf's residential ban, that they returned to Herrnhut in Saxony, where, after the death of their founder in 1760, a council of thirteen men, the Unitäts-Ältesten-Konferenz (Unity Eldest Conference, or UÄC), assumed the leadership for all communities worldwide and established itself permanently at Schloss Berthelsdorf near Herrnhut.[16]

Moravian women and men often realized their idea of a pious life in friction with their families of origin and questioning their expectations. They instead joined a new family, a chosen kin group organized around a strong belief system and the experience of being born again in Christ.[17] Becoming a Moravian quite often meant to break with the family of origin or at least to loosen family ties. It is frequently said in the members' memoirs that the decision to join the Brethren met with a great lack of understanding in their natural families and was often carried out against the family's express wishes. Sometimes Moravian memoirs provide accounts where family members unsuccessfully tried to force their kin who had become a member of the Moravians to leave the Brethren and to return home. Even when it did not result in an external conflict, an inner conflict between the commitment to family and the commitment to the chosen relations of the religious community is sometimes mentioned, as when the obligation to care for an older family member postponed a decision to move to a Moravian settlement.[18]

Leaving one set of kin and joining another set is often a normal issue in kinship relations. Whereas it is often expected that women will become part of a new kin group after marriage, among the Moravians women and men had to let go of their natural families to join the Moravian community. And whereas in the first case a system of exchanges and reciprocities often created bonds between old and new family, in the case of the Moravians contacts with the natural family were often interrupted. The Moravians exemplify an extreme case of the biblical notion (Luke 9:59–62; Mathew 12:48–50) of leaving father and mother behind to join the kingdom of God—which the Moravians hoped to help build with their worldwide missionary and evangelization campaign.

The inner organization of the community aimed at weakening traditional family structures. Families in the form of arranged marriages existed, but children were not raised in the family but rather in communal institutions.[19] In the Moravian settlements (*Gemeinorte*), the members were divided into so-called choirs, according to age, gender, and family status. In every settlement there was a boys' choir, a girls' choir, a choir of unmarried brethren, a choir of unmarried sisters, a choir of married couples, and a choir of widows and one of widowers. Not the families but those choirs were the main points of identification for the members. Even in graveyards, the members were buried in the order of their choirs.

In these choirs, not only did religious instruction take place, but the unmarried members also lived together in the houses of their respective choirs. In the eighteenth century, this system was so strictly administered that in some settlements, for example in Bethlehem, Pennsylvania, even the marriage partners lived in separate choir houses. The normal practice, however, was that a marriage constituted the founding of one's own household. Children were usually taken from the families when they were six years old and educated in the boys' or, respectively, the girls' choir houses.[20]

Life in the Moravian community offered women a variety of possibilities for work and development beyond the role model of wife and mother. Life as a single person, mostly in a "choir," was considered an acceptable alternative lifestyle to marriage, and even for the married sisters, motherhood was not the central part of their identity.[21]

The choir organization was the central means to control the members' behavior and to enforce a strict community discipline: the development of each person was noted in choir reports that were sent in regular intervals to the central leadership.[22] In the case of transgressions, the individual was "fondly rebuked" (as the sources call it rather vaguely) or temporarily excluded from the Lord's Supper.[23] The ultimate sanction was the expulsion from the community. In the settlement Herrnhut, for example, between 1773 and 1801, 132 people were excluded from a group of approximately 900 inhabitants, and in the American settlement Salem in the same period, 38 from 200.[24]

Marriage was seen as a powerful tool of strengthening group cohesion. All marriage partners were chosen by the Unity's leadership on the basis of the choir reports, whereby the leadership frequently mixed people from different communities and even countries. This rigid regulation had a considerable potential for conflict. The wish to marry without the consent of the leadership constituted the most frequent reason for the expulsion from the community. From 1773 to 1801, 29 individuals in Herrnhut and 19 in Salem were excluded for this reason.[25]

Often such relations ended with members leaving the community voluntarily, as for instance Jens Schmidt, who in 1780 in Salem was to be married to the widow Baumgarten. Schmidt, however, was convinced that the sister Eva Hein was the person the Savior had selected for him and all the leadership's "good willed persuasion" (as the sources call it) could not divert him from his desire. The conflict ended as Schmidt withdrew from the Moravian community.[26]

One decade after the establishment of Bethlehem, in neighboring Nazareth, the local leadership warned the central leadership in Herrnhut that some brothers would leave the community if the UÄC would not send sisters soon. These men had left Europe some years earlier with the assurance that the leadership would find them marriage partners. This promise had not been fulfilled, and the local leaders feared that the brothers would turn away from the community. In November 1753, they sent the categorical request: "Send sisters for the following brothers to marry."[27]

As with all important decisions within the Moravian community, the leadership's selection was subjected to lot, which the Moravians regarded as a means of manifesting Christ's will.[28] In the case of Moritz Christian von Schweinitz, several sisters whom the leadership selected for him were not confirmed by lot ("mehrere Schwestern, die für mich in Vorschlag gewesen, [wurden] von unserm l. Herrn … nicht approbirt").[29] As a determined Moravian, von Schweinitz seemed to have waited patiently until the lot finally confirmed a sister whom he then married. But the so-called marriage lot was not undisputed. At the Synod of 1801, several Irish and English settlements requested to waive the lot as precondition for marriages. Their request was rejected with the argument that uniformity in this matter was essential for the cohesion of the group: "Unsere Gesamtstruktur erfordert dies als eine Gepflogenheit ohne jede Ausnahme; denn sie würde aller Wahrscheinlichkeit nach keinen Bestand haben, wenn dieser Brauch nicht überall und ohne Einschränkung in den Ortsgemeinden beachtet würde" (Our overall structure requires this as a regular practice without any exception, because quite obviously it could not be maintained if the custom were not observed everywhere and without reservation in the communities).[30]

After 1818, the marriage lot was gradually abolished for the common members in the American and European settlements. For the Moravian leadership and office holders, it remained in use until 1825 and for missionaries until 1848.[31]

As the example of marriage praxis shows, the network that held the Moravian communities and missionary stations in Europe and overseas together was tight knit.[32] The sense of communal identity was maintained not only by close institutionalized links between the worldwide settlements and the group's leadership in Saxony, but also by shared rituals and festivities, commonly read magazines or other devotional literature, and the circulation of reports about various settlement's activities. The members of the Moravians operated within large structures and also within different cultures. But, at the same time, they always remained within the microcosm of their own communities, which were held together by a close network comprising organization, shared lifestyle and rituals, and communication.

From the outset, organization and finances were the charge of the central leadership. The complete development of institutional structures took place, however, only after the death of Zinzendorf, in 1760. Once his charismatic authority as the basis of group cohesion had ceased to exist, his successors in the Moravian leadership were challenged to stabilize relations among the global settlements institutionally. Now periodical synods with delegates from all Moravian branches decided upon uniform guidelines for all worldwide settlements, and the leadership in Herrnhut governed even the smallest details of everyday life in missions and settlements around the world. Decisions by local leadership had to be approved by the central ruling body in Herrnhut. The UÄC made decisions on the filling of positions, changes in residency of members, the purchase of land or houses, management of economic enterprises, etc. All settlements had to regularly contribute funds, including financial surpluses, to support the missionary activities of other Moravian locations in times of financial instability or crisis.[33]

The economic development in all settlements was subordinate to central planning, since all economic activities were meant to finance the worldwide Moravian missionary activities.[34] As a matter of principle, members were not allowed to engage in agriculture and thereby commit themselves to a place.[35] Typical work for the Moravians included often very successful trading enterprises that benefited from the community's international connections and highly skilled handicrafts such as cabinetmaking, gold smithing, fur trading, watch making, soap boiling, and textile production.[36]

The property question remained unclear until the end of the nineteenth century. Private property was permitted, but holders were seen merely as trustees rather than owners of their fortunes and had to put them at the community's disposal in cases of need.[37]

The settlements and mission stations all over the world were in constant contact via letters with the UÄC. From 1741 on—upon a decision of Zinzendorf—a member in every community was responsible for corresponding with the Pilgerhaus. Following the establishment of the director's office in Herrnhut, correspondents were also appointed here whose job was to maintain contact with the localities that were assigned to them. At certain intervals, the settlements and mission stations had to supply information, in the form of diaries, about the internal and external conditions of their respective localities. If the central leadership received information about grievances, they sent out newsletters demanding compliance with established norms. In 1813, for example, the diary of the American community of Salem noted that a newsletter from Herrnhut dealing with the observance of clothing regulations had been read publicly.[38]

In order to monitor compliance with community norms, from time to time the central executive also sent one or more of its members on extended visitation trips throughout Europe, to countries having mission stations, or to the settlements in North America.[39] The causes for such visitations varied and sometimes were apparently slight: In 1787 the UÄC sent one of their members to the Silesian settlement Neusalz after they learned about the "alarming" situation that female peddlers regularly had come into the choir house of the single brothers to sell milk and butter.[40]

This tightly woven system of controls secured the uniform development of the worldwide community during the eighteenth and early nineteenth centuries quite well. Not least, it was the strong in-group/out-group bias that secured the maintenance of clear group boundaries. As we have seen earlier, within the space of thirty years about 20 percent of the members were excluded, others left the community voluntarily, and sometimes whole settlements were closed down when their development went astray in the eyes of the leadership.

However, it would be wrong to reduce the relationship between the settlements all around the world and the headquarters in Herrnhut to the issue of control. The Moravians established themselves as a tightly woven global community of mutual exchange among like-minded brothers and sisters.[41] Without their high in-group identification and their commitment to submit themselves to the rigid community discipline in order to serve the common religious cause, all mechanisms of control would have failed to work.

First and foremost, it was a common rhythm of life that created a strong feeling of interconnectedness. There were many things that took place daily, weekly, monthly, or annually in the same way in all of the worldwide settlements and missionary outposts. The day began everywhere with the same *Losung* (watchword), which was always selected for one year ahead of time and then distributed to all communities around the world. The weekly schedule in all of the communities followed the same rituals of singing sessions, community meetings, bible readings, communal prayer, and love feasts. Each month, a so-called *Gemeintag* (community day) was held everywhere, and letters from Herrnhut or other communities, as well as the newest edition of the group's journal, *Gemeinnachrichten*, were read aloud. The annual course of events was shaped by a multitude of special celebrations and days of commemoration, which were an important means of safeguarding the group's collective identity by a common interpretation of the past. For example, the days when the different missions started were celebrated; on 4 May, the single sisters had their day that was celebrated worldwide; 2 February was the day of the widows and widowers. These forms of symbolic communication created strong bonds between the members and did not comprise a national community of remembrance but a rather global one. Everywhere, life among the Moravians was shaped by the same rhythm of weekly plans, ceremonies, and liturgical rituals. Life in the American town of Salem was similar to that in any other community, regardless of whether it was the English community of Fulneck, Christiansfeld in Denmark, or Gnadau in Germany. Thus, members of Moravian communities could feel at home, so to speak, anywhere in the world. Regardless from which country they came, in their communities they always found what for them was a familiar everyday life.

As a globally active group, the Moravian Brethren relied upon communication via written media in order to transmit information between the central leadership and the individual communities, as well as among the communities themselves. The most important medium of communication within the group was the periodical journal *Gemeinnachrichten*, which was in some sense the equivalent of a *Familienrundbrief*, with which transregional and transnational families kept in contact with each other.[42]

Beginning in 1747, the *Gemeinnachrichten* were published under various names, initially as handwritten copies; from 1818, they were printed with the title *Nachrichten aus der Brüdergemeine*. Each issue contained speeches, sermons, or addresses by leading members; detailed accounts from the individual communities and mission fields based on letters and reports that the settlements and missionaries sent regularly to the directorate in Herrnhut; and always several biographical sketches of deceased male and female members.[43]

Each month, the *Gemeinnachrichten* circulated around the globe among the various communities and were read there communally, generally on the monthly *Gemeintag*. As in Herrnhut in Saxony, so the members in Fulneck in England, for example—or in Zeist in the Netherlands, in Bethlehem in Pennsylvania, in Okak in Labrador, in Sarepta in Russia, in New Herrnhut in Greenland, in Gnadenthal in South Africa, in New Hope on Jamaica, in Gracehill on Antigua, in Paramaribo in Suriname, in Bluefields on the Mosquito Coast, in Montgomery on Tobago, and in Saron on Barbados—congregated on the first Sunday of each month in their community buildings, where the latest issue was read aloud. The communal readings made the *Gemeinnachrichten* an important means of interaction and group communication that bound its members together in a community characterized by a strong feeling of consensus. The information circulating around the globe made the events in the settlements of the various countries international reading material, so to speak, and served to direct the mental horizon of all members in the same direction. The printed speeches and sermons provided communities with standardized material for their many liturgical convocations and thus kept the "type of teaching uniform in all of our communities," as the Synod of 1764 noted. The reports on the work of missionaries and conversion successes among the "heathen" ensured the members of the importance of their global "mission." The *Gemeinnachrichten* were also the main means of communicating the group's theology and spirituality. Up to the middle of the nineteenth century, the Moravians possessed no comprehensive theological textbook of their doctrines; they rather constructed their religious identity within the context of a continuous narrative that extended over generations and continents.[44]

The *Gemeinnachrichten* was the most important periodical publication that kept the members in contact with one another. Month after month they disseminated the ideas and visions that structured the community and gave it a common identity. With the *Gemeinnachrichten,* members kept each other up-to-date about developments in the various communities and mission stations, and they were also able to participate in events in faraway lands where members of the group lived. The regular reading of reports from other communities created a strong feeling of togetherness and mutual solidarity, and the individual communities and mission stations could also count on support and aid during emergencies. In 1803, for example, in addition to the regular contributions for the missionary endeavors, the American community of Salem sent 500 pounds to the Silesian community Gnadenfrei in order to help members there cope with damages caused by a fire. The news of a major hurricane in Barbados and Jamaica also spurred the community of Salem to provide financial assistance to the affected Moravian mission stations. Following a catastrophic fire in the Russian community of Sarepta in 1823, which destroyed almost two-thirds of the village, 132,000 rubles were donated from other Moravian settlements.[45]

An important aspect of the global community's continuing self-assurance was the memoirs of recently deceased members, which were published in the *Gemeinnachrichten.* They served, first of all, as a notification of the death of a member and made members aware of an all-encompassing sense of unity, to which not only those living or dying in their respective settlements belonged.

The creation of meaning and identity by means of biographical narrative exemplified a comprehensive social practice for all members of the Brethren communities. Each member was required to leave behind his or her own personally written memoir, which was then read aloud as a farewell ritual upon the death of the particular brother or sister. The memoirs printed in the *Gemeinnachrichten* publicized this ritual, as it were, worldwide and made them aware of the universal scope of the community to which not only those living and dying in their own settlement belonged. Given the Moravian marriage practice and members' mobility, this ritual must have had especially deep resonances for people who knew each other or had complex familial ties although they lived far away from each other.[46]

Through their public use, the memoirs assumed a powerful role within the Moravian community. Again and again, they provided the Moravian brothers and sisters with exemplary models of successful lives in the Brethren communities. By being circulated among the various settlements, they linked the thought and behavior of people at completely different locations. In the practice of writing and speaking about one's own life in public, a canon of knowledge was created that was affirmed again and again by means of common usage. It served to strengthen the self-assurance of the members, but it could also be enriched by them with their respective interpretation of their religious experience. The Moravians thus constituted a global "narrative community" that created a common cultural memory and therefore its own collective identity by collecting, exchanging, and circulating exemplary biographies of brothers and sisters belonging to the fellowship.

The Moravians were not the only pietistic community that had its own newsletters as the preferred method of creating a sense of global community. Think of the Halle Mission, or the Christentumsgesellschaft, or in the Catholic context, the Jesuits.[47] But, compared to the Moravian Brethren, neither the Halle Mission nor the Christentumsgesellschaft had at its disposal a comparable diversity of "agencies" fostering community building via organization, communication, and rituals. The Halle Mission sent its missionaries out into the world from a central headquarters, but this did not result in the establishment of strong communities in other locations.[48] The Christentumsgesellschaft was a comparably informal network of awakened Christians all over Europe that had no strong administrative hub.[49] Conversely, the special challenge the Moravians had to face, as a polylocal group having strongly established communities in various countries, was to create a sense of unity by a continuous cultivation of collective rituals and memories, and to permanently stabilize group unity against the external influences of the countries of residency.

They succeeded in achieving this over a period of some fifty to sixty years, even in light of the most adverse conditions for communication. During the nineteenth century, however, the global connection of the Moravians became increasingly weaker, although the infrastructural prerequisites for exchange rapidly improved. Quicker transportation routes and lower shipping costs certainly simplified the possibilities of transatlantic communication; however, this did not automatically result in a mental "contraction of space" and a closer sense of community as it is often assumed in the literature of globalization.[50] On the contrary, the "experienced" distance even increased. Decisive for the feeling of proximity and distance were, ultimately, not the technical possibilities of communication, but rather the idea of community and the desire to communicate resulting from this. And this changed in parts of the Moravian communities during the nineteenth century.

Due to vast distances, from the very beginning it was frequently difficult for the Moravian communities to maintain regular contact. During times of war, it could happen that the foreign communities and mission stations were cut off for several months or sometimes, even years, from information from the Herrnhut headquarters and other branches of the Moravian Brethren.[51] The Continental Blockade during the Napoleonic Wars even made contact with England difficult. But to draw the conclusion that distance, transportation difficulties, or time delays in the exchange of information per se weakened global unity appears erroneous to me. On the contrary, during the eighteenth century, the utmost emphasis was placed upon remaining in spiritual contact in spite of what were frequently very difficult conditions—the voyage alone, across the Atlantic, could take months when conditions were bad. When the delivery of the *Gemeinnachrichten* was delayed or prevented due to wars or other postal delivery disruptions, the members helped themselves by rereading articles from the collections of older issues. If the year's supply of the daily *Losungen* did not arrive in time, then the members would read the watchword from the respective day of a previous year. As a replacement for missing news, other Moravian books were also read, for example, stories dealing with Moravian history or their various missions. Thus the time in which the actual connection was interrupted was effectively bridged by the knowledge of shared rituals and stories of communal experience, and contact was reestablished as quickly as possible. At the end of the Napoleonic Wars, the missionaries in South

Africa, after being almost completely cut off from contact to Herrnhut, even requested a visit to the cape by the central executive.[52]

The global social arena of the Moravians thus consisted primarily of an "imaginary order."[53] Ultimately, it was not the actual connection that was decisive, but rather the feeling of unity. As long as the concept of community was alive for its members, the global connection existed and functioned. For the decrease in worldwide cohesion, changes in the loyalties of the members caused by the successive infiltration of the external world into portions of the community were more decisive than the technical difficulties in communication. Precisely due to their relatively isolated situation for members in the mission countries, the "experienced" distance to their brothers and sisters in other parts of the world generally remained relatively small and unchanged during the nineteenth century. During the nineteenth century, above all North American members broke away from their strong inner connection to global group unity and increasingly oriented their loyalties and sense of belonging toward a national level.

The foundations for this development were already laid during the American Revolution. This had brought the Moravians into a difficult position. Based upon their refusal to bear arms, their missionary relationships to the Indians, and, above all, their connections to the brothers and sisters in England, the Moravians were mistrusted by the "Americans" around them. In North Carolina, the Brethren barely avoided having their land confiscated because their members there refused to take an oath of loyalty to the United States or to renounce their loyalty to the British Monarchy under oath.[54]

The Moravians did not want to endanger the unity of the global community and particularly the missionary activities in the English colonies by openly taking sides against England. They paid for substitutes and contributed to the costs of the war in other "nonmilitary" ways, such as caring for the wounded. Members who wished to participate militarily in the fight for America's independence were indeed expelled. Many young men left the group voluntarily. The Moravians' attempt to always remain neutral in political matters became more and more difficult, since the American Revolution—much more than the various monarchical governments under which they had lived in Europe and which only demanded neutrality—forced the members to clash with their fellow citizens. The European monarchies could live with subjects who kept out of things and otherwise caused no problems; the Revolution, on the other hand, demanded that one take sides—either as friend or foe. It thus called the global community of the Moravians strongly into question.

The members of the American branch of the Moravians identified more and more strongly with their environment. Global cohesion increasingly receded into the background. In the run-up to the General Synod of 1818, the American communities formulated various demands, for example, for more decision-making authority and for the abolition of the ban on military service. Even though the synod did not acquiesce to these demands, it became clear that the American members were beginning to go their own way.[55]

Over time, language differences also led to a weakening of the network. Into the nineteenth century, the German language was the lingua franca of the Moravians. Correspondence, diaries, instructions, and community news were all written in German; and in all communities, this was the main spoken language until after the beginning of the nineteenth century. The compulsory attendance of the members' children at a Moravian educational institution ensured that the non-German members continued to be exposed to the German language.

This obligation was less and less strictly observed during the nineteenth century. Education in a Moravian institution was still compulsory only for the children of members serving as missionaries. While the members of the European congregations still frequently continued to send their children to the Moravians' German schools, this practice became more and more infrequent in the American communities; and the use of the German language in the American communities became less and less common.

So that the American communities could still participate in the communication network of the larger community, in 1821, at the recommendation of the Pennsylvania communities, a portion of the *Gemeinnachrichten* began to be officially published in English. By the middle of the 1820s, however, the American communities had also established their own English-language publications, which increasingly supplanted the *Gemeinnachrichten*.[56] Even though the latter continued to be received by the American communities, beginning in the late 1820s and early 1830s, it was evidently read less and less.

The emergence of these new publications was another indication of an increasing national orientation in the American branch of the Moravians, since the new journals were no longer intended to address all members of the community, but were rather thought of as an internal means of communication among the American communities themselves.[57] In its first issue, the new English language periodical *Moravian Church Miscellany* nevertheless attested to the still existing ties between the old and the new continent. On its first page it brought the memoir of the deceased twenty-nine-year-old sister Caroline Hamilton to the attention of its readers: "Born at Quedlinburg, Germany, educated partly in our schools in Gnadau and Niesky, and partly in Paris, afterwards engaged in instructing the young in England then called as a missionary's wife, to the West India labor-field, our sister was finally, in the providence of God, brought to this country and into the midst of the Philadelphia congregation, in order here to die."[58] Despite their own newspapers and the increasing orientation of the American members on the American nation, personnel connections still held the global community together.

This chapter has focused on the mechanisms of cohesion of a religious community scattered across the globe. Though it looked at a system of spiritual kinship rather than at a family in the strict sense of the word, the issues raised here may be helpful in thinking through different issues of other transnational kinship as well. The close organizational links between the different branches of the Moravians and the strict control of their homogeneous development constitute an extreme case that all the more may highlight some factors that constitute, stabilize, or challenge transnational family systems. Structures of central authority and coordination; mechanisms of conflict resolution; marriage practices; shared rituals, festivities, lifestyles, and religious beliefs; communicative strategies to maintain feelings of connectedness and collective memory; travel activities and exchanges among members; and a common language as a tool of cohesion (or the creation of barriers when members begin to have linguistic differences) are important points to consider when dealing with transnational families of any kind, though every family played out those factors in its own way.

Notes

1. On the Pietistic notion of "work furthering the Kingdom of God" (*Reich Gottes Arbeit*), see, e.g., Hartmut Lehmann, "Horizonte pietistischer Lebenswelten," in *Protestantische Weltsichten: Transformationen seit dem 17. Jahrhundert*, ed. Hartmut Lehmann (Göttingen, 1998), 11–28; Jürgen Ohlemacher, *Das Reich Gottes in Deutschland bauen: ein Beitrag zur Vorgeschichte von Theologien der deutschen Gemeinschaftsbewegung* (Göttingen, 1986).
2. The Moravians drew a clear distinction between "friends" and members, the first being supporters of the Moravian cause gathered in conventicles all over Europe (the so-called diaspora) under the regular supervision of Moravian traveling preachers. Full members lived in self-contained settlements (*Gemeinorte*), that is, communities in which only members of the Moravians were allowed to reside who submitted themselves to the strict rules of the community. The average size of a settlement was roughly five hundred people.
3. In 1761, the global Moravian community had roughly 12,000 members: 5,747 on the European continent, 3,442 in Great Britain, and 3,015 in North and South

America. By 1857, the membership had increased to 20,000, with 6,188 of the members living on the European continent, 5,161 in Great Britain, and 8,414 in America. See Dietrich Meyer, *Zinzendorf und die Herrnhuter Brüdergemeine, 1700–2000* (Göttingen, 2000), 174.

4. In 1839 there were twenty-five Moravian missionaries in Greenland as compared to 2,000 converts. The ratio was 31/1,300 in Labrador, 5/150 in Canada, 3/100 in the United States, and 36/10,000 in the Danish West Indies. The following ratios are recorded in the British West Indies: 19/8,000 in Jamaica, 22/10,000 in Antigua, 10/4,000 in St. Kitts, 6/1,400 in Barbados, 4/700 in Tobago, 14/4,000 in Suriname. In South Africa the ratio was 39/2,745. See Martin Cunow, *Die Herrnhuter* (Weimar, 1839), 55–59.
5. There were only few exceptions to this rule, the most famous being Christian and Rebecca Protten. Christian Jacob Protten (1715–1769) originated from Guinea and was raised in Copenhagen. He joined the Moravians as a young man and worked as missionary in Guinea. Rebecca Protten (1718–1780) was a freed slave from St. Thomas. In 1738, she married the Moravian missionary Freundlich. Their marriage was annulled by the Danish colonial administration, and both were jailed. Only three years later, they were freed at the intervention of Zinzendorf. As a widow, Rebecca traveled in 1742 to Germany and later married Christian Protten; John Sensbach, *Rebecca's Revival: Creating Black Christianity in the Atlantic World* (Cambridge, MA, 2005) and Peter Sebald, "Christian Jakob Protten Africanus (1715–1769): Erster Missionar einer deutschen Missionsgesellschaft in Schwarzafrika," in *Kolonien und Missionen: Referate des 3. Internationalen Kolonialgeschichtlichen Symposiums 1993 in Bremen*, ed. Wilfried Wagner (Munich, 1994) 109–21.
6. Protocols of the Provincial Synods in London 1754, cited in Hermann Wellenreuther and Carola Wessel, eds., *Herrnhuter Indianermission in der Amerikanischen Revolution: Die Tagebücher von David Zeisberger 1772 bis 1781* (Berlin, 1995), 75.
7. Chorbericht Christiansfeld 1809; Unitätsarchiv Herrnhut (henceforth UA), R.4.C.III.
8. Protocols of the Provincial Conference in London 1749, cited in Wellenreuther and Wessel, *Herrnhuter Indianermission*, 75.
9. The memoir of Benigna Sophia Cunow (1765–1836) appears in the Moravian journal *Nachrichten aus der Brüdergemeine* (June 1839): 445.
10. Dienerblatt Johann Christian Bechler, in UA, Dienerblätter (comprehensive collection of personnel papers of the officeholders), without signature.
11. Vgl. Jørgen Bøytler, "Zinzendorf und Dänemark," in *Graf ohne Grenzen*, ed. Dietrich Meyer and Paul Peucker (Herrnhut, 2000), 77.
12. Paul Peucker, "Heerendijk: Link in the Moravian Network: Moravian Colonists Destined for Pennsylvania," *Transactions of the Moravian Historical Society* 30 (1998): 9–21.
13. Elizabeth W. Sommer, *Serving Two Masters: Authority, Faith and Community among the Moravian Brethren in Germany and North Carolina in the 18th Century* (Lexington, KY, 2000), 40. See also the protocols of the Salem Eldest Conference (8 March 1781) cited at 121.
14. See hymnal book of the Moravian Brethren: *Gesangbuch zum Gebrauch der evangelischen Brüdergemeinen* (Barby, 1778).
15. The Pilger house was the inner circle of the Moravian community. Its members were chosen by Zinzendorf on the basis of their religious "virtuosity." Some members of the Pilgerhaus had special functions such as "eldest" of the worldwide single brothers or "eldest" of the worldwide single sisters; others served as correspondents with the

settlements that were assigned to them, and others served as scribes to write down Zinzendorf's speeches, which then circulated among the worldwide communities.
16. The leadership of the Pilgerhaus included strong female figures. After 1760 the central leadership was exclusively male. For more details see Gisela Mettele, *Weltbürgertum oder Gottesreich: Die Herrnhuter Brüdergemeine als globale Gemeinschaft* (Göttingen, 2009).
17. As with the Quakers, Baptists, and Unitarians and—in the Reformation—the "Family of Love," the use of familial expressions was pervasive within the Moravian community. The use of the language of family stressed the horizontal images of brothers and sisters rather than the vertical images of parents and children. The expression "eldest" (*Ältester, Ältestin*) for leadership positions signified a hierarchical parent-like relation, but in the communication between Moravians, the eldest were referred to as brothers and sisters as well. Before 1760, the metaphor of the "mother" had several strong connotations: Zinzendorf's wife, Dorothea, and Anna Nitschmann, the eldest of the worldwide choirs of the single sisters, were referred to as "Mama'gen" and "community mother" (*Gemeinmutter*), respectively. On a different spiritual level, the Holy Spirit was characterized as a mother, and also Jesus was attributed some motherly qualities, since Moravians referred to the side wound as a "womb" from which believers were born again; Aaron Spencer Fogleman, *Jesus Is Female: Moravians and Radical Religion in Early America* (Philadelphia, 2007). Jesus was, however, not female in the understanding of the Moravians. Female and male members alike referred to him as their "husband" or "the Man." Fogleman rightly points to the fact that the Christo-centrism of the community in some sense disempowered God as the father figure. Likewise on the level of "earthly" leadership it is remarkable that Zinzendorf was not referred to as "father" but as "disciple" (*Jünger*).
18. See, for example, the memoir of Rosalie Schoen in *Nachrichten aus der Brüdergemeine* (August 1839), 601.
19. In the nineteenth century, there was increasing value placed on education in the family. The question of institutional education versus family education was, however, never clearly answered; both were still practiced. In particular for the children of church workers and missionaries, it was still normal in the nineteenth to live in the educational institutions.
20. Choir reports, Moravian Archives Herrnhut, R 4 C III (singles brothers), R 4 C IV (singles sisters).
21. See Beverly Smaby, *The Transformation of Moravian Bethlehem: From Communal Mission to Family Economy* (Philadelphia, 1988); Magde Dresser, "Sisters and Brethren: Power, Propriety and Gender among the Bristol Moravians, 1746–1833," *Social History* 21 (1996): 304–29; Katherine Faull, ed., *Moravian Women's Memoirs: Their Related Lives 1750–1820* (Syracuse, NY, 1997); Peter Vogt, "A Voice of Themselves: Women as Participants in Congregational Discourse in the 18th-Century Moravian Movement," in *Women Preachers and Prophets through Two Millennia of Christianity*, ed. Beverly Mayne Kienzle and Pamela J. Walker (Berkeley, CA, 1998), 227–47; Gisela Mettele, "Bürgerinnen und Schwestern: Weibliche Lebensentwürfe in bürgerlicher Gesellschaft und religiöser Gemeinschaft," *Unitas Fratrum: Zeitschrift für Geschichte und Gegenwartsfragen der Brüdergemeine* 45/46 (1999): 113–40.
22. UA, R.4.C.III (Brüder), R.4.C.IV (Schwestern), R.4.C.II (Ehechor).
23. Synodal-Verlaß von 1801, Ch. "Von der GemeinDisciplin," § 209; UA, R.2.B.47.
24. Sommer, *Serving Two Masters*, 61–73.
25. Ibid., 61f.
26. For more examples in North America and Europe see ibid., 71–78.

27. Fritz Tanner, *Die Ehe im Pietismus* (Zürich, 1952).
28. The lot was used to make or ratify decisions on all levels of Moravian life. Casting lots was a common practice within Pietism, but the comprehensive use the Moravians made of the lot was quite exceptional; Sommer, *Serving Two Masters*, 19. Erich Beyreuther, "Lostheorie und Lospraxis," in *Studien zur Theologie Zinzendorfs*, ed. Erich Beyreuther (Neukirchen, 1962), 109–39; Elisabeth W. Sommer, "Gambling with God: The Use of the Lot by the Moravian Brethren in the 18th Century," *Journal of the History of Ideas* 59 (1998): 267–86.; Hans-Jürgen Schrader, *Literaturproduktion und Büchermarkt des radikalen Pietismus: Johann Heinrich Reitz' "Historie der Wiedergebohrnen" und ihr geschichtlicher Kontext* (Göttingen, 1989), 296.
29. Memoir Moritz Christian von Schweinitz (1748–1822); UA, R 22.35.37.
30. Synodalverlaß 1801 § 319; UA, R.2.B.47.
31. Meyer, *Zinzendorf und die Herrnhuter Brüdergemeine*, 70.
32. The concept of network is here used with the qualification that, with its semantics alone, which suggests a more noninstitutionally safeguarded and less hierarchically conceived form of group formation, the Brethren community would be described only partially. On research related to the network concept, see Johannes Weyer, ed., *Soziale Netzwerke: Konzepte und Methoden der sozialwissenschaftlichen Netzwerkforschung* (Munich, 2000); Dorothea Jansen, *Einführung in die Netzwerkanalyse* (Opladen, 1999); Manuel Castells, *The Rise of the Network Society* (Oxford, 1996).
33. Adelaide Fries, ed., *Records of the Moravians on North Carolina 1752–1857*, 11 vols. paginated successively (Raleigh, NC, 1922–69), 1700, 2073, 2482.
34. See Peter Vogt, "Des Heilands Ökonomie: Wirtschaftsethik bei Zinzendorf," *Unitas Fratrum: Zeitschrift für Geschichte und Gegenwartsfragen der Brüdergemeine* 49/50 (2002): 158.
35. See memorandum UÄC 1758; Otto Uttendörfer, *Wirtschaftsgeist und Wirtschaftsorganisation Herrnhuts und der Brüdergemeine von 1743 bis zum Ende des Jahrhunderts* (Herrnhut, 1926), 51.
36. International connections as the basis for the economic success of Moravian enterprises are described in more detail in Gisela Mettele, "'Kommerz und fromme Demut': Wirtschaftsethik und Wirtschaftspraxis im Gefühlspietismus," *Vierteljahrsschrift für Sozial- und Wirtschaftsgeschichte* 92 (2005): 301–2.
37. Noncompliance could be sanctioned with temporary exclusion from the Lord's Supper or expulsion from the community; Protokoll der Generalsynode Marienborn 1764, 861 in UA, R.2.B.44.1.c.
38. Fries, *Records of the Moravians in North Carolina*, 2176f. The question of clothing was not insignificant, since in Moravian communities clothing was an essential symbol of unity and uniformity; Gisela Mettele, "Entwürfe des pietistischen Körpers: Die Herrnhuter Brüdergemeine und die Mode," in *Das Echo Halles: Kulturelle Wirkungen des Pietismus*, ed. Rainer Lächele (Tübingen, 2001), 291–314.
39. During the eighteenth century, twenty-three major visitation voyages took place, during each of which the inspectors visited the settlements of several countries; John C. S. Mason, *The Moravian Church and the Missionary Awakening in England 1760–1800* (Suffolk, UK, 2001), 25.
40. Sommer, *Serving Two Masters*, 70f.
41. The discussion about the formation of collective memories forms the backbone of my argumentation here. See Astrid Erll, ed., *Kollektives Gedächtnis und Erinnerungskulturen* (Stuttgart, 2005); Jan Assmann, *Das kulturelle Gedächtnis: Schrift, Erinnerung und politische Identität in frühen Hochkulturen* (Munich, 1999); Maurice Halbwachs, *Das kollektive Gedächtnis* (Stuttgart, 1967).

42. The function of *Familienrundbriefe* as a means of creating a collective memory is mentioned in Claudia Vorst, *Familie als Erzählkosmos: Phänomen und Bedeutung der Chronik* (Münster, 1995) and Miriam Gebhardt, *Das Familiengedächtnis: Erinnerung im deutsch-jüdischen Bürgertum 1890 bis 1932* (Stuttgart, 1999).
43. Many Pietist groups circulated genealogies, collections of letters, and memoirs. The scope of those circles was rarely as wide as in the case of the Moravians and often remained in the regional context; Ulrike Gleixner, *Pietismus und Bürgertum: Eine historische Anthropologie der Frömmigkeit* (Göttingen, 2005). Another difference with the Moravian case lies in the fact that identify formation and tradition building in the Württemberg *Bildungsbürgertum* gradually excluded women's memoirs: in the eighteenth century, men and women had equal part in the formation of Pietist communicative cultures in Württemberg; in the nineteenth century many memoirs of male Pietists circulated in published form whereas most women's texts now remained in the family archives. For the public use of male and female memoirs within the Moravian community see Mettele; *Weltbürgertum oder Gottesreich.*
44. For the concept of "narrative theology," see Michael Goldberg, *Theology and Narrative: A Critical Introduction* (Nashville, 1982), ch. 3 and 4.
45. Fries, *Records,* 1700, 2073, 2482.
46. More than thirty thousand memoirs are stored in the archives in Herrnhut alone (UA R 22). In the context of this article, I refer to the published memoirs since these versions were the ones that became part of the collective memory. With the published biographical writings, the question of polishing and editing changes naturally arises. There is no doubt that the editors of the *Gemeinnachrichten* selected and revised biographies corresponding to their own notion of a "successful" Moravian life. No discourse, however, can be fully controlled, and texts are never univocal; they could be interpreted or even misread. The "making and remaking" of community identity within the Moravians as a dynamic process with many interchanges and questions of editing and differences between the published and unpublished versions are discussed in Mettele, *Weltbürgertum,* 198ff.
47. A comparison between the Jesuits and the Moravians would be highly interesting, since their respective international structures seem to be very comparable in many respects. In the context of this article, such a comparison is unfortunately not possible.
48. Paul Raabe, ed., *Pietas Hallensis Universalis: Weltweite Beziehungen der Franckeschen Stiftungen im 18. Jahrhundert* (Halle a.d. Saale, 1995).
49. Eamon Duffy, "The Society of Promoting Christian Knowledge in Europe: The Background to the Founding of the Christentumsgesellschaft," *Pietismus und Neuzeit* 7 (1981): 28–42.
50. Critical assessment in Jürgen Osterhammel and Niels Peterson, *Geschichte der Globalisierung* (Munich, 2003).
51. Carola Wessel, "Connecting Congregations: The Net of Communication among the Moravians as Exemplified by the Interaction between Pennsylvania, the Upper Ohio Valley, and Germany (1772–1774)," in *The Distinctiveness of Moravian Culture,* ed. Craig Atwood and Peter Vogt (Nazareth, PA, 2003), 168.
52. Bernhard Krüger, *The Pear Tree Blossoms: A History of the Moravian Mission stations in South Africa 1737–1869* (Genadenthal, 1966), 121.
53. See in general Doris Reichert, "Räumliches Denken als Ordnung der Dinge," in *Räumliches Denken,* ed. Doris Reichert (Zürich, 1996), 15–43.
54. For this and the following see Gollin, *Moravians in Two Worlds;* Beverly Prior Smaby, *The Transformation of Moravian Bethlehem: From Communal Mission to Family Economy* (Philadelphia, 1988); Sommer, *Serving Two Masters.*

55. Synodalverlaß vom Jahr 1818 UA R.2.B.47, Beilagen zum Synodus 1818, UA R.2.B.50.f.
56. In 1822 the *United Brethren's Missionary Intelligencer* was founded; it was followed in 1838 by the *Moravian Church Miscellany.*
57. Beginning in 1790, the English branch of the Moravian Brethren had also published an English-language periodical, *Periodical Accounts.* This publication, however, was not intended for internal communication, but was rather aimed at external supporters of the Moravian community in order to provide such supporters with regular news from the mission field. Periodicals that, as internal communication pages, competed with and increasingly replaced the *Gemeinnachrichten* emerged only in North America.
58. *Moravian Church Miscellany* 1 (1850): 1.

Part II

Modernity

Chapter 9

Families of Empires and Nations

Phanariot Hanedans *from the Ottoman Empire to the World Around It (1669–1856)*

Christine Philliou

Phanariots were a series of interconnected Orthodox Christian elites that grew out of the social and political fabric of Ottoman governance, rising to power in the late seventeenth century and enjoying an ascendancy that lasted until the 1820s.[1] Their political success far surpassed their mercantile origins and connected them with Ottoman governance in several ways: they served as translators in strategic scribal offices in Istanbul and in the Ottoman military and as governors in the semiautonomous provinces of Eflak and Boğdan (Wallachia and Moldavia in today's Romania), all the while as their base of power rested on their association with the Ecumenical Patriarchate in Istanbul. With the outbreak of rebellions in 1821, which led to the Greek War of Independence—rebellions initiated by some from among the ranks of Phanariots—these elites split up, settling into lucrative positions in several empires and emergent nation-states. In a typology of transregional elites, Phanariots therefore share characteristics with those of mercantile diasporas, Muslim Ottoman grandees, and emergent transnational elites in the nineteenth century.

Family relationships were embedded in the larger structures of patronage for Phanariot elites as they were for Ottoman subjects of all confessions and social stations. In conventional scholarship, kinship ties are treated only in the context of a small and secretive clique of families who sponsored a "Greek Enlightenment" and facilitated the achievement of Greek statehood. Particular families, such as the Hypsilantis and Mavrocordatos clans, are renowned for abandoning their positions in the Ottoman Empire, ultimately to take part in establishing the independent state of Greece. Yet the processes in which Phanariots were involved from the mid-seventeenth and increasingly in the late eighteenth century—and the ways they instrumentalized family relationships—had consequences far beyond the movement for Greek independence, and the active families were more numerous and diverse than the handful of prominent names would suggest.

Phanariots in the Ottoman Empire have received much less scholarly attention than Greek mercantile elites in the larger Mediterranean world. Both enjoyed prominence in precisely the same period (late eighteenth to early nineteenth century) and were connected by ties of commerce, blood, and local origins.[2] The well-known story of the Greek merchant diaspora, operating from London to Marseille through Odessa, which amassed the capital, built the information networks, and imported the ideas necessary for a secessionist revolution and the establishment of an independent Greek state obscures the fact that there was also a Greek-identified elite within the Ottoman Empire.[3] This was an elite that can hardly be termed part of a diaspora, for its members were increasingly involved in the work of Ottoman governance and were concentrated at the Ottoman metropole, which had, of course, once been the chief city of Byzantium. Phanariots did not belong to the imperial ruling house nor did they share the dominant religion of Sunni Islam. And yet, while other transregional networks of "middleman minorities" could be deeply involved in the political economy of the states that gave them shelter, Phanariots went well beyond this arena to serve as functionaries—governors and diplomats—for the Ottoman state, and thus confound the national and diaspora frameworks.[4] It should not be a surprise, then, although it has been all but ignored up to now, that Phanariots deployed a number of strategies to gain status and legitimacy *within* the political culture of the Ottoman Empire. Key to these strategies was not just the mobilization of family relationships, but the formalization of those relationships in a specifically Ottoman Turkish idiom. In this chapter, I will focus on the fact that a significant faction of Phanariots was in the midst of consolidating transregional households—comparable to those of their Muslim peers in structure and function—at the turn of the nineteenth century. The term of choice for such households in the generation before 1821 was *hanedan*. After exploring the broader landscape of families and politics during the eighteenth century, I will examine the term *hanedan* for the range of meanings it had for both Ottomans and Phanariots and end by considering what became of the term and the Phanariots who used it after the outbreak of a Greek secessionist conflict in 1821.

A quantitative and comprehensive study of kinship patterns among Phanariots is not possible given the fragmentary evidence available. This is not merely because records have been lost, but because the very phenomenon of the Phanariot ascendancy, like the term *hanedan*, was not fully institutionalized.[5] While families formed webs of patronage ultimately replaced by institutions such as the Tercüme Odası, or Translation Office (est. 1833), they did so in what seems to have been an improvised way, and this is reflected even in the little we can glean about kinship patterns.[6] Thus, I have used anecdotal evidence from contemporary chronicles, personal correspondence, secondary sources regarding Phanariot genealogies, and Ottoman state archival sources that make reference to particular offices and functions performed for the Ottoman state in the hopes of capturing one thread of continuity and discontinuity before, during, and after the 1820s.

Kinship and Ottoman Households in the Eighteenth Century

In the context of the Ottoman state, three patterns associated with the pre-1821 Phanariot ascendancy stand out: 1) structural-functional similarities with other contemporary Ottoman elites in the instrumentalization of family relationships; 2) the control of information within the family for political advantage; 3) their dominance articulated in the idiom of Ottoman governance.

Historians of the Ottoman Empire have long noted the shift from a military to bureaucratic state emerging from the crises of the mid-seventeenth century.[7] This entailed changes on countless levels such as revenue collection and expenditure, provincial administration, trade and food provisioning, and writing about politics and statecraft.[8] But perhaps most important for the emergence of Phanariot elites in this transformation was the 1699–1700 Treaty of Carlowitz, which signaled the closing of the Ottoman frontier with Europe, the end of an expansion-driven regime, and the first official cession of territory to Christendom.[9] This treaty prompted a realignment of Ottoman diplomacy and a reconfiguration of administration in the border areas and populations as well as in the diplomatic apparatus in Istanbul. It also coincided with the rise of

Russia as a major power and threat to Ottoman ambitions for expansion and eventually political survival. Together, these changes offered a host of opportunities for an Orthodox Christian elite, such as the Phanariots, with linguistic and political knowledge useful for diplomatic intercourse with the states of Christendom.

A handful of individual Phanariots and families had already attained positions of great influence in the decades before Carlowitz. Panagiotis Nicousios, a native of the formerly Genoese island of Chios, and Alexander Mavrocordatos, from an already prominent Istanbul family, were the two major examples of this.[10] The Mavrocordatos family, like several other emerging Phanariot families in the seventeenth century, apparently accumulated capital from a monopoly of particular commodities, such as salt, meat, and grain, which were crucial to provisioning the capital city of Istanbul.[11] They then used this money to purchase titles in the Orthodox Patriarchate Church of St. George in the Phanar district of Istanbul, "a practice which eventually gave them complete control of the Patriarchate and its various functions."[12]

At the same time that particular families were accumulating wealth and influence within the Ottoman imperial domains, members of these same families seem to have also been sent abroad, often to Italian cities, to study medicine. This was the case with Panagiotis Nicousios, who studied in Padua, as well as with Alexander Mavrocordatos, who studied first at the College of St. Athanasius in Rome and then went on to study medicine at the universities of Padua and Bologna.[13] Upon their return to Istanbul, both took up positions teaching at the Patriarchal Academy and entered the service of the Ottoman grand vezir as physicians. Once they began working as physicians, they enjoyed privileged access to the grand vezir, who eventually came to see the usefulness of their expertise in the Italian language for the burgeoning area of diplomacy.[14]

In the aftermath of the Treaty of Carlowitz, diplomacy became more central to maintaining Ottoman power. There, in the realm of interimperial negotiations rather than through dominance on the battlefield, borders and commercial agreements were coming to be negotiated.[15] Particular Phanariot families on the rise were strategically placed to capitalize on what was no doubt an unpleasant reality for members of the Ottoman central state. Not only did they share Orthodox Christianity with the Russian Empire, which made them both valuable and threatening, but also some of those families from the formerly Genoese island of Chios had maintained ties with Italian states and possessed the ever more important knowledge of European languages such as Italian and French.[16]

Both Phanariot pioneers, Panagiotis Nicousios and Alexander Mavrocordatos, were granted the office of grand dragoman (interpreter) during the Grand Vezirate of Fazil Ahmet Köprülü (1661–1676), himself a member of the dynasty credited with restoring Ottoman imperial governance during the crises and rebellions earlier that century.[17] This fact points to two key conjunctures.[18] First, it was with the Köprülü Restoration that a model of politics based on the military/grandee household expanded beyond the sultan's palace throughout the Ottoman provinces.[19] We indeed find that many prominent Muslim Ottoman families of the eighteenth century—in *ulema* (religious learning and jurisprudence), bureaucratic office, regional commerce, or the military—traced their origins to the late seventeenth century.[20] As their dominance of the Orthodox Patriarchate led to a monopoly of the office of grand dragoman and the provincial *voyvoda* administrative offices of Moldavia and Wallachia (in 1711 and 1716, respectively), Phanariots borrowed kinship practices—and terminology—from their vezir and *ayan* counterparts.[21]

With the accession of Nicousios and then of his protégé Alexander Mavrocordatos to the office of grand dragoman, trade in information became central to Phanariot political livelihood and the basis for their further expansion of power. These initial appointees were said to have been valued for their knowledge of European languages and expertise regarding diplomatic negotiations. By the second decade of the eighteenth century, Alexander Mavrocordatos's son Nicholas was appointed *voyvoda* of Moldavia and then Wallachia, crucial border provinces in the continuing territorial conflicts among the bordering empires. Understandably, information about neighboring rivals and potential collaborators in the provinces was key to the maintenance of Ottoman power.

By 1800, the task of Phanariot *voyvoda*s-cum-ambassadors in Europe was repeatedly acknowledged to be "procuring news" (*celb-i havadis*).[22] In an early nineteenth-century investiture ceremony for Wallachian and Moldavian *voyvodas*, the sultan explicitly charged the initiate with the following duties and concomitant privilege:

> The arrangement demanded of you from my imperial pantries [coffers] is this: you bring back news from the European parts; the *hospodarship* [office of *voyvoda*] of Wallachia is granted to you with full freedom and plenipotentiary powers; in return, your loyalty is demanded.[23]

While contemporary Muslim Ottoman elites in the Balkans, Anatolia, and Arab lands were necessary for revenue collection and domestic stability, Phanariots supplied crucial information from abroad through posts in the border provinces, in their capacity as dragomans, and eventually in naval service alongside the *kapudan paşa* (admiral). The often exorbitant taxes they were allowed to collect in the Danubian principalities were a perquisite they received in exchange for procuring information and supplying staple foodstuffs, such as grains and meat, to the Ottoman capital.[24]

By the end of the eighteenth century, Phanariots had set up far-reaching webs for the transport of information and goods. Such webs were staffed by relatives stationed in Istanbul, the Danubian principalities, and beyond. Ottoman authorities described these networks this way: "Members of the Rum *ta'ifesi* who are in the Wallachian and Moldavian service, *like a chain* (*zincir mesellu*) have continual contact with their families across long distances."[25] From countless *yol tezkeresi*, or travel documents issued by the Ottoman authorities, we know that members of particular Phanariot retinues circulated with their families among designated nodes of this vast information network.[26]

Family members served a variety of purposes in this "chain." Male relatives (sons, brothers, and sons-in-law) of the reigning *voyvoda*s in Wallachia and Moldavia were kept in captivity in Istanbul as hostages (*esir*) to ensure loyalty, and since they were in communication with their families and important conduits of information, they might be interrogated whenever the Ottoman authorities found it useful.[27] The position of *kapıkahya* (or *kapıkethüdası*) was an important office often filled by a male family member (with ties of blood or marriage) of the reigning *voyvoda*.[28] The *kapıkahya* was the representative of the *voyvoda* to the Sublime Porte who would remain in Istanbul (in his own residence) and would regularly visit the Porte to convey information from his superior in the provinces and to keep abreast of goings-on at the palace that might affect the *voyvoda*.[29]

Women family members, too, were deemed important, even in official documents, for securing information. Arguing in favor of Phanariot *voyvoda*s-cum-ambassadors bringing their wives with them to their posts, an anonymous writer noted: "Given that it is obvious that in Europe the *ta'ife* of women have great insight, ambassadors should be permitted to have their wives and families accompany them, so that the latter can procure information (from the wives of European statesmen)."[30]

Family relationships, then, could facilitate the task of information management between Phanariot elites and the Ottoman central state in a number of ways.[31] Nevertheless, although the Phanariot specialization in procuring information perhaps made them functionally unique among eighteenth-century Ottoman elites and although they can be productively compared with trading diasporas discussed elsewhere in this volume, they still found it useful to adopt strategies and symbols of legitimacy from the Ottoman political environment in which they thrived. Although Phanariots could not have access to titles and status with particular Muslim significance, they were able to attach themselves to Ottoman political culture through confessionally neutral terms, first among which was *hanedan*.

Phanariot *Hanedans*

The term *hanedan* is of Persian derivation, meaning literally "a great tribe [or] family."[32] Once it passed into Ottoman-Turkish usage, it was used as a conventional label to refer to those ruling families going back to the Abbasid dynasty and to the Ottoman dynasty itself (*hanedan-ı Al-i Osmani*). It does not seem to have been used as a legal-administrative term within the classical Islamic-Ottoman order of *askeri* (rulers) and *re'aya* (ruled), within the world of office-holders and scribes (*kalem*), among ulema (religious-juridical experts), or among the elite *askeri* (men of the sword). Furthermore, it did not confer or confirm such status as could, for example, entitle a provincial family to a de jure privileged position within the central state. And yet, the term *hanedan* gained currency for Phanariots in the eighteenth century at the same time as its use spread throughout the Ottoman political system, and I would suggest that its adoption signifies their integration into the imperial regime. In the course of the eighteenth century, following the Köprülü Restoration, Ottoman provincial elites emerged in the context of what has been often described as "decentralization."[33] These elites (*ayan*) have been well studied for their involvement in *malikane* life-term tax-farming in Anatolia and much of the southern Balkans and for their accumulation of military power in the same areas during the late eighteenth century.[34] Their combination of military and tax-collecting functions, taking up operations of the state previously coordinated from the center, developed into provincial patronage networks and fostered connections to mercantile groups.

Phanariots mirrored the ad hoc accumulation of power that characterized *ayans* in the eighteenth century, with some important structural differences. Since as Christians they could not own slaves, their households composed family members and servants whose only obligations arose from social patronage. As a result, their households and those of other elites, such as those in Egypt during Mamluk and post-Mamluk Ottoman rule containing legally imported slaves from the Caucasus, cannot simply be equated.[35] Their status as Christians also kept them from direct access to military power in contrast with *ayans* who often began their careers as military leaders. Limited to service as scribes, the most the Phanariots could do was accompany the military on campaign as dragomans of the imperial army (*Tercüman-ı Ordu-yu Hümayun*), which they frequently did by the early nineteenth century.

These structural differences had a number of consequences. Although Phanariot princes in Wallachia and Moldavia did come to have personal militias (known as *arnavut neferleri*, or "Albanians") by the later eighteenth century, their base of power was not military as it was for most *ayans*. As a result they could be dismissed at the will of the sultan with no recourse to armed opposition. And there was another major structural difference—in most cases of *ayan* rule, one family dominated a province, often merging with settled, local *hanedan*, or dynasties. By contrast, among the Phanariots, several families vied for appointment to rotating positions of *voyvoda* and dragomans, making for a highly unstable, fluid, and costly modus vivendi as entire retinues of advisors, scribes, and servants moved back and forth with their families between Istanbul and the remote Danubian principalities with the unpredictable replacement of each *voyvoda*.[36]

Since tax farms (*timars*, by the eighteenth century, *malikane*) presupposed military office, Phanariot exclusion from the latter limited their ability to acquire such lucrative positions within Ottoman territory.[37] But Moldavia and Wallachia, although de facto part of the empire, were not de jure part of the Ottoman land and tax regime, and offered an area for Phanariots to extend their activities.[38] They purchased land and cultivated dense ties with the church hierarchy (installing male family members in lay church positions), whose officials managed much of the property in the principalities, and with the local boyar landowning elite (by marriage alliances with boyar families). As a result, even though the top offices for which these families competed were highly unstable, they were able to circumvent the structural obstacles they had as Christians to establish stable, land-based households. By the turn of the nineteenth century, exploiting the frontier status of Moldavia and Wallachia to their advantage, Phanariots were fashioning themselves as *hanedans*, or landed dynasties. Already during the eighteenth century, despite their lack of military power, they were commanding households that moved between Istanbul and the Danubian principalities. Despite the fact that they could not gain formal status as *askeri* (men of the sword) or as *malikaneci*, *mufassil*, or *mutesellim*—the official titles for tax farmers and other local tax officials—they had entrenched themselves in local and imperial rule in other ways. Already controlling land through church holdings, they continued to accumulate holdings through purchase and marriage alliances with indigenous boyars.[39] The writer of an Ottoman *irade* (sultanic decree) around 1800 claimed that the "beys, sons of beys, boyars, and sons of boyars ... are not descended from merchants and shopkeepers but are counted among the greatest dynasties (*hanedan*)."[40] It seems likely that, at least in the case of beys and their sons, if not boyars (who were indeed indigenous to Wallachia and Moldavia and whose power had long rested on their land-holding status), their commercial origins were being obscured to elevate them to the higher status of state officialdom.[41] The *irade* went on to say that *voyvodas* of Moldavia and Wallachia are "acknowledged in Europe to have a rank equivalent to that of kings" and used the term *hanedan* to render a European concept of landed nobility into an Ottoman idiom.[42]

The social composition of Phanariot *hanedans* points to a number of convergences with contemporary Muslim Ottoman *hanedans*. These dynasties, based in Wallachia, Moldavia, and Istanbul, like members of the Ottoman imperial and vezir households and those of eighteenth-century Egypt, were drawn from different areas of the empire and were of diverse ethnic-linguistic origins.[43] Even the most prominent Phanariot families established already from the late seventeenth century had gone "trans-ethnic" as well as transregional as a prerequisite to achieving power. The Ghikas family was originally Albanian, and the seventeenth-century ancestors of the eighteenth- and nineteenth-century Hellenized Phanariot Ghikases had reportedly arrived in Istanbul with patronage connections to their fellow Albanian countrymen, the Köprülü Vezirs.[44] The Aristarchis family, originally Armenian, had come to Istanbul in the late seventeenth century from the Black Sea coast as *sarrafs* (accountants) and had Hellenized by the later eighteenth century. The Kallimakis had likely started out as Romanians and had Hellenized to keep their hold on the rule of the Danubian principalities when the offices of prince passed into the hands of Phanariots in 1711.[45]

Further parallels exist between transregional Phanariot households and their more monoregional Muslim Ottoman counterparts. In providing background for her study on eighteenth-century Aleppo, Margaret Meriwether notes, "Certain occupations have always been highly regarded in Islamic societies, and the upper stratum of Ottoman provincial society was drawn from families associated with these respected careers: religious learning, mercantile activities, and service to the Ottoman state."[46] Career paths of members of Phanariot families reflected a similar strategy, not of specialization but of diversification, as one brother entered the clergy and another the service of an Ottoman military or scribal official or an already prominent Phanariot grandee, and a third went into commerce or became, for instance, a physician. Accumulation of a range of offices and titles, then, allowed for the building of influence by providing ever-wider access to information, expertise, and valuable goods. With regard to the eighteenth-century Aleppan monoregional elite families she examines, Meriwether writes that "the economic power of these families was not grounded in a single form of wealth, such as land or merchant capital, that would link them together through shared economic interests. … Instead what they had in common was the diversity of economic resources they controlled. They had acquired their wealth in different ways: by engaging in commerce and money-lending, by appropriating rural surpluses as tax farmers and owners of rural property, and by controlling *waqfs*."[47] Indeed we can say all of these things for Phanariots as well, replacing only the term *waqfs* (Muslim pious foundations) with church properties throughout the empire and in particular in the Danubian principalities, and the term *tax farmers* with *voyvoda*s, who were essentially tax farmers on a grand scale. While Meriwether's Muslim Aleppan families diversified within the economy and provincial government of Aleppo, Phanariots diversified across professions, but also across regions and ethnicities.

The similarities between Phanariots and Muslim Ottoman contemporaries do not stop there. Meriwether also notes the trend throughout the empire in the eighteenth century of acquiring family names, "with the –zade and –oghlu [-oğlu] suffix attached to a name or nisba being the usual form."[48] Many Phanariot families were also coming to add the Turkish *-oğlu* or even the Persian *-zade* suffixes to their names just at the time they were coming to be termed *hanedan*. The Hançerlizade (alternately known as Hançerli(s), Hantzeris, and Hançerlioğlu), İskerletzade Aleksandır (whom we would recognize as Mavrocordatos, but who, by the late eighteenth century, chose to be called İskerletzade, or the Turkish-Persian rendering of "son of Scarlatos") and the Phanariot-affiliated Armenian Düzoğlu (also known as Duzian) families are all evidence of this trend.[49] Ottoman documents at times referred in passing to *hanedanzadelik*, or the quality of being descended from a *hanedan*—better translated as "nobility," confirming that the choice to add *-zade* and *-oğlu* to one's family name signified such pretensions for Christians and Muslims alike.

Maintenance and expansion of *hanedans* through marriage and fictive kinship alliances also reflect parallels between Phanariots and Muslim Ottoman elites. Men who were already prominent in Phanariot networks would marry their daughters or nieces to aspiring men, bringing them into the household and larger network. The father-in-law/uncle would then be responsible for providing opportunities for the son-in-law/nephew (*damat*) and in turn would receive a client. Jane Hathaway notes the same pattern in eighteenth-century Egypt and points out that it is not only similar to European dynastic practices, but also to the sultans' practice of marrying a princess to a prominent vezir, thereby admitting him into the House of Osman.[50] In the case of godparentage, the specific custom of baptizing a child is a Christian practice, but the logic of expanding and reinforcing the patronage network through fictive kinship seems to have parallels in both the Ottoman imperial and Egyptian cases.[51] One need only consider the prevalent *ghulam/köle* system of elite slavery in the eighteenth-century Ottoman Empire, whereby a Muslim grandee would accumulate slaves, often from the Caucasus or the Balkans, and, much like a godfather would his godchildren, train them as client-protégés in his household, eventually placing his slave-progeny in key positions of power.[52]

Phanariots, then, were borrowing a number of features and strategies from their Muslim Ottoman counterparts, not least of which were specific practices of instrumentalizing family relationships for political and economic purposes. They were building and consolidating *hanedan*s outside the juridical mainstream of Ottoman land-holding and tax-collecting regimes as part of a larger project to gain de facto legitimacy and importance in the realm of Ottoman rule. A major difference between Phanariot and Muslim Ottoman elites, however, was that the Phanariot enterprise was being carried out on a geographically larger scale. While leaders of households in Egypt, Syria, and other Ottoman provinces diversified *within* the province (from military to tax-collecting and commerce, for instance), Phanariots, barred from direct access to military power, were building ever-denser relationships to Ottoman governance within the imperial capital as they were also cultivating ties beyond the empire—in the border zone of Moldavia and Wallachia as well as in European states and empires. And it is this difference, in part, which explains the divergent paths of Phanariot families from each other and from many of their Muslim Ottoman contemporaries in the course of the Greek War of Independence.

Institutions and Revolutions

By the turn of the nineteenth century, Phanariot affiliates were being appointed ambassadors to the first permanent embassies established by the Ottoman sultanate in London, Paris, and Berlin.[53] As part of the *Nizam-i Cedid* reforms, which are often heralded as primarily military in character, Sultan Selim III and his advisors also sought to institutionalize Ottoman diplomacy abroad, discussing how best to do it and whether to appoint members of Phanariot *hanedans*. Phanariots were in a precarious position throughout the period of their ascendancy, charged with conveying sensitive information between the sultan and European states and thus always vulnerable to accusations of treachery. When such accusations were leveled and the accused fled to Russia or Austria, as was often the case, Ottoman authorities at times punished family members by confiscating property, but rarely disqualified from other offices or physically harmed the entire family. Famous cases of early nineteenth-century *ayans* such as Tepedelenli Ali Paşa of Yanya, Osman Pasvantoğlu of Vidin, or Kavalalı Mehmet Ali Paşa of Egypt point to a pattern of negotiation—and success or failure—for the entire family/dynasty. When Tepedelenli Ali Paşa and Osman Pasvantoğlu fell from power, their sons were prevented from succeeding them; when Mehmet Ali negotiated with the Ottoman Porte in the 1830s and 1840s, it was on behalf of his dynasty, and his success resulted in the establishment of a hereditary dynasty in Egypt that lasted until the 1950s. Phanariot *hanedans* could and did remain intact even when an individual member suffered exile or death.

In the few years before 1821, there were two developments that helped usher in a new period of transnationalism and the breakdown of transregional *hanedans* by catalyzing a Greek national movement.[54] First, and more well-known of the two, was the establishment in Odessa in 1814–15 of the secret *Philike Hetaireia*, or Society of Friends, by three merchants not directly connected to Phanariot networks. This secret society gradually drafted Phanariot affiliates as well as clerics and other merchants into their ranks, lobbying for Russian support for a rebellion of Christians in the Ottoman Empire. The second development was in 1819, when, I argue, the symbiosis between Ottoman state and Phanariot networks was institutionalized in a long-overlooked reform known as the *Hanedan-i Erba'a*, or Dynasty of Four.[55] In this reform, eligibility for the top four Phanariot offices (dragoman of the court, dragoman of the fleet, princes of Moldavia and of Wallachia) was limited to four particular families, referred to as *hanedans*—that of the current Moldavian Hospodar Kallimaki, that of the current Wallachian Hospodar Drakozade Aleko Soutsos, that of Mihal Bey's line descending from the current imperial dragoman Drakozade Mihalaki Soutsos, and, finally, the "houses of the three brothers of the deceased Alexander Muruzis [would] have a monopoly" of the four high offices. The other families who would be excluded from the offices, such as Jacob Argyropoulos's and Hançerli's families, would be paid a pension of 60,000 and 40,000 guruş, respectively, by the four reigning families.[56]

While the power of these four families—now referred to unquestionably as *hanedans*—was bolstered by this reform, in having their power institutionalized these families were also being reined in and their power assigned limitations. And of course the other families who were not selected for eligibility were to be permanently excluded from political power (and given pensions by the winning families). Underneath these four and more top families were webs of patronage composed of scores, and likely hundreds of other families who were in the retinues and employ of the prominent Phanariots.[57] This innovation, we can only surmise, must have caused a disruption in entrenched patterns of politics and connections of family and patronage. Less than two years later, the flag of insurrection against the Ottoman sultanate was raised, first in Moldavia, then in the Peloponnese and Aegean Islands, where rebellions developed into a protracted war for independence.

The Breakdown of Dynasties and the Transition to "Multinationalism"

The events of the Greek War of Independence fall outside the scope of this chapter. Of greater relevance is the outcome of the war and the establishment of the Greek kingdom for the Phanariot-Ottoman *hanedans*. In the immediate wake of violence in the 1820s, members of the same household or family found themselves scattered across long distances and made choices to maximize their chances of survival. In Istanbul, early reprisals against prominent church officials prompted the escape of several prominent Phanariot families, who were presumably associated with these clerics: former Wallachian Hospodar Alexander Hançerlis; *Beyzâde* (Prince) Georgios Karaca; and Nicholas Soutsos, brother of Michael and the *kapıkahya* who had been first questioned by the Ottoman grand vezir upon receiving news of the insurrections in Moldavia.[58]

Many members of Phanariot *hanedans* who survived the immediate Istanbul aftermath of Greek insurgencies in Moldavia were exiled within Ottoman domains. The *voyvoda* Kallimakis was exiled to Bolu, in northern Anatolia, where he was subsequently murdered by the governor there.[59] Stavrakis Aristarchis, who has gone down in history as the last Phanariot dragoman, was soon removed from office and exiled with his family to Bolu as well, where he was killed, ostensibly by robbers, in 1822 as he was returning from hot springs with his teenage son Nicholas.[60] Other lesser boyars, such as Hatman Yorgaki Mano, Count Yorgaki Vogoridi, and one Ağa Yanko were exiled with their families to Anatolian towns like Zile, Tosya, Bursa, and Kangiri.[61]

Other Phanariots escaped abroad. The family of dragoman Kostaki Muruzis fled to Odessa and then returned to Moldavia in 1829 with the

Peace of Adrianople (now Edirne). Jacob Argyropoulos, aka Yakovaki (who had been imperial dragoman from 1812 to 1815, but excluded from eligibility for Phanariot high offices in the Tetrarchy Regulation of 1819), was first exiled to Çorum and then Ankara until 1825 and was moved to Bursa in 1829. Upon returning to Istanbul, he was asked to travel to Petersburg with another Phanariot associate, Stephanos Vogorides, to represent the Ottoman Empire in preparatory negotiations for the Peace of Adrianople. Argyropoulos pretended to accept the proposal but instead escaped to the island of Aegina, then to Athens, where he lived until 1850.[62]

There were also many Phanariots who took part in the Greek Revolution and settled in the new Greek capital of Athens and enjoyed a fraught relationship with the coalition of social groups vying for power in the new Greek state.[63] Alexander Mavrocordatos and Kostaki Karaca (son of the former Wallachian Hospodar), for instance, had been in Pisa when the Greek rebellions began.[64] They arrived at the site of rebellions in 1821 and immediately began trying to lead the provisional and local governments. They were joined by fellow Phanariot Theodore Negris, who had in 1821 just been appointed Ottoman chargé d'affaires to France but, while on the way to his post, defected and joined the Greek insurgency.[65] Michael (Mihalvoda) Soutsos (1778–1864), who had been imperial dragoman (1815–1818) and was *hospodar* of Wallachia when Hypsilantis declared uprisings in Moldavia in 1821, joined the revolution (having been a member of the Society of Friends) and was appointed by Greek king Otto as head of the Greek legation to Paris in 1833, then to Petersburg, Stockholm, and Copenhagen.[66]

Once the crisis subsided, Phanariots availed themselves of a number of strategies to recoup some of their power within and beyond Ottoman domains. The range of outcomes is clear even from the six families (the four who were included and the two who were excluded) mentioned in the *Hanedan-i Erba'a* resolution. Michael Soutsos had been *voyvoda* of Moldavia since 1818. He was inducted into the Society of Friends in late November 1820 (only two months before insurrection started in his principality). After the insurrection failed, he fled with his family to Bessarabia (after being excommunicated by Patriarch Gregorios V because of his role in the revolution), then went through Austria to neutral Switzerland. After the establishment of Greece in 1828, Greek president John Capodistrias appointed Soutsos representative of Greece in Paris. Soutsos eventually settled in Athens in a palace he built for himself. Other branches of the family, also mentioned in the 1819 *Hanedan-i Erba'a* resolution, remained in Moldavia as francophiles, like much of the Moldavian and Wallachian local aristocracy. Family members born during and after the 1820s were born in Athens, Odessa, and Paris.

Scarlatos and Ioannis Kallimaki did not survive the first year of the Greek insurrections—they were both exiled to Anatolia and eventually strangled there. The marriages of Kallimaki's daughters, however, indicate the continuity of Phanariot alliances: one daughter, Sevasti, married Michael Soutsos; another, Smaragda, married *voyvoda* Alexander Hantzeris; and a third, Maria, married Gregorios Stourzas, of a Moldavian boyar family.[67] Another member of the Kallimaki family settled permanently in Paris and served in the mid-nineteenth century in the Ottoman embassy there. Kostaki Mourouzi, the head of the fourth family named in the 1819 resolution, was killed while serving as grand dragoman in the early days of the Greek insurrections, as mentioned above. His family seems to have fled to Odessa; one son, also named Constantine, studied in France and served in the French navy before settling in Greece in the 1840s; another son, Panagiotis, became a Greek officer in the Russian army, dying in Vienna in 1859 with the rank of general.[68]

The two families who were excluded from eligibility for the top Phanariot offices in 1819, Argyropoulos and Hançerlis, add to the variety of national and career trajectories. Jacob Argyropoulos, as mentioned above, was out of office when the revolution erupted, and was exiled to Anatolia, where he remained until he fled to Greece. His son Manuel arrived in Greece with his father and was later appointed dragoman of the Greek embassy in Istanbul, where he served from 1836 until 1849. He was ultimately appointed dragoman of the Russian embassy in Istanbul and served there until 1863. His younger brother Pericles became a constitutional law professor and ultimately a member of parliament and foreign minister of Greece in the 1850s, just as his brother was serving the Russian Empire in Istanbul. The Hançerlis family had long been suspected of Russian sympathies. These suspicions were perhaps not unfounded, as Alexander Hançerlis (1759–1854) took refuge in Russia when insurrections began in Moldavia. While in Moscow, he compiled a French-Arabic-Persian-Turkish dictionary, and died at the age of 96. The younger generation, exemplified by Gregorios, Dimitrios, and Michael, all of whom were born around the time of the Greek Revolution, were schooled and/or settled in German states, demonstrating yet another possible trajectory.

There were of course families, often of second-tier Phanariot status in the period before 1821, who reconstituted *hanedans* in Ottoman territory, albeit on a smaller scale than before and, significantly, without using the term *hanedan*. Stephanos Vogorides and Nicholas Aristarchis are two such examples—the former allied with Britain and the latter with

Russia. Both built networks of clientage that connected the Ottoman central state, the emergent foreign ministry, the Orthodox Church, Moldavian and Wallachian administrations, and foreign states using a logic similar to that prior to 1821.[69] New families also emerged, such as the Karatheodoris and Musurus families, to be known as "neo-Phanariots."

The conventional understanding of Phanariots is that they all but disappeared from the Ottoman Empire and ended up in Greece with the conflicts of the 1820s. When we expand our scope of analysis beyond a single empire or nation-state, however, and view Phanariots as transregional dynasties that were based in Ottoman territory before 1821, we find that while their integrity and landed base of operations was shattered, they came to reconstitute divergent aspects of their pre-1821 repertoire on a transnational scale. In doing so, Phanariots that joined the "diaspora" fared better than their Muslim Ottoman counterparts, whose power was also threatened at the same time by a newly ambitious Ottoman central state. It is telling that neither Phanariots nor their Muslim Ottoman counterparts claimed the status of *hanedan* by the mid-nineteenth century—not only had Phanariot fortunes changed, but the power of Muslim provincial magnates had been suppressed by the 1830s (with the great exception of Mehmet Ali in Egypt), in both cases making the term *hanedan* much less relevant.

Conclusion

The case of Phanariots brings to the fore several important points for the larger discussion of transregional and transnational families that is the focus of the present volume. To begin with, Phanariots were, consciously it seems, eclectic in the strategies they used to instrumentalize family relationships for political and economic gain. This was a natural outcome of their location at the intersection of Ottoman state structures, Orthodox Christian ecclesiastical and lay hierarchies, European Christian states, and the Greek mercantile diasporas operating throughout the region, not to mention of their mobility between land and tax regimes of Ottoman domains proper and the autonomous Danubian principalities. While conventionally this openness to a wide array of influences is seen as the cause of their initiating the movement for Greek independence (as they were the first in the region to appropriate ideas of the Enlightenment and national self-determination), I have tried to show that such openness was also an important contributing factor to their simultaneous project within the Ottoman political context to fashion themselves as *hanedans* in the later eighteenth and early nineteenth century. In other words, Phanariots were borrowing strategies and symbols of family relationships from their Muslim Ottoman counterparts—provincial *ayans* as well as the Ottoman royal household—to build a base of power even as some among their ranks, and those who had already dispersed to mercantile centers of the Mediterranean and Black Sea, worked to undermine the Ottoman system and create a new polity.

Phanariots also demonstrate a range of strategies of adaptation from a transregional to a transnational environment. Regardless of the positions adopted by one or another Phanariot *hanedan*/household toward Greek independence, they all found themselves in a new political landscape after the 1820s. Branches of the same family could and did end up in Moldavia, Wallachia, Greece, the Ottoman Empire, Russia, France, and German and Italian states, marrying into national elites of those states or members of fellow Phanariot families. From anecdotal evidence it is clear that a marriage alliance to another established Phanariot family was as common as one to an elite family of the new nationality, whether Romanian, French, Italian, or British. Both strategies could help stabilize a highly indeterminate status as they transitioned away from operations in Ottoman government.

While it is clear that those Phanariots who remained in the arena of Ottoman rule went on to recoup power through reestablishing household-like affiliations, they no longer called themselves *hanedan* and no longer enjoyed official prominence in Ottoman diplomacy or provincial administration. One could also speculate that there was a continuous logic for Phanariots who dispersed to settle in the many states mentioned above. It would not be surprising to find out that brothers and cousins in several states continued to stay in contact or to cooperate in various business and/or political ventures. And yet the territorial base of power in Istanbul's Phanar district or the Danubian principalities seems to have fallen out of the picture. Consequently, transregional family enterprises that were taking on a legal status as landed dynasties in 1820 had by 1830 become uprooted transnational families. Ironically, it was the Greek national revolution that sent Phanariots into dispersal, adding a new dimension to the story that features Greek "diaspora" merchants leading the effort to create a nation-state and national metropole.

Finally, it is illuminating to compare this Phanariot break from transregional *hanedans* to transnational families with the trajectories of Muslim Ottoman mono-regional elites. In doing so, we see that the very transregional dimension of Phanariot activities, forced on them to a large extent by dint of their formal exclusion from military and landowning institutions, gave them an important advantage over monoregional Muslim Ottoman elites. Those monoregional elites, although showing themselves able to adapt to reforms emanating from the imperial center, had a limited array of options and could not easily relocate if adaptation proved impossible.[70] For them it was a zero-sum game to win—like Mehmet Ali of Egypt—or lose—like Ali Paşa of Yanya. For Phanariots, involvement in Ottoman governance, like the term *hanedan*, turned out to be one important piece of a broader portfolio.

Notes

1. The term *Phanariot* denoted association with the Istanbul neighborhood of Phanar (*Fener* in Turkish and Φανάρι in Greek). Literally meaning "lantern" or "lighthouse," Phanar was the name of the quarter in Istanbul where the Orthodox Patriarchate has been located since the seventeenth century. For a more comprehensive treatment of the Phanariot ascendancy and its Ottoman context, see Christine Philliou, *Biography of an Empire: Practicing Ottoman Governance in the Age of Revolution* (Berkeley, CA, 2010) and "Communities on the Verge: Unraveling the Phanariot Ascendancy in Ottoman Governance," *Comparative Studies in Society and History* 51 (2009), 151–81. Some of the material in this chapter is taken from my book.
2. The island of Chios, for instance, was the birthplace of prominent Phanariots such as Panagiotis Nicousios (see below) in the seventeenth and eighteenth centuries, as well as of large-scale mercantile families such as the Rallis and Argentis in the eighteenth and nineteenth centuries.
3. For structural analyses and typologies of Greek mercantile diaspora firms, see Gelina Harlaftis, "Mapping the Greek Maritime Diaspora from the Early Eighteenth to the Late Twentieth Centuries," Ioanna Papelasis-Minoglou, "Toward a Typology of Greek Diaspora Entrepreneurship," and Maria-Christina Hatziioannou, "Crossing Empires: Greek Merchant Networks before the Imperialistic Expansion," all in *Diaspora Entrepreneurial Networks: Five Centuries of History*, ed. Ina Baghdiantz-McCabe, Gelina Harlaftis, and Ioanna Papelasis-Minoglou (Oxford, 2005); Olga Katsiardi-Herring, "He hellenike diaspora: He geographia kai he typologia tes" [The Greek Diaspora: Its Geography and Typology], in *Hellenike Oikonomike Historia 15os-19os aionas* [Greek Economic History, Sixteenth to Nineteenth Centuries] (Athens, 2003), 237–47; Gelina Harlaftis, *History of Greek-owned Shipping: The Making of an International Tramp Fleet, 1830 to the Present*, ed. Spyros I. Asdrachas (Athens, 1996).

   The problem of terminology looms large here. All Orthodox Christians in the Ottoman Empire were termed *Rum* (Roman), but in practice this term also connoted what we could call Greek as opposed to Serbian, Bulgarian, or Albanian, for instance. Phanariot elites were not Greek identified in a national sense, but were speakers of Greek by birth or education, and they identified themselves with Greek as the predominant language and cultural force for Orthodox Christians in the Ottoman Empire.
4. Illuminating comparisons with Phanariots can be drawn from Niall Ferguson's *The House of Rothschild: Money's Prophets 1798–1848* (New York, 1998).
5. Access to more systematic records of marriage and godparentage alliances is also limited because the lion's share of the Ecumenical Patriarchate Archives in Istanbul is not open to researchers. Passing mentions of marriages, baptisms, and financial

property matters do find their way into the outgoing correspondence from the Patriarchate to Metropolitan Sees, which is the one section of the archive that is available to researchers.

6. Interestingly, the same has been said about Greek merchant coalitions in this period. Ioanna Papalasis-Minoglou, among others, has noted the "amorphous" structures of such coalitions. See her "The Greek Merchant House of the Russian Black Sea: A 19th-Century Example of a Traders' Coalition," *International Journal of Maritime History* 10 (1998): 61–104.
7. Halil Inalcik, "Centralization and Decentralization in Ottoman Administration," in *Studies in Eighteenth-Century Islamic History*, ed. Thomas Naff and Roger Owen (Carbondale, IL, 1977); Rifa'at Ali Abou-El-Haj, "The Ottoman Vezir and Pasha Households, 1683–1703: A Preliminary Report," *Journal of the American Oriental Society* 94 (1974): 438–47; Rifa'at Ali Abou-El-Haj, *Formation of the Modern State: Ottoman Empire, 16th to 18th Centuries* (Syracuse, NY, 2005); Leslie Peirce, *The Imperial Harem: Women and Sovereignty in the Ottoman Empire* (New York, 1993); Metin Kunt, *The Sultan's Servants: The Transformation of Ottoman Provincial Government, 1550–1650* (New York, 1983).
8. See Virginia Aksan, "Ottoman Political Writing, 1768–1808," *International Journal of Middle East Studies* 25 (1993): 53–69; Bernard Lewis, *The Muslim Discovery of Europe* (New York, 1982); Cornell Fleischer, *Bureaucrat and Intellectual in the Ottoman Empire: The Historian Mustafa Ali, 1541–1600* (Princeton, NJ, 1986); Abou-El-Haj, *Formation of the Modern State.*
9. Rifa'at Ali Abou-El-Haj, "The Formal Closure of the Ottoman Frontier, 1699–1703," *Journal of the American Oriental Societies* 89 (1969): 467–75.
10. Nicholas Mavrocordatos (1599–1649) was the first to move from his native Chios to Istanbul, and became prominent in the lay service of the Orthodox church there. Alexander *ex aporriton* (minister of secrets) the grand dragoman (1636–1709) was his son and Nicholas (1670–1730), the *voyvoda* of Moldavia and Wallachia, his grandson.
11. Damien Janos, "Panaiotis [*sic*] Nicousios and Alexander Mavrocordatos: The Rise of the Phanariots and the Office of Grand Dragoman in the Ottoman Administration in the Second Half of the Seventeenth Century," *Archivum Ottomanicum* 23 (2005): 189.
12. Sir Stephen Runciman, *Great Church in Captivity: A Study of the Patriarchate of Constantinople from the Even of the Turkish Conquest to the Greek War of Independence* (London, 1968); Janos, "Panaiotis Nicousios," 189. Unfortunately, neither gives us specific evidence as to the nature or implications of this control, nor about the internal workings of these entrepreneurial families.
13. Janos, "Panaiotis Nicousios," 193, without a citation for this information.
14. On the culture and activities of Venetian-Ottoman dragomans, see Ella-Natalie Rothman, "Between Venice and Istanbul: Trans-imperial Subjects and Cultural Mediation in the Early Modern Mediterranean" (PhD diss., University of Michigan, 2006).
15. Maurits H. Van den Boogert, *The Capitulations and the Ottoman Legal System: Qadis, Consuls and Beratlis in the 18th Century* (Leiden, 2005); Ali İhsan Bağış, *Osmanlı Ticaretinde Gayrî Müslimler* [Non-Muslims in Ottoman Commerce], 2nd ed. (Ankara, 1998).
16. For discussions of the range of factors that led to the systematic adoption of Phanariots as dragomans in the eighteenth century, see Janos, "Panaiotis Nicousios," and Christine Philliou, "Worlds Old and New: Phanariot Networks and the Remaking of

Ottoman Governance, 1800–1850" (PhD diss., Princeton University, 2004), chapter 1.

17. The grand dragoman was the interpreter at the Ottoman court. He would facilitate visits to the court by European envoys and would often manage negotiations between the Ottoman state and European states.
18. Janos, "Panaiotis Nicousios," 193.
19. See Metin Kunt, *The Sultan's Servants.*
20. For the ulema, see Madeline Zilfi, *Politics of Piety: The Ottoman Ulema in the Postclassical Age (1600–1800)* (Minneapolis, 1988). For the bureaucracy, see Carter Findley, *Bureaucratic Reform in the Ottoman Empire: The Sublime Porte, 1789–1922* (Princeton, NJ, 1980). For Egypt, see Jane Hathaway, *Politics of Households in Ottoman Egypt: The Rise of the Qazdaglis* (New York, 1997).
21. The term *ayan* varies in meaning between the Arab and non-Arab Ottoman provinces. In the Arab provinces, *ayan* were an "urban elite that occupied the top stratum of local society and acted as mediators between the population and the government. [This elite] existed as an identifiable group as early as the ninth century, and its formation was closely linked to the evolution and functioning of the city in Islamic society and the distinctive political structures in which it was embedded." Margaret Meriwether, *The Kin Who Count: Family and Society in Ottoman Aleppo, 1770–1840* (Austin, TX, 1999), 31. In non-Arab provinces, the term *ayan* signifies a new class that came to power in the late seventeenth century and came to combine formal office and military power and constitute a threat to the power of the central state by the later eighteenth century. Terms such as *hospodar, voyoda,* prince, and bey are interchangeable because they all refer to the same office.
22. Başbakanlık Osmanlı Arşivleri, Istanbul (hereafter BOA) HAT 13754-A.
23. Dionysios Photeinos, *Historia tes Palai Dakias* [History of the Former Dacia], 3 vols. (Vienna, 1819), 3:422.
24. The supplying of the imperial capital and Ottoman troops in the Balkans with grain became ever more important after the loss of Crimea, another major grain supplying region, to Russia in 1783. See Philliou, "Communities on the Verge," 156.
25. BOA HH 13745-A (h. 1216).
26. BOA Eflak/Boğdan Ahkam deftlerleri, various.
27. This seems to have been similar to the pre-1783 arrangement the Ottomans had with the Crimean Khans, although not with the Egyptian households and the *ayans.* See Athanasios Komnenos Hypsilantes, *Ekklesiastikon kai politikon ton eis dodeka biblion E' Th' kai I' etoi Ta Meta ten Alosin (1453–1789)* [Ecclesiastical and Political Events after the Fall of Constantinople in Twelve books] (Athens, 1972), 417.
28. The term *kapikahya/kapikethudas,* meaning "steward" or "scribe," was originally a guild office (*kahya/kethuda*). Guild terminology permeated many areas of Ottoman governance: note references to the Rum *ta'ifesi* above (*ta'ife* meaning guild).
29. See Marc-Philippe Zallony, *Essai sur les Phanariotes, ou l'on voit les causes primitives de leur élévation aux hospodariats de la Valachie et la Moldavie, leur mode d'administration, et les causes principales de leur chute; suivi de quelques réflexions sur l'état actuel de la Grèce* (Marseille, 1824), for an explanation of this system.
30. BOA HAT 13745-A.
31. One of many examples of the ways family relationships were embedded in Phanariot networks: "The old Callimachi, interpreter of the Porte, ceded his place to George Ghika, in order to take the reins of the Moldavian administration (7 August 1758). Ghika, son of the interpreter executed after the Convention of Constantinople, and cousin of the new *voyvoda* of Wallachia, Scarlatos Ghika, competed for this place

with Hypsilanti, physician of the Grand Vezir Raghip Mohammed, who, despite his merit, could not obtain the position." (Joseph Hammer-Purgstall, *Histoire de l'Empire ottoman, depuis son origine jusqu'à nos jours,* 18 vols [Paris, 1835–43], 16:39, cited in Hypsilantis, *Ekklesiastikon kai politikon ton*, 11).

32. See Francis Joseph Steingass, *A Comprehensive Persian-English Dictionary Including the Arabic Words and Phrases to be Met with in Persian Literature* (London, 1892; 1930), 443.
33. Inalcik, "Centralization and Decentralization."
34. For *ayan* in their Balkan and Anatolian contexts, see Bruce McGowan, "The Age of the Ayans, 1699–1812," in *An Economic and Social History of the Ottoman Empire*, 2 vols., ed. Suraiya Faroqhi, Bruce McGowan, Donald Quataert, and Sevket Pamuk (Cambridge, 1994), 2:637–758; Yuzo Nagata, *Tarihte ayanlar: Karaosmanoğulları üzerine bir inceleme* [*Ayans* in History: A Study of the Karaosmanogullari] (Ankara, 1997); Deena Sadat, "Rumeli Ayanlari: The Eighteenth Century," *Journal of Modern History* 44 (1972): 346–63; Robert Zens, "The ayanlik and Pasvanoğlu Osman Paşa of Vidin in the Age of Ottoman Social Change, 1791–1815" (PhD diss., University of Wisconsin-Madison, 2005); Rossitsa Gradeva, "Secession and Revolution in the Ottoman Empire at the End of the Eighteenth Century: Osman Pazvantoglu and Rhigas Velestinlis," in *Ottoman Rule and the Balkans, 1760–1850: Conflict, Transformation, Adaptation; Proceedings of an International Conference Held in Rethymno, Greece, 13–14 December 2003*, ed. Antonis Anastasopoulos and Elias Kolovos (Rethymno, 2007), 73–94; Rossitsa Gradeva, "Osman Pazvantoglu of Vidin: Between Old and New," in *The Ottoman Balkans, 1750–1830*, ed. Frederick F. Anscombe (Princeton, NJ, 2006), 115–62. For *malikane* in eastern Anatolia, see Ariel Salzmann, *Tocqueville in the Ottoman Empire: Rival Paths to the Modern State* (Leiden, 2005); Dina Rizk Khoury, *State and Provincial Society in the Ottoman Empire: Mosul, 1540–1834* (Cambridge, 2002).
35. See chapter 2 in this volume.
36. See Dionysios Photeinos, *Historia tes Palai Dakias.*
37. Halil Inalcik and others provide evidence that Metropolitans were granted *timars* early on, in fourteenth-century Arnavut (Albania) for instance, but it seems that by the sixteenth century the practice of granting *timars* to non-*askeri*, and therefore to Christians, had ceased. While *malikanes* in the seventeenth and eighteenth centuries did not carry with them military obligations, it does not seem that Christians were vying for them at auctions. See Karen Barkey, *Empire of Difference: The Ottomans in Comparative Perspective* (Cambridge, 2008).
38. See Viorel Panaite, *The Ottoman Law of War and Peace: The Ottoman Empire and Tribute-Payers* (New York, 2000).
39. See Nicolae Iorga, *Byzance après Byzance* (Paris, 1992), for a discussion of Orthodox Church connections in the Danubian Principalities.
40. BOA HAT 13745-A.
41. The fascinating point here is that this fact of their being a kind of landed aristocracy is being used to argue for their appointment as resident Ottoman ambassadors to European/Christian states. The writer of the document argues that European societies have always respected aristocratic descent (*hanedanzadelik*) (implying that this is not so much the case in the Ottoman context), and since ambassadors who will command respect in Europe should be appointed, Phanariots are the best candidates for the embassies. BOA HAT 13745-A.
42. Citation from a document in BOA HH 13745-A.

43. See Hathaway, *Politics of Households,* for the Caucasian slave and Anatolian Janissary origins of Egypt's eighteenth-century households.
44. "Ghikas," in *Megale Hellenike Enkyklopaideia* (Athens, 1956–65), 7:448–49.
45. The extent to which these ethnic and geographic origins persisted to influence marriage and factional alliances is unclear. It does seem that in the Phanariot case, exogamy was favored (first- and second-cousin marriage was prohibited in the Orthodox church, which was no doubt a structural incentive for exogamy).
46. Meriwether, *Kin Who Count,* 43.
47. Ibid., 44.
48. Ibid., 50–51.
49. See Abou-El-Haj, "The Ottoman Vezir and Pasha Households," for the same phenomenon among Muslim grandees of the late seventeenth and early eighteenth centuries.
50. Hathaway, *Politics of Households,* 110.
51. See Michael Herzfeld, *The Poetics of Manhood: Contest and Identity in a Cretan Mountain Village* (Princeton, NJ, 1985); John K. Campbell, *Honour, Family, and Patronage: A Study of Institutions and Moral Values in a Greek Mountain Community* (Oxford, 1970). See also Ecumenical Patriarchate of Istanbul archives (EPI), outgoing correspondence to Metropolitan Sees, various, for mention of godparentage among prominent Phanariots, even in the midst of the conflicts of the 1820s.
52. Husrev Paşa was among the most prominent examples, as he himself was bought as a slave in Circassia and then went on to be one of the most powerful of Ottoman statesmen in the late eighteenth and first half of the nineteenth century, installing scores of his slave-progeny in the Ottoman military and bureaucracy. See "Husrev Paşa," in *Islâm ansiklopedisi: Islâ âlemi coğrafya, etnografya ve biyografya lŭgati* [Encyclopedia of Islam: A Geographical, Ethnographical, and Biographical Dictionary of the Islamic World] (Ankara, 1940–1988).
53. See Findley, *Bureaucratic Reform* and *Ottoman Civil Officialdom: A Social History* (Princeton, NJ, 1989).
54. In the present discussion, the role of ideology is effectively excluded. This is in part because it is unclear what role ideology played in determining the outcome of the Greek Revolution in the early nineteenth century, and in part because the evidence of discussions within the Ottoman Empire and among Ottoman Phanariots does not present the split as an ideological one but instead one between loyalty and treachery.
55. See Philliou, "Communities on the Verge," and "Breaking the Tetrarchy and Saving the Kaymakam: To Be an Ambitious Ottoman Christian in 1821," in Anastasopoulos and Kolovos, *Ottoman Rule and the Balkans,* 181–94.
56. BOA Name-i Humayun #989.
57. BOA Name-i Humayun #989, the official document from the Orthodox Christian millet expressing gratitude to the Sultan for the Dynasty of Four Regulation. At the bottom of the document is a list of names, organized hierarchically, of the top officials in the retinue of each of the four *hanedans.*
58. See also Valeriu Veliman, *Relatiile Romano-Otomane 1711–1821: Documente turcesti* (Bucharest, 1984), 753, a published Ottoman document from March 1821 referring to Schinas as the brother-in-law (or son-in-law—*damat*) of the Moldavian hospodar Michael Soutzos and stating that he and his son fled form Istanbul with their possessions.
59. Mihail-Dimitri Sturdza, *Dictionnaire historique et généalogique de grandes familles de Grèce, d'Albanie et de Constantinople* (Paris, 1983), 247.

60. Nicholas Aristarchis would return to Istanbul two years later and start a long career as grand logothete for the Orthodox Patriarchate and Russian-aligned Ottoman court favorite.
61. BOA Cevdet Hariciye #148 (evasit-e Muharrem 1236; November 1820; these boyars were associated with Iskerlet Kallimaki, the hospodar of Wallachia who fled just before insurrections broke out).
62. Epameinondas Stamatiades, *Viographiai ton Hellenon megalon diermeneon tou Othomanikou kratous* [Biographies of the Greek Grand Dragomans of the Ottoman State] (Thessaloniki, 1865; 1973), 165–66.
63. See Spyridon Tricoupes, *Historia tes Hellenikes Epanastaseos* [History of the Greek Revolution], 4 vols. (Athens, 1888; 1968), 2:110–11, for the dissatisfaction of mainland Greeks after encountering their Phanariot potential leaders in 1821. See also John Petropulos, *Politics and Statecraft in the Kingdom of Greece* (Princeton, NJ, 1965).
64. Tricoupes, *Historia*, 2:108 and *passim*.
65. Ibid., 2:109.
66. Others escaped in the early days of the conflict and returned only two years later. In June of 1823 the British consul reported that "many Greeks who had fled to Odessa are now returning to Constantinople and Smyrna." National Archives, Kew Gardens (UK), FO 78/114.
67. "Kallimachis," in *Megale Hellenike Enkyklopaideia*, 17:572.
68. "Mourouzis," in ibid., 18:426.
69. Philliou, *Biography of an Empire*, chapter 5.
70. For their strategies of adaptation to Ottoman reforms emanating from Istanbul, see Albert Hourani, "Ottoman Reform and the Politics of Notables," in *Beginnings of Modernization in the Middle East: The Nineteenth Century, ed.* William R. Polk and Richard L. Chambers (Chicago, 1968), 41–68.

Chapter 10

Into the World

Kinship and Nation Building in France, 1750–1885

Christopher H. Johnson

This chapter examines the paths of several closely related families of Vannes in Brittany, perhaps the least "French" of France's provinces under the Old Regime, as members branched out into the nation. Its key sources are the extensive and untapped manuscript correspondence and journals from within these families.[1] As a chapter in this collection on transnational families, it serves as a reminder that while the emergent nation-state and national economies of the eighteenth and nineteenth centuries gradually brought an end to the transnational roles of aristocratic court-service dynasties and reoriented the transnational functions of families in business, another phenomenon, the growth of trans*regional* families in territorial entities that were only putatively "national" states during the early modern era, was the common bond that made the nation in human terms.[2] Here is another primordial function of kinship that historians tend to overlook. To have siblings, cousins, uncles and aunts, nephews and nieces deployed across the nation, but especially in Paris; to depend on them to advance your economic interests and deal with the legal entanglements; to have them directly serving the French nation in military or civil functions in such distant places; and to interact with family members and their associates in the French artistic and intellectual community: these were the sinews of nationhood that kinship gave life to. Although there is little doubt that people of substance and education became the most "national" of Frenchmen in the nineteenth century, it should not be forgotten that the common people sent their relatives hither and yon in huge numbers—some returning home, some not, including thousands of Breton-speaking peasants for service and common labor in Paris and elsewhere.[3] Historians who offer political, institutional, or ideological explanations of the forging of France (or any other modern nation-state) tell only part of the story.[4] For France was a nation of immigrants, not just from abroad, but from its provinces, who became more alike without losing many of their distinctive characteristics, a reality that contemporary French culture celebrates.[5]

The analysis centers on the kinship grid of the Galles, Jollivet, and Le Ridant families, but is supplemented by an examination of exogamous marriages and the relocation of other members of Vannes' bourgeois elite during the first three quarters of the nineteenth century. The original stimulus for this study was the realization that these families seemed to reserve at least one marriage with someone from elsewhere while also emphasizing close, often consanguineous, unions for a majority of their children.[6] Those venturing into the nation added luster to their hometowns by their accomplishments, while integrating into the society of their new environments. Simultaneously, those remaining to manage their natal *pays*' businesses, estates, and civic affairs flourished all the more by virtue of the exchanges of economic, social, and cultural capital that families' spreading wings articulated. The "pride of place" so characteristic of nineteenth-century local life would not have taken on the dimensions that it did without this interaction animated by kinship networks. Local pride and national pride grew together.[7]

Under the Ancien Régime, Vannes was Brittany's "second city" politically (after Rennes) and a stronghold of loyalty to the crown. Its economy combined administration with landholding and a weakening commerce in grain. Vannes' bourgeoisie inhabited two worlds, a region where a majority of the population spoke Breton and a city that was culturally French. If in the mid-eighteenth century their horizons extended to others like themselves across the province, their actual connections with France at large were limited.[8] How these ordinary bourgeois joined the nation and its repercussions for their ordinary city is the story I want to tell.[9]

Prologue: First Steps

Three families, Galles, Jollivet, and Le Ridant, who came together in a double wedding in 1787, are at its heart. The first made their fortune

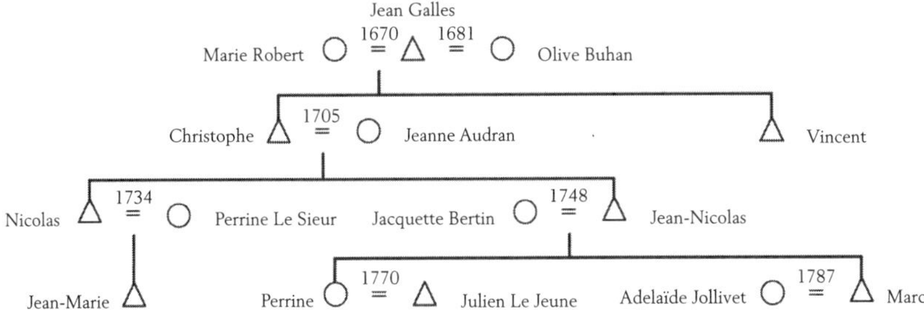

Figure 10.1. Galles kinship diagram.

in publishing, establishing by 1750 the largest firm in Lower Brittany mainly by printing for the renowned secondary school of Vannes, for the church, and for the government. Its first three generations benefited from advantageous marriages of talented printers with the daughters of rivals and finally with a distant cousin of bishop Jean-Charles de Bertin.[10] The other two came from substantial *roturier* farming stock whose sons at mid-century became *notaires* in Vannes, a profitable profession in an era of remarkable turnover in land.[11]

Jean-Nicolas Galles and Jacquette Bertin sought to expand their operations by opening a branch in Paris, initiating the families' first foray into the nation and a typical path for ambitious provincials. Their key contacts in the capital were Michel and Claude Audran IV, Galles' second cousins who at the time were the most revered and influential of the artists at the famed Gobelins tapestry works.[12] In 1760, they had saved Jean-Nicolas from prosecution for selling false lottery tickets, while introducing him to the key figures of the world of print, including the chief censor, Chrétien de Malesherbes.[13] Their nephew, Jean-Marie Galles, was selected to run the Paris business and did so with excellent results, living at first with the Audrans (whom he referred to as "Les Gobelins" in his correspondence) and exploiting all their connections.[14] Kinship did its work. Unfortunately, although young Galles succeeded sufficiently to rise to the rank of "Bourgeois de Paris," he did not found a collateral line of the family because he never married—for reasons that remain obscure—despite the fervent urging of his family back home.[15] During the Revolution, the Paris business declined rapidly, while that in Vannes did well even though the Galles family remained constitutional monarchists.[16] Jean-Marie retreated to more politically hospitable Orleans.[17] The family's first transregional endeavor was thus still born. Nevertheless, by the 1780s both Marc Galles and his mother were among the wealthiest bourgeois of Vannes, their firm clearly benefiting from Jean-Marie's work in Paris.[18]

With the disappointment over Jean-Marie's "celibacy," Galles and Son, mainly in the hands of Jean-Nicolas's widow, Jacquette, after his death in 1763, settled for regional connections. The matriarch convinced her daughter Perrine to marry Julien Le Jeune, heir to the largest publishing house of Lorient, in 1770. It turned out to be a disaster. Le Jeune was a classic old-regime wastrel—a gambler and a drunk—and it was not long before Perrine was back in Vannes with her daughter Angelique in tow. The latter was bravely betrothed to a printer of Saint-Brieuc, J.-P. Prud'homme, whose house, happily, became the major publisher in that growing city on the north Breton coast. It had strong reciprocal relations with the Imprimerie Galles.[19]

Meanwhile, Marc Galles pursued another form of national integration for the French speakers of Vannes: building cultural capital. He too had made the rounds of Paris and studied art and philosophy. Upon his return, he encouraged his mother to maintain the reins of the business, allowing him to combine civic duties with his love of the arts. Although details are sketchy, he brought together an informal circle of artists and intellectuals in Vannes, later enhanced by correspondents in Rennes and Paris. The men of this circle around the "Imprimeur-humaniste de Vannes" were variously related by kinship and could count on the hospitality of "les Gobelins" in Paris.[20] They formed a cultural nucleus that in the next generation would form Vannes' influential Société polymathique du Morbihan. Marc's son, Jean-Marie, was its founder in 1826, and his grandsons and nephews led scholarship that brought it to national prominence.

Act One: The Rise of the Jollivets and the Le Ridants

It is commonly understood that the French Revolution did more to create "the nation," not only in France but also in much of the world, than

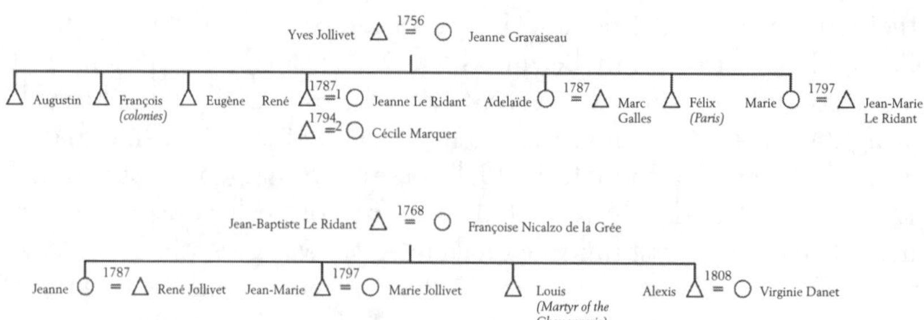

Figure 10.2. Kinship diagrams: The rise of the Jollivets and the Le Ridants.

any other single event.[21] For the Morbihan and much of Brittany, however, the centralization, standardization, and rationalization of government and infrastructure, the end of a society of orders, and the eclipse of the Bourbon monarchy were widely resisted, even if they were generally welcomed by the Francophone bourgeoisie. The guerilla revolt known as the Chouannerie arising after the declaration of the republic in 1792 was rooted in the countryside, led by nobles, a few bourgeois landowners, and village priests, and fought by Breton-speaking peasants.[22] The Janus face of the region now took the shape of *les bleus* versus *les blancs*. If our families and their widening kin networks ranged on both sides, the Galles/Jollivet/Le Ridant core remained royalists, though most were *constitutionnels*. Jean-Marie and Louis Le Ridant, however, became field leaders in the Chouannerie. Vannes embraced the Revolution, but support waned as it radicalized. The overall political atmosphere in the city was cautious and thoroughly moderate, whichever side one was on, and citizens readily adapted to the successive regimes that followed the Terror. Several figures in the kinship universe of the families considered here took significant positions in local government before 1815, but, with a slight nudge to the right, many did so afterwards as well. Politics had little bearing on marriage decisions, as the bourgeois elite of Vannes merged by the 1830s into a kind of Orleanist blur. Family, service, and power, not political ideology, motivated them.[23]

Although a handful of Vannetais played briefly on the national stage during the Revolution and empire, it was in the years after Waterloo that the "nationalization" of the city's bourgeoisie occurred, largely the work of men and women from the royalist camp rewarded for their loyalty to the Bourbons. Few were Ultras, thus allowing them and their descendants to segue smoothly as regimes changed. Among them were Galleses, Jollivets, and Le Ridants, several of whom, over three generations, came to play important roles on the national stage. Although all were male, their opportunities were enhanced by key women, thus continuing the work of Olive Buhan and Jacquette Bertin. And for all, despite the mythology of the "self-made man" and "careers open to talent," family ties always made a difference.

Before his marriage to Jeanne Le Ridant, René Jollivet seemed on track toward a career in wholesale commerce. But after a stint in Lorient, in mid-1786 an opportunity to seek a government position in Paris arose. His father's most prized client was the Marquise de Sérent, whose husband was "all-powerful and very well placed at Court, being the *gouverneur des princes* [the sons of Louis XVI] [and] the sole Breton able to obtain entry" for René. For her part, the marquise served as wardrobe manager for the royal sister, Madame Elizabeth, and developed a special relationship with the king's only daughter, Marie-Thérèse-Charlotte, who spent many hours with her stylish aunt.[24] René went to Paris and stayed with J.-B. Michel, a cousin of local businessmen. While waiting for a position to open up, René took a job with a *notaire* and enrolled in courses in law, which he enjoyed, though he feared that he "would cut a sad figure at the bar," an amusing comment in light of his future.[25] Although he visited all the sights, René was not dazzled by Europe's greatest capital. Paris seemed "bespotted with mud," with "horrible traffic" that made him late for appointments. Finally, a solid position in the Ministry of Justice arose. Mme De Sérent wrote a letter on his behalf, and an audience with the marquis was arranged. On the appointed day in January, René traveled to Versailles, but the great man was nowhere to be found. René kept his request afloat, continued to study the judicial system assiduously, but then, on 19 February 1787, abruptly informed his father that he was returning to Vannes to take his license in law.

René's first foray into the world thus ended unsuccessfully, an example, undoubtedly, of a majority of provincial bourgeois making the quest. It appears that one reason was Jeanne-Marie Le Ridant, whose one surviving letter to him speaks of their love.[26] René and Jeanne married—along with his sister Adelaïde and Marc Galles—just two months after his return. René would thus pursue a more mundane path to success, following in his father's footsteps as a *notaire*, adding his law license, becoming a landed proprietor, and extending his families' reputation.[27]

Their critical connection remained, despite the snub by her husband, the Marquise de Sérent. She grew even closer to the royal children after their parents were executed, visiting them regularly in the Temple until the death of young Louis "XVII," after which Marie-Thérèse, then seventeen, was to be released to the Austrians in Basel. Mme de Sérent was her choice for a companion, but the Republican officials rejected her, fearing a plot. They later reunited, and Sérent, elevated to duchesse, became her *dame d'honneur*. "Madame Royale," who married her eldest cousin, the duc d'Angoulême (after patriotically refusing the Austrian archduke), became a Bourbon hero, the last fragile link to their murdered monarch. With the Restoration, she emerged as a power in the court. And Louis XVIII himself had a fatherly fondness for her lady-in-waiting.[28]

She was, of course, little help during the Revolution and Empire, and René Jollivet made his way largely on his own, working hard for his clients, while benefiting himself en route. The loss of Jeanne to childbed fever in 1792 was recouped two years later by his marriage to Cécile Marquer. Her brother had emigrated and, in a move typical in the royalist world, René Jollivet had bought his "chateau" overlooking the Auray river for the ridiculous price of 1,285 francs on the promise to sell it back upon his return. But for now, the family had a superb residence, from which Cécile wrote her only surviving letter during a ball celebrating the second anniversary of the fall of Robespierre.[29] René bought a number of *biens nationaux* and negotiated the sale of many others, all with an eye to returning them with the anticipated restoration of the Bourbons. Needless to say, all were not repurchased, leaving *notaires* like Jollivet and Le Ridant vastly richer than they were at the beginning of the Revolution.[30] In all respects, young Jollivet had positioned himself brilliantly in the regard of potentially powerful people, while at the same time doing nothing to alienate himself from the current powers, at least once the clouds of the Quiberon disaster had passed.[31] René's sister Adelaïde Galles, writing in 1796 to their brother in Martinique, reported on René's happy marriage and their expected baby:

> You can see that his family is growing, though perhaps not at the same rate as his means of raising it. Nevertheless, he does well and would do better if he were less softhearted and more *intéressé*. He enjoys a reputation fit to satisfy the most ambitious of men of his status. He even has celebrity. … He has worked very hard and continues to do so without relaxing. It is time that he gathers the fruits of it.[32]

And gather he would.

Adelaïde also had something to say about their youngest sister. Marie-Joseph was a bit mercurial and self-absorbed, but very bright, and "more striking than pretty." Nineteen years old, she was engaged to Jean-Marie Le Ridant, who had now foresworn his Chouan connections (having miraculously survived the post-Quiberon executions) and would soon make his career as an officer in the imperial army. He never hid his royalist sympathies, but was a French patriot and willing to fight for the nation. Only when Napoleon proposed the Russian campaign of 1812 did Le Ridant withdraw his support and was imprisoned until the advent of the First Restoration. Like all of the family, he supported the Bourbons during the One Hundred Days, serving as the liaison with England, while his nephew Eugène Galles fought with the revitalized Chouan army in Brittany.[33] Jean-Marie thus remained an honorable royalist while his brother-in-law Jollivet defended the rights and lands of émigrés. But it was Marie Jollivet Le Ridant who had entered the society of the non-émigré royalists in Paris, where her husband was stationed when not on the battlefield. The prestige of Mme de Sérent opened doors for her, but her own vibrant personality won her a place in this world. She endured her husband's imprisonment with patience and basked in the glory that his resistance to the "tyrant" brought to their name.[34]

The fact that Marie and Jean-Marie had no children meant that she focused her attention on her nieces and nephews. This became all the more imperative in light of the continuing history of tragedy that beset these families. Her sister Adelaïde died in 1797, leaving behind six children, ranging from two to eleven. Marc Galles never recovered from the blow and passed away early in 1801. Although the house continued to print as "Les Enfants Galles" under grandmother Jacquette's direction, the affairs of these children became the official responsibility of Uncle René Jollivet, their guardian. But he himself had lost his "dear Cécile" the previous year. He would marry again (to Désirée Kercado) in 1802. René had five children in the same age range (he would have six more with Désirée), and his male siblings were flung far and wide, pioneer cosmopolites of this family.[35] Thus "Aunt Marie" at an early age became the obvious female friend and role model for the entire brood of her departed sister as well as those of her brother René. In 1804, she and Jean-Marie bought an estate not far from Auray called Pont-Sal. It provided a wonderful country environment for all the children, who lived as "brothers and sisters" in Vannes since the Galles and Jollivet houses were virtually contiguous. Even if Marie was not there, the families were always welcome, and memories of Pont-Sal fill their writings. Aunt Marie was their glamorous link to the world of Tout-Paris. She became the source of information about politics and international affairs. Her opinions with regard to the royalist cause came from the inside. All in the family came to idolize Madame Royale as well as her uncle Louis. When he took the throne, Marie became the kingpin of the families' destiny.

René Jollivet shared his sister's passion for the cause, but had been more circumspect with his opinions locally and blended amicably with the imperial officials, while keeping up with the royalist program via correspondence and frequent visits with Marie. As one of the wealthier commoners in Vannes (he too had a country house, called Truhélin, in nearby Arradon), René could not be denied a spot on the imperial city council. Then, bouncing from a top position with the First Restoration to a principled opponent of the One Hundred Days, he was selected in the Second Restoration as president of the electoral college of Vannes' arrondissement. Following the vision of Louis XVIII, the city labored to bring reconciliation and peace to its divided inhabitants, including a parade uniting young men who fought on both sides in the "Chouannerie of 1815." Jollivet's presidential address carried the same message: "Let no prejudice, no memory, no preoccupation with the past place obstacles before the reestablishment of mutual confidence." Jollivet was one of two commoners among the six men elected from the Morbihan to the famous "Chambre inouïble," where he and three others resisted the Ultra-royalist majority.[36] He would be returned to the more moderate chamber of 1817, but lost to the Ultras in 1819. Louis XVIII did not forget his loyalty, appointing him *procureur-général* of Angers (the top judicial post overseeing several départements), which he held until the Ultras took full control of the government in 1821. René Jollivet was thus the first in the family to carry the standard of the Breton bourgeoisie onto the national stage. Talented as he may have been, his sister's crucial friendships certainly did not hurt.

Act Two: Eugène Galles, Adèle Jollivet, and the Post-Revolutionary Generation

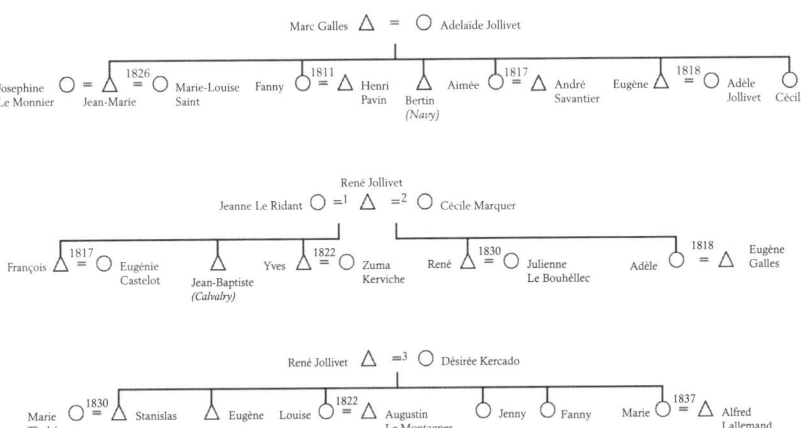

Figure 10.3. Kinship diagrams: Eugène Galles, Adèle Jollivet, and the post-Revolutionary generation.

After his service in 1815, Jean-Marie Le Ridant was soon appointed *chef de bataillon* in the Royal Army. His military career had stimulated the dreams of his nephews, and they were not alone among young bourgeois in Vannes. The city's best-known imperial officer, General de Bonté, ennobled by Napoleon and married to an aristocrat, added further inspiration.[37] Bertin and Eugène Galles, as well as Jean-Baptiste and René Jollivet, all became career officers, trained (save René) at Saint-Cyr and recommended by their uncle. Jean-Baptiste, the oldest, was a cavalry officer, Eugène went to the infantry, while Bertin and René chose the navy.[38] All fought for the Empire in its last days. Eugène spent his leaves with his Aunt Marie in Paris and was introduced to her influential network.[39] Jean-Marie Galles took full charge of the publishing house with the death of his grandmother when he was eighteen (1808), becoming "Galles," the head of the family. In 1811, his eldest sister Fanny married Henri Pavin, a distant relative and bureaucrat from Redon. Although the couple had spent time together on family outings along the banks of the Vilaine, it was Aunt Marie who made the arrangements and gave the final blessing. This was the first of many: none of this generation (or the following one) married without her input and approval. She was the family doyenne, a striking example of the pivotal role played by women, many of them aunts, not only in orchestrating marriage and inheritance decisions, but in enhancing their kinfolk's place in the larger world.[40] And in this, they were full participants in the process of nation building.

The closeness of the Galles/Jollivet siblings was not at all unusual in this age.[41] A culture of consanguinity was emerging, where "mari, cousin, frère" could be uttered in the same breath.[42] This world of horizontal kin connection and familial intimacy underlay a process of consolidation of bourgeois social, economic, and political power on the local and regional level, as close and homogamous marriage created a broad *cousinage* uniting the elite. And nobles, though rarely marrying bourgeois, often attended their weddings and joined them in civil society, thus forming a personally connected notability.[43] The Galleses and Jollivets participated fully in this local process of bourgeois class formation. The union of cousins Adéle Jollivet and Eugène Galles (1818), who had "loved each other all their lives as brother and sister," was the key event reconsolidating these families. Aunt Marie approved and simultaneously arranged Aimée Galles' marriage to André Savantier, a family friend from Auray. Bertin, alas, died at sea the same year, 1817. "Galles" married distant relative Josephine Le Monnier in 1822, then her cousin Marie-Louise Saint in 1826 after yet another postchildbirth death.[44] Jollivet males wed nonrelatives, though wives from Republican backgrounds, further homogenizing this elite.[45] Only François Jollivet, the eldest, married out—to a Lorient merchant's daughter, Eugénie Castelot, in 1819.[46]

This generation therefore stayed close to home, following the lead of their parents. But, among the males, only the heads of the family, Jean-Marie Galles and Yves Jollivet, actually built their lives in Vannes, taking command of the family fortunes there, while the rest went "into the world."[47] And unlike René Jollivet I, whose national stature was rooted firmly in his local roles, they played out their careers in the larger nation, most of them in its service. The following generation became even more "national," though no one in either, except possibly unmarried Jean-Baptiste Jollivet, forgot that they were Vannetais.

Eugène and Adèle Galles corresponded weekly during his long periods on duty as an infantry officer. Their letters open a window on one route into the nation. After the Napoleonic epic, even in defeat, soldiers, symbols of glory, were held in the highest regard. Royalists like Le Ridant and Galles emerged during the Restoration with added luster. Nobles might be favored over *roturiers* in recruitment and advancement, but Eugène never mentions being passed over because of his social status.[48] Indeed, he only notes one snub in all his letters. His aunt Marie, bridging both worlds, laid out her program for him.

The earliest example of her work came in the summer of 1817. Eugène was at that time assigned to Belle Ile off the coast from Vannes, making the courtship with Adèle easy and romantic.[49] Jean-Marie Le Ridant was between assignments and living in Paris with his wife. The Belle Ile base was about to close, and Le Ridant awaited a satisfactory post. So Aunt Marie swung into action, inviting Eugène to Paris to show him off. The command of the Loiret legion was available, and Le Ridant sought that promotion. Eugène might be placed as a captain under his uncle. Marie arranged dinners and balls, and it made sense that Eugène should have a beautiful (and politically connected) young woman on his arm. Thus did Adèle Jollivet come to Paris in July. Love bloomed and society swooned: a woman in the next box at the opera sighed that the young couple "came out of a novel."[50] The plan worked perfectly. The positions secured, uncle and nephew would be stationed in pleasantly conservative Orléans after the wedding in June 1818.

Eugène's routine involved military exercises with his men and endless meetings. His own quarters were spacious and the mess food good, but he had a social life far beyond that. As legion commander, uncle Ridant lived in a fine townhouse and, to the envy of Eugène, could have his wife by his side while on duty. Mme Le Ridant was fully in her element, arranging soirées with officers, public officials, and Orléannais high society. Eugène, a guest invited everywhere, was impressed by the charm of his hostesses (though not by their husbands) and seemed oblivious to their social status. Politics did make a difference, but the young man chose his words carefully.[51] Galles thus honed his social skills among the elite, noble and bourgeois, of this major city. Contacts for the future abounded as his aunt paved the way.

At the same time, he and his fellow officers, because of their mobility, acted as agents tying the national elite together, a fact little emphasized by historians. The crises unfolding from the assassination of the duc de Berry in 1820 to the French invasion of liberal Spain in 1823 took Le Ridant and his legion north to secure those borders as the main body of the French army marched south. Wherever they went, whether Paris or Valenciennes, the same reception awaited them. Aunt Marie also had time to promote, successfully, the career of her nephew René Jollivet by making the appropriate *démarches* (solicitations) in the Parisian offices of the Marine. In August 1824, Le Ridant's regiment was reassigned to Brest—and the time for socializing was over. He, his nephew, and their men were slated for Guadeloupe to fortify the Antilles. Marie remained in Paris, seeking rapid action on Eugène's promotion to *chef de bataillon* in recompense, perhaps, for this rugged assignment, but, in the name of military honor, she did not try to forestall his deployment. Adèle, however, desperately wrote her stepmother Désirée in Paris to ask Mme de Sérent to use her influence on Eugène's behalf, but to no avail. Things evolved so rapidly that Eugène barely had time to see Adèle and his growing family before he and his uncle shipped out on 10 December 1824. Marie bravely joined them later, her influence spent. Many letters of news and love crossed the Atlantic until the fateful one from Aunt Marie arrived in November 1825: "Pleure, mon enfant, pleure. Tu as perdu le meilleur mari qui existait, peut-être, sur la terre [Weep, my child, weep. You have lost the best husband who perhaps ever existed on this earth]."[52] Adèle's life transformed, and Marie's first grand project came to an end.

Act Three: The Triumphs of General René Galles and His Generation

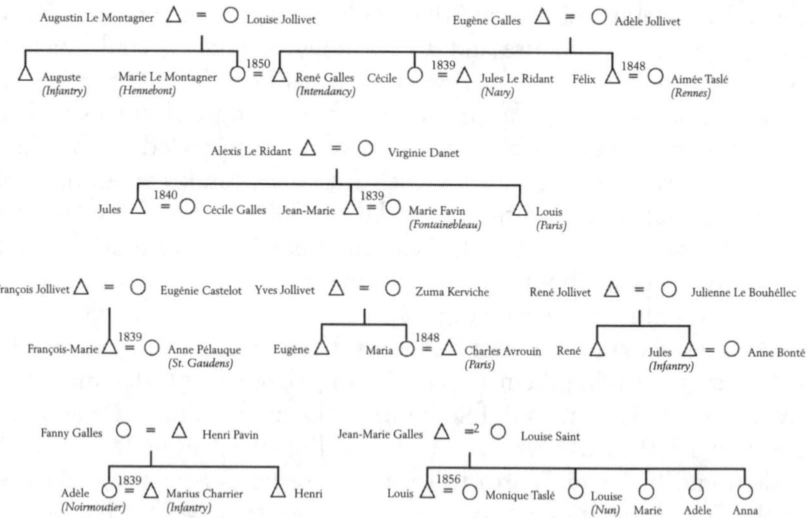

Figure 10.4. Kinship diagrams: The triumphs of General René Galles and his generation.

The widow had three children, René, age six; Cécile, four; and Félix (whom his father held but once), one. Aunt Marie now showered her attention on them, especially the eldest. She set up a secret trust that would assure René's education and provide him with the funds necessary for his establishment. Eugène's thwarted future would now be René's. Marie had the family live with her at Pont Sal until Adèle had had enough of her domination, which she thought was harming the children's development.[53] Adèle, well educated herself, taught René at home until he went to an elite *pension*, followed by a year at the Collège de Vannes. At the age of ten, René was admitted to the Collège Royale in Nantes, the best military preparatory school in the west, where he remained at the top of his class. All was quietly financed from René's trust.

Adèle's letters to her son and his memoirs provide a Bildungsroman about the families' most successful figure in the nation and a window on his entire generation's progress beyond the confines of their *pays*.[54] Adèle's love for and expectations of Eugène transferred to her son; she did not remarry. She did what she could to provide the boy with a father figure, finally settling on her brother René, who wrote his godson stirring letters about hard work and intestinal fortitude. But he had his own growing family to worry about and was captain of a formidable warship out of Lorient. René Jollivet II rewarded his nephew's high marks with visits shipboard and as the new *gentilhomme* of Truhélin saw to it that René spent delightful summers there with his siblings and cousins.[55] But in the end, it was the boy's father's memory, evoked in many ways by his mother as a shining light on his pathway to success (as well as an occasional source of guilt when he stumbled), that served best.

In fact, Adèle herself became the father, both uncompromising taskmaster and best friend. And as mother, she swore unconditional love and forgiveness of René's foibles. Regarding the latter, his aunt Marie and other worried about his *légèreté*, characterized as a lack of seriousness and a far too eclectic range of interests, which often caused him to lose focus. Adèle defended him, emphasizing that a person of his intelligence and sensitivity would naturally have catholic tastes and vary his levels of concentration. René wrote a good deal about his relative disinterest in mathematics and science, generally preferring literature, philosophy, and history, and his mother's understanding made him all the more determined to succeed in the former. He knew (and was regularly reminded) that if he did not master them, he would not be admitted to the École Polytechnique and thus qualify for a brilliant military career, both of which were slated for him from the beginning. Adèle paid for extra tutoring in mathematics, though the subject still held him up as he fell short on his first admission examination for the école. René then was admitted to the famous Pension Bourdon in Paris, financed by his aunt and facilitated by Parisian contacts of uncle Yvon Jollivet. This special year of intense advanced study won him entrance into what was at the time (1837) the grandest of the Grandes Écoles.[56] René did well on his exams and was ranked a remarkable fourth in the nation in philosophy and mathematics by Auguste Comte.[57] He got the word of his triumph in "une enveloppe à grand cachet rouge." Emotions ran high in Vannes, with tears of joy from Cécile and Félix, who "would not have traded their brother for Charlemagne," a moment of fulfillment with *tante* Le Ridant, and raptures of joy from Adèle: "Thus my beloved mother had succeeded; for it was her, much more than myself, who had guided me, not without pain, to the realization of her precious project."[58]

Initially, most of his friends in his entering class were fellow Bretons, participants in the flood of young men from the provinces to reach the pinnacle of academic achievement and a place in the elite of the nation. The Morbihan ranked, over the century, in the upper third of departments sending their sons to the école, but few came from the far-west Finistère. Overall, the entrance of Bretons into the elite of the nation, at least as measured by the "anciens elèves" of the École Polytechnique, was modest, but significant. But the École Polytechnique was a melting pot, probably the central institution, along with the École Normale Supérieure, in the forging of a national haute bourgeoisie, and young Galles rapidly shed his Breton label.[59] The school, selecting at random, ensured that students from diverse geographical and social origins interacted in housing and study units called *salles d'étude,* which often formed lifelong friendships. René Galles understood well how the école shaped an integrated national elite. His "society" in later life, inaugurated in his *salle d'étude,* would be that of his fellow *polytechniciens* and their various circles: nearly all of the men of his promotion when they met for their fiftieth reunion were "general officers or occupying the highest levels in the hierarchy of civil careers," both within the government and in the private sector.[60]

At the école, René did very well, enjoying most his studies in the humanities, but letting science and engineering slide. Adèle reminded him of his destiny in no uncertain terms: "[Your] distaste for the sciences concerns me a great deal. But I count on your reason and good sense. You are in a position that is the object of envy of many people. You must achieve a high rank in the school. You have to keep this alone in mind." She softened the stricture by pointing out to him that a high rank would open the way toward rapid success in the military and hence make it easier "to give vent to your taste for literature, which I personally find delightful."[61] René kept his nose to the grindstone. His final exams placed him in position to garner nomination for his second choice (after the Marine, to his family's relief) as an artillery officer, where advanced math and science were essential.[62] He had also become integrated into Parisian society via contacts of his great-uncle and aunt, who adapted easily to Orleanism after 1830, and various cousins there in other pursuits. *Polytechniciens* themselves held a special place in Parisian life during the July Monarchy, having helped to bring it into being and watch-dogging its progress thereafter. René Galles was a convert to the secular *juste milieu*, to the consternation of his more religious mother, and retained throughout his life a philosophical outlook allowing him to adapt easily to the changing fashions of French politics. In this, he was quite typical of the national elite of which he became a part.

After artillery school in Metz and a whirlwind of posts from Fez to Paris by 1848, he moved on to various ordinance commands before being tapped for the intendancy. This was the army corps reserved only for officers of higher rank whose functions were largely administrative, overseeing finances and pay, provisioning, outfitting, transport, housing, marches, and field encampments. A brilliant manager, René rose quickly through the ranks, serving as *sous-intendant militaire* (to his delight in Vannes from 1862 to 1869), then *intendant militaire* in Algeria through the period of the Franco-Prussian War (thus untainted by the scandalous mismanagement that many blamed for the French defeat at Sedan) and at Nantes during the seventies, finally becoming an *intendant général* in Paris before his retirement in 1880. At all posts, the regular hours allowed him to pursue his true passion, historical and archeological research, and serve as president on several occasions of learned societies, precisely fulfilling his departed mother's vision.

René Galles's combination of state service and academic achievement was perhaps his extended family's most inspiring story in the journey of Vannetais bourgeois into the world. But there were many others. His brother Félix studied law in Paris and Rennes and embarked on a career in the Ministry of Justice, culminating in a *procureur-generalship* and then a place in the Cour de Cassation shortly before his death in 1870. He was aided in this pursuit by Stanislas Jollivet, first *conseiller* of the Cour d'Appel of Rennes by 1846, who not only facilitated his placement in the judiciary, but also served as go-between for his marriage into the Taslé family, powerful figures in civil society and politics across Brittany. François-Marie Jollivet-Castelot, moved from Vannes' city council to mayor during the Second Republic and to the Corps Législatif thereafter before he was struck down by an early death in 1854. Jules Jollivet, a Saint-Cyrien, became a general in the infantry, heading the mission in Algeria in the late sixties, and was a key figure in the renovation of the military during the Third Republic. Louis Le Ridant, Alexis's son, rose to prominence as a Parisian lawyer and was René Galles' closest confidant in the capital. His brother Jules, another Saint-Cyrien, in 1840 wed Cécile Galles over the opposition of Aunt Marie, who took revenge by cutting her out of her will.[63] Young Ridant was on his way to a brilliant career in the Navy when he too died at sea. Jules Jollivet remembered fondly Adèle and Cécile, "the two gracious widows, mother and daughter" at the family gatherings at Truhélin. The third Ridant brother, Jean-Marie, went on to a career in Paris in the high echelons of the postal service. Jules Trochu was a cousin by marriage and one of Adèle's favorite visitors.[64] A decorated hero of the Algerian, Crimean, and Italian wars, he was also a highly regarded military analyst, reformer, and anonymous author of a critical study of the army of the Second Empire.[65] Trochu had the misfortune of being the military commandant of Paris and interim head of government during the darkest days of the Siege and the Commune.[66] Adolphe Billault was Josephine Le Monnier's cousin. He made his career in law in Nantes and became a moderate republican politician, then appointed minister of the interior by Napoleon III before his death in 1863.[67] These kinfolk only begin the list of Vannetais whose state service carried the banner of their home town into the nation. They usually could count on relatives and friends wherever they went, more so indeed than pioneers like Eugène Galles.

Participation in intellectual and cultural pursuits was equally important. The city would claim one of the most active and influential learned societies in the nation, the Société Polymathique du Morbihan (SPM), founded by Jean-Marie Galles in 1826.[68] Like its many counterparts elsewhere, the work of society members was largely local and often practical.[69] But from the beginning it benefited significantly from the input of people from elsewhere who usually came to the city with administrative or academic appointments.[70] Such people also entered the social and political life of the city, enhancing a cosmopolitan atmosphere that encouraged an outward gaze among the natives. Becoming national was thus a two-way street. As the nineteenth century advanced with improving communications and ever-growing administrative and educational integration, so too did this interactive process.

After establishing a reputation in biology and paleontology in one of the most ecologically complex regions in Europe, the SPM made a lasting mark in prehistorical archeology for its work on the hundreds of nearby tumuli and megaliths, above all at Carnac.[71] The research was spearheaded by René and Louis Galles and culminated in proof that these monuments, like Stonehenge, predated the Celts, much to the disappointment of the noble-led *bretonniste* movement, whose glorification of the "Celtic race" contributed to the backward-looking antinational and antiurban conservatism that pervaded rural Brittany.[72] The SPM membership, though not class-bound and comfortable with a Breton identity, nevertheless exhibited strong support for Third Republic educational reforms and other aspects of French patriotism of the era. Its various historical studies delved into the Breton and Catholic past, but sought to integrate them into the national network of *monuments historiques* designated by the centralized Comité des travaux historiques. In all this, SPM members participated in building the nation culturally through their research locally. They were also widely connected with other learned societies, corresponding with seventy-five in France and ten internationally in 1885, the last year of René Galles' presidency.[73]

The nature of the membership of the SPM had changed dramatically by 1885 as well. Although old, kin-connected Vannes families—Galles, Taslé, Le Mené, De la Gillardaie, Lallemand, Burgault, Huchet—were well represented, compared to the rolls of the 1840s and fifties, their numbers were dwarfed by men from elsewhere, but many of whom had married there. Among the latter was secretary Léon Lallement, a lawyer and member since 1877, whose father Jean, also a lawyer, came to Vannes with his family in 1833 from Guérande (Loire-Inf.) and was appointed mayor by Napoleon III from 1854 to 1869. Leon married into the prestigious Caradec family. The SPM had been constantly renewed by talented outsiders, while sons and daughters of its indigenous members relocated and often married elsewhere, nevertheless often retaining nonresident status in the society. As time passed, more and more members of both types had no obvious roots in Vannes, a fact underlining its "national" character.

Kinship and Nation Building

The SPM, comprising mostly men of elite status in the city or elsewhere, was a microcosm of the shifting relationship of Vannes to the nation at large, one in which its leading citizens were thoroughly integrated into a national bourgeoisie. Marriages continued to take place among locals and indeed among relatives, but also reached out across the land. It is this combination of endogamy and exogamy within the same families that needs emphasis, because it appears to be the classic nineteenth-century pattern, especially among the *classes dirigeantes.*

To actually plot this process in detail, even for the Vannetais influx and diaspora, would require research throughout France and another book. But my careful analysis of marriages among the city's bourgeois elite in the first half of the century can make some suggestions about it. The critical point is that most families, all in practicing close or at least endogamous marriage for most of their children, seem to reserve at least one either with someone from beyond the Vannes orbit now resident in the city or with someone residing beyond that orbit.[74] And such marriages became more frequent as time went by.

Our families illustrate the phenomenon. Once established in the city, the first generations married almost exclusively among Vannes natives (including those emigrating to the colonies), though Jacquette Bertin Galles valiantly sought regional printing alliances. The children of Marc Galles and René Jollivet, if not all marrying locally, still married close by to family friends. The first-cousin marriage (Eugène and Adèle) and other close unions (Jean-Marie's) occurred as well. Only François Jollivet branched out to the Castelots of Lorient. In the next generation, five cousin marriages took place, but were joined by six important exogamous unions: Jollivet-Castelot to Anne Pélauque, whose father was a career customs inspector, now division chief in Vannes; Adèle Pavin to Marius Charrier, an architect from Noirmoutier who came to Vannes as its chief city planner; Jean-Marie Le Ridant II to Marie Favin, the daughter of a deceased elite army officer and born in Fontainbleau who came to Vannes with her uncle, a tax official; Maria Jollivet to Charles Avrouin, born in Paris, whose father was the head of Morbihan tax services and an SPM activist; and the marriages to the Taslé sisters, nieces of the mayor of Vannes, daughters of an appeals court judge in Rennes, by Félix Galles and Louis Galles.

This inward-outward character of provincial bourgeois ascendancy was replicated by many other families in Vannes and no doubt throughout the nation. We can document them briefly with the following families.

Marriages (1800–1852) and Career Paths (to 1880) of Vannetais Elite Families[75]

Name	**Endogamous[76]**	**Career(s)**	**Exogamous[77]**	**Career(s)**
Marquer	3 (1 cousin)	*notaires* (Vannes)	0	
Lorvol	3 (1 cousin)	medicine	0	
Lallemand	5 (2 cousin)	military, waw	1 (Ploërmel)	judiciary
Danet	5	adm, prop, *négoce*	0	
Taslé	4 (1 cousin)	*notaire*, politics	2 (Rennes)	judiciary
Boullé	4 (2 cousin)	politics, military	3 (Paris)	politics, adm
Thubé	4	military, judiciary	1 (Lyon)	military
Delorme	3 (1 cousin)	*négoce*	1 (Versailles)	mil. surgery
Claret	3 (1 cousin)	judiciary, medicine	1 (Rennes)	education

Morand	2	*négoce*, adm.	2 (Rennes)	education
Burgault	5 (1 cousin)	prop, *nég*, law, adm	2 (Rennes)	law
Huchet	4	jud, adm, *not*	1 (Guer)	judiciary
Jamet	4 (1 cousin)	law, *négoce*	1 (Dordogne)	adm
Jourdan	3	law, politics	2 (Caen)	adm
Caradec	3	law, politics, judiciary	1 (Paris)	law
Lucas de Bourgarel	3	law, politics	1 (Caen)	adm
Le Febvrier	6 (1 cousin)	law, adm, jud, med	1 (Versailles)	military
Le Bouhéllec	3	law, military, adm	0	
Mahé de Villeneuve	3	law, politics, military	1 (Paris)	law
Pradier	5 (1 cousin)	pol, adm, mil, med	3 (Paris)	edu, adm
Rialan	5 (1 cousin)	law, jud, mil	2 (Bath, Eng.)	military
Thomas-Ducordic	2	law, *not*, politics	1 (Paris)	military
Thomas-Clomaduec	3	medicine, *nég*, adm	1 (Paris)	education
Guillo Dubodan	4	politics, jud, military	2 (Paris)	military

This snapshot obviously does not do justice to the complexity of the lives and careers of these families, who were chosen because they had deep roots in the city and played significant roles in its life. Many individuals left Vannes without marrying there and many others married into families not included here. Prominent among these are several of the most active men in the SPM, such as Cayot-Delandre, Jan de la Gaillardaie, and Blutel. The numbers above only cover two generations. Most of the Vannetais indicated under "career" (in both columns) achieved success mainly in some form of public service, as was the case with our families. Included are three *procureurs-général*, two prefects, and three court of appeals judges. Moreover, six families produced ten deputies and senators, with the Caradecs and Guillo Dubodans leading the way.

Within the category of public service, the military stands out the most. Besides our families' high officers, the numbers above include five generals or navy captains. Although Brittany was one of the less militarized of France's border provinces under the Old Regime, the Belle Ile base and the counterrevolutionary struggle heightened the prestige of military involvement in the Vannetais.[78] According to William Serman's figures for 1825–1865, if the numbers of officers from the Morbihan fell short of the land-border departments and Paris, only a tiny percentage were nobles, and it ranked high among departments where the officer corps was a family tradition. Within the department, Vannes' arrondissement accounted for nearly two-thirds. In part because of this growing reputation, the city would acquire early in the Third Republic garrisons for three regiments, a masterstroke promoted by generals Trochu, Jollivet, and Galles.[79]

Conclusion

Vannetais thus took their place in the nation. Public service, especially military and intellectual, led the areas of excellence. Geographical location and local history had something to do with this. But there was another reason. These are fields where merit counted for a good deal, and most of these men were highly talented and raised, indeed selected, to make the most of it. And coming from a backwater like Vannes in misty Lower Brittany made the concerted role of kin on behalf of the chosen ones all the more important if they were to successfully make their way in the nation.

Breaking into the highest echelons of the national elite was not easy. René Galles' letter of admission to the École Polytechnique was signed by the minister of war, General Bernard, whose Parisian-born son had been in René's Pension Bourdon and would be his classmate at the école. In neither was he anywhere close to René's intellectual equal. Although the level of nepotism at the école in the early days has not been scientifically evaluated, it influenced military recruitment and advancement, where certain *polytechniciens* of great family stature had advantages over others.[80] Moreover, although members the Galles family circle were comfortable enough economically, their income was rather modest compared to that of the average student.[81] Having neither family connections among alumni nor great wealth, René Galles was thus a pioneer, one of a relatively small group of young men whose hard work and academic brilliance consistently saved the reputation of these elite institutions as symbols of post-Revolutionary equality of opportunity, essential components in the mythology of the Revolutionary tradition.[82] It should nevertheless be recalled that even this "scholarship boy" had benefited from his great-aunt's largesse for tuition payments at the best *collège* in the west as well as the preparatory pension in Paris, and he possibly owed his admission to the latter to his uncle Yves's well-placed friend, Erdevan. Without his mother's constant prodding and solicitude, the encouragement of her generation's near relatives, and her aunt's iron-clad expectations of him, René would not have made it to the École Polytechnique. His history, which we have the rare privilege to follow from the inside, illuminates vividly the workings of social ascent in the world of the nineteenth-century notability. It was never just about money and never just about power or even family connection; it was what family members, particularly "those closest to you," one's horizontal kin network, actually *did* that made the final difference. It is here where the intimate study of kinship in this era adds a dimension to the study of modernization and makes its fundamental contribution, for we then abandon correlations and their derivative abstractions about class and power. We watch them happen.

Notes

1. Archives Départementales du Morbihan (henceforth ADM), Fonds Galles, 2 J 1–262, which includes over 1,600 letters, mainly from the first half of the nineteenth century, exchanged by members of the three multiply intermarried families; many genealogies; and a detailed manuscript autobiography concentrating on his early years by general René Galles (1819–1889), and the Fonds Jollivet, which, though less extensive, includes earlier correspondence and the reminiscences of general René Jollivet (1832–95). These collections form the foundation of my book, "Becoming Bourgeois: Kinship, Love, and Power in Provincial France (1670–1880)," in progress.
2. This is not the place to rehash the arguments regarding the extent of cohesion and sense of nationhood among even the most territorially unified of states in early modern Europe, but the consensus today is that until the eighteenth century, "national states" were only tenuously connected provinces governed by a central government largely for the purposes of collecting taxes and raising armies, where a majority of local populations did not speak the official language nor did they partake in something that might be called a national culture. In France, according to David Bell, only in the eighteenth century did even the elites begin to evince national feeling, love of and loyalty to *la patrie.* It arose from a concerted political effort by the state to create a "cult of the nation," forging an ideology that combined Gallican Catholicism with the mystique of the king. The results of this campaign were more successful in some provinces than others, with the Breton west (Lower Brittany)—save for its urban notability and court-connected aristocrats—being the least affected. See David Bell, *The Cult of the Nation in France: Inventing Nationalism, 1680–1800* (Cambridge, MA, 2001). Caroline Ford presents a picture of the belated integration of Lower Brittany into the nation—the last part of France to do so, occurring only in the late nineteenth and early twentieth centuries—that emphasizes the importance of religion as well, in this instance a social Catholicism that reconciled traditional religious practices and cultural peculiarities with a national and republican movement, culminating in Christian Democracy in the 1920s and beyond. It marked the entrance of ordinary people, mostly rural and many Breton-speaking, into the national political arena. See Caroline C. Ford, *Creating the Nation in Provincial France: Religion and Political Identity in Brittany* (Princeton, NJ, 1993).
3. See above all, Abel Châtelain, *Les migrants temporaires en France de 1800 à 1914*, 2 vols. (Lille, 1977). On Breton migration see Leslie Page Moch, "Bretons in Paris: Regional Ties and Urban Networks in an Age of Urbanization," *Quaderni storici* 106

(2001): 177–99; "Networks among Bretons? The Evidence from Paris," *Continuity and Change* 18 (2003): 431–55; "Migration and the Nation: The View from Paris," *Social Science History* 28 (2004): 1–18.

4. The best set of studies along these lines is in Geoff Eley and Ronald Grigor Suny, eds., *Becoming National: A Reader* (Oxford, 1996). See as well Benedict Anderson, *Imagined Communities: Reflections on the Origin and Spread of Nationalism* (London, 1983).
5. Gérard Noiriel, *The French Melting Pot: Immigration, Citizenship, and National Identity,* trans. Geoffroy de Laforcade (Minneapolis, 1996).
6. Christopher H. Johnson, "Kinship, Civil Society, and Power in Nineteenth-Century Vannes," in *Kinship in Europe: Approaches to Long-Term Development (1300–1900),* ed. David Warren Sabean, Simon Teuscher, and Jon Mathieu (New York, 2007), 258–83.
7. See the remarkable study by Stéphane Gerson, *Pride of Place: Local Memories and Political Culture in Nineteenth-Century France* (Ithaca, NY, 2003).
8. Joël Cornette, *Histoire de la Bretagne et les Bretons* (Paris, 2005), vols. 1 and 2, 4e partie. The great work on the Vannetais is Timothy Le Goff, *Vannes and its Region: A Study of Town and Country in the Eighteenth Century* (Oxford, 1981).
9. My goal here is to follow the pathways of typical French bourgeois (and how different were other western and central Europeans of their circumstances?) coming from a typical—though a bit more off the beaten track—town in the revolutionary age. I take my cue from studies such as Gerson, *Pride of Place;* Carol Harrison, *The Bourgeois Citizen in Nineteenth-Century France: Gender, Sociability, and the Uses of Emulation* (Oxford, 1999); and especially Joël Cornette, *Un révolutionnaire ordinaire: Benoît Lacombe, Négociant, 1759–1819* (Paris, 1986). Although members of the Vannes families studied here went on to some fame, their "ordinariness" is signaled by the fact that few appear in national biographical dictionaries or secondary works beyond local studies. Vannes, a town increasing from ten to twelve thousand in the first half of the nineteenth century, was an average provincial capital with an average mix of professions. Industrialization was weak, but so it was in most French towns of this era. Ted Margadant, *Urban Rivalries in the French Revolution* (Princeton, NJ, 1992), esp. chapter 1, presents a magnificent overview of French cities at the time: Vannes is at the median and remained so. For my perspectives on the nature of the French bourgeoisie (and why I believe those of Vannes are at least as typical as the industrialists, say, of Lille or Lyon, or the bankers of Paris), see Johnson, "Kinship, Civil Society, and Power," 263–64 and note 18.
10. Fonds Galles ADM 2 J 71. For brief biographies of the more prominent Galles men, see René Kerviler, ed., *Répertoire général de Bio-Bibliographie bretonne* (Rennes, 1904, repr. 1978), s.v. "Galles." Georges Lepeux, *Gallia typographique ou Répertoire biographique… de tous les imprimeurs de France,* (Paris, 1914), vol. 4, s.v. "Vannes: Jean Galles, le sieur du Clos; Christophe Galles;" and ADM, B 1359, "Reception de Jean-Nicolas Galles." Marriages are recorded in the parish registers of Saint-Mené, assembled with all état civil records, ADM, Ec Vannes (microfilm), 1670, 1681, 1705, 1737, 1741. On wealth, see ADM, B 676, "Inventaire des effets de la communauté de Nicolas Galles avec feue demoiselle Perrine Lesieur Son Epouse pour arrester de la ditte Communauté avec son fils, Jean Marie," 6 April 1745. Later: ADM, C (non-classé) Rôles d'impositions, Capitation, 1780–89. On the size of publishers' operations in Brittany and royal regulation of the book trade, see Jean Quéniart, *Culture et société urbaines dans la France de l'ouest au XVIIIe siècle* (Paris, 1978), 343–48, 357, 360. The tendency of state policy (whatever its rationale) to favor industrial and

commercial concentration at least from the time of Cardinal Fleury on, has been a theme in several studies. See the summary view in Christopher H. Johnson, "Capitalism and the State: Capital Accumulation and Proletarianization in the Languedocian Woolens Industry, 1700–1789," in *The Workplace before the Factory: Artisans and Proletarians, 1500–1800*, ed. Thomas Max Safley and Leonard N. Rosenband (Ithaca, NY, 1993), 37–62.

11. See Le Goff, *Vannes and its Region*, 151–204. On the Jollivets and le Ridants, see ADM 1049–1107, Famille Jollivet.
12. On the Audrans, see Thomas Crow, *Painters and Public Life in Eighteenth-Century Paris* (New Haven, CT, 1985), 58–60; Audran, *Histoire généalogique de la famille des Audran* (Rennes, 1754); Quéniart, *Culture et société urbaines*, 371; and Lepeux, *Gallia typographique*, vol. 4: *Vannes: Nicolas Audran*.
13. Bernard Frélaut, "Un Vannétais à la Bastille: Jean-Nicolas Galles à la Bastille en 1760 d'après sa correspondance inédite," *Mémoires de la société polymathique du Morbihan* 116 (1990) : 173–83.
14. The heaviest concentration of Jean-Marie's letters to be retained is a total of thirty-four from 1761 through the summer of 1763; ADM, 2 J 76. The power of the Audrans lay in part due to a giant government subsidy overseen by Audran, père; Archives Nationales, Paris (AN), F 12 639A, document dated 11 June 1764. Jean-Marie thought the trade in Paris was too free, corrupt, and arbitrary: letter of 8 February 1761. Among the many books on the subject, Daniel Roche, *France in the Enlightenment*, trans. Arthur Goldhammer (Cambridge, MA, 1998) remains the most insightful, for he captures the schizophrenia of the age. For details on governmental regulation in this era, see Thierry Rigogne, *Between State and Market: Printing and Bookselling in Eighteenth-century France* (Oxford, 2008). Jean-Marie was in Paris when the Jesuits were expelled and feared, unnecessarily, that it might hurt their business. On the interplay of religion and politics in these years, see Dale Van Kley, *The Religious Origins of the French Revolution* (Princeton, NJ, 1998). On the image of the Jesuits, see Dale Van Kley, *The Damians Affair and the Unraveling of the Ancien Régime, 1750–1770* (Princeton, NJ, 1984), ch. 2.
15. He had a love affair with a *courtière de commerce* that his family opposed, but that also did not go well emotionally. Whether his decision was related to this experience cannot be determined. His cousin Perrine sent him a brochure about his "national duty" to produce children in this imagined time of fertility crisis. Both the love letters from his sweetheart and Perrine's correspondence are in ADM, J 2 73.
16. The family was intellectually similar to Jean-Marie's friend La Harpe, who in the end condemned the Revolution for its attack on Roman Catholicism. See Christopher Todd, *Voltaire's Disciple: Jean-François de La Harpe* (London, 1972).
17. See his correspondence from there in ADM, 2 J 74.
18. This can be followed in the Capitation roles: ADM, C (non-classé), Rôles d'impositions, 1765–89.
19. Jean-Marie's correspondence about Perrine is in ADM, 2 J 73; Galles genealogies, 2 J 71. Angélique's betrothal is in ADM, Ec Vannes, 13 Messidor, an V (1797).
20. The remarks are based on detailed research for my book manuscript, "Becoming Bourgeois," ch. 3.
21. See especially Isser Wolloch, *The New Regime: Transformations of the French Civic Order 1789–1820s* (New York, 1994) and Eric Hobsbawm, *The Age of Revolution, 1789–1851* (New York, 1975).
22. Donald Sutherland, *Les Chouans: Les origines sociales de la Contre-Révolution populaire en Bretagne, 1770–1796* (Rennes, 1990) is the best introduction to this vast subject.

23. See Johnson, "Kinship, Civil Society, and Power." I argue here that this was typical of local elites throughout France.
24. Vigée-Lebrun has a marvelous painting of Elizabeth, whose clothes are magnificent! Quotation from René Jollivet to Yves Jollivet, 31 December 1786 in ADM, Papiers Famille Jollivet, E 1050.
25. René to Yves Jollivet, 12 October 1786, Papiers Jollivet.
26. Jeanne-Marie Le Ridant to René Jollivet, 6 August 1786, Papiers Jollivet.
27. Their status before the Revolution can be gauged by the list of signatories on their marriage documents. Although it included names from their more modest roots in Sarzeau, Lanouée, and Vannes' extramural parishes (Le Gueranic and Maguero, kin of the Le Ridants, Granelle and Berugeay, kin of the Jollivets, and the ubiquitous Galpins for the Galles), there were no less than four members of the Serres family, the now wealthy *négociants* whose very name (for they came from the Galpin male line) signaled turning one's back on an insignificant past. Two male Col de la Chapelles, Le Ridant god-kin and *financiers-propriétaires,* witnessed the marriage, as did the Latours, *père et fils,* cloth merchants, linked through the father's wife, a Housset, to the Jamets and Jourdans. The big grain merchant contingent was represented by Pierre-Marie Danet and L. M. C. Gravé de la Rive; ADM, Ec Vannes, 16 April 1787.
28. Evelyne Lever, *Louis XVIII* (Paris, 1988), 175, 214–16, 235–36, 265–68, 460, 469–71; Ernest Daudet, *Madame Royale* (Paris, 1912); Marie-Thérèse de France, duchesse d'Angoulême, *Journal de la duchesse d'Angoulême, corrigé et annoté par Louis XVIII* (Paris, 1893).
29. ADM, 2 J 81, Cécile Marquer Jollivet to Marie-Joseph Jollivet, 28 July 1796.
30. ADM, Q 28 178, 180, 233, 228, 124, 165 and 191; Q 26 199; Q 2897.
31. This invasion of exiles in 1795 on the Quiberon peninsula was the last gasp of the counterrevolution, brutally repressed by Republican General Hoche. It entered royalist mythology in a manner similar to "the forty-five," Bonnie Prince Charlie's effort to restore the Stuarts and Scottish independence. See Patrick Huchet, *1795: Quiberon, ou le destin de la France* (Rennes, 1995).
32. ADM, 2 J 81, Adelaïde Jollivet Galles to Augustin Jollivet, 1 September 1796.
33. On Marie-Joseph, see letter of 1 September 1786. References to Ridant's career are in family letters in ADM 2 J 79, 1810–15; Archives Nationales de la Guerre personnel files; and Roger Grand, *Les Cent-jours dans l'Ouest: La Chouannerie de 1815* (Paris, 1942), 61, 82, 191.
34. Marie's correspondence from before 1815 is lost, so we can only rely on retrospective remarks in later correspondence about this era. René Galles would write in his memoirs: "Our great-aunt Le Ridant had a genius for intrigue on behalf of those she loved. She spent most of her time in Paris where she had numerous acquaintances in high society, even intimate relations at court. Mme de Sérent, dame d'honneur de la duchesse d'Angoulême, was her good friend. She set this world in motion for her husband and nephews. She would not rest until she succeeded." René Galles, "Journal," cha1, 7, ADM, 2 J 79. On royalism during the Empire, see Lever, *Louis XVIII,* 243–33.
35. Unfortunately we have little information about them other than via family correspondence and genealogies. Eldest brothers Augustin and Jean-Baptise were notaries in Martinique and François a landowner in Réunion, while the youngest, Félix, became a royalist journalist in Paris. None figure in secondary literature on the era. Further primary research might be fruitful, but neither the AN nor the ADM have yielded anything.

36. R. M. Jollivet, *Discours prononcé par M. le Président du Collège électoral de l'arrondissement de Vannes à l'ouverture de sa session, le 14 août 1815* (Vannes, 1815). Grand, *Les Cent Jours,* 233; Leguay, *Histoire de Vannes,* 202. On the political atmosphere after Waterloo, see Guillaume de Bertier de Sauvigny, *La Restauration* (Paris, 1955), 146–67. Jollivet to Jullien, 9 May 1815, and other materials relating to the Conseil Général, ADM, 2 M 66; Conseil de la Préfecture, 2 M 53. If Jollivet spoke for reconciliation of interests, however, he only went so far. He became a floor leader on behalf of a proposed law to limit free speech, the vaguely worded bill to outlaw "seditious cries," defined as both direct attacks on the king and those tending "to weaken respect due to the authority of the king" (such as "Long live the Emperor" or waving the tricolor). This bill, passed on 9 November 1815, was part of an omnibus package of four laws often known as the "legal white terror." Adolphe Robert and Gaston Couguy, *Dictionnaire des Parlementaires français* (Paris, 1889), s.v. "Jollivet"; Bertier de Sauvigny, *La Restauration,* 176–78. On the elections in the Morbihan, see ADM, 3 M 233.
37. Bonté was close to the Galles, a signatory at several weddings.
38. Bertin chided Eugène for not following him; ADM, 2 J 79, Bertin to Eugène Galles, 18 July 1812.
39. ADM, 2 J 79, Aimée to Eugene Galles, November 1813.
40. David Warren Sabean, *Kinship in Neckarhausen* (Cambridge, 1998), ch. 23; Christopher H. Johnson and David Warren Sabean, "From Siblingship to Siblinghood: Kinship and the Shaping of European Society (1300–1900)," in *Sibling Relations and the Transformations of European Kinship, 1300–1900,* ed. Christopher H. Johnson and David Warren Sabean (New York, 2011), ch. 1.
41. Johnson and Sabean, "From Siblingship to Siblinghood."
42. Christopher H. Johnson, "Das geschwister Archipel: Bruder-Schwester-Liebe und Klassenformation im Frankreich des 19. Jarhunderts," *L'Homme: Zeitschrift für feministische Geschictswissenschaft* 13 (2002): 50–67.
43. Jean-André Tudesq, *Les grands notables en France, 1840–1849)* (Paris, 1964); Johnson "Kinship, Civil Society, and Power."
44. See Irvine Louden, *Death in Childbirth: An International Study of Maternal Care and Maternal Mortality, 1800–1950* (Oxford, 1992) for this nineteenth-century plague.
45. Johnson, "Kinship, Civil Society, and Power."
46. Genealogical information drawn from marriage registers is in ADM, Ec Vannes, and correspondence, 2 J 79.
47. The phrase in René Galles, upon his graduation from the École Polytechnique ("Journal," ch. 3, 26.)
48. It was true, nonetheless, that entrance into the elite services and certain regiments was much easier for aristocrats. Serman summarized it this way: "Ainsi, le corps d'Etat Major et la cavalerie ont une allure aristocratique: le recruitement de leurs officiers n'exclut pas les hommes du peuple, mais il accorde une place relativement large, sinon priviligé, aux nobles, aux fils d'officiers et aux héritiers des notables civils." William Serman, *Les origines des officiers français (1848–1870)* (Paris, 1979), 337.
49. See Johnson, "Das geschwister archipel."
50. This story became a family tradition and is told by René Galles in his memoirs ("Journal," ch. 1, 10.)
51. ADM 2 J 79, Eugène to Adèle Galles, 35 letters, 1818–1820.
52. Adm 2 J 79, 132 letters exchanged between Adèle and Eugène Galles, 1820–1825; 2 J 81 (letters from Marie Le Ridant).

53. Galles, "Journal," ch. 1, 7. Also letters from Adèle to her son after he went away to school hint at the tension in the household. They returned to Vannes and her house across from Alexis Le Ridant in 1829.
54. ADM, 2 J 80.
55. These are rhapsodically described by Jules Jollivet, René's eldest, in "Mes souvenirs," ADM, E 1050.
56. See above all, Bruno Belhoste, *La formation d'une technocratie: L'École polytechnique et ses élèves de la Révolution au Second Empire* (Paris 2003). The best appreciation of the Polytechnique's economic role remains Rondo Cameron, *France and the Economic Development of Europe, 1830–1880* (Princeton, NJ, 1963). On the history of the school, see Terry Shinn, *L'École polytechnique, 1794–1914* (Paris, 1980) and Bruno Belhoste et al., eds., *La France des X: Deux siècles d'histoire* (Paris, 1995).
57. In his oral exam with the great man, René had one of those magical moments: "I answered all the questions that were put to me. I remember that in finishing, the mathematician-philosopher asked me one that I answered intuitively, nearly by chance; it was one of those moments when the overheated mind takes on a strange lucidity; I had answered wonderfully well. And when since I have tried to recall the reasoning behind my answer, I cannot; I left it in the Salle St. Jean where it would still be, if not for the petrol and the Commune." Galles, "Journal," ch. 2, 56.
58. Galles, "Journal," 56–61. As Flaubert put it: "Polytechnique, rêve de toutes les mères." Belhoste, *La formation*, 329.
59. In one incident, at the beginning of his second year during the hazing of new arrivals, he even denied any connection with a fellow Breton. When, amid the shower of insults, his schoolmate at Nantes, Jollan de Clerville, recognized a friendly face, he offered his hand and said "Bonjour, Galles," to which the latter replied coldly that he was surely mistaken, that "I do not have the honor of your acquaintance." This then became the rallying cry of the assembled, who relayed in mockery, "Who is the *conscrit* who pretends to know *un ancien*? Get him out of here!" Although the two saw each other often in the ensuing years, "There long remained a shadow between us." Galles, "Journal," ch. 3, 4–5.
60. Ibid., 23.
61. Undated (first page missing), but marked by René in sorting it "1839," in ADM, 2 J 80.
62. His mother remembered the fate of Bertin Galles in her letter of 7 January 1840; ADM, 2 J 80.
63. This caused an enormous rift in the family. Marie's objections centered on her disapproval of the Bonapartism and corruption of Virginie Danet Le Ridant's brother.
64. René Galles' story of the Thubé-Trochu wedding underlines their closeness ("Journal," ch. 3, 22.
65. Jules Trochu, *L'armée en 1867* (Paris, 1867)
66. He defended his much-criticized role in *Pour la vérité et pour la justice* (Paris, 1873).
67. See Adolphe Robert, Edgar Bourloton, and Gaston Cougny, *Dictionnaire des parlementaires fraçais* (Paris, 1890), s.v. "Billault."
68. On its early history and kinship networks and the founding role of Jean-Marie Galles, see Johnson, "Kinship, Civil Society, and Power," 269–75.
69. See Jean-Pierre Chaline, *Sociabilité et érudition: Les sociétés savantes en France, XIX*[e]*–XX*[e] *siècles* (Paris, 1995). For Chaline's high regard for the SPM, see 222.
70. The Collège de Vannes was the major attraction for the latter. On its history and importance, see J. Allanic, *Histoire du Collège de Vannes* (Rennes, 1902). Jules Simon,

who attended the *collège* in the early thirties, seemed certain that it contributed significantly to his success at the École Normale Supérieure, not so much because of the knowledge imparted, but for the scholarly discipline and love of learning its "family" of instructors rendered; Simon, *Premières années* (Paris, 1901), 69–112.

71. It is today a World Heritage site.
72. On the historiography of the problem, see Jean-Yves Guiomar, *Le bretonisme: Les historiens bretons au XIX*[e] *siècle* (Mayenne, 1987), ch. 9.
73. "Allocution de M. Galles," *Bulletin de la société polymathique du Morbihan* (1885): 1–2. Individual "nonresident" and "corresponding" members included many leading figures in French intellectual life such as Jules Simon, historians Henri Martin and Arthur de la Borderie, and other members of the Académie française and the Institut.
74. Roughly, a circle bounded by La Roche Bernard and Rochefort on the east, Sérent and Saint-Jean Brévelay on the north, and Auray on the West. Established relations could stretch to Redon, Josselyn, Pontivy, and Lorient, but they had their own orbits.
75. This table is created from my database largely drawn from 120 very detailed *actes de mariage* provided by the commune after 1804; ADM, Ec Vannes. All regimes until 1848 required indications of social status ("Monsieur/Madame, le Sieur/la Dame," and no title) to be judged by the officers of the *état civil* (the chief judge of the civil tribunal assisted by the *premier adjoint du Mairie*), which roughly corresponded to the noble and bourgeois elite (about 10 percent in the case of Vannes, with only a handful of nobles), the *classe moyenne* of merchants, master artisans, *employés,* and the like (some 30 percent), and wage earners of all sorts. Economic status can easily be determined from the *cens* lists (taxes necessary to be electors under the narrow suffrage of the Restoration and July Monarchy) (ADM, 3 M 25) as well as the list of "Notables" under the empire. I am working with 416 surnames and 1,042 individuals—males well outnumber females because of the four witnesses signing for every wedding, though many women did sign the document as well-wishers. Mothers of bride and groom are listed by their maiden names, one of the main reasons these documents are so useful to kinship studies. The same can be said for the fact that all witnesses indicate their kinship relationship to the bride and groom (or both, given the number of cousin marriages). The families chosen for this list are based on their multiple appearances in the marriage documents (giving weight to larger families) and because I am familiar with their histories due to my intensive study of the city in this period. They also appear regularly in the Galles/Jollivet/Le Ridant correspondence and by the second half of the nineteenth century many were their relatives. See Johnson, "Kinship, Civil Society, and Power."
76. Vannes' "orbit." See note 83. The term *endogamous* refers to both geographically and genetically close marriages.
77. In the cases where more than one was exogamous, only the most distant city of residence of the bride or groom is indicated due to space. These numbers include both people who have migrated to Vannes and those where the groom or bride (mostly the latter) will likely reside in their spouse's city. In either case, these are indicators of establishing kinship connections elsewhere.
78. Stéphane Perréon, *L'armée en Bretagne au XVIII*[e] *siècle* (Rennes, 2005).
79. Serman, *Les origins des officiers,* 272–74. See also, Jean-Pierre Leguay, *Histoire de Vannes et de sa région* (Toulouse, 1988), 217–19.
80. Pierre Chalmin made the point nicely: "Let us agree: [the officer corps] was widely and democratically open to all, especially after the institution of examinations and

competitions. It was the opposite of a caste. Anyone could become an officer and advance by his own talents, but advancement did not favor [everyone] equally depending on merit. One made one's way with ease and especially rapidly only on the condition of having at one's disposal several well-placed protectors. The army was constituted of diverse clienteles—in the old meaning of the word—living in the comfortable wake of relatives or friends. … Sometimes birth could serve; a father, an uncle is already in place; other times an opportune and profitable marriage … could procure a powerful protector." This led to "*familles militaires*" often extending for several generations. We have evidence of this among the military men of Vannes, modest as their place may have been. Chalmin, *L'officier français de 1815 à 1870* (Paris, 1957), 360. Belhoste, who rather downplays the oft-repeated notion of "Polytechnique dynasties," estimates "autorecruitment" at around 8 percent based on surnames of students from 1794 to 1870, thus by no means including all relatives. *La formation*, 337.

81. Shinn, *L'École Polytechnique*, 63–80. Belhoste assembles the various studies of the social origins of *polytechniciens* (also noting that this word was rarely used at the time) and argues that Shinn overestimated the level of wealth of their fathers based on their occupations (especially *propriétaire*); I am not sure I agree with him, but in any case, the only true measure would be family wealth at the time of admission, which would involve a detailed examination of a range of local documents such as I have worked with. Such a study would be impossible on a global basis, of course. However, a good measure (and not one pursued as far as I know) would be to discover how many students' fathers and grandfathers were to be found on the *cens* lists of the Restoration and July Monarchy. It should also be remembered that a growing majority of the students went to special preparatory schools in Paris before admission, which were quite expensive. The Bourdon cost three thousand francs for the year, about four times as much as the average annual wage of a worker. Belhoste makes the convincing point that the largest proportion of Polytechnique students came from families already involved in state service and secondly from economic professions. In this, René was more typical, of course.

82. Pierre Bourdieu, *La noblesse d'État: Grandes écoles et esprit de corps* (Paris, 1989), has most effectively argued this point, but nothing, perhaps, about the nature of French society is better known to the public at large for at least 150 years. Christophe Charle's exhaustive study, *Les élites de la République (1880–1900)* (Paris, 1987), explores the intertwining of influence and power at the highest levels of government and society during an era when the democratic promise of the Revolution was supposedly fulfilled.

Chapter 11

German International Families in the Nineteenth Century

The Siemens Family as a Thought Experiment

David Warren Sabean

During the nineteenth century, property-holding families within all stations and classes throughout Europe developed systems of marriage that linked the same families across generations. Chronicles of individual families present many forms of systematic and unsystematic repeated exchanges, and while many particular marriages may seem arbitrary, when viewed in the context of all the alliances established by a set of kin, they often fit into a logic of reciprocity or demonstrate systemic features. Certainly there were no rules that created the expectation or the necessity of marrying kin or prescribing choices directed towards particular kindred, clans, lineages, or patri- or matrilines. And while the new structures were to be found among small peasant producers and aristocratic landowners, within petit-bourgeois and great entrepreneurial milieus, and throughout cultural and political elites, they were by no means developed by all families. Exactly how the new forms developed or why people sought out members from within their kin groups for spouses is open for considerable investigation, but the phenomenon can be observed in many corners of Europe throughout the long nineteenth century.[1] An older understanding of repeated marriages put them down to localism or provincialism, with the proverbial inbred village symptomatic of a pathological obsession with property, immobility, or fear of change. Other examples of inbred ethnic or religious groups or ruling houses often stirred the imaginations of political pundits, social commentators, or biologists. But we are now able to see that from the middle of the eighteenth century until the aftermath of World War I, a familial dynamic developed that sets this epoch off from the periods both before and after.

Some observers have organized analysis of the forms that characterize the long nineteenth century around the figure of "cousin" marriage.[2] Certainly cousins as central for the pool of marriageable suitors emerged in all propertied classes during this period, but the phenomenon of marital reciprocity goes well beyond the specific marriage between the children or grandchildren of siblings.[3] It can be shown that once a marriage was concluded between two families or lineages, many more marriages might occur between and among the same groups without there being ties of blood between the new pairs.[4] There were various possible forms to link families across generations, but there was also a substantial increase in single-generation alliances, such as the marriage of cousins with siblings, sets of siblings together, and with a deceased spouse's sibling. What characterizes all of these kinds of marriages is a search for people from within the same milieu, from similar class backgrounds, and for familiarity.[5]

With these considerations in mind, it is possible to broaden the perspective on reciprocity and to think of the marriage strategies of the period as oriented towards developing broad, extensive, and well-integrated groups of kin, linked together through horizontally constructed networks. Even when such networks in part could be diffuse or meander off into relative obscurity, they might be mobilized from time to time for placing this or that family member, scraping together capital for some business venture, or offering temporary aid in unfamiliar territory. Of course, not all marriages were within already well-charted relations. Pierre Bourdieu made the point some time ago that even in societies with high rates of endogamy, familial strategies would always be balanced between socially close and socially distant marriages, since both consolidation and innovation are important for individual and familial protection and aggrandizement.[6]

Until now, most studies of kinship have been carried out in local, regional, or national frameworks. But many of the same considerations I have pointed to might fruitfully be examined by looking at the social dynamics of those families that spread themselves across different nations. The point is all the more important in the light of recent work by Johnson, Delille, and Kuper, who have shown how new kinship features could be mobilized to construct classes and cultural and social milieus and to create crucial forms of national integration among political and social elites. In the situation under consideration here, hundreds of German families in the nineteenth century coordinated their activities across national boundaries in global networks in which mechanisms similar to those within localities, regions, and nations acted as effective instruments of cohesion. The analysis of familial reciprocities should not be limited to the study of marriage alone. There are many ways that linked families could carry on regular exchanges, such as providing guardians or godparents for each other, passing children back and forth for education, training in a craft or business, companionship or care, or as business associates. Regular and irregular visiting, celebration of weddings and anniversaries, vacationing together, periodic family gatherings, dense networks of correspondence—all of these forms flourished in the nineteenth century. Exploring familial reciprocities among those German families dispersed across different nations or allied with families in different cultures and regions will contribute to understanding the effectiveness of the new kinship networks and perhaps their limitations, while at the same time offering insight into the specific features of late-nineteenth-century globalization.

To carry out this project will involve reading through many volumes of biographies, autobiographies, and family and firm histories. In this preliminary study, I will be concentrating for the most part on one particular industrialist family in Germany, the Siemens, that came to prominence in the second half of the nineteenth century. I want to use their example to explore a number of themes, and although I do not want to minimize the peculiarities and specificities of their history, I want to carry out the exercise to suggest the contours of a possible research problematic.

Patrilines

Recent research has placed a great deal of emphasis on the rise of restrictive forms of inheritance and succession during the early modern period. Unigeniture, entail, and fidei commissum developed in this or that stratum or region in fits and starts from the early fifteenth century onwards and emerged for the most part fully formed by the beginning of the eighteenth century.[7] Families became organized around estates, benefices, offices, privileges, and properties that gave continuity to male lineages over many generations. Just as these tendencies emerged in full flower, they were challenged by a number of changes in the way wealth was accumulated and the way it was distributed from generation to generation. Middle-class bureaucrats, theorists, and commentators launched an attack on closed forms of inheritance, arguing for an equal distribution of familial resources to all inheriting children.[8] The new capitalist relations that restructured the economy put a premium on invention and entrepreneurial activity and were less concerned with preserving a particular privilege or pieces of land intact than in taking advantage of expanding economic activities. Studies of the Rhineland industrialists have shown, however, that with rare exceptions, the families that developed the new mining, metallurgical, and trading firms, that took advantage of the new economic opportunities, and that developed new kinds of wealth were all descendants of substantial burghers of the eighteenth century.[9] In the process of forging their industrial power, they reconfigured their families around new forms of agnatic lineage and familial cohesion. Middle- and upper-class familial dynamics demonstrate a concern for maintaining coherence by cultivating identity with a surname or male-defined line. I will illustrate this with the Siemens family, but preliminary research on family associations (*Vereine*) and foundations (*Stiftungen*) in the decades around 1900 shows an obsession with protecting, celebrating, and researching patronyms and gathering into association all the people who can be shown to share a particular lineage name through blood descent. The difference between the earlier form of line or lineage construction can be seen in the models that the different periods used to construct familial identity. In the early modern construction, a person traced back his line according to the privileges and rights he won through inheritance and through the differentiation of life chances accorded to the siblings of each generation. Reference was to the stem, the line of succession, perhaps from eldest son to eldest son. What emerged in the nineteenth century was a way of thinking of the family as a group of people descended from an apical ancestor. And as I will show, this group was characterized by surname identity and linkages down the generations through men.[10]

The problem for historical analysis is to see how these families linked up with other families, to get a sense of the distinctions that might be drawn between affinal and consanguineal kin and between relatives linked through fathers and those through mothers, and to explore the possibilities that lay in the lively exchanges that characterized cousin networks. But the first thing to do is to investigate some of the dynamics of family consciousness, the identity of the group that entered into exchange with other similarly structured groups, for the system of reciprocities seems to have been based upon ever-greater cohesion within agnatically structured lineages. I began a study of the phenomenon of constructing these new forms of identity in *Kinship in Neckarhausen* and will paraphrase a few paragraphs to sketch in some of the nineteenth-century developments among middle-class and upper-class families.[11] During the second half of the nineteenth century, family members within bourgeois milieus devoted more and more time to narcissistic reflection on their own genealogies and newly constructed chronicles.[12] It was then that many families founded archives and formally entrusted them to a particular member, sometimes the same person who produced the family newspaper—a good example, of course, was the founding of the Siemens family archive. Collections of letters and diaries of grandparents or great-aunts and uncles were privately published at the end of the nineteenth and beginning of the twentieth century for family members. Most of these documents originated during the *Vormärz* or in the course of time from the decades following the mid-century Revolutionary period, testimony to a growing interest in maintaining a trail of family tradition but also to founding generations that documented themselves ever more volubly and self-consciously. The publications of old family papers celebrated a lineage and provided a practical exercise in building familial attachment.

Many families—I think the decade of the 1870s was a crucial one in this regard—went so far as to institutionalize themselves as associations (*Vereine*). It appears that families before 1900 could establish formal foundations (*Stiftungen*) like the Siemens's or informal associations (*Vereine*). After 1900, they could formally register with the courts as family associations (*eingetragene Vereine*). Fifty-six members of the Siemens family gathered together in Burgberg near Harzburg in 1873 to erect a family foundation.[13] Apparently they were accompanied by their wives and children, since reports often referred to two hundred or more people taking part in such family celebrations. In 1875, fifty-five members of the association approved the formal constitution when they met at another hotel in the Harz region, and four years later the foundation was formally registered with the city court in Berlin. For the most part, the members of the association met every five years and built a considerable fund for the use of family members. One of the tasks the family set itself was the periodic publication of the Siemens genealogy. By 1900, the family published an annual newspaper, something that many families of the period were doing. They paid an archivist from Goslar, where the family had originated from, to write a history of the family, and by 1915 the children of Werner Siemens decided to purchase the original Siemens house in Goslar and establish the archive there. In 1920, the family association, now twice as large as at its first meetings, met for the first time in the Goslar *Stammhaus*.

As many other such documents, the constitution of the family foundation asserted as its purpose to help needy members of the family and to assist in the costs of education of the young people. Only those people found in the official genealogy together with their descendants could become members, and the document specifically excluded adopted children even when they carried the name Siemens. No descendants of female members could continue membership in the association. All the elements of constructing male lineage consciousness can be found in this example. While daughters were conspicuous as active members, their children, in turn, were expected to become attached to other male lines. Institutionalized meetings cultivated those relationships that, well before the 1870s, families like the Siemens' maintained through more informal visits, vacations, and family festivals. Perhaps organizational innovation became necessary to establish familial coherence as relations became ever more extended with each generation. Or perhaps the new tourist infrastructure—railroads and hotels—made it attractive to gather together periodically in a central place. Whatever prompted the spurt of foundations and associations from the 1870s onwards, three principles of family cohesion were underscored and given special emphasis—recognition through surnames, coordination of educational and other opportunities for children, and maintaining respect for the name by ensuring that no one—especially the elderly—slipped into conspicuous poverty.

Throughout the nineteenth century, while lineages were being constructed through cultivating surname ties transmitted through men, alliances were also constructed with other similar lineages. Such alliances themselves gained meaning and shape from the fact of coherently constituted lines. Despite the necessity of opening up to other families, however, there was always a good deal of marriage back into a line. Continual intercourse among people with the same surname, coupled with narcissistic celebration, provided the grounds for endogamous desire. Reading through genealogies, one continually stumbles across marriages where the partners carried the same surname. Good examples are provided by the Siemens family themselves or by other entrepreneurial families like the Deliuses from Bielefeld. Or to take another example: the Remy family from Bendorf, early entrepreneurs and merchants in mining, iron, and steel, offers an instance of repeated marriage back into the male lineage. The author of a recent genealogical study constructed five kinship diagrams (*Stammtafeln*) at the end of her article, in which one out of five (19.5 percent) of the 92 marriages depicted since the founding generation around 1700 involved both partners with the surname Remy.[14] The concern with male lineages, of course, made the necessity of male heirs all the more urgent, indeed emotional, and for historians of industrialist families working closely to their sources, the word *Stammhalter* (son and heir, literally: "lineage preserver") flows easily and unconsciously from their pens.

The strong sense of lineage correlated closely with the systematic cultivation of alliances: two or more families in continual exchange with each other within a generation, and, with repeated marriages between lines, over several generations, in many cases lasting longer than a century. Relationships between individuals opened up whole families and their surrounding relatives and friends to each other. And the particular alliance between partners constituted by marriage never isolated a couple and their children—much of the literature on the "rise" of the nuclear family fails to balance the story with an account of the dynamics of larger groups accessible to each other through the mediation of their particular marriages.

Siemens

There is nothing natural about the development of cohesive family feeling; or the coordination of economic, political, or cultural capital; or the promotion of relatives through family networks. If kinship networks are to have any meaning in practice, they have to be cultivated and maintained through considerable labor. And for the nineteenth century, we can see that particular family members specialized in the work that kept the strands of familial sentiment knit together. There is considerable evidence to show that a great deal of this activity was in the hands of the wives, mothers, sisters, and aunts. The family in the center of focus here, the Siemenses, involves a set of brothers, four of whom became major industrial figures in the second half of the nineteenth century, with four others who played considerable roles in the family fortunes. Hans, Walter, and Otto died too young for their full potential to emerge, while Ferdinand became a substantial estate owner. The four industrialists, Werner, Wilhelm, Carl, and Friedrich, coordinated their activities under the considerable influence of the eldest, Werner. Each of them, however, at one time or other played an important role in helping out all of the other brothers and involved themselves in the activities of the larger set of Siemens relatives. As in most industrialist families, success was only to be had by the initiative and risk taking displayed by particular individuals. This, of course, made for considerable tension, and the history of many industrialist families over the nineteenth century reveals a succession of reorganizations, mergers, personal initiatives, alliances, autonomous foundations, mutual investments, and bitter, sometimes irreconcilable splits. The kinship business required labor, time, and investment to bridge differences, coordinate energies, combat indifference, and counteract diverging desires.[15] But it is also important to think of kinship not simply as a matter of cohesion but as a map with riffs and breaks as much as points of connection. In the case of the Siemens family, kinship coordination can be considered on two planes, but the one is quite shadowy. Werner refers to the "female correspondence" of the kinship network in one of his letters, making it clear that all kinds of news, gift transactions, commemorations, and mutual aid circulated in channels parallel to the business and technical correspondence between the male members of the family, although I do not want to underestimate the considerable number of "private" matters that arise in the latter.[16] Werner began each of his marriages by encouraging his fiancées to enter into an active correspondence with a wide set of his female relatives. In terms of the larger network of Siemens family members—the descendants for the most part from the apical ancestor, Ananias, back in the late sixteenth century—Werner pointed to one of his paternal aunts who had become the center of the very large interacting set of relatives.[17] There may yet be the possibility of giving more definition to the labor of women in developing and maintaining the contacts with kin, but in my consideration here, I will focus on Werner as the key player in familial politics, since for him there is considerable published documentation.[18]

Brothers Siemens

The brothers established themselves across Europe. Werner (1816–1892) centered his activities in Berlin, but his entrepreneurial activities took him to St. Petersburg, the Caucasus, the Red Sea, the Mediterranean coast, France, and England. Wilhelm, later William (1823–1883), established himself primarily in England, but the telegraphy and cable laying took him also to the edges of Europe and to the Near East. Carl (1829–1906) for many years represented the family in St. Petersburg, spent years in the Caucasus, contemplated going off to America with Wilhelm and Friedrich (gold mining), spent ten years in England with Wilhelm, and ended up in Berlin as the survivor of the four entrepreneurs.[19] These three brothers were all ennobled, respectively, in Germany, England, and Russia, and Wilhelm became an English subject and Carl, a Russian subject. Friedrich (1826–1867) worked with Werner in Berlin and then with Wilhelm in England developing industrial furnaces. After Hans (1818–1867)—who had begun in agriculture, established a distilling company, and finally a glass factory in Dresden, using the furnace technology of his brothers—died, Friedrich moved to Dresden to take over the firm and built up a large industrial complex, which included factories in Dresden, Bohemia, and England.[20] Walter (1833–1868) learned the trade of telegraphy through his brothers and became established in the Caucasus, in Tiflis (Tbilisi), where he managed a mine owned by Werner and Carl and negotiated across the border in Persia for the establishment of the Indo-European telegraph line that Werner, Wilhelm, and Carl were building. His early death brought Carl down to manage the mine for a few years. Otto (1836–1871), the youngest, also worked for his older brothers in Berlin and England and even set out for Australia with the idea of setting up a branch of the Siemens concerns equivalent to that of Carl in St. Petersburg, but he was soon back and ended up in the Caucasus with Walter and Carl before his early death.[21]

The practical meaning of family for Werner, of course, changed over his lifetime with the nature of the family's wealth and activities.[22] As the oldest son, he considered himself responsible for the education and placement of his younger siblings, especially after the early death of his parents and the dispersal of the children to different relatives.[23] We know from later statements that his parents had instilled in the children a strong sense of belonging together and of responsibility for each other. Werner was particularly impressed by the historical lessons of one of the family tutors, who impressed upon his mind the story of the great German Renaissance merchant and eventually noble family of the Fuggers.[24] Perhaps the model of such families was in his mind from the beginning, but as he grew older his vision widened and he spoke of the family business in imperial terms, bringing in the Fuggers and Rothschilds as models for how an integrated international family could work.[25] A crisis between Werner, Wilhelm, and Karl emerged in the 1860s, and the correspondence between the brothers reveals a number of things: the critical importance of a leading personality to do the work of keeping alliances going, the strong assumptions about inclusion and exclusion, the vision that establishes a sense of purpose, and, just as important, the material mediations that help give shape to the commitments that family members are willing to make to each other.

The Crisis

Werner had sent the twenty-year-old Wilhelm to England to see about selling a patented process Werner had developed to great success, after which the younger brother decided to settle in England as an inventor and consultant.[26] When Werner established a firm with the mechanic, Johann Georg Halske (1814–1890), based on production of telegraph equipment and the building of telegraph lines in 1847, Wilhelm became the representative of the company in England. Werner saw that the telegraph was destined to become an international affair and first sent his brother Carl to France to play a similar role. St. Petersburg turned out to have more promise, and Werner got Carl established there, where Carl came to manage the business of Siemens and Halske, which already by 1850 was a successful international enterprise. While both Carl and Wilhelm represented the Berlin business, each developed sidelines of his own, with the English brother becoming a major inventor, particularly with developments in the technology of heating and furnaces. Werner had hired almost all of his brothers at one time or another to work for Siemens and Halske, and many other relatives filtered through as well, and by the early 1860s Halske was loudly complaining. Werner wrote to Wilhelm: "I have to admit that he is not completely unreasonable. The interests of my siblings have in fact had more influence on the course of our business than was fair for an outsider to the family."[27] It is interesting that Werner cooperated well with Halske and utilized many of his early acquaintances and friends in building up the business, over the course of time promoting promising young men to positions of responsibility and power in the various firms he directed. Still, the coordination of family members composed a sort of skeleton around which everyone else was organized. And familial aggrandizement gave focus and purpose to the whole enterprise.

The crisis of the 1860s had several dimensions. With Carl in St. Petersburg, there was considerable loss of money through the sidelines that he got into, buying up several estates and planning a brewing business. Werner accused him of *Interesse-Particularismus* and encouraged him to pay attention to the interests of the whole (*Gesamt-Interessen*). "We always have to reckon what the common business (*Gesamtgeschäft*) wins or loses with any particular measure. Even though we have to take particular interests into consideration, we cannot allow them to dominate."[28] Werner kept worrying about the splintering of interests, and both he and Halske wrote in 1863 warning Carl to take only those decisions that would be in the common interest and not pay attention to any personal motives of any kind. Werner wrote to him: "We know very well that you would never act against this principle intentionally, but experience teaches that your good nature and inability to say no easily leads you unwillingly astray, which can be very destructive."[29] At this point, "centrifugal developments" were also happening in London. Wilhelm too was losing money for the firm, apparently, and he was spending a great deal of his time involved in other pursuits, also losing money, in which Werner had invested and then invested heavily again. He wrote to Carl: "Wilhelm and I have carried out our entire technical careers faithfully alongside each other, and I could not therefore let him drop."[30] Unable to get along with each other, Halske and Wilhelm confronted a number of issues. Wilhelm wanted to develop the international laying of cable, which Halske did not want to pursue.[31] And he also thought that the business arrangement between Siemens and Halske in Berlin with him in London was to his disadvantage, an issue that blew up over the question of the pricing of Berlin goods to be sold on the English market.[32]

Continually circling around the exchanges between the brothers was the problem of "outsiders." Of course, each of the brothers felt loyal to some of his own partners or officers, who the other brothers might consider intruders into family affairs. Wilhelm certainly felt this way about Halske and was quite willing to let him drop.[33] Carl too came to see Halske as holding the progress of the family back. In England, one of the business associates, L. Loeffler, who had started out in the Berlin firm but now worked with Wilhelm in England, was suspected by Werner of instigating Wilhelm's discontent and trying to make the London business independent.[34] So in different constellations, the brothers took aim at outsiders. It is interesting that the rhetoric that Werner used in cajoling and encouraging continuously mixed business and family, while in other contexts, he argued for their strict separation, as we will see. He pleaded with his brother to have the one *business* act in a "brotherly" fashion to the other.[35] Wilhelm's complaint about the pricing of the apparatuses that he was to sell had led to distrust and implied dishonesty on the part of the Berlin firm, which Werner energetically denied. But he began to see that because the Berlin firm had interests in the profits of the London firm and Wilhelm had no part in the Berlin firm, their respective interests could not be identical. He suggested to Wilhelm that they combine the two operations: "I passionately wish a real brotherly and friendly relationship between our businesses."[36] Wilhelm at that point was pushing for separation on the grounds that it was impossible to mix business and personal interests—businesses haggle over prices, while partners cannot introduce particular interests. Werner put his stamp on the future relationships between the brothers with this thought: "That dear Brother must become otherwise, and we have to come to an agreement over it."[37] He emphasized the international nature of the business where each branch brought advantages to the others. There was no question of competing among themselves. The Berlin firm sold much more cheaply to the London firm so that it could make a profit, and if

Loeffler was not mistrustful and jealous and misled Wilhelm, he would see how it works.[38] He appealed for getting back to a brotherly tone.

To Carl, Werner laid out the global strategy: "For our business, the London firm is an arm that has to work with the rest of the body harmoniously. England is the world market, and without England we cannot continue our telegraphy business."[39] Werner was absolutely clear that he did not want to lose the English business and its coordination with Berlin. Wilhelm had made a considerable name for himself and had significant influence in England. It was he who made things possible for them all, and as their agent, he established their reputation. To Wilhelm: "It all comes out the same, when the business here in all its parts considers the London one as part of its own flesh and blood, as indeed in reality is the case."[40] In the dispute, Wilhelm found little future selling Berlin-produced apparatuses, but wanted to shift their business in the direction of submarine cable—and that was precisely where the mechanic Halske had no interest in going.[41]

The three-year conflict convinced Werner that Wilhelm was right about the future. With the prospect of Halske retiring, he began to think strategically not so much about where the business had its branches and made its income but where the brothers were located.[42] To Wilhelm in 1863, he wrote that Carl had become an influential personality in St. Petersburg, almost more than Wilhelm himself in England. Walter had been developing his own reputation in Russia and had a large area of activity in Tiflis. Werner was now looking toward a great future for the Siemens family. His solution to Wilhelm was to found a business in 1867 at the retirement of Halske with the three brothers as partners, to be called the "Gebrüder Siemens."[43] There would be three independent houses in St. Petersburg, Berlin, and London, with each brother sharing in one-third of the profits of each house. "Private business would be, as previously, forbidden."[44] What exactly Werner meant by that is unclear, since he had continuously invested privately in Wilhelm's activities and in those of his other brothers and together with Carl bought a mine in the Caucasus. In any event, his vision was now fixed on business structured around an agnatic lineage: "My leading idea to this suggestion was to found a lasting firm that perhaps later could become, under the leadership of our sons, a world firm like the Rothschilds among others and could bring fame (*Ansehen*) in the world for our name. For this great plan the individual, if he finds it a good idea, must be ready to make personal sacrifice. A simple, clear and healthy foundation is the main thing."[45]

Up until the founding of the new firm, the brothers fought over many things. Wilhelm found the Caucasus mine not worth the trouble and warned against investing any money in Walter. Wilhelm did not want to work any more with Halske, while Carl defended him.[46] Werner played the mediator, pointing out to each brother that they found each other's ideas risky. And he constantly counseled Wilhelm to act in a brotherly fashion. Wilhelm, however, felt undervalued and was jealous of the position of Berlin.[47] There was a constant shifting of ideas about agreement and about who was to share with whom. At one point, Carl seemed excluded, and he insisted on being part of any deal. He wrote to Werner: "My inmost interest is always and everywhere to see my interests united with yours."[48] In all of the shifting conflict, Werner had the goal of creating a single business combining the interests of the three brothers. In the end, in 1867, the brothers founded the Siemens Brothers firm.[49]

It became clear to Werner that the business had become bureaucratic and the business correspondence far beyond his own capacities. In the past he had been used to mixing personal and business matters in the same letters, but within a year of the founding of the firm based on the ownership of the three brothers, he wrote to Wilhelm that from now on they had to keep the two kinds of correspondence completely separate and that the business correspondence would be carried on by the officers of the firm.[50] Yet private correspondence would be absolutely essential to iron out conflicts among the directors. He was well aware that a business empire based on a family had to have a way of dealing constantly with personal issues—family and business would run along two separate paths, but they would continually track each other.[51]

Siemens Clan

To this point, I have been following the interplay between family and business. There is much more to say about the importance of other Siemens family members and relatives for the crucial provision of investment capital at different points in the development of the Siemens family firms. But it is also important to understand that beyond the business connections themselves, there was a whole range of family activities and sociability within which all the particular relationships were embedded. And Werner's two marriages were themselves very much in the nineteenth-century tradition—the first with the daughter of a Königsberg professor related to him through a maternal uncle, who was among the early investors in Werner's activities.[52] Such a marriage represents the alliance of two families over more than one generation. His second was with a third cousin—a Siemens, daughter of a professor in Hohenheim—with whom he had active contact.[53] And this kind of marriage, like that of one of his sons, who married the daughter of his brother Ferdinand, followed the pattern of endogamous strengthening of agnatic lineage ties.[54] In 1861, Werner suggested that the family should found a regular family meeting to which everyone would be obligated to come.[55] About a decade later, as we have seen, the Siemens family established their foundation (*Stiftung*), expressly dedicated to fostering family feeling among people of the same name and with a demonstrated genealogical connection.[56] As we have seen, the family met periodically in groups of up to two hundred people, taking over entire hotels in the Harz.[57] There were various members of the family engaged in the Siemens businesses, and room was frequently made for a young man connected through marriage. Tracing out the relations of the second and third generations will be part of the larger project, but I want to take up three moments in the family history that illustrate ways in which family egoism played a role.

Georg Siemens

The first moment has to do with the career of Georg Siemens (1839–1901), the son of Werner's cousin Johann Georg Siemens, *Justizrat* in Berlin and the first major source of investment funds.[58] The latter was a partner in Siemens and Halske and at the beginning of the firm lived with his family in the same house as Werner and various of his assorted siblings—and apparently with Halske himself.[59] After his father broke off business relations with Siemens and Halske and moved out of the house, personal relations with Werner still remained warm, and Werner took considerable interest in his first cousin once removed, becoming influential in decisions about Georg's education.[60] At one point a maternal uncle, Wilhelm von Sperl, was ready to will his entire fortune to Georg if he changed his name, but young Georg refused.[61] Werner brought him into the firm and promoted him rapidly until he became the secretary of the business. During the early 1860s, the young man was sent to England to help set up the international directory of Siemens and Halske, with Georg himself as a member.[62] After Walter died, Georg was sent to Persia to carry on very successful year-long negotiations for the Indo-European telegraph line.[63] Clearly Werner was grooming Georg as his successor. By 1869, he was promoted within the firm in Berlin, and Werner made him the guardian of his children in case of his own death, precisely because at that point his brother Carl was unwilling to move to Berlin should the need arise.[64] Werner even wrote to Carl that "the dynasty is to be rescued through Georg."[65]

It is at this point that an interesting shift in the relationships took place. In many families with talented young men, some of them insisted on striking off on their own, and this is precisely what Georg did. He became one of the founders of the Deutsche Bank, bringing in Werner himself to serve on the board (*Verwaltungsrat*).[66] Almost as soon as he became independent, in 1868, with a crisis in financing in the London firm, Georg underwrote the debts on his own reckoning—actually taking large losses.[67] Even in this early part of his career, like with many members of industrialist families of the time, it was precisely his independence that operated strategically to support a network of family members. This is not the place to chronicle Georg's role in the rise of the huge electrical conglomerate, AEG, and its rivalry with Siemens. Georg was on the board of the AEG, but all along took great interest in the Siemens family business.[68] In the early 1890s, he even brokered a deal between the two giant firms, which when it came to an end in 1894 led to the renewal of their rivalry.[69] Georg advised turning Siemens and Halske into a joint-stock company (*Aktiengesellschaft* [AG]), but for Werner it was always a question of keeping the firm as a family undertaking.[70] Still, the advantage of an AG, as Georg pointed out, was its ability to have access to the financial markets.[71] Werner in his autobiography took up the question of whether large commercial houses should remain permanently in the family of the founder. The problem for him was that corporations were purely gain-seeking enterprises that could by their very nature only pursue maximum profit. Crucial for him was the idea of risk as the most successful path of innovation, which in turn required a larger store of knowledge and experience than could be found in a non-family-owned company. "Such an aggregation of capital, knowledge, and experience can only be formed and maintained in long established commercial houses, remaining by inheritance in the same family."[72] In accord with Werner's vision, Georg pioneered a practice of limiting dividends in order to continue developing the internal strength of the firm.[73] Even after Georg succeeded in setting up Siemens as an AG in 1887 (two years before Werner retired), all the shares remained in the hands of the Siemens family. By 1894, Georg wrote that while his own business interests lay on the side of the AEG, his sentiment was on the side of Siemens and Halske.[74] He had been instrumental in the success of the AEG and was chairman of the board, but he nonetheless resigned in 1896 in order to devote his energies exclusively to Siemens and Halske. His brother-in-law, Hermann Görz, was sent to St. Petersburg to represent the interests of the firm.[75] There is a great deal to explore in this fascinating evolution, which I have to leave aside here, but the principal markers along the way are important: refusal to abandon the family name, training and socialization within the family firm, developing an independent position strategic for family success at crucial points, and a willingness to put family aggrandizement ahead of personal interests.

Alexander Siemens

Werner's hopes in Georg Siemens lay precisely in the fact that he carried the Siemens name and represented the larger kinship group. And all along Georg played a key role in support for his cousin's firm, turning it into a modern joint-stock company while protecting familial ownership and directorship. A similar situation arose with the London branch of the family business. Wilhelm had married the sister of one of his closest associates in London, who in turn married a women from Hannover, whose sister was married to Gustav Siemens, a high court judge in Hannover. The latter's son, Alexander, was another Siemens hired on by Werner and educated and promoted within the firm, one of the young men sent off as an engineer to construct the Indo-European telegraph line. In 1871, Wilhelm brought him to England and adopted him, with the intent of making him his successor.[76] Many kin worked for the Siemens brothers; the point seems to have been to provide space for individuals to show talent and then to promote them up through the ranks. All the brothers called upon Siemens relatives as distant as third and fourth cousins to play key roles in their firms, and they were often traded back and forth, getting education and experience in one country and then traveling on to the next. In the genealogy provided by Hermann Siemens, I counted twenty-six men who worked for the firms: businessmen, salesmen, managers, technicians, engineers (lots of them), chemists, lawyers, and inventors. They held positions as section directors, members of the high administration and boards of directors, chairmen, partners, head clerks, and CEOs. It is hard to locate in the Siemens genealogy, which is based on a single surname, all the relatives by marriage that ended up in the firm as well, although there are many examples of allied employees and investors to be found in a detailed reading of the secondary literature on the Siemens.

Carl had come to England for a decade, where he and Wilhelm built houses side-by-side with a communicating passageway, but by 1881, Wilhelm had largely withdrawn from the business, and Carl was itching to return to St. Petersburg.[77] In 1880, with the floating of Siemens Brothers & Co. Ltd., there were seven subscribers: Werner, Wilhelm, Carl, Loeffler, Arnold (Werner's eldest son), Georg Wilhelm (Werner's second son, and successor as director of Siemens and Halske in Berlin), and Alexander. We have already heard about Loeffler, whom Werner had suspected of instigating Wilhelm's mistrust of the parent firm in Berlin.[78] After Wilhelm's death in 1883, Loeffler became managing director and ended up suing the German company in the name of the English company. By 1888, he was forced to resign and was replaced by Alexander (who had become, like his adopted father, a British citizen) because he represented the family and carried the name.[79] Without going into detail here, the Stafford works of the firm were eventually put under Werner's youngest son (from his second marriage), Carl Friedrich, whose elder brother Wilhelm eventually brought him back to Berlin to establish his credentials and to succeed him there.[80]

The Problem of Allied Families

In the early modern period, there had been widespread prohibitions against marrying kin connected through heredity or through marriage. In Protestant countries (except for England), people were forbidden to marry as far as second cousins and in Catholic countries as far as third cousins without dispensations, which until the early eighteenth century were difficult to come by. During the course of the eighteenth century, most countries either abrogated the prohibitions beyond the nuclear family or constructed a policy of pro forma dispensations. The upshot of the prohibitions, on the one hand, and the strict rules of succession and subsequent differentiation of siblings, on the other, meant that any family or lineage could only reproduce itself through marriage with "strangers," that is, with people not closely related to themselves. Beginning in the eighteenth century, this slowly changed, and family members eventually were able to find marriage partners not only with allied families but from within the lineage itself, which in turn was thought of as a surname group descended from a particular ancestor.

Hermann Siemens, a population biologist, wrote a study in the *Archiv für Rassen- und Gesellschaftsbiologie* in which he chronicled the history of the Siemens family in all of its branches from the sixteenth century onwards.[81] From the mid-eighteenth century, marriages back into the various branches of the Siemens family proliferated as did marriages between linked families.[82] There were always, of course, marriages outwards with new families, but they tended, for the most part, to be in similar milieus (for example, one of Werner's sons married his friend von Helmholtz's daughter, while another married his brother's daughter). Relationships could be very close between allied families, but when we look at the generation of Werner and his brothers, they distinguished carefully between family members carrying the Siemens surname and family members who were merely allied through marriage. Allies could be crucial for business connections, but they had to be shown careful limits. I want to deal rather extensively with Carl's marriage to show the ideas and values that motivated Werner and became part of his strategy for family coordination and aggrandizement.

When Werner first went to St. Petersburg to investigate the possibilities of setting up telegraphy in Russia, he developed a close relationship with Baron von Kap-herr, a banker and businessman with considerable experience and connections. When Werner sent his brother Carl (in his early twenties) in 1855 to head the office of Siemens and Halske, he recommended Kap-herr as an important associate and financier. When Carl and Kap-herr soon got into conflict, Werner counseled his younger brother to try to get along. After all, Kap-herr was useful for the business when Carl was away in southern Russia supervising cable construction.[83] Kap-herr had even run the St. Petersburg office, and although he had acted more independently than was in the Siemens's interests, he was very useful and hard to dispense with. The problem arose from Carl leaving Kap-herr signature rights while he was out of town, and now he continued to sign papers in the name of the firm.[84]

Because of Carl's inexperience, Werner had surrounded him with the best business people available. But he now advised Carl to take everything into his own hands and make everyone, including Kap-herr, fall into line.[85] Carl later wrote notes on the margin of Werner's letter: "While I was in southern Russia dealing with the building of the line, he [Kap-herr] made himself lord of the situation," but upon his return he had to reestablish his dominance. His brother Werner overvalued Kap-herr's services.[86] Apparently the tensions between the two men were somewhat resolved once Carl became engaged to and married Kap-herr's daughter.[87] Even during the period of his engagement, however, he was complaining about interference of his fiancée into the firm's affairs. Werner wrote that Carl was right to forbid her intrusion into business questions and to counter the objectionable Kap-herr house practice of confusing business and the domestic sphere.[88] There needed to be clear boundaries, and Kap-herr himself needed to be put in his place.

Once Carl was married, Werner relied on Scripture to tell his brother that a wife's duty was to leave father and mother and to follow her husband.[89] Carl needed to be self-conscious about his own rights and not allow his wife or her family to infringe upon them even in inessential things. Werner feared that Carl's father-in-law would attempt to utilize the ties of kinship to establish his own dominance. In a letter to Kap-herr, Werner wrote about the ties of kinship that now united their families and made them closer than before, but also lead to the kind of transitory friction characteristic of business and family life: "I hold it as very dangerous for business and family life when the matters of both are not kept strictly separate."[90] Werner then brought up his long-time, trusted associate Meyer, whom he had sent to work with Carl in St. Petersburg. He was annoyed that Kap-herr's son Hermann on a trip to Berlin had had the temerity to tell him that he was too swayed by Meyer's judgment. While he would not assert that Meyer was always right, he had worked with him for twenty years and trusted his judgment. But the important point in the matter was the way the incident illustrated ill-judged mixing of family with business—that is, *allied* family, Kap-herr doing an end-run through his son. To Carl he wrote that conflicts could not be avoided and had to be fought through. While it was understandable for Carl's wife, Marie, to want to defend her father's actions, she could not be spared the sad battle between marital and filial love.[91] Kap-herr's chief failure lay in intrigues, and he was blind to the interests of others. He needed to be limited to a restricted field.

The battle for Carl's soul went on for several months. While Carl was traveling, Marie called one of the chief officers of the firm, Elster, into the courtyard "like a common servant" and reprimanded for not doing something promptly. She was reading Elster's correspondence and interfering in other ways. Werner was full of advice, and full of contemporary notions about the characteristics of the sexes: "With women, feeling and fantasy are more lively than with us. … when they get an idea into their heads, it easily runs away with them."[92] Carl's wife suffered from a fundamentally false view about her own position, considering herself a Frau Meisterin, capable of running things when her husband was away, something she should be "weaned" of. It was all right for a woman to rule in her proper sphere, the house, but she should have absolutely no place in business. The ultimate issue had to do with whether Carl could assert his own independence and forbid his wife or anyone else to do anything that displeased him.[93] "You have to teach your wife to honor your will as the highest law." "Once you have decided a matter, you should not allow it to come up again, even if you were wrong."

Finally, Werner got to the point that had motivated him all along: Kap-herr wanted to tie the Siemens business to his own family's interests. And he wanted to do this through Carl. Carl had to block the channel Kap-herr built through marriage to his daughter: "You have to allow not the slightest influence on your business dealings of her biased and one-sided judgment that is a consequence of her upbringing and the continuous influence of *her blood relatives* [my emphasis]."[94] Carl would have to decide if he wanted to move to open battle with his father-in-law and if need be with his wife, to bring her to reason. Once he won the battle, then he could leave St. Petersburg, secure that the administration of the firm would be able to carry on without interference. And if there was no satisfaction, then Kap-herr's son should be kicked out of his apartment! "Show them that there will be no *Weiberregiment* in our business." In one of the last letters on this issue, Werner said that the manner of thought and action of the Kap-herrs was too different from that of the Siemens.[95] The men of the family put ideas into Marie's head, precisely as a way to exercise their own interests. He advised Carl to write to Kap-herr and tell him that the family should never discuss business in Marie's presence and that he would break off family relations or leave St. Petersburg if they did not agree to his will. "Misunderstandings and misjudgments are quite usual with young wives, who come into a circle where other views dominate than those from home."[96] In a final letter, Werner advised: "Ban systematically any kind of business from the family circle," meaning from the in-laws, of course.[97] It seems to me that all of this correspondence offers a textbook case about the issues of lineage aggrandizement and the necessities and dangers of alliance.

Conclusion

There were many ways that families could organize themselves in the nineteenth century, and, of course, the Siemens clan offers only one possibility. Nonetheless, their history provides an insight into certain features of kinship relations that are to be found throughout Germany and most of Europe. An important aspect of many entrepreneurial families is the fact that they burst the bonds of nationality and reached into many parts of the world. And it seems important to understand that while Germany may not have had an empire or only a small, lately acquired one, Germans used the empires of other nations to expand their economic reach. Far more important for them than any particular colonies that Germany stumbled into were the empires of England, France, Russia, Austria, and the Ottomans. Furthermore, the extension of German economic interests frequently was made possible by the coordinated activities of families, whose structural lineaments looked similar whether international or contained within the confines of the nation. The features of endogamy, patrilineal construction, and systematic exchange created important resources for enterprising individuals to build upon. Beyond the specific relations of core individuals—brothers, fathers and sons, and the like—some family "workers" put a great deal of effort into creating a strong identity among a large and growing number of people through genealogical investigation, founding family associations, arranging periodic gatherings, establishing institutions, and cultivating name recognition. The Siemens family fits very nicely into these dynamics. And it illustrates one major aspect of kinship relationships of the nineteenth century—the dialectic between strong lineal recognition and the pragmatic use of networks constructed out of friends, allies, and consanguines. There were significant ambivalences at every level: Georg, Wilhelm, and Alexander all profited from being part of the Siemens clan, but insisted on striking off in their own directions—but, as we have seen, this could be part of the strength of this particular kinship system. It was outfitted to promote the most able of its members. And there were significant tensions and possibilities inherent in relationships through maternal kin and through in-laws. Given some of the structural possibilities of nineteenth-century kin, it is still important to see that cohesion did not arise from nature but was the result of the intense labor of developing identities, moral claims, and practical networks.

Notes

1. The evidence is summarized in David Warren Sabean, *Kinship in Neckarhausen, 1700–1870* (Cambridge, 1998), 428–48; David Warren Sabean and Simon Teuscher, "Kinship in Europe: A New Approach to Long-Term Development," in *Kinship in Europe: Approaches to Long-Term Development (1300–1900)*, ed. David Warren Sabean, Simon Teuscher, and Jon Mathieu (New York, 2007), 16–24. See also the essays in the same volume by Christopher H. Johnson, "Kinship, Civil Society, and Power in Nineteenth-Century Vannes," 258–83, and Elisabeth Joris, "Kinship and Gender: Property, Enterprise, and Politics," 231–57.
2. Nancy Fix Anderson, "Cousin Marriage in Victorian England," *Journal of Family History* 11 (1986): 285–301; Adam Kuper, "Incest, Cousin Marriage, and the Origin of the Human Sciences in Nineteenth-Century England," *Past and Present* 174 (2002): 153–83.
3. It should also be clear that while cousin marriages appeared in all propertied classes in Europe, not all families practiced them, and in any one locality or milieu, different classes pursued different marriage strategies.
4. Both Sabean and Delille offer examples. Sabean, *Kinship*, 281, 285, 392. Gérard Delille, *Famille et propriété dans le royaume de Naples (XVe–XIXe)* (Paris, 1985). His argument is summarized in Sabean, *Kinship*, 399–407.
5. This is documented more fully in David Warren Sabean, "Kinship and Issues of the Self in Europe around 1800," in *Sibling Relations and the Transformations of European Kinship, 1300–1900*, ed. Christopher H. Johnson and David Warren Sabean (New York, 2011), ch. 11.
6. Pierre Bourdieu, *Outline of a Theory of Practice* (Cambridge, 1977), 57; Pierre Bourdieu, *The Logic of Practice* (Cambridge, 1977), 187.
7. See David Warren Sabean, "From Clan to Kindred: Kinship and the Circulation of Property in Premodern and Modern Europe," in *Heredity Produced: At the Crossroads of Biology, Politics, and Culture, 1500–1870*, ed. Staffan Müller-Wille and Hans-Jörg Rheinberger (Cambridge, MA, 2007), 37–60, and Sabean and Teuscher, "Kinship in Europe," 4–16.

8. See Ulrike Vedder, "Continuity and Death: Literature and the Law of Succession in the Nineteenth Century," in Müller-Wille and Rheinberger, *Heredity*, 85–102.
9. Friedrich Zunkel, *Der Rheinisch-Westfälische Unternehmer 1834–1879: Ein Beitrag zur Geschichte des deutschen Bürgertums im 19. Jahrhundert* (Cologne, 1962), 9–23.
10. A good example is found in the text of the Siemens family foundation (*Stiftung*), printed in Hermann Werner Siemens, *Stammbaum der Familie Siemens* (Munich, 1935), 28.
11. The following text is taken from Sabean, *Kinship*, 452–54.
12. Hermann Siemens in *Stammbaum*, 22, points out that the Siemens genealogy was first put together in 1829 and then revised several times until Hermann himself totally redid it twice, with the definitive construction published in 1935.
13. A list of Siemens family association meetings is given in Hermann Siemens, *Stammbaum*, 22–26, and the statutes of the family foundation, 28–31.
14. Brigitte Schröder, "Der Weg zur Eisenbahnschiene. Geschichte der Familie Remy und ihre wirtschaftliche und kulturelle Bedeutung," in *Deutsches Familienarchiv: Ein genealogisches Sammelwerk* (Neustadt an der Aisch, 1986), 91:3–158.
15. This is discussed in Sabean, *Kinship*, 449–89.
16. Werner von Siemens, *Werner Siemens, Ein kurzgefaßtes Lebensbild nebst einer Auswahl seiner Briefe: Aus Anlaß der 100. Wiederkehr seiner Geburtstages*, ed. Conrad Matschoß (Berlin, 1916).
17. Werner von Siemens, *Personal Recollections* (London, 1893), 7.
18. Hermann Siemens in *Stammbaum* gives considerable credit to Leo Siemens for the labor (establishing the foundation and publishing a genealogy) for creating and maintaining family identity and cohesion.
19. William Pole, *The Life of Sir William Siemens* (London, 1888), 71.
20. On Friedrich, see Richard Ehrenberg, *Unternehmungen der Brüder Siemens*, vol. 1, *Bis zum Jahre 1870* (Jena, 1906), 308–41.
21. Siemens, *Werner Siemens*, 228–29.
22. In 1833, he wrote to his son Wilhelm: "Our task is to maintain the position that our family has achieved in the world," in Friedrich Heintzenberg, ed., *Aus einem reichen Leben: Werner von Siemens in Briefen an seine Familie und Freunde*, 2nd. ed. (Stuttgart, 1953), 320.
23. Siemens, *Werner Siemens*, 8–9.
24. Ibid., 2.
25. Kurt Busse, *Werner von Siemens* (Bad Godesberg, 1966), 31.
26. Ehrenberg, *Unternehmungen*, 38; John D. Scott, *Siemens Brothers 1858–1958: An Essay in the History of Industry* (London, 1958), 21.
27. Siemens, *Werner Siemens*, 212.
28. Ehrenberg, *Unternehmungen*, 411–12.
29. Ibid., 413.
30. Ibid., 414–15.
31. Ibid., 403–7.
32. Ibid., 421–23.
33. Scott, *Siemens Brothers*, 51–52.
34. Ehrenberg, *Unternehmungen*, 419–20, 424.
35. Ibid., 422.
36. Ibid.
37. Ibid., 423.
38. Ibid., 421–24.
39. Ibid., 424.

40. Ibid., 425.
41. Ibid., 426–27.
42. Ibid., 427–28.
43. Ibid., 429.
44. Ibid., 430.
45. Ibid.; Siemens, *Werner Siemens,* 218.
46. Ehrenberg, *Unternehmungen,* 431.
47. Ibid., 433–34.
48. Ibid., 444.
49. Ibid., 454–56; Scott, *Siemens Brothers,* 52ff.
50. Siemens, *Werner Siemens,* 110.
51. Ibid., 289.
52. Kurt Busse, *Werner,* 10. On how kinship played a role in his courtship, see Heintzenberg, *Aus einem reichen Leben,* 21–22.
53. Busse, *Werner,* 22.
54. Heintzenberg, *Aus einem reichen Leben,* 311.
55. Ibid., 183.
56. Hermann Siemens, *Stammbaum,* 22–31, with the text of the *Stiftung.*
57. Scott, *Siemens Brothers,* 29; Pole, *William,* 16.
58. Scott, *Siemens Brothers,* 25; Georg Siemens, *History of the House of Siemens,* 2 vols. (Freiburg, 1952), 1:17.
59. On the early financing of Siemens and Halske through family connections, see Siemens, *Werner Siemens,* 31; Carl Helfferich, *Georg von Siemens: Ein Lebensbild aus Deutschlands großer Zeit,* 2nd. ed., 3 vols. (Berlin, 1923), 1:6–7.
60. Helfferich, *Georg von Siemens,* 13.
61. Ibid., 1:42.
62. Ehrenberg, *Unternehmungen,* 205; Georg Siemens, *House of Siemens,* 1:56.
63. Ehrenberg, *Unternehmungen,* 224; Helfferich, *Georg von Siemens,* 101–3.
64. Ehrenberg, *Unternehmeungen,* 297.
65. Helfferich, *Georg von Siemens,* 2:20–21.
66. Ibid., 1:188; 2:17.
67. Ibid., 2:20–21.
68. Georg Siemens, *House of Siemens,* 1:99–100.
69. Ibid., 1:154.
70. Ibid., 1:156; Helfferich, *Georg von Siemens,* 2:3–57.
71. Georg Siemens, *House of Siemens,* 1:154–56.
72. Werner von Siemens, *Recollections,* 359. See Helfferich, *Georg von Siemens,* 2:106.
73. Helfferich, *Georg von Siemens,* 2:106.
74. Ibid., 2:123.
75. Georg Siemens, *House of Siemens,* 1:315; Helfferich, *Goerg von Siemens,* 2:138.
76. On Alexander's training and career, see Scott, *Siemens Brothers,* 69.
77. Pole, *William,* 274.
78. Scott, *Siemens Brothers,* 65, makes the general point that Loeffler and Halske clashed with the "family principle."
79. Ibid., 67–8: the brothers agreed that "outsiders were outsiders."
80. Ibid., 75; Georg Siemens, *House of Siemens,* 311–12.
81. "Über das Erfindergeschlecht Siemens," *Archiv für Rassen- und Gesellschaftsbiologie* 12 (1916–18): 171–90.
82. Ehrenberg, *Unternehmungen,* 84–86, 89–91.
83. Heintzenberg, *Aus einem reichen Leben,* 99–103.

84. Ibid., 100.
85. Ibid., 101.
86. Ibid., 103.
87. Ibid., 107.
88. Ibid., 113.
89. Ibid., 114.
90. Ibid., 116.
91. Ibid., 117.
92. Ibid., 124.
93. Ibid., 125.
94. Ibid., 128.
95. Ibid., 131–32.
96. Ibid., 133.
97. Ibid., 134.

Chapter 12

The Culture of Caribbean Migration to Britain in the 1950s

Mary Chamberlain

> SCANTLEBURY–Ethel Eudine, aged 90 years, late of Easy Hall, St. John. Wife of the late John 'Alsa' Scantlebury; mother of Randolph Toppin and Ophelia Clarke (USA), Seymour Scantlebury and Heather Gollop (of UK), Elinda Scantlebury (of Saudi Arabia), Byron and Orrendelle Scantlebury (of Canada), Richard Scantlebury, Leroy Scantlebury (of Health Ministry), Venilla Callender (of Data Processing Department), Cirleine Scantlebury and the late Everton Toppin; grandmother of Richard Toppin, Delcina Kellman, Dr. Decourtney Scantlebury (World Renowned Pianist), Merton King and Doriel Scantlebury (of UWI), Celestine Kellman and 27 others; great grandmother of 51; sister of Vernita Wiltshire (of Ruby, St. Philip), Eureta Goddard (of Easy Hall, St. John), Errol, Kirkland, Dorothy and Mervene Beckles (of USA), the late Joseph Belgrave, Violet Edgehill, Cynthia Greaves and Wesley Grant; aunt of Ulric Spooner, Herman Spencer and Carlyle Sobers; relative of the Toppin, Kellman, Spencer and Sobers families; friend of the many.
>
> —Obituary in *The Sun* (Barbados), May 2004.

While the changes in Europe's flows of sentiment and flows of money reflected and resulted in its modernizing process and the concomitant reconfiguration of Europe's political frameworks, economic institutions, and domestic arrangements, the same processes resulted in very different political and social configurations in Europe's earliest colonies in the West Indies.[1] From the start the Caribbean was at the center of the global experiment, a region whose formation was, as Don Robotham has argued, "within the framework of global capitalism," and whose strength and livelihood was intimately bound up with the commercial, military, and imperial ambitions of Europe.[2] Certainly for many of the wealthier Europeans from the sixteenth and seventeenth centuries, transnationalism was a central feature of their settlement as lives in the Caribbean became enmeshed with activities and ambitions (both professional and familial) in the metropolises of Europe, and vice versa. Their presence, however, and their profits, were increasingly dependent upon another transnational community—the Africans imported into the Caribbean to act as slave labor. This forced migration (which we may legitimately call a diaspora) of between eleven million and eighteen million men and women brought to the Caribbean between the sixteenth and nineteenth centuries, was the largest forced migration in modern history.[3] Africans were plucked from their routines of culture and kin and thrust into the logic of the plantation regime. This logic, as Sidney Mintz argued, transformed not only the pattern of production and the organization of labor, but the social and family life of the laborer. The Caribbean peoples were the first *modern* people.[4]

By the early years of the nineteenth century, a pattern of family formation could be discerned that followed peculiar chronological and kinship rules, typified (as Jean Besson usefully summarized) by three key elements:

- *a dynamic complex marriage system*, based on multiple conjugal forms and sequential unions or serial polygamy
- *ego-focused bilateral kinship networks*, recognizing relatives for each individual on both parental sides
- *ancestor-orientated nonunilineal or cognatic descent lines,* traced from a common ancestor of either gender through both males and females.[5]

The logic of Caribbean families originated not in the conjugal unit (as emphasized in the European Christian tradition) but in descent through the maternal and paternal lines, and in resulting kin connections. Siblings could, however, have different fathers or mothers and still regard themselves as "full" siblings (the concept of "half" and "step" relatives is not used). Each sibling could belong to a different kinship constellation, sharing some kin and ancestors but not others. "Outside" kin could also be incorporated in family membership, on more or less equal terms.[6]

These creolized families that emerged out of the trauma of the African diaspora and slavery were broad, inclusive, and flexible and as such could maximize scarce resources (in contrast to some European models where scarce resources would be an argument for restricting family entitlement). While these characteristics became uniquely suited to the large-scale migrations from the region in the nineteenth and twentieth centuries, they were often identified during slavery and, particularly, after as evidence of dissolute and deviant lifestyles, and an inability to conform to "civilized" principles of family formation.[7] Most commentators—from the nineteenth century onwards—focused on what they perceived as the high rates of illegitimacy, the high proportion of female-headed households (leading to what R. T. Smith defined as "matrifocal" families), and the marginalization of men, blaming the situation on slavery or promiscuity and characterizing it as an exclusively lower-class phenomenon.[8] At the same time, they downgraded, ignored, or even condemned the broad and inclusive structures of kinship that supported what Thomas Simey, the social policy adviser to West Indian Development and Welfare, characterized in the 1940s as "casual" and "disintegrate" family life.[9] Indeed, much to Simey's consternation, "Not a single [household] consisted only of parents and their children," and subsequent critics pointed to patterns of childrearing that engaged a range of adults other than the parents.[10]

As Caribbean families continued to reconstitute themselves after slavery, they also migrated. During the nineteenth century, migration was broadly confined within the region, but the relaunch of the Panama Canal project by the Isthmanian Canal Commission in 1904 enticed laborers to Panama. Between 1904 and 1914 approximately ninety thousand Jamaicans and sixty thousand Barbadians—one in four of the population—left for Panama; from Panama many traveled to other destinations within the Caribbean and to North, South, and Central America.[11] From the late nineteenth and early twentieth century, however, a number of characteristics emerged that distinguished Caribbean migration. While it may have been individuals who migrated, this migration was with, and for, the support of the family in the Caribbean. It was, in this sense, a family endeavor. For the most part, despite poor communications, nineteenth- and twentieth-century migrants maintained links with family members across the oceans and the generations through letters and remittances.[12] Many of the migrants (who included independent women as well as men) eventually returned home to the Caribbean.[13] Those who remained in their host societies built new communities while retaining many of their cultural attributes and family contact with the Caribbean.[14] By the early decades of the twentieth century, out-migration had become an integral feature of the Caribbean and an increasingly important component of the family and national economy.[15] Out-migration had become, in other words, an active ingredient in the culture of the region, each migration reinforcing its "image" as a positive activity while family strategies evolved, and family structures accommodated, to facilitate it.[16] As a result, the Caribbean remained a constant feature in the lives of migrants, while for those who remained in the region, migration was seen as a link with "foreign," not a severance from home, an opportunity to extend, not disrupt, the family links. In other words, *transnational* activity was built into the fabric of migration.

Despite the centrality of migration in Caribbean society, the links between families and migration have been relatively underexplored. Migration scholars, such as Elizabeth Thomas Hope, Bonham Richardson, Karen Fog Olwig, or myself, have noted the more complex links while some scholars of the family have examined the relationship between male absence and migration.[17] Yet the links with family and the features identified in earlier migrations (such as the rates of return or the implementation of family strategies) make sense of contemporary elements such as those described by Thomas-Hope as the "homeward orientation" of Caribbean migrants, or by others as "circularity."[18] Moreover, many overseas Caribbean communities of long standing maintain family links over generations and have prompted further insights into the links between families and migration. Olwig, for instance, has highlighted the internationalization of families through the extension of their domestic organization abroad and pointed to ways in which family and neighborhood structures in the Caribbean were well adapted to enable and support the process of migration, less likely to be fractured by its effects, and more likely to replicate or reproduce comparable structures or comparable values for survival in the host community.[19] Such adaptations may be interpreted as a continuation of the process of "creolization," the processes of change and synthesis arising as opposing cultures accommodate to each other.[20] These processes, which necessarily contain transnationalism as their central agent, have already been noted among the Caribbean community in the United States, but are less remarked upon in the British context.[21] Indeed, the proximity of the Caribbean to North America and regular, easy, and relatively cheap communications have resulted in a strengthening of the social, cultural, and domestic links between West Indians in North America and the Caribbean to the point, as Nancy Foner has observed, that returning "home" permanently has become less imperative. Regular visits and extended stays have become sufficient to sustain an imaginative engagement with, and commitment to, "home."

Migration influences, as we shall see, the gestalt and the identity of the family, while the family provides a way of looking at, interpreting, and organizing the world—an example of what Sidney Mintz and Richard Price term "cognitive orientations," or shared and inherited values—a key resource when family belongings extend beyond national boundaries and when the world's resources can be utilized to further family ends.[22] Thus the integration of migration into the organization of families may be seen as evidence of their adaptability and flexibility.

Family Case Study

Let me offer a case study based on oral and life histories, which best illustrates these points. Although critics of qualitative methods may doubt the veracity of a single account or the ability of a numerically small sample to exemplify larger group behavior, a qualitative approach to a subject as complex and as intimate as the family can exemplify its beliefs, mores, and activities. In terms of family and household, life stories may reveal detail on membership, organization, functions, and change within the life cycle or course of the individual and of the family. Life stories can remind us of the movement and flexibility within families, and lead away from an essentialist position on all families (and *the* Caribbean family in particular). They can also provide information from perspectives often ignored or undocumented—of children, for instance, or the elderly—or reveal emotions or feelings, or uncover the inner dynamics of family life, particularly when two or more generations of the same family are interviewed. Above all, they can hint at the meanings that families and family practices have for their members, and the intimate worlds that these meanings inhabit, articulate, and replicate. While every family may have its own subculture, they cannot be isolated from their environment. No life story can be told without reference to the broader milieu as it interacts with the individual and the family—through work, play, and education; health, death, and consumption; and a host of other major and minor interventions.

Lloyd migrated from Jamaica to Britain in 1957 and was "received" into Britain by his wife's cousin. Two years later, he was joined by his wife, Hyacinth, who left their five children in Jamaica under the care of her sister and other kin. Such patterns of child fostering had been noted in the nineteenth century in relation to plantation labor and clearly proved adaptable to the exigencies of migration, where childcare abroad was difficult to find.[23] At the same time, the remittances returned by the migrants helped support not only their children, but also the wider family. In time, four of those five children were brought over to join their parents and two more British-born siblings. Lloyd's migration to Britain paralleled other family members who migrated to the United States, Canada, and, unusually, Japan.

Hyacinth's mother, Lucretia, had married twice and had had four children from her first marriage and two from her second. Hyacinth and her brother from the second marriage lost their father when she was two. Lucretia's first husband, a Chinese man (from mainland China), had also died when his children were small. Lucretia supported all her children from her earnings as a laundress and lived close to her mother (Hyacinth's grandmother) and her mother's six uncles and aunts (another uncle had migrated to Panama). This grandmother was a "beauty" who

> used to love me so much and love all the grandchildren. She would hold at least six, seven, eight of us on her knees. She used to be so good. … she used to be so sweet. Everybody say I look like her sometimes. But her hair was like satin. Like satin. When you plait her hair, it just flicks up, soft, soft, soft.[24]

Her maternal grandfather died when she was small, although she remembers that he "work hard" and "loved children, love his family."[25] She grew up "very, very. Very, very. Very, very close"[26] to her siblings, with no distinction made between fathers and, in this case, mixed-race siblings. She remained close to all the family, "up to the fourth cousin," despite the fact that most of her siblings and cousins were now dispersed around the world. Indeed, through telephone conversations, letters, and keeping up with family developments, she maintained that she kept regular contact with, and was certainly informed about,

> all the family, everywhere, everyone. … because the way we grow up, our family was so loving and people know us to be so loving and kind and everything else. Why shouldn't you want to know them?[27]

Leaving her children behind in Jamaica, was, without any question, full of anguish, but she found work and saved hard and "in no time" had saved sufficiently to bring four of her children to England to join her and her husband and to send a fifth child, the eldest, to cousins in Canada. Her son Jerry was eleven when he joined his parents in 1966. He was six when his mother left, and although he lived with his aunt in a tenement yard in Kingston,

> the extended family that we came from, everybody shared in what we did, you know, we could stay with Uncle this or Auntie that, or what have you, so everybody had a responsibility to bring up everybody else's children. They weren't restricted to any one particular pair.[28]

The first- and second-hand memories of his grandparents—from both sides—are strong. Jerry never knew his maternal grandparents, but from family stories his mother "has taken a lot from her, from the way she's spoken of by other members of the family."[29] In particular, the family legend recalls his grandmother as "such a strong woman. And one of the things she taught her kids was 'Always be there for each other, no matter what'"[30] Significantly, therefore, as Jerry stressed,

> the way that my mother has kept us all together … is identical … [to the] family unit there [in Jamaica]. … That's the same sort of thing that my parents, especially my mother, has tried to maintain. … So each of the siblings that's gone off, have … kept like the family thing going. … it's so much instinctive. … We're spiritual people … and our history is more of somebody telling you what's happened, and you never forget it. It's not a case of "Oh, I can't remember." It's there with you all the time. … it's sort of passed down, which is good. It's nice because … especially living in this country, where there's a lot of pressures … especially because we're an ethnic minority, the family unit provides the type of solace, stability, that is needed to go ahead. … we're always looking out, or thinking about the other one, or the two that's not here, or the three that's not here. … it's as if we're carrying on a tradition that we're not even fully aware of.[31]

As a result of such sentiments, the family members in England—siblings and cousins—lived close to each other in South London. In Jerry's family, as in so many, it was the mothers and grandmothers who were instrumental in ensuring that family members remained in touch with each other. In the study, there were several instances of grandmothers spending their retirement visiting family members around the globe for extended periods.[32]

When Jerry was sixteen, his mother went to the United States to visit her sister-in-law who was looking after three nieces from Jamaica. Hyacinth's mother-in-law was also staying in the United States with this sister. In the course of the visit, the sister-in-law became ill and required hospitalization. Without hesitation, Hyacinth called her husband and informed him that she would be staying. She looked after the children until her sister-in-law was better, then cared for her mother-in-law until her death, then, at her sister-in-law's suggestion and with her help, got a job, while her husband took care of their children in England. She stayed for three years, sending over money and goods, and had planned to stay long enough to earn the right to live and work in the United States. However, she learned that her sixteen-year-old daughter was pregnant and that Jerry, too, aged nineteen, was fathering a child. She returned home immediately: "After I spoke my piece, what could I do … but love them [the grandchildren]? Let them know that I'm their grandmother."[33]

Hyacinth did more than love them. She allowed Jerry and his girlfriend to live in her home until they were able to live independently and helped bring up this grandchild along with her existing—and subsequent—grandchildren. She now has fifteen grandchildren and through regular and sustained periods of childcare has played an active role in their upbringing: "I don't mind at all. … if I only have the strength and the help that I need, financially, I don't mind at all. I love it."[34] The help was both practical and symbolic as she recounted to her grandchildren stories of Jamaica and their family and acculturated them with their origins and values. As she said, (and the comment is representative of this generation of migrants) "We are the grandparents, we know we are West Indians, we are not white English, so they have to have a background of their own."[35]

Significantly, however, it was not only Hyacinth who contributed to the care of Simon, Jerry's child. Simon's paternal grandfather, Lloyd, was influential in his childhood, as was his maternal grandmother, from St. Vincent, who helped out in his childcare, along with Jerry's sisters. "The extended family" as Jerry described "that's been there. You know, if it wasn't my side, it was [my partner's], so, you know, it didn't really matter."[36] Simon, aged twenty-two, lived with his maternal grandmother in a neighborhood filled with both maternal and paternal kin—"We're a close-knit family"—and was as preoccupied with the importance of family as his father, and grandmother, traveling back to the Caribbean, Jamaica, and St. Vincent and to North America to meet relatives.[37] He inherited a wide kinship network from his father and from his mother: "Another family tree. Very big … I went to Canada to visit my grandfather, my mum's dad, … and my auntie and uncle."[38] Jerry has three sons, one of whom was an "outside" child. Although Simon was not close to this brother, "He's still my brother … he's still part of me, he's still blood, at the end of the day, you know?"[39]

In this family, the family values, which actively incorporated wider kin within the socialization of children, have been translated across the ocean and inherited through the generations. "What's helped [my sons] more than anything else," Jerry argued,

> is this network that we've got, the family network. It's given them stability, because they know they've got us to fall back on, should they fall by the wayside in any way. … Whatever happened to them out there may affect them more than it would have done, had they not had this.[40]

Thus Lucretia's dictum to stay together has been an ethos inherited across the generations. More particularly, the importance of the Caribbean and of the family in the Caribbean in providing a sense of identity offered a further ethos that runs through the generations, and was well articulated by Jerry:

> I see myself as a human being first, and as a black person of African-Caribbean descent. I've become a British person through rules and regulations, but I can never be English. Not even my sons, who were born here. They might be English on paper, but they will not … be regarded as such. They will always be Afro-Caribbean, or West Indian. … *And this is why I'm insistent about them learning about where their parents are from. … I always thought that we've got this escape hatch in the back of our minds, those of us who are not born here, where we can always go back to*. But those who are born here haven't got that, it's just stories to them, you know. But they're always being portrayed as being from somewhere else. Now, if you keep telling a young black kid that he's a West Indian, when he was born here, I mean, how does he feel? What sort of things are happening to his head all his life? To be apart from the society that he's grown up in? … *The one thing they will feel, having gone back [to the Caribbean] … is that they realize, for the first time, that they are part of something … part of something else. … [The Caribbean] will always be there for them as part of something that is their heritage.*[41] (Emphasis added)

Discussion

Four interrelated issues arise from these sources: first, this family articulated both the symbolic and the practical discourses of a transnational family narrative. A global context was part of the everyday milieu in which they operated, and the benefits resulting were considered there for the reaping—Canada or the United States, Europe or Japan, St. Vincent or Jamaica. National borders were no barrier to family connectedness, while the idea of family as a *Caribbean* family centered the sense of identity of family members.

Migrants do not leave the old country behind, but remain in an imaginative continuity with it, maintaining it in emotional dialogue, material support, and where possible "traditional" practices. Jerry relied on his mother and his (former) partner's parents to help in the upbringing of his son, Simon. As we have seen, Simon lives close to family members, as preoccupied as they with the wider family network. Other informants stressed the need and desire to impart to their children the foundations of their Caribbean origins and a positive avowal of Caribbean culture, for, as one argued, "I strongly believe that you should never forget your roots."[42] Many British-born (or brought up) African-Caribbeans had a clear sense of the difference of the African-Caribbean family and a pride not only in individual members but also in the system as a whole. As another British-born woman described it, "The sense of family, the sense of unity, was much stronger [than with English families]. … I'm actually really proud of Caribbean families, that was something that we will always retain."[43] These stories of pride in the family, of its importance for support and solace, identity and differentiation, were replicated frequently. Benson, for instance, wanted

> [his children] to know a bit of their history, where they're coming from … not just Jamaican, but black culture. … it's very important, me telling them my background and things like that … [and] it's good to know that family keep in touch. They should know who their cousins are, aunties are, whoever.[44]

The forces of social exclusion in Britain mesh with family histories of other exclusions, and many British-born Caribbeans, in addition to espousing Caribbean culture, have adopted mobile allegiances. "I belong to whoever wants me," argued one informant. "If British people don't want me, what's the point of making yourself part of something that doesn't want you?"[45]

Second, African-Caribbean family narratives focus on the celebratory rather than on the problematic aspects of their relationships.[46] This is not to say that there are no problems. Extended periods of separation resulted, in some cases, with children failing to bond with parents who left when they were babies or to adjust to new siblings born in the United Kingdom. Maternal separation has also been identified as a possible causal element in schizophrenia among second-generation Caribbeans in Britain. Equally, sibling tensions have arisen when one sibling was '"chosen" as the one to migrate and enjoyed greater social mobility. Returning migrants sometimes experienced problems rehabilitating with families left behind, particularly if there was a marked disparity in perceived wealth. Some men migrated and abandoned their families. A contemporary issue in the United Kingdom concerns young Caribbean-heritage men turning to drugs and violence as a source of income and an affirmation of masculinity.[47] There are also demographic changes that threaten the long-term functioning of Caribbean families. In the United Kingdom, grandmothers are often in paid employment and may not have the flexibility or freedom to assume care and control of grandchildren. Smaller family sizes mean that the kinship networks will also diminish over time, which could further threaten the informal systems of family support.

Nevertheless, narratives of family difficulties took a secondary position in the accounts of families. This was sometimes because the problem may have involved only one or two family members, small cogs in the wider wheel of family involvement, or because the tensions were temporary, or because families, in the narratives they inhabited, stressed harmony and not dysfunction—and for practical reasons. Linked with this positive avowal of Caribbean culture was the language of the family that stressed its "closeness," its "loving," while family members could be galvanized to provide support or advice in times of trouble. The emphasis on closeness extended the meaning of the narratives by encoding values and prescriptions for loyalty, love, and "living good." They were particular ways of talking about particular relationships. These narratives linked families across the oceans and the generations. They strengthened family membership and ties that had very practical implications in enabling migration and facilitating return. But they were also increasingly powerful as expressions of, and foci for, a Caribbean cultural identity abroad and in the Caribbean itself. As African-Caribbean family patterns in Britain continued to conform to those identified in the Caribbean and as transnational links continued to affirm the influence of the Caribbean, the idea of family and the meanings attached to it emerged as key elements in narratives of belonging and identity. It was not just that you came from Jamaica (or Trinidad or Barbados) but that you came from particular Jamaican (Trinidadian, Barbadian) *family or families* and kinship constellations that stood for identifiable beliefs and values and that represented a formidable network of kin whose loyalty—as members of a shared lineage—could be taken on trust:

> We have a family reunion now … in New York. … Two years ago … [it was] in Canada … the one before that was in Jamaica. … Every two years, yes … every year it become bigger … a few hundred I would say.… How many tables it was? About 30![48]

Indeed, as Sutton argued, family reunions, as rituals, were visible affirmations of family identity that overrode all other affiliations.[49] What linked the family is kinship and lineage, neither of which relied on place for meaning. The longevity of migration as a feature of Caribbean life has arguably reinforced the sense of kinship and lineage as unifying features of family life and as a distinguishing feature of Caribbean diasporic communities.

But if the language of families was symbolic, it also contained practical elements. Loyalty to members of a shared lineage could be assumed and trust guaranteed. Members of a transnational family, of close transnational networks, were provided with opportunities to utilize the networks to enhance their material or occupational world, to broaden their experience, or to provide support when required. Hyacinth flew across the Atlantic to support her sister-in-law, and she, in turn, provided her with employment in America as recompense. This employment helped her children in England. Membership of a transnational family contains within it a transnational imagination. The links and networks are both multinational as well as transnational. Indeed, the spreading or dispersal of material and emotional resources throughout the diasporic trajectory of each family provided diversity and security, strength and opportunity. Family members provided important points of contact, facilitating migration, remigration and, of course, return. When the family was both the source of belonging and the resource for survival, then identity was both portable and secure.

Third, the trend to return, first noted for Britain by Ceri Peach[50] for the 1980s, accelerated in the 1990s and continues, now supplemented by numbers of British-born Caribbeans "returning" to the Caribbean.[51] Returning residents, from Europe and North America, and "new" migrants to the Caribbean have been able to call on the support of Caribbean-based kin to assist their settlement in the Caribbean. In other ways the revolution in communications has changed the shape of migration itself. As Nancy Foner has indicated for the United States, cheap flights have obviated the need to return permanently and have made possible a pattern of migratory "commuting," particularly for elderly African-Caribbeans.[52] A comparable pattern is emerging with British-based West Indians who either return to the Caribbean for protracted periods or play host to Caribbean family members for up to six months (the legal maximum).[53] Many informants indicated a desire on retirement to alternate periods spent in Britain and the Caribbean. This has important implications for families, enabling them to keep in close touch and to replenish cultural contacts. Even without protracted visits, cheap communications—email, Skype, the telephone—allow both close and distant kin, in the Caribbean, Europe, and North America, to maintain contact. Easy communications and the possibility of dual nationality also means that migrants are prepared to spend longer in their country of destination.

This pattern of migration that links with new generations can be easily maintained or renewed, links that continue to replenish family values, models, and behavior and enable a continuity across generations between family members in Britain, North America, the Caribbean, and elsewhere, renewing for another generation the cycle of transnationalism. Aging parents in the Caribbean have heightened the emotional intensity felt by their children and grandchildren abroad, giving a fresh urgency to the frequency of contact and visits and the desire to flesh out "roots" for younger British-born generations. Visits home, as one Trinidadian informant described, are "important, to see Mum and Dad regularly … [and] because I would like my kids to keep in touch with Trinidad and all the relatives there … to appreciate the other part of the culture. … I think that makes them a better individual."[54]

Such patterns of migration and return are not, however, without pain and are marked, in both cases, by the absence of this older generation. One returnee's daughter felt that "now she's [her mother] gone it's like losing my right arm."[55] Her mother, now settled in Trinidad, justified the arrangement, saying, "It's not far. It's just an eight hours' journey to come, so [she] can always come along, or we can always come across."[56] But families are able to withstand the absence of members. The power of this linkage has roots within the family nexus that has been accommodated to migration, rather than disrupted by it, and should be recognized as a central element of African-Caribbean family culture.

Finally, the need to maintain contact with family and the knowledge, for a diasporic people, of a contingency or safety net has been historically important for other reasons. The trauma of the slave trade and the history of slavery—or, rather, its subsequent denial and silencing—is not part of the direct diasporic memory (in ways in which Exodus or the leitmotif of suffering is for the Jews). But it is what drives it. Understanding the rupture and shame of slavery makes sense of the subsequent stories that families have told about themselves and continue to tell. The stories celebrate family and affirm survival, and surviving slavery was arguably possible only through the formation of kinship networks and assumptions of trust and affection. Indeed, these stories could *only* be told as a result of the particular history of slavery. Simultaneously, and paradoxically, they conceal and reveal this history. Families need to *tell*, to pass on to the generations a sense of continuity, a coded explanation as to why they are no longer where they could or should be. No wonder then that families hold to the same or similar stories. In doing so, these become the badge of *connectivity*. Family stories work as engines of inclusion, not exclusion, emphasizing global linkages, shared lineages, and communities who speak the same normative shorthand. Even those who set themselves outside the family narrative can only do so by colluding with the family narrative. There is no escaping, and this connectivity is one implicitly recognized by all across the diaspora.

Furthermore, West Indians have long been unsure of their tenure in modern nation-states, and with reason. Few West Indians had the franchise in their respective West Indian colonies until the 1940s and 1950s; Caribbean migrants were expelled from Panama in the 1920s, Cuba and the Dominican Republic in the 1930s, and effectively excluded from the social polities of the United States and the United Kingdom by social practices and formal legislation.[57] With the ever-present threat of exclusion if not expulsion, maintaining contact provided security. As Roy argued,

> Imagine me in Britain. I'm not writing to my brother. I'm not writing to my niece. … should I be surprised if when I come they resent me? … or imagine that I going to be in England forever, in the English way of life, then. … circumstances dictate and … [I] have to be back here. … [Remember] they didn't come out of Panama because they wanted to. They were thrown out.[58]

"If I fly to Barbados tomorrow," another British born informant pointed out, "I know that I can go at any one of my sisters, and I have a bed to sleep on. … if I go to Toronto and I seek out my cousin, I know he's going to open the door to me."[59]

It was precisely the flexibility of the African-Caribbean family at home and abroad that provided it with the means to survive and to support the high levels of migration that accompany it. For African-Caribbean migrants, the borders of the nation may, like the family, be emotional rather than geographic, political identities and belongings shaped by the networks of transnational kin, citizenship contingent on a diasporic imperative. For, these African-Caribbean families were also black families. They held a peculiar and precarious position in the grand narratives of globalization that brought them to the New World, and in the narratives of citizenship, nationhood, and national identity that subsequently emerged. "I am," as one informant said, "a citizen of the world." "I belong," said another, "to whoever wants me." Diasporic memory is a necessarily layered one that links with the black experience and provides a cultural continuity with those back home and overseas. For a community with a tenuous hold on the white narrative of modernity, this was and remains an important asset.

Notes

1. David Warren Sabean and Simon Teuscher, "Introduction: Transregional and Transnational Families: European History in Comparative Perspective," in this volume.
2. Don Robotham, "Transnationalism in the Caribbean: Formal and Informal," *American Ethnologist* 25 (1996): 307–21.
3. See Robin Cohen, *Global Diasporas: An Introduction* (London, 1997).
4. Sidney Mintz, "The Caribbean as a Socio-Cultural Area," *Journal of World History* 9 (1966): 916–41.

5. Jean Besson, *Martha Brae's Two Histories: European Expansion and Caribbean Culture-Building in Jamaica* (Chapel Hill, NC, 2002), 27 (original emphasis). See also Barry Higman, *Slave Population and Economy in Jamaica 1807–1834* (Cambridge, 1976).
6. "Outside" children and "outside woman" refer to relationships and families maintained outside the permanent or "inside" relationship.
7. Edward Long, *The History of Jamaica*, (London, 1774), vol. 2; Edward Bridges, *The Annals of Jamaica* (London, 1827), vol. 2; Roderick A. McDonald, ed., *Between Slavery and Freedom: Special Magistrate John Anderson's Journal of St. Vincent during the Apprenticeship* (Kingston, 2001).
8. R. T. Smith, *The Negro Family in British Guiana* (London, 1956); Franklin Frazier, *The Negro Family in the United States* (Chicago, 1939); Melville Herskovits, *The Myth of the Negro Past* (Boston, 1941); Orlando Patterson, *The Sociology of Slavery* (London, 1967); Fernando Henriques, *Family and Colour in Jamaica* (London, 1953); Edith Clarke, *My Mother Who Fathered Me* (Kingston, 1999 [1957]); Sidney Mintz and Richard Price, *An Anthropological Approach to the African-American Past: A Caribbean Perspective* (Philadelphia, 1976).
9. Thomas Simey, *Welfare and Planning in the West Indies* (Oxford, 1946), 84.
10. Ibid., 84. See also Clarke, *My Mother;* Henriques, *Family and Colour;* Erna Brodber, "African Jamaican Women at the turn of the Century," *Social and Economic Studies* 35 (1986): 23–50.
11. Velma Newton, *The Silver Men* (Kingston, 1987).
12. George Roberts, "Emigration from the Island of Barbados," *Social and Economic Studies* 4 (1955): 245–87; Bonham Richardson, *Caribbean Migrants, Environment and Human Survival on St. Kitts and Nevis* (Knoxville, TN, 1983); Bonham Richardson, *Panama Money in Barbados, 1900–1920* (Knoxville, TN, 1985).
13. Roberts, "Emigration"; Richardson, *Panama, Money*; Philip Kasinitz, *Caribbean New York: Black Immigrants and the Politics of Race* (Ithaca, NY, 1992).
14. Kasinitz, *Caribbean New York;* Winston James, *Holding Aloft the Banner of Ethiopia: Caribbean Radicalism in Early Twentieth Century America* (London, 1998); Irma Watkins-Owens, *Blood Relations: Caribbean Immigrants and the Harlem Community* (Bloomington, IN, 1996); Mary Chamberlain, *Empire and Nation-Building in the Caribbean: Barbados 1937–1966* (Manchester, UK, 2010).
15. Richardson, *Panama Money.* The remittances returned by Barbadians for instance, were significant and substantial, and outweighed the potential deleterious impact of so large a migration, as the registrar general commented in his 1921 report: "In years past public opinion strongly advocated the emigration of the people and steps were taken to give effect thereto. The idea was that the surplus population should find an outlet and settlement elsewhere. Whether it was an advantage to the Island to lose the better class of agricultural labourer and industrial worker is another matter, anyway, it stands out as an indisputable fact that it has proved a valuable asset to the Island owing to the money they have sent back." CO21/107, Documents laid at Meeting of Assembly of 22 November 1921, 86.
16. Elizabeth Thomas-Hope, *Explanation in Caribbean Migration* (London, 1992).
17. Karen Fog Olwig, "Constructing Lives: Migration Narratives and Life Stories among Nevisians," in *Caribbean Migration: Globalised Identities,* ed. Mary Chamberlain (London, 1998), 63–80; Karen Fog Olwig, *Caribbean Journeys: An Ethnography of Migration and Home in Three Family Networks* (Durham, NC, 2007); Mary Chamberlain, *Narratives of Exile and Return* (New Brunswick, NJ, 2006 [1997]); Mary Chamberlain, *Family Love in the Diaspora: Migration and the Anglo-Caribbean Expe-*

rience (New Brunswick, NJ, 2006); Christine Barrow, "Finding the Support: Strategies for Survival," *Social and Economic Studies* 35 (1986): 131–76.

18. R. Palmer, ed., *In Search of a Better Life: Perspectives on Migration from the Caribbean* (New York, 1990); Dennis Conway, "Conceptualising Contemporary Patterns of Caribbean International Mobility," *Caribbean Geography* 2 (1988): 145–163; George Gmelch, *Double Passage: The Lives of Caribbean Migrants Abroad and Back Home* (Ann Arbor, MI, 1992).
19. Olwig, "Constructing Lives." See also Thomas-Hope, *Explanation;* Chamberlain, *Narratives;* Constance Sutton and Elsa M. Chaney, eds., *Caribbean Life in New York City: Socio-cultural Dimensions* (New York, 1994); Linda Basch, Nina Glick Schiller, and Cristina Szanton Blanc, *Nations Unbound: Transnational Projects, Post-Colonial Predicaments, and Deterritorialized Nation States* (Langhorne, PA, 1994); Nina Glick Schiller and Georges Fouron, *Georges Woke Up Laughing: Long-Distance Nationalism* (Durham, NC, 2001).
20. Edward Kamau Brathwaite, *The Development of Creole Society in Jamaica, 1770–1820* (Oxford, 1971); Verene A. Shepherd and Glen L. Richards, eds., *Questioning Creole: Creolisation Discourses in Caribbean Culture* (Kingston, 2002).
21. Basch et al, *Nations*, Kasinitz, *Caribbean*; Sutton and Chaney, *Caribbean Life*; Susan Craig James, "Intertwining Roots," *Journal of Caribbean History* 25 (1992): 216–18; Harry Goulbourne, *Caribbean Transnational Experience* (London, 2002).
22. Mintz and Price, *Anthropological Approach*, 14. They argue that cultural continuities from Africa among New World enslaved peoples are more likely to have occurred at the "deeper" level of values and attitudes.
23. The Select Committee on West India Colonies noted in 1842 that in Barbados parents removed their children from the estates and "carried them away and distributed them among friends and family." The National Archive (TNA), *Parliamentary Papers*, XIII, 479 (1842), para. 1452.
24. JF020/1/1/1/13. Names have been anonymized. Interviews (unless indicated otherwise) from H. Goulbourne and M. Chamberlain, *Living Arrangements, Family Structure and Social Change of Caribbeans in Britain*, financed by the Economic and Social Research Council (Award Number L315253009). Approximately fifty families, across three generations, were interviewed between 1995 and 1998 by Dr. Dwaine Plaza, research assistant on the project, except those in Trinidad, which were carried out by Mary Chamberlain. References are to recording and transcript pages. Recordings and Transcripts lodged in Qualidata Archive, University of Essex.
25. JF020/1/1/2/16.
26. JF020/1/1/2/17.
27. JF020/1/1/18.
28. JF022/2/1/1/6.
29. Ibid.
30. JF022/2/1/1/15.
31. JF022/2/1/1/10–11.
32. See Dwaine Plaza, "Transnational Grannies: The Changing Family Responsibility of Elderly African Caribbean-born Women Resident in Britain," *Social Indicators Research Journal* 11 (2000): 180–201.
33. JF020/1/2/1/38. There is a discernible migrant flow from the United Kingdom to the United States. Many West Indians in Britain are in poorly paid work so remigrating to the United States—where they will join other family members—makes economic sense.
34. JF020/1/1/2/26.

35. JF020/1/2/1/42.
36. JF022/2/2/2/32.
37. JF021/1/1/6.
38. JF021/1/1/10–11.
39. JF021/1/2/1.
40. JF022/2/2/41.
41. JF022/2/2/42–43.
42. JD013 2/1/2/34.
43. JC011.
44. JG025/2/2/143.
45. Chamberlain, *Narratives*, 120
46. Constance Sutton, "Celebrating Ourselves: The Family Reunion Rituals of African Caribbean Transnational Families," *Global Networks* 4 (2004): 243–58.
47. For examples of family issues see case studies in Chamberlain, *Family Love.* For studies of schizophrenia, see Dinesh Bhugra, "Migration and Schizophrenia," *Acta Psychiatrica Scandinavia* 102, suppl. 407 (2000): 68–73. Young male underachievement has often been blamed on single mothers (the Caribbean heritage population has the highest proportion of single mother–headed households in the UK) who are more likely to be poorer, and to live in deprived areas with poor educational facilities and limited employment prospects. Here, however, social and economic factors (and institutional racism) need to be factored into explanations of dysfunctional behaviors.
48. JL0351b.
49. Sutton, *Celebrating Ourselves.*
50. Ceri Peach, *The Caribbean in Europe: Contrasting Patterns of Migration and Settlement in Britain, France and the Netherlands* (Warwick, UK, 1991)
51. Goulbourne, *Caribbean Transnational;* Frank Abernaty, "The Dynamics of Return Migration to St. Lucia," in *Caribbean Families in Britain and the Transatlantic World*, ed. Harry Goulbourne and Mary Chamberlain (London, 2001), 170–87; Denis Conway and Rob Potter, "Caribbean Transnational Return Migrants as Agents of Change," *Geography Compass* 1 (2007): 25–45.
52. Nancy Foner, "West Indians in New York City and London: A Comparative Analysis," in Sutton and Chaney, *Caribbean Life;* Nancy Foner, "Towards a Comparative Perspective on Caribbean Migration," in Chamberlain, *Caribbean Migration*, 47–62; Basch et al., *Nations Unbound;* Carol Boyce-Davis, *Black Women, Writing and Identity: Migrations of the Subject* (London, 1994).
53. Dwaine Plaza, "Frequent Flyer Grannies," paper presented to the Caribbean Studies Association, San Juan, Puerto Rico, 27–31 May 1996.
54. TB018.
55. TR038.
56. TR097.
57. The Immigration Act of 1924 and Nationality and Immigration Act of 1952 in the United States, and the 1962, 1968, and 1971 Immigration Acts in the United Kingdom.
58. Chamberlain, *Narratives*, 87.
59. BB056/2/2/2/41.

Chapter 13

Exile, Familial Ideology, and Gender Roles in Palestinian Camps in Jordan, 1948–2001

Stéphanie Latte Abdallah

Camp refugee families in Jordan, who have been crucial in the reconstruction of Palestinian national identity after 1948, have produced what Pierre Bourdieu calls "a family of words": a fixed representation of family values and practices that has transcended exile.[1] This representation is best understood as a "social fiction," whose aim has been to counterbalance the harsh events of history.[2] Most social and political actors in Jordan have shaped and encouraged the idea of traditional family values. As Olivier Schwartz shows, for the contemporary context of workers' families in the North of France, a social condition of subordination can indeed fix sexual roles.[3] In her study of refugee populations in Tanzania, Lisa Malkki identifies an increased need for ethnic identity in family and matrimonial practices.[4]

And yet, gender roles and family practices within Palestinian camp families have changed since 1948. I intend to analyze how exile in Jordan has had an impact on the construction of Palestinian refugee families and gender relations on both a social and a symbolic level. This chapter will show how the conditions of exile created a specific "familial ideology," while they also brought major social changes among camp families. I argue that this social reality remains largely unaccounted for in scholarship and other public discourses.

This study is grounded in fieldwork done from 1999 to 2002 in two camps in Jordan: the Jabal Hussein camp in Amman and the Jerash or Gaza camp. The Jabal Hussein camp was created after 1948 and is today part of the urban configuration of the Jordanian capital. The camp's inhabitants came mainly from villages and small towns. The Jerash or Gaza camp was created in the wake of the 1967 exodus and has been populated mostly by Bedouin refugees from Bir al Saba in the Negev, who found refuge in the Gaza Strip after 1948 and were later displaced to Jordan in 1967. Unlike most of the refugees in Jordan, as former Gazans, the Jerash camp's inhabitants are not Jordanian nationals.

Binational Histories and Familial Ideology

In the camps, the guilt felt by fathers of the first generation (men born before 1938) after the 1948 exodus strengthened the values of family honor and women's honor.[5] The value of honor has been a historical agent in Palestinian wars and exoduses. In exile, the preservation of women's honor from actual and feared Israeli military practices, especially as a result of stories about rape cases and direct experiences, along with the more general insecurity created by the 1948 war and later the 1967 Israeli occupation of the West Bank and the Gaza Strip, became a discourse aimed at defending family unity. This discourse compensated for men's failure to keep the land. Within families, the protection of sexual honor (*'ard*) legitimated the decisions to leave the villages, the towns, and the land in Palestine. It overshadowed the feeling of loss of social honor (*sharaf*) and alleviated the continuing sense of guilt in the first generation, among its men in particular.

During the first decade of exile, the family unit was the fragile refuge of Palestinian identity. Family networks and traditional leadership (such as the *mukhtars*) inherited from village, city, and Bedouin social organizations were only partially rebuilt.[6] Both humanitarian agencies dealing with the refugees (the Red Cross from 1948 to 1950 and the United Nations Relief and Works Agency [UNRWA] from 1950 to the present) and Jordanian governments reinforced the power of these hierarchies.[7] Indeed, the *mukhtars* were the main go-betweens in the organization and its delivery of humanitarian assistance until 1955 and remained the chosen and reliable interlocutors of Jordanian authorities in the administration of the camps.

Families have played a key role as symbolic and effective solidarity networks against the harsh and uncertain conditions of camp life. Since the beginning of exile, forced displacements, migrations, and the dispersion of clans (*hamulas*) in multiple places contributed to the creation of a public image of the family as an immutable institution. Until the renewal of the national movement in the mid-1960s, the family was the only social and political institution that remained in place. Until the mid-1960s, camp society was characterized by an absence of political leadership and by the contingent management of humanitarian assistance. These "refugee years" (or "lost years") were imbued by a feeling of failure, of a political and social void. But families have elaborated a self-representation able to maintain continuity beyond the exodus, to link past and future times. As such, this representation can be understood as an act of memory that denied the historical experience of loss and change. This image has been a way to resist, an alternative reality made of words, which compensated for and encouraged rapid social changes linked to the major rupture of exile. This image of the family played a critical political role by reproducing Palestinian identity and traditions before the new emergence of a national movement, which later fulfilled this role.

This narrative about family identity has been, first of all, shaped on the idea of maintaining hereditary qualities, values, and shared social attitudes and choices. For example, the daughters of the Suleiman family bestowed upon themselves their father's qualities (such as frankness, honesty, generosity, independence of mind, originality, and a certain avant-garde spirit), even though they suffered from what they called his "dictatorial" power.[8] Family unity has meant common choices, such as to be involved or not in partisan activism, and ways of behaving. In Palestinian camps in Jordan, militant involvement has frequently been a familial issue. Leïla K., a leader of the Popular Front for the Liberation of Palestine (an influential leftist faction of the Palestine Liberation Organization [PLO]), explained her political activism first as a result of her condition as a refugee and secondly as a result of her family identity, "a political family."[9] If family identity has often determined the affiliation to a precise party, its primary influence has been upon socialization and the values that have been key identity markers, such as family values or the ones conveyed more broadly by political activism and party culture.[10]

An image of perpetuation of family structures and marriage practices, notably endogamy, also shaped the discourse of family unity and identity. This narrative has promoted the idea of the reproduction of what is called here "tradition." In the camps, this discourse has been held mainly by men of the first generation, for whom family, conceived outside of history, has been a way to circumscribe exile to a limited moment. The discourse of endogamy has been primarily geared towards the marriage of women, given the role that women have had in representations of genealogical identity. For Moussa Suleiman, from the Jabal Hussein camp, familial traditions linked to the village of origin were maintained by three conditions: abiding to sexual moral and women's honor prescriptions; the will to marry his daughters to men of his village of origin (Dawaimeh); and refusing his daughters access to higher education or the permission to work for wages outside the house. These three conditions were a way, as he stated, to make sure that "everything stays the same, that nothing has changed when we return to Dawaimeh."[11] His role in the camp, as sheikh and social leader, contributed to his rejection of social change in his family.[12] The old discourse of social endogamy was maintained by Moussa Suleiman in order to serve a high social position and Palestinian political identity.

Like the main social and political actors in Jordan, the Palestinian national movement did not challenge family power and values during this period of intense political activism in Jordan (1968–1971).[13] Its main focus was to involve camp families, seen as socially conservative, in the resistance movement and, above all, to involve men in the armed struggle. Camps became the avant-garde of the nation, and "popular memory (of the villages and rural life) and Palestinian nationalism became interlinked."[14] In Jordan, camp families got heavily involved in the national struggle, emphasizing their family values to influence resistance institutions during these few years. Thereafter, most of the families withdrew from the national movement. Palestinian women's activism did not develop much during this period, and its effect did not last once the national movement's institutions were expelled from the country in 1971 after the Jordanian civil war. Sharing many of these family values, activists and leaders of Fatah, as well as leftist parties, did little to challenge them. It can be said that the national movement utilized rather than questioned traditional family values. Indeed, it gave women's honor a national dimension, as stated in the famous slogan "land before honor" (*al-ard qabl al-'ard*), and promoted the notion of motherhood as a political act.[15] Yet, with the national value given to honor, in practice women's agency and political involvement became less controlled. Moreover, the Palestinian national movement gave precedence to the conjugal bond: direct economic assistance was given to widows of martyrs, and not only to mothers and families of martyrs, recognizing them in the representations of national symbolism. This policy contributed to women's economic independence from their families of origin and in-laws and allowed them to keep and raise their children as de facto heads of families in spite of customary practices prescribing that women return to their parents' houses and leave their children in their in-laws' houses.

The Jordanian state also reinforced traditional family values and women's honor in the way it dealt with Palestinian refugees and, more broadly, because its social and political system has encouraged the power of family groups. The work of the jurist Lama Abu-Odeh, for instance, has revealed the role given to family honor and private justice in the Jordanian penal code. Her work shows that Jordanian elites reproduced the discourse of "tradition" and contributed to the emergence of a new nationalist patriarchy system in which the role of women is modernized but submissive to the institution of the family, which has remained the basis of national culture.[16] Traditional family values have also been promoted in order to counter partisan opposition to the regime and circumscribe the political arena. After the expulsion of the Palestinian resistance movement in 1971, the official state discourse and its strict monitoring of lay political activity encouraged a fallback on community and conservative family values, leading to a resurgence of the emphasis on family honor and virtue.[17] Meanwhile, the Muslim Brotherhood's social and charitable activities contributed to spread religious values notably in poor areas like the camps. While it proscribed the social activities of the secular Palestinian movement, the Jordanian monarchy allowed these programs to flourish.

The emphasis on familial values and on the family's political role has targeted the influence of party culture. It was first geared towards the secular culture of Palestinian movements and pan-Arabism and, second towards political Islam. Indeed, the latter became a new political force with the beginning of the Intifada in 1988 in Palestine and with the democratization process and the parliamentary elections of 1989 in Jordan. As soon as the political wing of the Muslim Brotherhood, the Islamic Action Front (IAF), opposed the peace treaties signed by Israel and the Palestinians (the Oslo agreements of 1993 and 1995) and by Israel and Jordan (the Wadi Arraba agreement of 1994), the Jordanian regime sought to reduce the IAF's influence, especially by changing the electoral law in 1993 and 1997. The aim of the electoral system of "one man, one vote" was at that time to increase tribal and family clans' political representation in parliament and, consequently, to reduce political party representation.[18] Consequently, the IAF's strong representation diminished by half.

Familial Ideology versus Social Change in the Jabal Hussein and Jerash Camps

Camp society, the avant-garde of an exiled nation until the Oslo agreements, was especially encouraged to act and represent itself as one *social body* in the actual and symbolic struggle for Palestine.[19] However, in practice, the conditions of exile have brought major social changes that have challenged this constructed image of social unity and, indeed, specific family forms: to be sure, extended families persist, but more families are fragmented or led by women.

The 1970s and 1980s were decades of relative prosperity that allowed the diffusion of the conjugal model, thanks notably to the new conditions created by Gulf migrations (during this period, migrations were mainly familial—married men brought their wives and children with them) and the increase in the value of remittances. But exile trajectories and camp life, especially during the 1950s (the "lost years") and again since the 1990s, have strengthened family structures and networks, which provide resources and compensate for economic hardships. Indeed, in the 1990s, camp inhabitants were pauperized by the effects of structural adjustment policies aimed at the Jordanian economy and by the first Iraq war, which led to the return of many migrants from the Gulf countries. Since then, their economic situation has continuously worsened. During these harsh decades, inhabitants of the camps relied heavily on closed family networks on the man's and the woman's side—*ai'la*—by which I mean the parents, children, sisters, and brothers, and their nuclear families. On the other hand, these conditions also led to familial breakups and the emergence of what I will call "families of women."

Losing Palestine meant the failure of the male figure. When men were unable to sustain and protect their families during the reestablishment in exile, tensions between the sexes rose. Women made independent choices and enjoyed greater mobility, notably grounded in the resources provided by the UNRWA and the Jordanian state's social and educational system. For example, in the first years of exile, women gained the opportunity to obtain a tent, humanitarian assistance, and, later on, a house. More directly, after the 1980s, the UNRWA has encouraged and supported women who wanted to live alone after being divorced or separated, mostly in order to raise their children, by granting them the status of "special hardship cases" when their households lacked an adult or an able-bodied man.

Early age mortality among the men of the second generation (who were born between 1939 and 1953) and the rise of divorce among the third generation (those born between 1954 and 1968) led to an increase in widows and divorcees.[20] Caught between individual choices, changes in gender roles, and the weakening of patriarchal power, marriage bonds have suffered from exile conditions. From the 1980s onwards (i.e., from the third generation onwards), matrimonial conflicts have been on the rise, and women have ceased to remarry as often as they used to. In the early 2000s, women head 37 percent of the families in Jerash and 33 percent in Jabal Hussein.[21] If we consider also the families in which the husband migrated or became unable to provide for his family, by the 2000s, more than half of the camp families are families of women.

Moreover, the impact of exile history is shown in the differences in marriage practices and changes in the Jabal Hussein and Jerash camps. In Jabal Hussein, exile reduced significantly the agnatic representation of family ties while the lost village has been reproduced among Jordanian refugee families through marriages. In Jerash, patriarchal power as well as agnatic and cross-border national bonds have been maintained more often through marriages with kin living in the Gaza Strip.

Jabal Hussein: Embodying the Lost Village in Jordan

In Jabal Hussein, where most inhabitants come from villages or small towns, my informants no longer mentioned the family lineage (*hamula*); their focus shifted instead on the village of origin (*balad*) and the closed family on both sides (*'ai'la*).[22] The village of origin became the new extended family of exile: in the early 2000s marriages between persons belonging to the same village of origin represented a third of all the unions that occurred in exile.[23] Another third was between persons of the same closed family (15 percent of this third was between a woman and her paternal uncle's son –*ibn 'am*[24]). Most of these marriages were between Jordanian Palestinian refugees, especially as the West Bank was officially in Jordan until 1988.

These unions show the vivacity that village identification in the camps retained in the memories of the old generation (i.e., that of those born before 1938), and how it has been embodied in actual marriage practices. Village identification has been vital in all historical periods. It was a key criterion in the settlement organization of the camps, in the distribution of humanitarian aid and in the deployment of family networks. In the 1970s, it was utilized politically and transmitted by the Palestinian national movement in Jordan, and after 1994 by the Palestinian National Authority (PNA) in Palestine. In Jordan, aside from the official social representation of the camps into the Camp Improvement Committees, camp society created *balad*-based associations, at first informal (*rabitas*).[25] From the 1980s onwards, official associations (*jama'iyehs*) representing villages and small towns have been created in camps or in the surrounding districts. This associative movement was initially meant to be a part of the democratization process in Jordan. It was supposed to foster a better political integration of the refugees, but it has been finally reduced to symbolic social representation. The men of the second generation (born between 1939 and 1953) have been the main active members of these associations. Thanks to money collected among members (*sanduq al-balad*), these associations have encouraged village solidarity and bonds: in their meeting places, marriage can be celebrated at a low cost, or condolences can be offered.

In the Jabal Hussein camp, among the four generations and since exile, very few marriages occurred between camp inhabitants and Jordanians, whatever length of Palestinian refugees' settlement in Jordan.[26] Among the 11 percent of unions between camp inhabitants and non-Palestinians, less than 4 percent were with Jordanians (men and women), around 5 percent were with other Arabs (this group is mainly constituted by men marrying Egyptian or Algerian or Lebanese women; only one of the women whom I interviewed had an Egyptian spouse), and even fewer marriages were with Europeans. These unions outside the nation have concerned mainly men; women are seen as having a specific role in preserving social, cultural, and religious boundaries and are thus less likely to marry outside the community. The strictly masculine, paternal laws and rules of transmission of the Jordanian nationality and of refugee status (according to the UNRWA registration system) have enhanced these practices. Moreover, there has been no intermarriage with nationals of Gulf countries, which have been the main destinations for camp families who migrated, because of social barriers between migrants and host societies. Finally, most migrants to other countries—whether they left to pursue their studies, because of their political activism, or in search for work—have been men.

Jerash: Between an Agnatic Identity and Palestinian Identity Reproduced Beyond Borders

In the Jerash camp, the boundaries separating camp members from Jordanian society have been even more marked. Most of the camp's inhabitants were not given Jordanian nationality. Since the camp's creation in 1968, its inhabitants have maintained close social, political, and administrative links with the Gaza Strip. Less than 1 percent of all the marriages that occurred in exile took place between Jordanians and Palestinians of the camps, and 4 percent with non-Palestinians (Egyptians, Americans, and Europeans). Here, unlike in Jabal Hussein, only Jordanian men came to ask for a fiancée and have done so rarely; reciprocity is difficult to establish since a Jordanian woman who marries a foreigner cannot give nationality to him or her children, and, until 1987, she even lost her own nationality. In spite of the resources that could have favored such intermarriages with Jordanians, the aristocratic spirit among most Bedouin clans has made it difficult for these relationships to develop. These marriages are not reciprocal and signify a lower status in a country where tribal values and perceptions are still strong.

Since 1967, the camp has been closely linked to the Gaza Strip through marriages and social, economic, and political networks. The historical, political, and national role of Jerash camp (visible in the involvement of camp inhabitants in the resistance movement of the 1970s, in their involvement in the Palestinian Liberation Army and in the police of the Palestinian National Authority) has been, indeed, embedded in matrimonial links. Even so, the strong national identity of the camp did not prevent old divisions from being maintained and indeed increased among camp inhabitants, such as the one between peasants and Bedouins. Bedouins hardly married peasants from the camp. According to reciprocity practices and because they knew that Bedouins have feelings of superiority linked to their qualities, the strength and size of their clans, and the activities they conducted before exile in Palestine, peasants also refused these intermarriages and have developed unions with camp dwellers originally belonging to other villages or small towns.

In Jerash, marriages within tribes (*'ashiras*) have been much less frequent than before 1948, but agnatic bonds and patriarchal ideology have been nevertheless reproduced by a high number of unions in the closed family (45 percent), among which 25 percent occur with the son of the paternal uncle (*ibn 'am*)—who was in most cases also a maternal relative. Strong ties and exchanges have been maintained beyond national borders and the new localization implicated by exile, mainly with kin.

Necessities and Chances of Exile: Family Choices and Gender Roles

Men and women's roles have varied according to family status before exile and to the geographic mobility and social resources of families. Indeed, the collective interests of families have determined individual choices and life histories, especially those of women who have been constantly inscribed in the collective destiny of the community, whether familial or national. What has been expected of women heavily depended on family choices. The choices made in the first years of exile and migration trajectories strongly influenced family reconstructions and status afterwards. Three different family histories can be distinguished. First are those families who privileged family resources and maintained strategies of reproduction rooted in prior village or Bedouin socioeconomic organization: their trajectories have been centered on a paternal figure (they represented 9 percent of my sample from both camps). Next are those families who, out of necessity or choice, immediately upon their arrival started acquiring new resources such as education, wage work, or the benefits of national political activism. They achieved upward social mobility. In these families, daughters' education and their wage work in Jordan and in Gulf countries have contributed to familial well-being, and responsibilities have been shared among all conjugal family members (35 percent of families of both camps). Finally come families who had simple survival strategies (the most numerous, 56 percent of the families): they had to rely on many kinds of resources. In those, women's roles have been fundamental for families who relied largely on their labor.

Affirmed Family Identity and Founding Paternal Role

The loss of livelihood after 1948 was a deep and harsh rupture. Relatively well-off families, who had previously diversified their activities and were trading farm goods, suffered from fewer hardships, unless there was a conjugal breakup, which at this time was due to the death or invalidity of the father or husband. Thanks to extended family status and bonds before exile, the father was able to maintain a high social status through the reconstruction of a network of village relations. These families, driven by a strong paternal figure who influenced generations born in exile, reestablished themselves by developing small family businesses or shops and did not experience repeated migrations. The creation of familial businesses has granted those families independence and unity by maintaining an autonomous family economy (the preferred choice for those who can afford it). This situation limited children's individual choices, professional careers, and mobility, notably for the eldest. The eldest sons generally followed their father's path. Children reproduced family activities and stayed within its social network, especially young women. Indeed, familial values superseded higher education, careers, and wage work as well as political activism, which were considered important only in diversifying symbolic and material resources or as supplementary strategies. In some of those families, for example, sons migrated to Gulf countries because their family business was unable to provide enough income to support all its members. One or two among the sons also had the opportunity to study abroad. But daughters had more limited choices. Indeed, women's education has been all the more circumscribed and considered useless; paying jobs have often not followed for these women, as the family sustained all its members by itself, reaching a comfortable economic level.

In the Jabal Hussein camp, the Suleiman family exemplifies the reproduction of this sort of familial identity in the first years of exile. They come from a village with a strong historic and social identity, Dawaimeh, near Hebron, and the clan (*hamula*) of the father, Haj Moussa, was one of the biggest, though his own family was a minor branch. But his personal qualities, the village social capital he could rely on, and, above all, the fact that he did not concentrate all his resources in the land—meaning he left with a small amount of money—helped him become a traditional leader of the camp. In 1948, Moussa's family owned 600,000 square meters of farmland, a good-sized piece. While his uncles, father, and brothers were farming the land, Moussa sold the farm's products in surrounding villages and in Yaffa. He also owned a shop in the village and was a sheikh, known for his capacity to give advice and ability to solve conflicts. After the exodus from Dawaimeh, Moussa first spent some time in Jericho, where he obtained a tent in the huge camp of Ein al-sultan and opened a small shop. Newly wed, he settled there with his younger brother, a bachelor, and his sister, who became a widow during the 1948 war, and her children. From the beginning, he tried to expand his activities on the East Bank of Jordan, focusing on remote places lacking commodities where his small grocery and kitchen utensils shop could be in demand, while keeping his shop and his house in the camp in Jericho (which were lost after 1967 Israeli occupation of the West Bank). The Suleiman family moved from one place to another in the East Bank of Jordan, came back to Jericho during the winters, bought land in the East Bank, and started new farming activities. They settled in Jabal Hussein camp in the late 1950s. He bought a house, renovated it to enlarge it, and opened the first household appliance shop of the camp on the ground floor. His trade expanded rapidly with the growth of the camp and the town around it. Thanks to social resources developed by his commercial activity and to his previous village reputation, he continued to perform his traditional role as a mediator of conflicts between individuals and families. He became responsible for the camp and eventually the head of the Camp Improvement Committee, a position he held for many years.

In families such as the Suleimans, the father's personality played a major role in postexile life. Most of the families of the first generation are large (between seven to ten children), and the age gaps between children are frequently wide. Families have been often split into two groups of children who had different roles and future perspectives: the older children have usually embodied maternal and paternal roles, while the younger ones who were brought up by the eldest siblings could have more personal choices benefiting from symbolic and actual resources acquired by the eldest. However, in failed marriages, the presence of numerous children has been a major drawback and caused backward social mobility. In polygamous families with many children, opportunities for the children have been limited because half-brothers and half-sisters rarely benefited from each other's resources. They had separate trajectories that favored one group to the detriment of the other.

In the Suleiman family, despite and, in a sense, thanks to familial ideology, all children (three boys and seven girls), daughters included, reached high educational levels. Four entered universities and two studied in community colleges where they pursued a two-year vocational training. The social status and good economic situation of the family, along with the fact that he only had two sons at that time, encouraged Haj Moussa to send his eldest son, Omar, to Holland to study medicine. Meanwhile, Moussa withdrew his eldest daughter from school when she reached the age of fifteen. Omar's return, without his diploma and with a Dutch wife, reinforced traditional familial values and cohesion. Moussa's two sons had to take over the shop's management. Omar divorced his foreign wife partly because of his father's repeated interventions in their marriage and his patriarchal attitudes. Omar remarried later with a young woman from his village of origin, Dawaimeh. Haj Moussa could only conceive his daughter's future through marriage with relatives or men originating from Dawaimeh.

Such a large family has favored the younger children, and often daughters, too: they could challenge their father's will, relying on the solidarity as well as the material, cultural, and symbolic resources of the eldest. Once married, Moussa's eldest daughter went back to school, migrating to Saudi Arabia with her husband, and took university classes. The next two oldest daughters, Izdihar and Amal, fought to study Arabic and English in community colleges in Amman. The youngest daughter, Nada, studied English at the University of Jordan, and the youngest boy entered Yarmouk University in Irbid (northern Jordan) to study Applied Arts. The eldest son's role shows the supportive and emulating dynamics that can develop in large families and the importance that privileged bonds between brothers and sisters can play in young women's access to education, paid jobs, and individual choices in families that do not rely on women's wage work. Izdihar, who was the first one to confront her father in order to complete her studies, credited her brother with her commitment to education: through him she discovered books, poetry, music, and a free attitude in life. Paradoxically, what these young women individually have attained against their father's will can be credited to the example the father himself set for his children: his idea of maintaining the family's social status, his independence of mind, and his constant efforts to create new opportunities in harsh conditions.

Diversification of Resources and Upward Social Mobility: Sharing Responsibilities within the Conjugal Family

Upward social mobility, frequently based on the acquisition of new resources, has rewarded families who have been able to invest immediately in the father or the elder sons' secondary or higher education. In these families, the father relied on different members of the conjugal family, men or women, according to the opportunities offered to each of them, and there were no early ruptures of marriages caused by widowhood or divorce.

These families encouraged their children to migrate for work, especially to seek opportunities after graduation as teachers for young women in Saudi Arabia and Gulf countries.[27] Whatever the number of children, all continued their studies after high school, whether in community colleges or universities, and worked afterwards, wherever possible. The first families who settled in the Gaza Strip (administratively ruled by Egypt from 1948 to 1967) or in Egypt benefited from good education facilities early in the 1960s, whereas those who came to Jordan only gained access to higher education in the late 1960s and 1970s. And even then, university education was available only through migration: to Egypt, Algeria, or Europe, mainly to Eastern Europe or the USSR. According to agreements with the PLO and with Jordan, students could receive a scholarship from the PLO or from governments of these countries in order to leave. In Jordan, in 1952, there were effectively only four secondary public schools—in Salt, Amman, Irbid, and Kerak.[28] There was one women's section in the school of Amman. The first university was opened in Amman in 1962 (the University of Jordan). During the 1960s, 1970s, and 1980s, a wider education system was implemented, including technical and vocational training centers and community colleges set up by UNRWA and the Jordanian government, sometimes in close cooperation. Refugee families at this time sent their children in great numbers to such education institutions.

Refugee families who settled in the Gaza Strip after 1948 benefited, early on, from the postgraduation facilities offered after UNRWA primary and secondary classes. Indeed, higher education opportunities had already developed thanks to the proximity of Egypt and its established university education. In Gaza at the beginning of the 1950s, the Egyptian government implemented a Teacher Training Center. The UNRWA system of loans and university scholarships, starting from the end of the 1950s, and the low cost of education and student housing in Egypt also allowed for such opportunities, however limited they were.

Thanks to the administrative links and trade networks between Egypt and the Gaza Strip, fathers were able to work there as taxi drivers, while their children were studying and their families benefited from shelter in the camps. If migrations to Egypt favored higher education, qualified job opportunities did not follow for those who settled there because of their foreign status as Palestinians in Egypt. Higher education and professional training permitted a massive familial migration to Gulf countries during the 1970s and the oil boom era. Most of the families who migrated from the Gaza Strip, the West Bank, or Jordan before 1967 had striking upward social trajectories and, generally, left the camps for good or stayed in the Gulf. Among those who came back after the first Iraq war in the 1990s, few needed housing in camps.[29]

Hatim's life story shows the key role of the Egyptian education system. Hatim became the chief of the Relief and Social Services Department at the UNRWA headquarters in Amman.[30] Originally from Ramleh, he took refuge in the Bureij camp in the Gaza Strip. As in many accounts of exile, his extended family broke up and followed different itineraries during the exodus. His father and one of his uncles went to the Gaza Strip while his other uncles took the road to the West Bank and Jordan. His father could never rejoin his brothers because of the fighting, and died, one year later, from the shock of exile. Hatim's mother also died at age forty-five. For a while, the five children stayed with their uncle in Gaza. Then they set off on their own, because he could not afford to raise them. They received UNRWA rations. The eldest worked in the building trades, and the second child, Hatim, also worked part time while he was in school. In 1958, the eldest daughter married a cousin and settled in Jordan. The eldest brother went to Mecca, as a pilgrim, found a job there and stayed, without sending much money to his siblings left in the Gaza Strip. Hatim thereafter became responsible for his siblings and adopted a paternal role.

In 1961, he graduated and received a small loan from the UNRWA. He then studied sociology and social work at the University of Cairo. Completing his BA in 1965, Hatim was employed by the Egyptian government as a social worker on the Aswan dam project. In April 1967, during a visit to his family in Jordan, unable to return to Egypt, he was forced to remain in Jordan. Joining his eldest brother, he settled in Qatar where he worked for the Ministry of Education. Hatim, alone at the beginning, and later with his new family, alternated work migrations in Qatar and Saudi Arabia, with stays in Jordan. Finally, he obtained a temporary Jordanian passport and married his cousin. After eight years in Saudi Arabia, he returned to Jordan and bought land under the name of his wife. Being a Gazan, he could not find work in the public sector, but he was finally employed by the UNRWA in 1977. He was, then, the only one holding a BA among the UNRWA's employees in Jordan.

The resources and networks of political activism ought to be mentioned, for they played an important role in families' upward mobility, helping their children further their education, even if it is hardly mentioned in oral interviews. Indeed, even more than activist salaries or pensions for widows of martyrs, the system of scholarships implemented by the PLO heavily contributed to these upward trajectories.

Failure of the Paternal Figure: Survival Strategies and Women's Roles

For the majority of families, exile's disruption of socioeconomic organization required survival strategies that have continued for generations. Frequent displacements (after 1948, after 1967, and then after the 1990–91 first Iraq war, for instance) or broken marriages often led to precarious living conditions.

When, due to hardship, the father failed to provide schooling opportunities for his children and/or the mother had been left as the sole breadwinner because of widowhood, illness of her spouse, divorce, or her husband's remarriage, families have relied on makeshift survival strategies. They have been often dependent on the social welfare system of the UNRWA, the Jordanian government, the assistance of the committees of *zaqat*, and especially Islamic charitable societies. Not all of these families were living in great poverty, but most of the boys could not study and thus have had the same precarious and low-skilled jobs as their fathers: craftsmen, sometimes self-employed, workmen, agricultural laborers, taxi drivers. Daughters either married early or worked to compensate for the men's absences or scarce resources.

Life stories of the second generation indicate that families have not favored sons' education over that of daughters, but chose according to the economic opportunities available. When young women were needed to work, they were encouraged to direct their studies toward jobs that have been perceived as honorable. This has been a form of protection. Positions in civil service and administration or in occupations in which the sexes are separated, such as teaching (the schools not being mixed), have been the most desirable. Young women were also trained in fields that facilitate self-employment or domestic work, such as craftsmaker, aesthetician, or hairdresser. Notably in Jerash, the parents have aimed to safeguard their daughters from the jobs their mothers often had to perform in the Gaza Strip and in the camp: temporary agricultural work on big farms, poultry farming, or small trades.

In Jerash, because of the few opportunities provided by high education, especially for nonnationals, young women have generally reached higher education levels than young men. For many years, for a young woman, being a secondary school graduate meant being able to be a teacher and migrate to Saudi Arabia with a male relative, who could then study and find a job.[31] But more boys have entered universities than girls. Moreover, access to public universities has been even more restricted for foreigners; the UNRWA has limited seats in its vocational training centers, and private community colleges or private universities have been expensive. In order to reduce university costs or to be able to register their children, families have been sending them to Cairo or, until 2003, to Iraq, a country that used to have a free and good university system.

In the camps, several familial responsibilities have been feminizing. On the one hand, this transformation is a consequence of the evolution of family structures due to the early deaths of men of the second generation and the multiplication of ruptures in the family life cycle. Early widowhood was a frequent consequence of the 1948 war, the 1970 civil war in Jordan, and, above all, the Lebanese conflict (especially from 1976 to 1983). On the other hand, this feminization results from the lack of male employment and an evolution within the camp, which has become since the 1990s a place of residence for the poor, for those who could not afford housing elsewhere. Last, it is the result of some women's choices.

From Jerash, many young men went to the Gaza Strip to become policemen after the Oslo agreements. Others migrated, alone, to Europe or other places and accepted poorly qualified jobs in order to sustain their families. In both camps, many women returned from Saudi Arabia, with their children, for life there became more difficult for migrants.

Men's inability to maintain their role as breadwinners has been all the more destabilizing when, as in Jerash, patriarchal structures and men's power have been sustained through marriages. This has increased familial tensions and fueled splits. In this camp, men have controlled the money earned by women; working has given women little power. On the contrary, the responsibilities they have assumed tend to increase the "natural" value given to men in order to reestablish the gender balance.

Daughters, generally the eldest ones, have played a key role in sustaining their families. Because of familial hardships, they often replaced the men as the only breadwinners, and, later on, when they could stop working and were too old for marriage, they have often assumed their mothers' roles, taking care of the house. Indeed, burdening economic roles have frequently meant celibacy for women, which has not been the case for men. But one must draw a distinction: some women have chosen celibacy while others have suffered it as a result of passive choices made by the families who have benefited from it. For families of the latter, this reality has been a painful sign of failure, especially for mothers who felt unable to give to their daughters a future of marriage and children. Young women have had a shorter window of years during which they could marry than men; thirty years old has been perceived as the limit, after which it has seemed almost impossible to find a spouse. Consequently, it was hard for women to be economically responsible for their family when they were young and yet hoped to get married afterwards. Moreover, even when their wage work was supplementary rather than necessary, in families with numerous children, mothers needed one of the eldest daughters to become responsible for the house. This role has been highly valorized; many women have complied without feeling that they have sacrificed their personal life to the collective well-being.

Oum Yussef was deeply hurt by the fact that her whole family (thirteen persons) has relied on UNRWA's assistance and on the wage work of her second child (out of seven), her daughter Leila.[32] At the time of the interview, Leila was close to forty years old and unmarried. The family was originally from Bir al-Saba in the Negev and took refuge in the Maghazi camp in the Gaza Strip from 1948 to 1968. Oum Yussef's husband was a workman before he retired. Oum Yussef worked hard until 1999 as an agriculturalist on relatives' farms in Sahab, in the Jordan valley, and in Mafraq. Each summer, when their children were young, they all went to do seasonal farming. The eldest son worked after graduating, and Leila studied in a community college until the late 1970s, when she left to teach in Saudi Arabia. Since she came back in 1992, Leila has been working as an administrative secretary at the UNRWA. Among Oum Yussef's five sons, three finished secondary school. The youngest even studied Arab literature at a university, but none of them found a job. Leila's mother was convinced that with Jordanian nationality, they would. Sometimes, her sons found temporary work; but one of them has been in Saudi Arabia for eleven years with his wife, who is a teacher, but he has remained unemployed. Jamal, the third son, was expelled from Jordan because of his political involvement. Leila has been employed in the UNRWA branch office in Amman and living in a women's dormitory to avoid a daily commute. She was earning 170 Jordanian dinars (about US$240) per month, was paying 70 JD for rent, and has been giving almost all the rest of her salary to her parents.

Many women who wanted to keep and raise their children after an early failed marriage had a fragile existence.[33] In general, their family wanted them to return home, provided they leave their children with their father or in-laws, who were supposed to cover their needs. Doing so, they could most probably remarry. If they did not accept such choice, they were poorly supported by their family, were not helped by their husbands and their family, and have had to cope with all their responsibilities alone.

Widows who lost their husbands later in life were protected by their older children, allowing them to stay home without familial conflict.

Nevertheless, the interventions of their fathers, brothers, or sons in the matrimonial choices of their daughters frequently brought about unstable marriages. The arrangements the widows' brothers (or less frequently sons) made were often hurried. The haste to marry the young women came from the family's desire to lessen their own duty to help the single mother and her children. Moreover, the constant rise of celibacy among women since the 1980s has been encouraging such haste, and daughters have been rushed into possible marriages also in order to preserve their reputation.

Nisreen's mother, Oum Ala, who was in her fifties at the time of my fieldwork, was widowed in 1983. She had nine children (five daughters and four sons). The eldest had just turned thirteen. With her brother's help, she bought the house they were renting in Jabal Hussein camp since they arrived there in 1970. The two families, originally from Yaffa, lived in the Gaza Strip until 1967:

> At the beginning, I thought of giving my children to my in-laws who live in the camp; then I managed to take care of them. They did not ask for them. I told them, if you help me, they are your children, if you don't, they are mine. They did not give me anything. Nisreen's paternal uncle would not even recognize her; we don't have any relations with them.[34]

Like her mother, an early widow who sustained her family when her father passed away after the 1948 exile, Oum Ala raised her children, helped by her brother, social assistance, and later by the work of her eldest son, Ala, who could not finish primary school and had various jobs. The other children stayed in school longer, but none of them graduated. Two girls married before reaching the age of twenty. At the time of my fieldwork, Abed, age twenty, and Mohamed, age sixteen, were working together as self-employed electricians. Ala was unemployed. When the boys reached age eighteen, the family could no longer benefit from the UNRWA's Special Hardship program, so they received the assistance of the Islamic center. Since Oum Ala became a widow, her brother became responsible for the family. He decided to marry off Nisreen, without her consent, when she was fifteen to a young man he hardly knew. Three months later, after many disputes and physical violence, the couple separated. In spite of repeated violence, her uncle encouraged Nisreen to remain with her husband. They had one daughter and divorced four years later.

Oum Ala and Nisreen decided to go to the Jordanian Women's Union to ask for legal assistance. She obtained a favorable divorce: a deferred dower (*mu'akhar*); a small, temporary alimony for her; and, most importantly, one for her daughter (36 Jordanian dinars, that is, roughly US$50).[35] Nisreen's uncle failed to protect her and, since then, Oum Ala has prevented him from intervening in their familial affairs.

These difficult relations between single mothers, their own families, and their in-laws have often led to conflicts and ruptures. When women took on the responsibility of head of family, not relying on their kin, the family has moved up socially but such improvement has been deferred to the next generation, i.e., the generation of their grandchildren. But their children had to contribute early to domestic economy: they left school early, and daughters generally married early. Yet these families have avoided the more familial breakups when the mother's family, notably her brothers, lacked effective committed interest in her and in the futures of her children. Effectively, children of single mothers have been perceived as belonging first to their father's family. As a result, limited investment has been made in their future; daughters were married off precipitously and received little protection. That opportunities are scarce for all has only aggravated the situation.

This situation was most probably what led Lina, a divorcee, to confront her relatives with the decision to leave her mother's house and live alone with her children when she was thirty years old. A house obtained by the UNRWA and the assistance given by the Special Hardship Program provided the means of realizing her goal. She knew that her work alone could not permit her to live independently. Until 1967, Lina's family had lived in the Gaza Strip, where her father was a taxi driver. In 1973, her father abandoned her mother and married another woman. He remained in the Jerash camp, but Lina hardly ever saw him. Her brothers married and bought houses in the camp. They were earning just enough to maintain their wives and children. Lina reproaches her father for his remarriage and lack of interest in and financial support for her and her eight siblings, who all had to leave school at the age of fifteen, while the eight children of his new wife continued their studies. Lina divorced when she was nineteen. Her husband had been trading between the camp and the Gaza Strip and stayed there. She held different jobs, most recently trading clothes between the camp and Mafraq. In her view, it was her father's failure that broke familial solidarity and unity:

> The person who makes a family, who brings people close to each other, is the father, and we do not have a father, so each one does whatever he feels like. He is the reason for all my misfortune.[36]

Lina's father did not support her when she encountered problems with her husband, although it was her father who had chosen him as her husband—he was his neighbor. She did not obtain her rights after divorce, neither the deferred dower (*mu'akhar*), nor the alimony for her children (*nafaqa*). Her husband owed her about JD 2,000 for the *mu'akhar* and the furniture of their house, which belonged to her according to their marriage contract. Her father refused to help her or to go to court to support her efforts to obtain what she deserved.

In Lina's and Nisreen's stories, the uncle and the father, having asserted both real and symbolic power in matrimonial choice, soon showed no real concern about these women's futures. They took no responsibility for and gave no guarantees to the unions they wanted, and through their inaction, passed down a reproduction of conjugal ruptures, from mothers to daughters.

The time periods in a woman's life I relate here are moments of transition that can bring a woman and her family to a point of tremendous insecurity. The women in this situation were not protected. But the power of family ideology induced them to remain within the family circle and not to seek other interventions, help, or resources, particularly those that would shame them and their families (*'eib*) by revealing the family's fragility, failure, private life, or absence of men. In both case studies, the women waited in vain for a traditional official intervention—meaning a masculine one. Nisreen and her mother waited, but in the end decided to seek other solutions, the only ones available to them. For Lina, it was too late because her husband did not come to Jordan. Finally, however, these three women abandoned the hollow myth of masculine protection and took their families' destinies into their own hands, whether individually or collectively.

Conclusion

In spite of the public discourse of camp families and the creation of a "family ideology" by most social and political actors in Jordan, exile has brought major social changes in Palestinian society. In both camps examined here, a small, better-off minority has adapted and more or less reconstituted the social and familial conditions of the past, but even here, daughters, especially younger ones, have achieved a degree of autonomy, spurred by the reality of exile. Another larger group of families had the resources to retool their existence principally through education, but the process has been made possible in part by considerable contributions of daughters and sisters, who have thus acquired greater status. Indeed, in the 1980s, women of the third generation in the camps were more educated than Jordanian women in general.[37] But the majority in both camps only had enough resources to eke out survival, and here the feminization of the family was most complete, as death and divorce challenged male authority and made the monetary contributions of women, sometimes with greater job opportunities than their husbands and brothers, absolutely essential.

Since the 1980s, average rates of celibacy, divorce, and separation have been much higher in the camps than in Jordan, and widows or divorcees have preferred not to remarry in order to raise their children.[38] Among the third generation, for instance, twice as many women from the camps chose celibacy.[39] These changes have been the result of the history and conditions of exile: its circumstances undermined the patriarchal family system, to a lesser or a greater extent depending on the standard of living of each family group—and most extremely among the poorest majority. But these changes have also been the results of women's personal choices. What I call "popular feminism" has indeed been grounded in three main trends: women's refusal to remarry after the frequent ruptures of matrimonial bond; women's independence from their family of origin and their in-laws in order to raise their children; and since the 1980s, the emergence of women's celibacy.[40] Nevertheless, this popular feminism has relied on an idea of traditional family values and has not overtly challenged the patriarchal family system.

The Jordanian state, while praising democracy and human and women's rights and constructing an international self-image of modernity, is rooted in and has been structured by traditional patriarchy. On the other hand, despite the image spread by Jordanian and Palestinian elites regarding their conservative values, camp inhabitants have challenged patriarchal family structures. Moreover, the Jordanian Women's Union, an independent, oppositional feminist group, within which a large number of activists are originally from the camps, is aiding camp women's contestations and camp families' social changes through its commitment toward women and its programs targeting family issues, especially in the camps. More acutely since the 1990s, its programs have been strengthening individual and couple choices, have supported spouses against their families of origin, and have contested the role given to familial honor. Given the fundamental role played by family and kinship in support of political power since the creation of Jordan, its actions are highly subversive.[41] Thus, it is the transnational enclave of the Palestinian camp refugees in Jordan that has become one of the leading edges in exposing the contradictions of the regime with regard to social and political change and to its alleged commitment to democratization.

Notes

I would specially like to thank Christopher H. Johnson for his careful and insightful critical reading of this chapter.

1. Pierre Bourdieu, "À propos de la famille comme catégorie réalisée," *Actes de la recherche en sciences sociales* 100 (1993): 32–36.
2. Pierre Bourdieu, *Langage et pouvoir symbolique* (Paris, 2001).
3. Olivier Schwartz, *Le monde privé des ouvriers: Hommes et femmes du Nord* (Paris, 1990).
4. Liisa Malkki, *Purity and Exile: Violence, Memory, and National Cosmology among Hutu Refugees in Tanzania* (Chicago, 1995).
5. In my research, I distinguished four age groups or historic generations among the interviewees, mostly women, following women's way of naming them. I call women who are born before 1938 (i.e., who were above sixty-five years old at the end of my fieldwork in 2003) the "old generation" or the "generation of Palestine." I described women born between 1939 and 1953, who were between fifty and sixty-four in 2003, as the "girls of the catastrophe" (*banet al-nakba*), with reference to the 1948 exodus. Women of the "third generation" are those who were born between 1954 and 1968, and women of the "new generation" are those born between 1969 and 1983. I understand generations as "groups of persons who have been through the same historical periods and political and economic situations at the same period of their life cycle." See Maurizio Gribaudi, *Itinéraires ouvriers: Espaces et groupes sociaux à Turin au début du XXème siècle* (Paris, 1987), 141.
6. *Mukhtars* are social leaders who, upon the government's nomination, represent a village, tribe, clan, district, or community. In pre-1948 Palestine, and in the region more generally, they were the main go-betweens connecting the population and the central administration. This office was largely based on the traditional leadership of the *sheikhs* (see note 12). It was instituted by the Ottomans and was strengthened under the British mandate. *Mukhtars* had administrative functions and were notably registry officers.
7. From 1948 to 1950, the Quakers in the Gaza Strip, the International Committee of the Red Cross in the West Bank, the League of National Societies of the Red Cross, and the Red Crescent in Lebanon, Syria, and Transjordan assisted Palestinian refugees under the supervision of the United Nations. In December 1949, the UNRWA (United Nations Relief and Works Agency for Palestine refugees in the Near East) was created and took over in April 1950. Since then, its mandate has been renewed, and it has employed more and more (and today mostly) Palestinian refugees (only the top positions are still reserved to an international staff). It became an administration of the refugees delivering key services in Education, Health, and Social Services.
8. Jabal Hussein camp, 3 May 1999, interview by the author. All the names of the interviewees from the camps have been changed.
9. Amman, 15 December 2000, interview by the author.
10. Family members can indeed be active in different parties but they share a common concern for political involvement.
11. Jabal Hussein camp, 21 April 1998, interview by the author.
12. A sheikh is a traditional community leader. In another context, it can also designate a religious leader.

13. Fatah, Yasser Arafat's party, was created in 1959 in Kuwait and started its military operations in Israel primarily from its bases in Jordan (West Bank) in 1965. In 1969, Fatah took the lead of the PLO, created in 1964. The other influential party was the Popular Front for the Liberation of Palestine.
14. Randa Farah, "Popular Memory and Reconstructions of Palestinian Identity: Al-Baq'a Refugee Camp, Jordan" (PhD diss., University of Toronto, 1999), 288.
15. See for instance Julie Peteet, *Gender in Crisis: Women and the Palestinian Resistance Movement* (New York, 1991); Valérie Pouzol-Ershaidat, "La nation contestée: Luttes féministes, combat pour la paix des femmes palestiniennes et israéliennes (1948–1998)" (PhD diss., École des Hautes Études en Sciences Sociales, Paris, 2001).
16. See Lama Abu-Odeh, "Feminism, Nationalism and the Law: the Case of Arab Women" (PhD diss., Cambridge University, 1993); "Crimes of Honour and the Construction of Gender in Arab Societies," in *Islam and Feminism: Legal and Literary Perspectives,* ed. Mai Yammami (London, 1996), 141–94.
17. Laurie Brand, *Women, the State, and Political Liberalization: Middle Eastern and North African Experiences* (New York, 1998), 124.
18. By changing from a plurinominal electoral system to a strict uninominal electoral system for multiple district seats, the electoral system has encouraged people to cast their vote for a member of their family group. This effect has been enhanced by an unbalanced districting that favors the political representation of constituencies less populated, mainly rural and/or populated by Bedouins.
19. I follow Pierre Bourdieu in stressing what he calls in French "logique du corps," that is, the symbolic process through which male domination constructs the family as a unity deprived of all internal conflict. See Bourdieu, "À propos de la famille."
20. On the issue of generations, see note 5.
21. These statistics are based on data about 54 families and 78 women gathered during my fieldwork in 1999 and 2002.
22. Other scholars have found a similar pattern in interviews conducted in Palestinian camps in Lebanon among camp dwellers of peasant origin in the late 1980s and early 1990s. See Rosemary Sayigh, "Palestinian Camp Women's Narratives of Exile: Self, Gender, National Crisis" (PhD diss., University of Hull, 1994).
23. Compare to the percentages given by the study of Hilma Granqvist in the village of Artas in the 1920s and the 1930s (where 33.7 percent of the marriages took place in the lineage—*hamula*) or on Palestinian society in the West Bank or in Israel after 1948. See Hilma Granqvist, *Marriage Conditions in a Palestinian Village,* 2 vols. (Helsingfors, 1931–35; repr., New York, 1975); Ibrahim Wade Ata, *The West Bank Palestinian Family* (London, 1986); Henry Rosenfeld, "An Analysis of Marriage and Marriage Statistics for a Muslim and Christian Arab village," *International Archive of Archaeology and Ethnography* 68 (1957): 32–52 and "Social and Economic Factors in Explanation of the Increased Rate of Patrilineal Endogamy in the Arab Village in Israel," in *Mediterranean Family Structures,* ed. John G. Peristiany (Cambridge, 1976), 115–36.
24. The incidence of this preferred marriage, which in Arabic is simply called "marriage," did not differ from the pre-exile period and Granqvist's data.
25. Camp Improvement Committees are institutions in between the Jordanian administration, the UNRWA, and the refugees, which make most daily administrative and infrastructural decisions concerning the camp. Their members are nominated by the Jordanian administration according to their social status and to what they represent for camp inhabitants.

26. This data refer to the post-1948 marriages in my samples of the four generations of refugees surveyed in 1999 and 2002. See note 21. I mean here the nationality of reference of the interviewees, not their legal nationality. Most of the refugees in Jordan have Jordanian nationality.
27. This migration was especially important until the 1980s. Thereafter, the two years of postgraduate studies that are required to become a teacher reduced opportunities, especially in Jerash, where education is more costly for nonnationals.
28. The first one was established in 1926.
29. Between 1990 and 1992, 300,000 expatriates from Palestinian returned to Jordan.
30. Amman, 26 February 2000, interview by the author.
31. The Saudi authorities request that most migrant women be sponsored by a male relative who acts as a guarantor.
32. Jerash Camp, 13 March 2000, interview with the author.
33. Since 1976, a mother can have the custody of her children, who are legally under the authority of their father or their paternal grandfather or uncles, until puberty, provided that she does not remarry. Before, according to a 1951 law, the age limit was nine for girls and eleven for boys. See Annelies Moors, *Women, Property and Islam: Palestinian Experiences 1920–1990* (Cambridge, 1995), 138.
34. Oum Ala, Jabal Hussein camp, 15 June 1999, interview by the author.
35. She was divorced by the Court (*tafriq*). Her husband did not decide unilaterally to divorce her (*talaq*) nor did she lose her financial rights, because she was the one to take the initiative (*khulu'*). According to the law, in the marriage contract an amount of money is given to the bride when the union is concluded (*muqqadam*), and another one is provided for in case of divorce (*mu'akhar*).
36. Jerash camp, 10 October 1999, interview by the author.
37. For average figures, see Stéphanie Latte Abdallah, *Femmes réfugiées palestiniennes* (Paris, 2006), 230.
38. For average figures, see Latte Abdallah, *Femmes réfugiées palestiniennes*, 229. This pattern contrasts with the general decline of divorce in Jordan and in most Arab countries during the twentieth century. See Philippe Fargues, *Générations arabes: L'alchimie du nombre* (Paris, 2000), 129 and 142–46.
39. For average figures, see Latte Abdallah, *Femmes réfugiées palestiniennes*, 229.
40. On the concept of "popular feminism" to describe forms and ways of women's resistance within civil society, see Cécile Dauphin, Arlette Farge, and Geneviève Fraisse et al., eds., "Culture et pouvoir des femmes: Essai d'historiographie," *Annales ESC* 2 (1986): 287.
41. See also Latte Abdallah, *Femmes réfugiées palestiniennes*, 59–79; "Les femmes des camps à l'avant-garde de la contestation du système patriarcal en Jordanie," in *Les Cahiers de l'Orient contemporaine* (Special issue: *Le Royaume Hachémite; De Abdallah Ier à Abdallah II —Un demi-siècle d'histoire*) 75 (2004): 77–100; "Le débat sur la criminalité liée à l'honneur en Jordanie: le genre comme enjeu politique et question sociale," *Monde arabe, Maghreb-Machrek: Les constructions sociales de la question féminine* 179 (2004): 29–45.

Chapter 14

Mirror Image of Family Relations

Social Links between Patel Migrants in Britain and India

Mario Rutten and Pravin J. Patel

By the end of the twentieth century, about two million people of South Asian origin resided in Europe, the United States, and Canada. The majority of them, about 1.26 million, lived in Britain.[1] Geographically, the Indian migrants in Britain are concentrated in the urban counties of England, from Kent in the southeast to Lancashire in the northwest. The largest number, about 36 percent of the total Indian population, live in Greater London, while 22 percent have settled in the Midlands area.[2] By far the largest Indian communities in Britain originate from Gujarat and Punjab.[3]

Gujarat is one of the most prosperous states of India. Being a coastal state, it has a long tradition of overseas trade. Gujarati business houses have existed in Africa since the thirteenth century, and Gujarati businessmen, particularly Ismaili Muslims, have been bankers and moneylenders of high reputation.[4] Among the Hindus of Gujarat, the members of the Patidar caste from central Gujarat have emigrated to East Africa in large numbers since the late nineteenth and early twentieth centuries.

The Patidar community is an upwardly mobile, middle-ranking peasant caste, which can be found in several regions of Gujarat but has its main concentration in the Charotar tract of Kheda and Anand districts in central Gujarat.[5] With about 15 to 20 percent of the district population, the Patidars form a substantial minority that has been able to acquire economic, social, and political dominance since the early part of the twentieth century, both at the regional and state levels.[6]

Participation of the Patidars from central Gujarat in the process of migration abroad has a long history. From the late nineteenth and early twentieth century onwards, family members of Patidar businessmen had already started migrating to Madhya Pradesh, Orissa, West Bengal, Andhra Pradesh, and other states of India to trade in the locally produced biddy tobacco. This form of migration was mainly confined to the upper stratum of the business community in central Gujarat. A more spectacular form of migration, which was one of the first streams of migration among the middle-class Patidars in central Gujarat, was the migration to foreign countries, especially to East African countries such as Kenya, Uganda, and Tanzania. This pattern of migration started during the period of economic deterioration around the turn of the century and accelerated during the 1920s and 1930s. Many Patidars who had never traveled any farther than Ahmedabad or Baroda began to pick up the trade connection that had existed for two thousand years between Gujarat and Africa.[7]

This early migration abroad from the Charotar tract was closely related to the job opportunities offered by British colonial rule in East Africa. During the first decades of the twentieth century especially, many Patidars from middle-class and lower-middle-class peasant backgrounds migrated as passage or free migrants to countries like Kenya, Tanzania, and Uganda. Colonial rule and the completion of the East African railways offered these educated middle-class Patidars white-collar clerical occupations and initiated a new era of economic opportunities to be exploited by members of this peasant caste, who took up a variety of commercial and professional activities. Most of these Patidar migrants went to East Africa on the basis of work permits provided by fellow villagers who had gone earlier or through marriage with a Patidar girl or boy living in an East African country. These marriages were known as *permitian lagn* (marriage arranged with a view to get a permit to go to Africa) because the main purpose for the Patidar family in the village was to provide one of their sons or daughters with an opportunity to migrate to East Africa. It was usually through the help and support of their new families-in-law along with that of other relatives and fellow villagers that these young migrants, who had never traveled beyond their own regional towns, were able to settle down in their new environment.

The colonial period and the 1950s saw only a very small trickle of Patidars to Britain. From the mid-1960s onwards, however, the pattern of migration of the Patidar households changed very quickly from East Africa to Britain. As a result of radical Africanization programs in these countries and the fear that immigration restrictions would soon be implemented by the British government, many of these East African Indians left for Britain in a relatively short time span. Between September 1967 and March 1968 alone, twelve thousand South Asians from Kenya entered Britain, and twenty-nine thousand more Asians arrived in 1972 after being expelled from Uganda.[8] Although a relatively prosperous minority of these so-called twice migrants had already begun to invest in Britain in the 1950s and early 1960s—mainly through the purchase of houses where young relatives could stay while studying—most of those who migrated from Africa to Britain at the end of the 1960s and early 1970s arrived practically empty handed and were usually fully dependent on friends and relatives.[9]

As a result of these patterns of migration, the Patels constitute one of the largest groups among the Gujarati Hindus in Britain. Not surprisingly "Patel" is one of the most popular Indian surnames abroad along with "Singh." According to a conservative estimate of the membership of associations of all the marriage circles in Britain, there were about thirty thousand Patels from central Gujarat living in Britain in the early 1990s, of which 90 percent resided in London.[10]

Social Differentiation

The main part of the findings presented in this chapter are based on fieldwork conducted in 1998 among members of the Patidar community in rural central Gujarat and among their relatives in London in 1999, followed by subsequent visits since then. In order to study the links between the Patidars of India and Britain, we collected information through a survey from 313 households in six villages in central Gujarat who have relatives in Britain, out of which 157 were selected for in-depth interviews. This was followed by a survey among 159 Patidar households in Greater London, of which 80 were selected for in-depth interviews. Members of the Patidar households in Greater London originated from these same six villages in central Gujarat.[11] The reason for selecting six different villages is related to the fact that the Patidars of central Gujarat are not a homogenous group but an internally differentiated one with several hierarchically organized subgroups having a preoccupation with the competitive display of social status. In their selection of marriage partners, the Patidars confine themselves to their own subdivision within a specific group of villages, based on an extended hierarchical system of endogamous marriage circles.[12] These marriage circles (*ekada* or *gol*) have retained their social significance for the Patidars living in Britain, where they have established associations that organize social and cultural activities for its members.[13]

In order to have a fairly representative picture of the socioeconomic-cultural links among the Patidars in central Gujarat and their relatives in Britain, we decided to select villages of both high-ranking and medium-ranking marriage circles. For this purpose, we divided the villages of central Gujarat into two major strata recognized as socially significant: *Mota Gam* (big villages) and *Nana Gam* (small villages). The six villages belonging to the marriage circle known as *Chha Gam* (six villages) are considered *Mota Gam*, while almost all the other villages are generally known as *Nana Gam*. From *Mota Gam* we selected two villages from the *Chha Gam* marriage circle. The big villages are actually rural towns compared to the smaller villages; however, this distinction reflects not only difference in size but also difference in social status. The Patidars of the big villages are considered to be of the highest social status among all the hypergamously organized marriage circles of villages in central Gujarat, in which girls marry into a family of higher or at least equal status (outside their village of birth).[14]

Except for the *Panch Gam* (five villages) marriage circle, whose status is ambiguous, all the other marriage circles belong to the *Nana Gam* category. From these marriage circles we selected four villages from two medium-status marriage circles: *Sattavis Gam* (27 villages) and *Bavis Gam* (22 villages).[15]

The selected stratified sample of villages within both *Mota Gam* and *Nana Gam* marriage circles allows for comparison between Patidars from high-status and medium-status villages. This difference between high-status and medium-status villages is an important aspect within the Patidar community with its strong sense of hierarchy and practice of hypergamy. An important reason for selecting these three specific marriage circles is that their members make up the largest share of the central Gujarat Patidar migrants in Britain. Based on information provided by Lyon and West on the number of Patidars in London, it turns out that 70 percent of the thirty thousand Patidars from central Gujarat in London belong to the *Chha Gam*, *Sattavis Gam*, and *Bavis Gam* marriage circles.[16]

Within the Patel community in Britain, there are differences related to their patterns of migration. First of all, there are those who belong to so-called twice-migrant families. These Patels entered Britain from East Africa, especially from Kenya, Uganda, and Tanzania. In our sample of 159 households in Greater London, they make up three-fourths of the total number of household members who were not born in Britain. This figure includes those who came to Britain after a temporary stay in India following their departure from East Africa. The remaining one-fourth of the immigrants consists of those who migrated directly from India to Britain without having any previous migration history.

In his overview of differentiation among the British Gujarati, Steven Vertovec extensively discusses the difference between these "East African" and the "Indian" Gujaratis. In general, he emphasizes, "East African" Gujarati are viewed within the Gujarati community in Britain as having a higher educational and occupational background and being wealthier and of higher status compared to those who directly migrated from India.[17] Our analysis of the migration history of the Patels from central Gujarat points to the fact that there are also social differences among East African Gujarati in Britain that belong to the same caste group. Most of the East African Patels settled in Britain came from Kenya and Uganda. There are slight social differences between those Patels who came to Britain from Kenya and those who came from Uganda. One of the reasons for this process of social differentiation within the Patidar community seems to be partly related to a difference in their patterns of migration.

It appears that due to an earlier process of urbanization and education, and a subsequent greater exposure to the outside world, the Patels of the *Mota Gam* villages started emigrating to East Africa earlier than their counterparts from the *Nana Gam* villages. Perhaps the fear of losing status by their inability to marry their daughters and sisters in equal or higher status families within their own marriage circle, due to a combination of higher dowries and an increasing scarcity of land, may also have compelled them to look for better opportunities outside India. As a result, most of those Patels who emigrated to East Africa at an early stage originated from one of the *Mota Gam* villages that belong to the *Chha Gam* marriage circle. Since Mombassa was the port of arrival in those days, the large majority of the *Mota Gam* Patels settled down in Kenya.

After they had established themselves, these migrants started to encourage and help those relatives who were interested in migrating to East Africa. This applied especially to those who were in need of assistants and other junior staff members to help them run their businesses. Due to the prevailing system of hypergamy among the Patidars of central Gujarat, some of these relatives originated from *Nana Gam* villages that belonged to other marriage circles. As a result, an increasing number of *Nana Gam* Patels started to emigrate to East Africa. Being latecomers and relatively less educated compared to the *Mota Gam*

Patels, many of them encountered difficulties in finding employment in Kenya. In search of new opportunities, these *Nana Gam* Patels started moving further inland and settled down in large numbers in British protectorate Uganda.

Thus, it seems that the majority of Patels who settled down in Kenya originated from the *Mota Gam* villages, while among those who settled down in Uganda, the proportion of Patels from *Nana Gam* villages is higher. This difference in geographical pattern of migration reflects a relatively invisible but nevertheless significant difference of status within the Patidar community of central Gujarat. In general, the Patels that belong to the *Mota Gam* villages are usually associated with higher status and greater wealth as compared to those who originate from the *Nana Gam* villages. Therefore, most of those who came from Kenya to Britain were relatively better-off and higher-status Patels than many of those who came from Uganda. Moreover, the Patels of the *Mota Gam* villages who had migrated earlier to Kenya also had a stronger tradition of retaining links back home than those who came later and settled in Uganda. This different tradition of maintaining links back home in India seems to be reflected in these two groups even in Britain.

Another reason for the social differentiation between those Patels in Britain who came from Kenya and those who came from Uganda is in the manner in which they migrated to Britain. The Patels who migrated from East Africa to Britain came in two waves. Those who came from Kenya arrived mainly in the mid- and late 1960s, while those who were settled in Uganda entered Britain in the early 1970s. Patels who came from Kenya could usually plan their migration in advance. Due to the continuing Africanization programs in Kenya, they could anticipate their departure and were able to transfer part of their wealth to Britain relatively easily. This was much less so for those Patels who had settled in Uganda. Their departure from Uganda was the result of a sudden and unexpected expulsion by Idi Amin. Being forced to leave the country at very short notice, they arrived in Britain as political refugees with very little personal property left over.

Social Links

Regardless of whether they migrated from East Africa or India, and whether they belonged to the *Mota Gam* or *Nana Gam* villages, the Patel community we studied in London remained attached to Indian culture and to the social relations of their Gujarati background. Most of the older generation have retained their Patidar identity by organizing themselves on the basis of their village of origin and marriage circle (*gol*). These village-based associations and organizations of village circles in Britain publish directories with details about Patidar family members that are used to help to arrange marriages. For this purpose, the associations also organize marriage *melas*, in which young boys and girls publicly introduce themselves and try to find suitable life-partners. In addition, village associations and marriage-circle associations of Patidars in Britain organize meetings to celebrate *Nav Ratri*, *Diwali*, and other important Indian festivals and have functions like dinner-and-dance parties on weekends, where they eat, drink, and dance to Hindi songs late into the night. Moreover, many Patels participate in religious activities, for which the Swaminarayan temple in North London is often a focal point.[18] Although most of the active members in these associations belong to the older generations of Patidar migrants, many organizations also have youth committees in which youngsters are involved and encouraged to organize and participate in various activities.

Along with organizing social and religious events, members of the Patidar community in London have started efforts to teach Gujarati to the younger generation. Children belonging to the second and third generation of migrants are mostly able to understand functional Gujarati, but they find it difficult to speak it, and are often unable to read and write the Gujarati script. This problem, of course, is not confined to the Patel community in Britain. The Gujarati community as a whole has become more conscious about teaching Gujarati to its children. There are about five hundred classes that teach Gujarati throughout Britain, often for two hours a week on Saturdays and Sundays. By the end of the 1990s, about one thousand to fifteen hundred students were taking Gujarati language examinations annually.

On the whole, village life in Gujarat still has a profound effect on the first generation of Patidar migrants. They grew up in the villages during their formative years, where they studied and spent their childhoods. Moreover, many of them were raised during the patriotic period of the national independence movement, which made them even prouder of their Indian culture and heritage. The social, religious, and cultural bonds with their home villages and with other Patidar migrants from the same region when they lived in East Africa and later in Britain further cemented ties with their villages of origin. As a result of all of this, the social identity of the first generation of Patidar migrants remains deeply embedded in village life, and ties with their places of origin and with their relatives and friends in Gujarat still continue to be quite strong.

One of the indicators of social links between the Patidar migrants in Britain and their relatives in the villages in Gujarat are the intense contacts that exist between the members of both groups. Until recently, letters were the main type of communication between Gujarati migrants and their relatives in India. Today, phone calls are an important way of keeping in touch, although pricing dictates that calls from India to Britain are usually very brief and often made in emergency situations or for very specific purposes. Patidars in Britain, on the other hand, make phone calls to their families in the villages more frequently; some even phone from Britain almost every week. During these calls information is exchanged about the well-being of relatives on both sides.

In terms of financial assistance, more than 40 percent of the selected households in Gujarat had received some kind of monetary help from relatives in Britain in the period between 1993 and 1998. Most of this financial help and support was given to cover part of the maintenance of the family in the village, to pay for part of the repair costs of the house, or to contribute to marriage expenses, religious rituals, or other social occasions. Almost half of the households have relatives in Britain who made investments in India during this five-year period. By far the most important type of investment by these relatives from Britain are financial investments in banks and shares. Parts of these investments are related to the various schemes that have been set up for Non-Resident Indians (NRIs) by the Indian government. Another important type of investment by relatives from Britain is the purchase of property. This includes farmland, residential plots, or houses and apartments. Family members in the village are often asked to help relatives in Britain to buy and afterwards to maintain the property.

Another important form of contact between households in Gujarat and family members in Britain are visits by relatives from Britain to their home villages. More than 90 percent of the selected 313 households in the six villages were visited by relatives from Britain in the period between 1993 and 1998. Altogether, 768 different relatives visited India, an average of 2.7 per household, with a substantial number traveling to India more than once during this five-year period. Most visits were relatively long: almost 50 percent lasting one to three months, and 9 percent from four to six months. About 40 percent of the relatives who visited their home villages stayed in India for less than a month.

In recent years, when many of the older migrants retired from active employment, a movement from Britain back to India during winter has emerged. Among the older generation of Patidar migrants in Britain, there are quite a few who could be called "international commuters," traveling to India every winter for stays of one to five months. In most cases, they live in Gujarat in their own apartment or bungalow in one of the nearby towns or on the outskirts of their home village. Some of them have actually for all practical purposes reemigrated to India as they spend more time in their country of origin than in Britain. Although most of these people did return to spend their retirement in India, some returned because they no longer wanted to live with their families in Britain. Having returned to their village of origin, some of them realized, however, that they are no longer at home there either, as is shown in the following case study.[19]

Shamalbhai is seventy-two years old, and since 1994 he has been living again in the village in which he was born in 1925. In 1953, at the age of twenty-seven, Shamalbhai left his native village when he was already married. He was invited to come to Tanzania by his father's eldest brother's son whose family had been living there since the 1930s.

In 1956, Shamalbhai came back to his village to collect his wife and three children. The highly unstable political situation around 1963 made the couple decide to take their children back to Charotar and to leave them with Shamalbhai's nearest relatives in his native village where they could attend the local schools. Although his wife stayed with their children for some months, she again joined her husband in Tanzania in 1964. Together, they lived and worked in Tanzania until 1973 with only one visit to their children in Charotar in 1969.

After their visit in 1973, his wife remained behind in the village, while Shamalbhai returned again to Tanzania in 1974. From there he applied and was allowed to enter Britain in 1979. Within one year after his arrival in London, Shamalbhai called his wife and their three children to join him in Britain. But Shamalbhai and his family were only able to get unskilled work during the early period in Britain. "I could only get a job in a factory," Shamalbhai mentioned to us.

> In Tanzania I had a big shop with assistants and drove around in a Jaguar car, but I had to leave almost all my property behind when I migrated to the UK and had to start again from scratch. I was not really happy in London. It was hard work that my wife and I had to perform in those factories for very low pay, but we did it for our children. By migrating to the UK, we wanted to give them a better future, because they would not have these opportunities in India, being relatively low educated and without much property in the village. After my retirement in 1990, however, my wife and I started to visit India very regularly. In fact, we used to often stay several months per year in India. In 1994, we even returned and took up permanent residence again in my native village, because after my father's brother's daughter had left for the US, there was no one left in the village to take care of my old father. We then built a new house on the outskirts of the village, and since then we live here the whole year around and only occasionally visit the UK.

Although at first, Shamalbhai returned to the village only because of his father, he visibly enjoys being part of the village life. Every day he makes his rounds of the village, and on various evenings one can meet him in the village square, talking to old friends. On the other hand, however, he occupies a marginal position in his home village.

> Although I was born and brought up here, even after four years of my permanent return, I still do not feel that I am really part of village society. We participate in various activities, but somehow we have difficulties really mixing with our relatives in the village and force ourselves to attend their gatherings. But to be honest, we used to have the same feeling when we were living in the UK, because I arrived there at the age of 55 and only worked there for about ten years.

After Shamalbhai left the room for a short while, his wife also started to express her views:

> Yes, we were also not at home in London, but at least we had our children and grandchildren nearby. I don't like it here at all and hardly leave our house. My whole life I have been able to live and adjust in different countries. I have lived in Charotar, in Tanzania, and in London, but now that we are old, I sometimes feel that we no longer feel at home anywhere and therefore it is better to keep to ourselves inside our own house.

As is to be expected, there are fewer visits by Indian relatives to Britain than by Patidar migrants to India. However, members of more than 20 percent of the selected households visited Britain between 1993 and 1998. In total, 128 members visited Britain in this five-year period, an average of 1.6 relatives per household. Clearly, substantial numbers of household members from the villages have visited Britain, often for long periods of time: only 8 percent stayed for less than a month. About 45 percent of them stayed between one to three months, while the visits of 33 percent lasted four to six months, with the remaining 14 percent for more than half a year.

The 313 households in the six selected villages with relatives in Britain have a total of 3,624 relatives in Britain, an average of 11.6 relatives per household. Although the selection of households in the six villages for in-depth interviews was done on the basis of the existence of relatives in Britain, 133 of the 157 families also have relatives outside Britain, altogether 1,469 relatives, with an average of 9.4 per household. After the imposition of rigorous immigration restrictions, emigration to Britain decreased rapidly from the late 1970s and early 1980s. Since then, the United States and Canada have become the most popular destinations for Patidar migrants.[20] Almost 75 percent of the 1,469 relatives of the selected families in central Gujarat live in the United States, while almost 16 percent live in East Africa.

One of the consequences of this scattered migration pattern of the Patidar community is the emergence of a category of people that we would describe as "world citizens." They are usually older people who, although they have a residence in one country, often travel between Britain, India, North America, and East Africa throughout the year, staying in each destination for a few months at a time. These people sometimes meet each other in different countries where they exchange information about relatives. There are even some cases of transnational holidays in which Patidar relatives from different parts of the world come together to spend their vacation by traveling to several countries.

Different Views

The above brief account indicates that members of the Patidar community in London frequently maintain long-distance family links with their home region in India. Regular visits and frequent contacts keep many of the Patidar migrants in London well linked to villages in Gujarat and vice versa. However, these visits and contacts are not without their problems. The following examples will show in more detail that there are sometimes differences of opinion between the Indian migrants in London and their relatives in Gujarat on the nature of their relationships and on the types of help rendered.

In many instances, the visits of the Patidar migrants to India and of their Indian relatives to Britain are related to the marriages of one of their family members in Britain or India, mostly with marriage partners from both countries. During the visits of the Patidar migrants to India, religious activities are also very common. In the last twenty-five years, the popularity of the Swaminarayan sect has increased among the Patels in Britain.[21] Although many Patels in central Gujarat have been followers of this Hindu sect for a long time, the shift to the Akshar Purushottam branch is a more recent phenomenon and one that is linked to the Patel community in Britain.

The popularity and powerful position of the Swaminarayan sect in Gujarat is also a fairly recent phenomenon, determined to a large extent by the influence of the Gujarati community in Britain and in North America. The construction of a large number of Swaminarayan temples in the villages in Gujarat over the past few decades has been financed largely by Gujarati immigrants. Because of its influence in the Gujarati diaspora—first in East Africa, later in Britain and North America—the

Akshar Purushottam branch of the reformist movement of Swaminarayan centered in Gujarat has gained in strength, allowing it to play an important social role and building up political influence.

During their visits to Gujarat, many Patel migrants make tours of several temples in the region, donating substantial amounts and participating in rituals and gatherings. Because of their substantial donations to local temples, they are often given special treatment in terms of comfortable and prominent positions. This emphasis on religion by the relatives from Britain and the special "VIP" treatment they receive in the temples in central Gujarat is viewed by some local Patels with jealousy and ridiculed in private conversations.

In 1988, Mohanbhai retired from his clerical job in London, while his wife Vimlaben retired in 1991. Since then, the two of them have been visiting Gujarat every year during the winter season for a period of two to three months. In 1994, they bought their own apartment in the nearby city of Baroda.

During their stay in Gujarat, Mohanbhai and Vimlaben spend most of their time in Baroda and from there they also make trips to Charotar to visit friends and relatives in their native village. Alongside these social visits, they take the opportunity during their stay to visit temples in Gujarat and usually also make a tour of a few days to other religious places in India. Mohanbhai emphasizes his religious nature, and indicates that he regularly makes donations to local temples. "Also, when I am in London," he told us, "I very often make visits to the temple. In London, I am a member of the temple of Akshar Purushottam. Whenever we stay in Gujarat, we make it a point of going to the big temple of Akshar Purushottam in Gandhinagar."

During one of their trips to their native village, Mohanbhai and Vimlaben showed some relatives the photographs of the Yagna ritual in which they had participated in the village temple a few weeks earlier. While showing the photographs, Vimlaben pointed out several of her relatives and friends from Britain and America. They were in fact easily recognizable, because Vimlaben and the other women from Britain and America were in the first row in the group photo, sitting in chairs with their plates on a table in front of them, while the women from the village sat on the floor behind them. Mohanbhai explained that Vimlaben and the other women from Britain and America had been the honored guests at the Yagna ritual in the village temple. While explaining this, he took a letter from his wallet that he showed to us and his local relatives with some pride. It was a letter of recommendation from the Swaminarayan Mandir in London in which Mohanbhai is mentioned as a member of the Mandir in London and was allowed to stay in any of their temples in Gujarat for two days with as many as eight persons. "In this letter, the temples in Gujarat are requested to provide me with boarding and lodging, and to enable me to pray and to have conversations with the priests," Mohanbhai told us. "About two years ago, the Swaminarayan Mandir in London started to issue these letters in order to ensure that only genuine and honest people can make use of the facilities of the temples in Gujarat. And because of this letter, I will get special treatment during my stay in the temple," Mohanbhai added. "We will be given a clean, private room furnished with a table and a chair, and air conditioning if available. They will prepare food that is not too spicy and give us mineral water. This 'VIP treatment' is usually given to every NRI (Non-Resident Indian) who visits a temple in Gujarat," Mohanbhai told us before he and Vimlaben left the house to visit some of Mohanbhai's old school friends in the village.

Shortly after Mohanbhai and Vimlaben left, local relatives started to make some critical remarks about the earlier discussions. One of Mohanbhai's cousins remarked:

> This VIP treatment is given to the NRIs only because they donate in pounds or dollars instead of Indian rupees. Many of them were never very religious when they were in Africa or went to Britain. But now that they are retired, they suddenly have a need for Indian culture and to rediscover religion. However, many of them have already become too Westernized. They are not even able to sit cross-legged on the floor for a long time and their stomachs can no longer stand our drinking water.

The other relatives agreed with him in their mild attempt to ridicule the NRIs emphasis on religion, but could at the same time also not hide their jealousy regarding the special treatment the NRIs receive in the local temples.

Another characteristic feature of the behavior of the Patel migrants in London is the absence of productive investments in India. This lack of enthusiasm regarding the maintaining of financial links and investments in Gujarat by the Patel migrants in London is part of lively discussions both in India and Britain. Among the Patel migrants in London there are those who emphasize that they consider the lukewarm response accorded them by the Indian government in the early 1970s more of a shocking experience than their sudden and unexpected expulsion from Uganda by Idi Amin. In those days, the Indian government did not realize the importance of the Non-Resident Indians. Therefore, many of those who settled in Britain, after being expelled from Uganda, ironically translate "NRI," the much trumpeted term by the Indian government, as "Non-Required Indians," and their bitterness is also reflected in their lack of enthusiasm for maintaining links back home in the form of investments in India.

It is partly due to these feelings that there are no strong developmental links between the villages in Charotar and the Patel community in Britain, despite the size and frequency of monetary help and financial transfers of the Patel relatives from Britain. Many Patels in the villages express their negative views about the fact that migrants from Britain do not contribute as much to the development of their home village as they did in the past. Although they seem to understand the economic problems faced by the Patels in Britain today, they strongly believe that the latter shirk their responsibilities by not contributing to the welfare of their home villages.

Sureshbhai's family belongs to one of the economically most well-to-do families in the village. They own about twenty acres of land and have a large cold-storage building, a tile factory, and several other undertakings. Sureshbhai's younger brother Mahendrabhai is a regional politician who is also quite active at the local level. Among other things, he is the chairman of the educational board and secretary of the village cooperative bank.

On various occasions, Sureshbhai and Mahendrabhai criticized the large-scale migrations of members of the Patel community to Britain and America. "Not one of our direct relatives has migrated abroad," Sureshbhai used to say with some pride. "We are happy to live here and are not like all those Patels who do anything to go abroad." Mahendrabhai adds:

> And when they leave, they forget all about their native place. In the past few years, there has hardly been any financial support to our village from the Patels who live in the UK. Until the 1960s, Patels who migrated to East Africa from our village used to make regular donations to the educational board and village *panchayat* [local government]. It was because of these donations that our village was among the first in the area to have a high school. Since they migrated from East Africa to the UK, however, we have hardly received any donations from our fellow villagers abroad. Even though they established a *samaj* [community organization] from our village in London, this has not resulted in substantial support for the development of our village. We realize that it is expensive to live in London, but compared to Gujarat, the Patels in Britain have hardly any social obligations and therefore less expenses in this regard. I personally feel that Patels in the UK are only after money and obsessed with saving as much money as they can. They hardly care about their relatives back home, and seem to have become misers who do not want to spend money on their social obligations.
>
> When they are in the UK, they don't think about the welfare or development of their native village, but when they visit their village, they start to empha-

> size that we are all part of the same village and *samaj* [community]. They even expect us to treat them with the highest respect because they have come from abroad. But to be honest, I don't think the Patels in Britain from our village are part of our community anymore; they have become strangers to us, strangers who are no longer really concerned about the welfare of their native village.

Family property issues in the village are also not without their problems. In several cases, relations between relatives in Britain and family members in the Gujarat village have become severely strained due to property conflicts. Members of the households in the village often believe that they are entitled to the total amount of ancestral property, because they looked after the family's property and often after their parents and other elder relatives in the village as well. The relatives in Britain, however, are sometimes of the opinion that they have a right to an equal share of the family's property, which they then will try to sell off.

Thus, at the beginning of the twenty-first century, the Patel community in India and Britain seems to be at the crossroads in every aspect of life. On the one hand, the relationships are becoming more transnational and extending their links into different countries from India to Britain and to the United States. On the other hand, it is struggling to maintain its traditional culture in Britain by reclaiming the younger generation and by redefining its links with the relatives in the home region of central Gujarat. This continuing process of both closeness and antagonism between the two sides of the transnational family, and the way in which they interact and influence each other, is not a new phenomenon for most of the Patel migrants in London.[22] This has been part of their daily existence as migrants who maintain intense and frequent links with relatives in their home villages.

Conclusion

Although in the past few decades social scientists have increasingly paid attention to processes of "globalization" and "transnationalism," there is a lack of research to offer detailed insight into these processes. Empirical studies of international migrants—sometimes referred to as "the exemplary communities of the transnational moment"—can provide an opportunity to contribute to a deeper and concrete understanding of the various aspects and implications of the globalization process.[23] Most of the earlier studies on international migration are characterized by a one-sided approach to the subject, i.e., they usually either focus on the effects of emigration for the home area or deal with problems of integration of the migrants in the host country. The research presented here has concentrated on the interrelation between the migrants and their family members in the home area. It has taken as its point of departure both the social environment of the locality of origin of the migrants and the social environment of the locality to which they have migrated. By studying the social linkages between people of the same community who are geographically separated, this research hopes to contribute to a better understanding of the existence of long-distance family relations and other networks beyond the nation-state and thereby to a new conceptualization of the transnational society in the making.

With the worldwide improvements in communications, the continuous interactional relationship between the migrant and the home community is more efficient and more evident. In contrast to the ex-indentured populations, contemporary Patidar migrants have been able to maintain extensive ties with India. Marriage arrangements, kinship networks, property, remittances, and religious affiliations keep many migrants well linked to their places of origin. However, this does not mean that all of the parties involved form a static and homogenous community. It is true that migrants in London and their relatives in India do view themselves as part of one and the same community. But at the same time, this transnational community is subject to ambivalence as its members disagree on the kinds of obligations they have towards one other. Relations are burdened with expectations that are not met, resulting in many frictions. The first-generation Patidar migrants in Britain seem to have an ambivalent attitude towards their home region and their relatives in the native villages. They are very much attached to Indian culture and emotionally depend upon their social links with their relatives and friends in Gujarat. They want to be respected by their relatives, and at the same time they criticize them on numerous occasions and are not always willing to accept the social obligations that are part of these links, or only do so very hesitantly.

To conclude, this chapter has shown that migrants in Britain and their relatives in Gujarat should not be viewed as separate communities, but should be considered in the same unit of analysis. At the same time, the findings of our study also indicate that they can not be considered a *homogenous* transnational community.[24] Social links keep many of the Patidar migrants in London well linked to their Gujarat villages and have resulted in a two-way flow of people, capital, and ideas. These links are reinforced by frequent personal visits, continuous communication, and also by regular transfers of money and/or material goods. At the same time, however, these links between India and Britain are not without problems. Several of the cases presented here show that there are substantial differences of opinion between Indian migrants in London and their relatives in Gujarat on the nature of their relationships and on the types of help to be rendered. Therefore, these linkages between the Patidars in India and their migrant relatives in Britain have important consequences not only for the integration of the migrants in the host country, but also for the home area, which is affected by the departure, return, money transfers, information, and frequent contacts with the migrants abroad.

Notes

1. Ravindra K. Jain, *Indian Communities Abroad: Themes and Literature* (Delhi, 1993), 34–35.
2. Sodhi Ram, *Indian Immigrants in Great Britain* (Delhi, 1989), 101–2.
3. Jain, *Indian Communities,* 36.
4. Christine Dobbin, *Asian Entrepreneurial Minorities: Conjoint Communities in the Making of the World Economy, 1570–1940* (Richmond, UK, 1996), 109–30.
5. David F. Pocock, *Kanbi and Patidar: A Study of the Patidar Community of Gujarat* (Oxford, 1972).
6. David Hardiman, *Peasant Nationalists of Gujarat: Kheda District 1917–1934* (Delhi, 1981); Mario Rutten, *Farms and Factories: Social Profile of Large Farmers and Rural Industrialists in West India* (Delhi, 1995).
7. Pocock, *Kanbi and Patidar,* 63; M. B. Desai, *The Rural Economy of Gujarat* (Bombay, 1948), 18 and 141; Harald Tambs-Lyche, *London Patidars: A Case Study in Urban Ethnicity* (London, 1980), 35–40.
8. Maureen Michaelson, "The Relevance of Caste amongst East African Gujaratis in Britain," *New Community* 7 (1978–79): 351.
9. Parminder Bhachu, *Twice Migrants: East African Sikh Settlers in Britain* (London, 1985); Michaelson, "Relevance of Caste," 350; Tambs-Lyche, *London Patidars,* 41.
10. Michael H. Lyon and Bernice J. M. West, "London Patels: Caste and Commerce," *New Community* 21–23 (1995): 407.
11. This research was funded by the Indo-Dutch Programme on Alternatives in Development (IDPAD).
12. Pocock, *Kanbi and Patidar;* Hardiman, *Peasant Nationalists.*
13. Lyon and West, "London Patels," 407; Michaelson, "Relevance of Caste," 355.
14. Pocock, *Kanbi and Patidar;* Hardiman, *Peasant Nationalists.*
15. Viewing the differences in village size between the Mota Gam and Nana Gam villages, and in order to have a fairly evenly sized sample in both categories, we selected two Mota Gam villages and four Nana Gam villages.
16. Lyon and West, "London Patels," 406–7.
17. Steven Vertovec, *The Hindu Diaspora: Comparative Patterns* (London, 2000), 90–91.
18. See also Raymond Brady Williams, *A New Face of Hinduism: The Swaminarayan Religion* (Cambridge, 1984).
19. All the names in the case studies presented in this chapter are pseudonyms in an attempt to preserve some measure of anonymity.

20. Jain, *Indian Communities;* Arthur W. Helweg, "Why Leave India for America? A Case Study Approach to Understanding Migrant Behaviour," *International Migration* 25 (1987): 165–78; Arthur W. Helweg, "Sikh Identity in England: Its Changing Nature," in *Sikh History and Religion in the Twentieth Century,* ed. Joseph T. O'Connell et al. (Delhi, 1990), 356–75.
21. D. F. Pocock, "Preservation of the Religious Life: Hindu Immigrants in England," *Contributions to Indian Sociology* 10 (1976): 341–65.
22. Harold S. Morris, *The Indians in Uganda* (London, 1968).
23. Khachig Tölölyan, "The Nation-state and Its Others: In Lieu of a Preface," *Diaspora: Journal of Transnational Studies* 1 (1991): 3–7.
24. See Gerd Baumann, *Contesting Culture: Discourses of Identity in Multi-ethnic London* (Cambridge, 1996), 23.

Bibliography

Abernaty, Frank. "The Dynamics of Return Migration to St. Lucia." In *Caribbean Families in Britain and the Transatlantic World*, edited by Harry Goulbourne and Mary Chamberlain, 170–87. London, 2001.

Abou-El-Haj, Rifa'at Ali. *Formation of the Modern State: Ottoman Empire, 16th to 18th Centuries.* Syracuse, NY, 2005.

———. "The Formal Closure of the Ottoman Frontier, 1699–1703." *Journal of the American Oriental Society* 89 (1969): 467–75.

———. "The Ottoman Vezir and Pasha Households, 1683–1703: A Preliminary Report." *Journal of the American Oriental Society* 94 (1974): 438–47.

Abu-Odeh, Lama. "Crimes of Honor and the Construction of Gender in Arab Societies." In *Islam and Feminism: Legal and Literary Perspectives,* edited by Mai Yammami, 141–94. London, 1996.

———. "Feminism, Nationalism and the Law: The Case of Arab Women." PhD dissertation, Harvard University, 1993.

Adams, Julia. *The Familial State: Ruling Families and Merchant Capitalism in Early Modern Europe.* Ithaca, NY, 2005.

Aksan, Virginia. "Ottoman Political Writing, 1768–1808." *International Journal of Middle East Studies* 25 (1993): 53–69.

Alioth, Martin. *Gruppen an der Macht: Zünfte und Patriziat in Strassburg im 14. und 15. Jahrhundert: Untersuchungen zu Verfassung, Wirtschaftsgefüge und Sozialstruktur.* 2 vols. Basel, 1988.

Allanic, A. *Histoire du Collège de Vannes.* Rennes, 1902.

Altman, Ida. *Emigrants and Society: Extremadura and Spanish America in the Sixteenth Century.* Berkeley, CA, 1989.

———. *Transatlantic Ties in the Spanish Empire: Brihuega, Spain, and Puebla, Mexico, 1560–1620.* Stanford, CA, 2000.

Andenna, Giancarlo, ed. *Comuni e signorie nell'Italia settentrionale: La Lombardia.* Vol. 6, *Storia d'Italia.* Turin, 1998.

Anderson, Benedict. *Imagined Communities: Reflections on the Origin and Spread of Nationalism.* London, 1983. Revised, 1991.

Anderson, Nancy Fix. "Cousin Marriage in Victorian England." *Journal of Family History* 11 (1986): 285–301.

Annibaletti, Giuliano. "Ein irreversibler Niedergang? Die Beziehungen zwischen Mantua und dem Reich nach 1627." *Zeitenblicke* 6 (2007). http://www.zeitenblicke.de/2007/1/Annibaletti/ (accessed 30 June 2008).

Antenhofer, Christina. "Briefe, Besuche, Hochzeiten: Die Gonzaga im Kontakt mit deutschen Fürstenhäusern." In *Le corti come luogo di comunicazione: Gli Asburgo e l'Italia (secoli XVI–XIX) / Höfe als Orte der Kommunikation: Die Habsburger und Italien (16.–19. Jh.): Tagungsband zur gleichnamigen Tagung in Trento 8.–10. November 2007*, edited by Jan Paul Niederkorn. Berlin, 2010.

———. *Briefe zwischen Süd und Nord: Die Hochzeit und Ehe von Paula de Gonzaga und Leonhard von Görz im Spiegel der fürstlichen Kommunikation (1473–1500)*. Innsbruck, 2007.

———. "Letters across the Borders: Strategies of Communication in an Italian-German Renaissance Correspondence." In *Women's Letters across Europe 1400–1700: Form and Persuasion*, edited by Jane Couchman and Ann Crabb, 103–22. Burlington, VT, 2005.

Arcangeli, Letizia, and Susanna Peyronel, eds. *Donne di potere nel rinascimento: Atti del convegno a Milano, 29 novembre—2 dicembre 2006*. Rome, 2009.

Aslanian, Sebouh. "From the Indian Ocean to the Mediterranean: Circulation and the Global Trade Networks of Armenian Merchants from New Julfa, 1605–1748." PhD dissertation, Columbia University, 2007.

———. "Social Capital, 'Trust' and the Role of Networks in Juflan Trade: Informal and Semi-Formal Institutions at Work." *Journal of Global History* 1 (2006): 383–402.

———. "The Circulation of Men and Credit: The Role of the Commenda and the Family Firm in Julfan Society." *Journal of the Economic and Social History of the Orient* 5 (2007): 124–71.

Assessorato alla cultura e alle belle arti. *Venezia e la Peste, 1348–1797*. Venice, 1979. Revised edition, 1980.

Assmann, Jan. *Das kulturelle Gedächtnis: Schrift, Erinnerung und politische Identität in frühen Hochkulturen*. Munich, 1999.

Ata, Ibrahim Wade. *The West Bank Palestinian Family*. London, 1986.

Audran. *Histoire généalogique de la famille des Audran*. Rennes, 1754.

Autrand, Françoise, ed. *Prosopographie et genèse de l'état moderne: Actes de la table ronde, org. par le Centre National de la Recherche Scientifique et l'École Normale Supérieure de Jeunes Filles, Paris, 22–23 Octobre 1984*. Paris, 1986.

Ayalon, David. "Studies in al-Jabarti: Notes on the Transformation of Mamluk Society in Egypt under the Ottomans." *Journal of Economic and Social History of the Orient* 3 (1960): 275–325.

Ayalon, David. *Studies on the Mamluks of Egypt*. London, 1977.

Babel, Rainer, and Werner Paravicini, eds. *Grand Tour: Adeliges Reisen und europäische Kultur vom 14. bis zum 18. Jahrhundert*. Stuttgart, 2005.

Badalo-Dulong, Claude. *Trente ans de diplomatie française en Allemagne: Louis XIV et l'electeur de Mayence, 1648–78*. Paris, 1956.

Bağış, Ali İhsan. *Osmanlı Ticaretinde Gayrî Müslimler* [Non-Muslims in Ottoman Commerce]. 2nd ed. Ankara, 1998.

Bamyeh, Mohammed A. "Transnationalism." *Current Sociology* 41 (1993): 1–95.

Bang, Anne K. *Sufis and Scholars of the Sea: Family Networks in East Africa, 1860–1925*. London, 2003.

Barkey, Karen. *Empire of Difference: The Ottomans in Comparative Perspective.* Cambridge, 2008.

Barrow, Christine. "Finding the Support: Strategies for Survival." *Social and Economic Studies* 35, no. 2 (1986): 131–76.

Basch, Linda, Nina Glick Schiller, and Cristina Szanton Blanc. *Nations Unbound: Transnational Projects, Post-Colonial Predicaments and Deterritorialized Nation States.* Langhorne, PA, 1994.

Battifol, Louis. *Les Anciennes Républiques alsaciennes.* Paris, 1918.

Baumann, Gerd. *Contesting Culture: Discourses of Identity in Multi-Ethnic London.* Cambridge, 1996.

Bekius, René. "A Global Enterprise: Armenian Merchants in the Textile Trade in the 17th and 18th Centuries." In *Carpets and Textiles in the Iranian World, 1400–1700.* Oxford, 2010.

Belhoste, Bruno, ed. *La France des X: Deux siècles d'histoire.* Paris, 1995.

———. *La formation d'une technocratie: L'École polytechnique et ses élèves de la Révolution au Second Empire.* Paris, 2003.

Bell, David A. *The Cult of the Nation in France: Inventing Nationalism, 1680–1800.* Cambridge, MA, 2001.

Beltrami, Luca. "L'annullamento del contratto di matrimonio fra Galeazzo Maria Sforza e Dorotea Gonzaga (1463)." *Archivio storico lombardo* 6 (1889): 126–32.

Benecke, Gerhard. *Society and Politics in Germany, 1500–1750.* London, 1974.

Bertier de Sauvigny, Guillaume de. *La Restauration.* Paris, 1955.

Bertini, Franco. "Le società di accomandita a Firenze e Livorno tra Ferdinando III e il regno d'Etruria." In *Istituzioni e società in Toscana nell'età moderna: Atti delle giornate di studio dedicate a Giuseppe Pansini*, 538–63. Rome, 1994.

Besson, Jean. *Martha Brae's Two Histories: European Expansion and Caribbean Culture-Building in Jamaica.* Chapel Hill, NC, 2002.

Bhachu, Parminder. *Twice Migrants: East African Sikh Settlers in Britain.* London, 1985.

Bhattacharya, Bhaswati. "Armenian European Relationship in India, 1500–1800: No Armenian Foundation for European Empire?" *Journal of the Economic and Social History of the Orient* 48 (2005): 277–322.

———. "Making Money at the Blessed Place of Manila: Armenians in the Madras-Manila Trade in the Eighteenth Century." *Journal of Global History* 3 (2008): 1–20.

———. "The 'Book of Will' of Petrus Woskan (1680–1751): Some Insights into the Global Commercial Networks of the Armenians in the Indian Ocean." *Journal of the Economic and Social History of the Orient* 51 (2008): 67–98.

Bhugra, Dinesh. "Migration and Schizophrenia." *Acta Psychiatrica Scandinavia. Supplementum* 102 (2000): 68–73.

Bischoff, Georges. *Gouvernés et gouvernants en Haute Alsace à l'époque autrichienne.* Strasbourg, 1996.

———. "Une enquête: La noblesse austro-bourguignonne sous le règne de Maximilien I." In *Les Pays de l'entre-deux au moyen-age: Questions d'histoire des territories d'empire entre Meuse, Rhône et Rhin.* Paris, 1990.

Black, Jeremy. *Kings, Nobles and Commoners: States and Societies in Early Modern Europe: A Revisionist History.* London, 2004.

Bodian, Miriam. *Hebrews of Portuguese Nation: Conversos and Community in Early Modern Amsterdam.* Bloomington, IN, 1997.

Bonacich, Edna. "A Theory of Middleman Minorities." *American Sociological Review* 38 (1973): 583–94.

Boulaire, Alain. *Les Rohan: 'Roi ne puis, duc ne daigne, Rohan suis!'.* Paris, 2001.

Boulton, D'Arcy J. D., and Jan R. Veenstra, eds. *The Ideology of Burgundy: The Promotion of National Consciousness, 1364–1565*. Leiden, 2006.

Bourdieu, Pierre. "A propos de la famille comme catégorie réalisée." *Actes de la Recherche en sciences sociales* 100 (1993): 32–36.

———. "Avenir de classe et causalite du probable." *Revue française de sociologie* 15, no. 1 (1974): 3–42.

———. *Langage et pouvoir symbolique*. Paris, 2001.

———. *La noblesse d'État: Grandes écoles et esprit de corps*. Paris, 1989.

———. "La parenté comme représentation et comme volonté." In *Esquisse d'une théorie de la pratique précédé de trois études d'ethnologie kabyle*. Paris, 1972. Reprinted, Paris, 2000, 83–186.

———. "Marriage Strategies as Strategies of Social Reproduction." In *Family and Society: Selections from the Annales*, edited by Robert Forster and Orest Ranum, translated by Elborg Forster, 117–44. Baltimore, 1976.

———. *Outline of a Theory of Practice*. Cambridge, 1977.

———. *The Logic of Practice*. Cambridge, 1977.

Boyce-Davis, Carol. *Black Women, Writing and Identity: Migrations of the Subject*. London, 1994.

Boyd-Bowman, Peter. "Patterns of Spanish Emigration to the Indies until 1600." *Hispanic American Historical Review* 56, no. 4 (1976): 580–604.

Bøytler, Jørgen. "Zinzendorf und Dänemark." In *Graf ohne Grenzen*, edited by Dietrich Meyer and Paul Peucker, 73–81. Herrnhut, 2000.

Brand, Laurie. *Women, the State, and Political Liberalization: Middle Eastern and North African Experiences*. New York, 1998.

Bras, Hilde, and Theo van Tilburg. "Kinship and Social Networks: A Regional Analysis of Sibling Relations in Twentieth-Century Netherlands." *Journal of Family History* 35 (2007): 296–322.

Brathwaite, Edward Kamau. *The Development of Creole Society in Jamaica, 1770–1820*. Oxford, 1971.

Brodber, Erna. "African Jamaican Women at the Turn of the Century." *Social and Economic Studies* 35, no. 3 (1986): 23–50.

Brulez, Wilfrid. *De Firma della Faille en de internationale handel van Vlaamse firma's in de 16e eeuw*. Brussels, 1959.

Brunner, Otto. "Das 'ganze Haus' und die alteuropäische 'Oekonomik'." In *Neue Wege der Verfassungs- und Sozialgeschichte*, 103–27. 2nd ed. Göttingen, 1968.

Bryceson, Deborah. "Europe's Transnational Families and Migration: Past and Present." In Bryceson and Vuorela, *Transnational Family*, 31–57. Oxford, 2002.

Bryceson, Deborah, and Ulla Vuorela, eds. *The Transnational Family: New European Frontiers and Global Networks*. Oxford , 2002.

———. "Transnational Families in the Twenty-First Century." In Bryceson and Vuorela, *Transnational Family*, 3–30.

Busse, Kurt. *Werner von Siemens*. Bad Godesberg, 1966.

Cabourdin, Guy, ed. "Les temps modernes — 1. De la Renaissance à la guerre de Trente ans." In *Encyclopédie illustrée de la Lorraine*. Nancy, 1991.

Caferro, William. *John Hawkwood: English Mercenary in Fourteenth-Century Italy*. Baltimore, 2006.

Cahen, Gilbert. "La Région Lorraine." In *Histoire des Juifs en France*, edited by Bernhard Blumenkranz, 77–136. Toulouse, 1972.

Calonaci, Stefano. *Dietro lo scudo crociato: I fedecommessi di famiglia e il trionfo della borghesia fiorentina (1400 ca-1750)*. Florence, 2005.

Cameron, Rondo. *France and the Economic Development of Europe, 1830–1880*. Princeton, NJ, 1963.
Campbell, John K. *Honour, Family, and Patronage: A Study of Institutions and Moral Values in a Greek Mountain Community*. Oxford, 1970.
Capitani, François de. *Adel, Bürger und Zünfte im Bern des 15. Jahrhunderts*. Bern, 1982.
Carmona, Maurice. "Aspects du capitalisme toscan aux XVIe et XVIIe siècles: Les sociétés en commandite à Florence et à Lucques." *Revue d'histoire moderne et contemporaine* 11 (1964): 81–108.
Carrière, Charles. *Négociants marseillais au XVIIIe siècle: Contribution à l'étude des économies maritimes*. Marseilles, 1973.
Carsten, Francis Ludwig. *Princes and Parliaments in Germany from the Fifteenth to the Eighteenth Century*. Oxford, 1959.
Castells, Manuel. *The Rise of the Network Society*. Oxford, 1996.
Castignoli, Paolo. *Studi di Storia: Livorno dagli archivi alla città*. Livorno, 2001.
Chaline, Jean-Pierre. *Sociabilité et érudition: Les sociétés savantes en France, XIXe–XXe siècles*. Paris, 1995.
Chalmin, Pierre. *L'officier français de 1815 à 1870*. Paris, 1957.
Chamberlain, Mary, ed. *Caribbean Migration: Globalised Identities*. London, 1998.
———. *Family Love in the Diaspora: Migration and the Anglo-Caribbean Experience*. New Brunswick, NJ, 2006.
———. *Narratives of Exile and Return*. New Brunswick, NJ, 1997. Reprinted, 2006.
———. *Empire and Nation-building in the Caribbean: Barbados 1937–1966*. Manchester, UK, 2010.
Chambers, David Sanderson. *Renaissance Cardinals and Their Worldly Problems*. Hampshire, UK, 1997.
Charle, Christophe. *Les élites de la République (1880–1900)*. Paris, 1987.
Châtelain, Abel. *Les migrations temporaires en France de 1800 à 1914*. 2 vols. Lille, 1977.
Chatziioannou, Maria-Christina. "Crossing Empires: Greek Merchant Networks before the Imperialistic Expansion." In *Diaspora Entrepreneurial Networks*, edited by McCabe, Harlaftis, and Pepelasis Minoglou.
Chauvard, Jean-François. *La circulation des biens à Venise: Stratégies patrimoniales et marché immobilier (1600–1750)*. Rome, 2005.
Chiappa Mauri, Luisa, ed. *Contado e città in dialogo: Comuni urbani e comunità rurali nella Lombardia medievale*. Milan, 2003.
Clark, Samuel. *State and Status: The Rise of the State and Aristocratic Power in Western Europe*. Cardiff, UK, 1995.
Clarke, Edith. *My Mother Who Fathered Me*. Kingston, 1957. Reprinted, 1999.
Cobos de Belchite, Julio de Atienza, baron de. *Nobiliario Español*. Madrid, 1954.
Cogswell, Neil, ed. *1758: Zweybrücken in Command: A Journal of the Speedy Army of Execution of the Empire under the Orders of His Most Serene Highness the Prince von Pfalz-Zweybrücken in 1758*. Guisborough, UK, 1998.
Cohen, Robin. *Global Diasporas: An Introduction*. London, 1997.
Coles, Paul. "The Crisis of Renaissance Society Genoa, 1488–1507." *Past & Present* 11, no. 1 (1957): 17–47.
Colorni, Vittorio. *Legge ebraica e leggi locali: Ricerche sull'ambito d'applicazione del diritto ebraico in Italia dall'epoca romana al secolo XIX*. Milan, 1945.
Contamine, Philippe. "Le problème des migrations des gens de guerre en Occident durant les derniers siècles du Moyen Âge." In *Le migrazioni in Europa secc. XIII–XVIII*, edited by Simonetta Cavaciocchi, 459–76. Florence, 1994.

Conway, Dennis. "Conceptualising Contemporary Patterns of Caribbean International Mobility." *Caribbean Geography* 2, no. 3 (1988): 145–63.

Conway, Dennis, and Rob Potter. "Caribbean Transnational Return Migrants as Agents of Change." *Geography Compass* 1 (2007): 25–45.

Cornette, Joël. *Histoire de la Bretagne et les Bretons.* Vols. 1 and 2. Paris, 2005.

———. *Un révolutionnaire ordinaire: Benoît Lacombe, Négociant, 1759–1819.* Paris, 1986.

Courcelles, Jean-Baptiste de. *Histoire généalogique et heraldique des pairs de France, des grands dignitaires de la couronne, des principales familles nobles du royaume, et des maisons princières de l'Europe.* 12 vols. Paris, 1822–1833.

Crow, Thomas. *Painters and Public Life in Eighteenth-Century Paris.* New Haven, CT, 1985.

Cunow, Martin. *Die Herrnhuter.* Weimar, 1839.

Dangeau, Philippe de Courcillon, marquis de. Journal, Eudore Soulié, Louis Dussieux, et al., eds., with *Additions inédites du duc de Saint-Simon.* 19 vols. Paris, 1854–1860.

Darling, Linda. *Revenue-Raising and Legitimacy: Tax Collection and Finance Administration in the Ottoman Empire, 1560–1660.* Leiden, 1996.

Daudet, Ernest. *Madame Royale.* Paris, 1912.

Dauphin, Cécile, Arlette Farge, Geneviève Fraisse et al. "Culture et pouvoir des femmes: Essai d'historiographie." *Annales ESC* 2 (1986): 271–93.

Davari, Stefano. "Il matrimonio di Dorotea Gonzaga con Galeazzo Maria Sforza." *Giornale Ligustico* 17 (1890): 3–43.

Davis, James C. *The Decline of the Venetian Nobility as a Ruling Class.* Baltimore, 1962.

Davis, Ralph. *Aleppo and the Devonshire Square: English Traders in the Levant in the Eighteenth Century.* London, 1967.

De Fraine, Piet. "Gouvernés et gouvernants au Pays et Duché d'Aerschot." *Anciens pays et assemblées d'états* 33 (1965): 181–94.

Delcourt, André. *Le duc de Croÿ, maréchal de France, 1718–1784: Un grand seigneur au siècle des lumières.* Saint-Amand-les-Eaux, 1984.

D'Elia, Anthony F. *The Renaissance of Marriage in Fifteenth-Century Italy.* Cambridge, 2004.

Delille, Gérard. *Famille et propriété dans le royaume de Naples (XVe–XIXe).* Rome, 1985.

———. *Le maire et le prieur: Pouvoir central et pouvoir local en Méditerranée occidentale (XVe–XVIIIe siècle).* Paris, 2003.

Derouet, Bernard. "La terre, la personne et le contrat: Exploitation et associations familiales en Bourbonnais (XVIIe–XVIIIe siècles)." *Revue d'histoire moderne et contemporaine* 2 (2003): 27–51.

———. "La transmission égalitaire du patrimoine dans la France rurale (XVIe–XIXe siècles): Nouvelles perspectives de recherche." In *Familia, casa y trabajo.* Vol. 3, *Historia de la Familia,* edited by Francisco Chacón Jiménez and Llorenc Ferrer Alós, 73–92. Murcia, 1997.

———. "Les pratiques familiales, le droit et la construction des différences (XVe–XIXe siècles)." *Annales HSS* (1997): 369–91.

———. "Parenté et marché foncier à l'époque moderne: Une reinterpretation." *Annales HSS* (2001): 337–68.

———. "Pratiques de l'alliance en milieu de communautés familiales (Bourbonnais, 1600–1750)." In *Le choix du conjoint,* edited by Guy Brunet, Antoinette Fauve-Chamoux, and Michel Oris, 227–51. Lyon, 1998.

———. "Pratiques successorales et rapport à la terre: Les sociétés paysannes d'ancien régime." *Annales ESC* (1989): 173–206.

———. "Territoire et parenté: Pour une mise en perspective de la communauté rurale et des formes de reproduction familiale." *Annales HSS* (1995): 645–86.

Derry, D. E. "The Dynastic Race in Egypt." *Journal of Egyptian Archaeology* 42 (1956): 80–85.

Desai, M. B. *The Rural Economy of Gujarat*. Bombay, 1948.

De Schepper, Hugo. "Le voyage difficile de Marguerite de Parme en Franche-Comté et en Flandre, 1580–1583." In *Margherita d'Austria (1522–1586): Costruzioni politiche e diplomazia, tra corte Farnese e Monarchia spagnola*, edited by Silvia Mantini, 127–40. Rome, 2003.

Diamond, Jared. *Collapse: How Societies Choose to Fail or Succeed*. New York, 2005.

Dilcher, Gerhard. *Die Entstehung der lombardischen Stadtkommune: Eine rechtsgeschichtliche Untersuchung*. Aalen, 1967.

Dion, Marie-Pierre. *Emmanuel de Croy (1718–1784): Itinéraire intellectuel et réussite nobiliaire au siècle des Lumières*. Brussels, 1987.

Dizionario Biografico degli Italiani, Rome, 1960 et seq.

Dobbin, Christine. *Asian Entrepreneurial Minorities: Conjoint Communities in the Making of the World Economy, 1570–1940*. Richmond, UK, 1996.

Donati, Claudio. "The Italian Nobilities in the Seventeenth and Eighteenth Centuries." In *The European Nobilities*, edited by Hamish Scott. Vol. 1, 237–68. London, 1995.

Dresser, Magde. "Sisters and Brethren: Power, Propriety and Gender among the Bristol Moravians, 1746–1833." *Social History* 21 (1996): 304–29.

Duby, Georges. "Au XIIe siècle: Les 'jeunes' dans la société aristocratique." *Annales ESC* 19 (1965): 835–46.

Duffy, Eamon. "The Society of Promoting Christian Knowledge in Europe: The Background to the Founding of the Christentumsgesellschaft." *Pietismus und Neuzeit* 7 (1981): 28–42.

Duvernoy, Emile. "Recherches sur le Traité de Nuremberg de 1542." *Annales de l'Est* 4, no. 1 (1933): 153–70.

Ehrenberg, Richard. *Unternehmungen der Brüder Siemens*. Vol. 1, *Bis zum Jahre 1970*. Jena, 1906.

Ehrmann, Gabriele, ed. *Georg von Ehingen: Reisen nach der Ritterschaft: Edition, Untersuchung, Kommentar*. Göppingen, 1979.

Eldem, Edhem. *French Trade in Istanbul in the Eighteenth Century*. Leiden, 1999.

Eley, Geoff, and Ronald Grigor Suny, eds. *Becoming National: A Reader*. Oxford, 1996.

Elliott, John. *Imperial Spain, 1469–1716*. London, 1990.

Eltis, David, and Stanley L. Engerman. "Was the Slave Trade Dominated by Men?" *Journal of Interdisciplinary History* 23, no. 2 (1992): 237–57.

Erll, Astrid, ed. *Kollektives Gedächtnis und Erinnerungskulturen*. Stuttgart, 2005.

Esch, Arnold. "Gemeinsames Erlebnis: Individueller Bericht." *Zeitschrift für historische Forschung* 25 (1984): 385–416.

Farah, Randa. "Popular Memory and Reconstructions of Palestinian Identity: Al-Baq'a Refugee Camp, Jordan." PhD dissertation, University of Toronto, 1999.

Fargues, Philippe. *Générations arabes: L'alchimie du nombre*. Paris, 2000.

Fasano Guarini, Elena. "La popolazione." In *Livorno e Pisa: Due città e un territorio nella politica dei Medici: Livorno, progetto e storia di una città tra il 1500 e il 1600*, 199–215. Pisa, 1980.

Faull, Katherine, ed. *Moravian Women's Memoirs: Their Related Lives 1750–1820*. Syracuse, NY, 1997.

Favero, Giovanni, and Francesca Trivellato. "Gli abitanti del ghetto di Venezia in età moderna: Dati e ipotesi." *Zakhor: Rivista della storia degli ebrei in Italia* 7 (2004): 9–50.

Ferguson, Niall. *The House of Rothschild: Money's Prophets 1798–1848*. New York, 1998.

Fichtner, Paula Sutter. "Dynastic Marriage in Sixteenth-Century Habsburg Diplomacy and Statecraft: An Interdisciplinary Approach." *American Historical Review* 81 (1976): 243–65.

Filippini, Jean-Pierre. "Gli ebrei e le attività economiche nell'area nord africana (XVII–XVIII secolo)." *Nuovi studi livornesi* 7 (1999): 131–49.

Findley, Carter. *Bureaucratic Reform in the Ottoman Empire: The Sublime Porte, 1789–1922*. Princeton, NJ, 1980.

Fischer, Daniel. "La France révolutionnaire face à l'affaire des princes d'Empire possessionnés en Basse Alsace, 1789–1801." In *Chantiers historiques en Alsace: Jeunes Chercheurs en Histoire de l'Université Marc Bloch de Strasbourg* 8 (2005–6): 125–35.

Flandrin, Jean-Louis. *Familles, parenté, maison, sexualité dans l'ancienne société*. Paris, 1976.

Fleischer, Cornell. *Bureaucrat and Intellectual in the Ottoman Empire: The Historian Mustafa Ali, 1541–1600*. Princeton, NJ, 1986.

Fogleman, Aaron Spencer. *Jesus Is Female: Moravians and Radical Religion in Early America*. Philadelphia, 2007.

Foner, Nancy. "Towards a Comparative Perspective on Caribbean Migration." In Chamberlain, *Caribbean Migration*, 47–62.

———. "West Indians in New York City and London: A Comparative Analysis." In *Caribbean Life in New York City: Socio-Cultural Dimensions*, edited by Constance R. Sutton and Elsa M. Chaney, 108–20. New York, 1994.

Ford, Caroline C. *Creating the Nation in Provincial France: Religion and Political Identity in Brittany*. Princeton, NJ, 1993.

Foucault, Michel. *La volonté de savoir*. Vol. 1, *Histoire de la sexualité*. Paris, 1976.

Fraisse, Geneviève. "Gouvernement de la famille, gouvernement de la cite." In *Le Lien familial*. Comprendre no. 2, edited by François De Singly and Sylvie Mesure, 169–82. Paris, 2001.

Frattarelli Fischer, Lucia. "Per la storia dell'insediamento degli Armeni a Livorno nel Seicento." In *Gli Armeni lungo le strade d'Italia: Atti del convegno internazionale (Torino, Genova, Livorno, 8–11 marzo 1997): Giornata di studi a Livorno*, 23–41. Pisa, 1998.

———. "'Pro Armenis Unitis cum conditionibus': La costruzione della Chiesa degli Armeni a Livorno: Un iter lungo e accidentato." In *Gli Armeni a Livorno: L'intercultura di una diaspora*. Interventi nel Convegno "Memoria e cultura armena fra Livorno e l'oriente," edited by Gian Giacomo Panessa and Massimo Sanacore, 27–41. Livorno, 2006.

———. "Proprietà e insediamento ebraici a Livorno dalla fine del Cinquecento alla seconda metà del Settecento." In *Quaderni storici* 54 (1983): 879–896.

Frazier, Franklin. *The Negro Family in the United States*. Chicago, 1939.

Frélaut, Bernard. "Un Vannétais à la Bastille: Jean-Nicolas Galles à la Bastille en 1760 d'après sa correspondance inedite." *Mémoires de la société polymathique du Morbihan* 116 (1990): 173–83.

Frensdorff, Ferdinand, and Matthias Lexer, eds. *Die Chroniken der schwäbischen Städte: Augsburg*. Vol. 2, 122–43. Leipzig, 1866.

Fries, Adelaide, ed. *Records of the Moravians in North Carolina 1752–1857*. Raleigh, NC: 1922–1969.

Fulaine, Jean-Charles. *Le Duc Charles IV de Lorraine et son armée, 1624–1675*. Metz, 1997.

Gabaccia, Donna R., and Fraser M. Ottanelli. "Introduction." *Italian Workers of the World: Labor Migration and the Formation of Multiethnic States*, edited by Donna R. Gabaccia and Fraser M. Ottanelli, 1–17. Urbana, IL, 2001.

Galasso, Cristina. *Alle origini di una comunità: Ebree ed ebrei a Livorno nel Seicento.* Florence, 2002.

Galles, René. "Allocution de M. Galles." *Bulletin de la société polymathique du Morbihan* 28 (1885): 1–2.

Gebhardt, Miriam. *Das Familiengedächtnis: Erinnerung im deutschen-jüdischen Bürgertum 1890 bis 1932.* Stuttgart, 1999.

Gerson, Stéphane. *Pride of Place: Local Memories and Political Culture in Nineteenth-Century France.* Ithaca, NY, 2003.

Geyl, Pieter. *History of the Dutch-Speaking Peoples, 1555–1648.* London, 2001.

"Ghikas." In *Megale Hellenike Enkyklopaideia.* Vol. 7, 448–49. Athens, 1956–1965.

Gianighian, Giorgio Nubar. "Segni di una presenza." In *Gli armeni e Venezia: Dagli Sceriman a Mechitar: Il momento culminante di una consuetudine millenaria,* edited by Boghos Levon Zekiyan and Aldo Ferrari, 59–92. Venice, 2004.

Gilomen, Hans-Jörg, and Martina Stercken, eds. *Zentren: Ausstrahlung, Einzugsbereich und Anziehungskraft von Städten und Siedlungen zwischen Rheinlauf und Alpen.* Zürich, 2001.

Gleixner, Ulrike. *Pietismus und Bürgertum. Eine historische Anthropologie der Frömmigkeit.* Göttingen, 2005.

Gmelch, George. *Double Passage: The Lives of Caribbean Migrants Abroad and Back Home.* Ann Arbor, MI, 1992.

Goez, Werner. *Geschichte Italiens in Mittelalter und Renaissance.* 3rd ed. Darmstadt, 1988.

Goldberg, Michael. *Theology and Narrative: A Critical Introduction.* Nashville, 1982.

Gollin, Gillian Lindt. *Moravians in Two World: A Study of Changing Communities.* New York, 1967.

Goodman, Jordan. "Financing Pre-Modern Industry, An Example from Florence, 1580–1660." *Journal of European Economic History* 10 (1981): 415–35.

Goulbourne, Harry. *Caribbean Transnational Experience.* London, 2002.

Gowers, Emily. "The Anatomy of Rome from Capitol to Cloaca." *Journal of Roman Studies* 85 (1995): 23–32.

Gradeva, Rossitsa. "Osman Pazvantoglu of Vidin, Between Old and New." In *The Ottoman Balkans, 1750–1830,* edited by Frederick F. Anscombe, 115–62. Princeton, NJ, 2006.

———. "Secession and Revolution in the Ottoman Empire at the End of the Eighteenth Century, Osman Pazvantoglu and Rhigas Velestinlis." In *Ottoman Rule and the Balkans, 1760–1850: Conflict, Transformation, Adaptation: Proceedings of an International Conference Held in Rethymno, Greece, 13–14 December 2003,* edited by Antonis Anastasopoulos and Elias Kolovos, 73–94. Rethymno, 2007.

Graf, Klaus. "Geschichtsschreibung und Landesdiskurs im Umkreis Graf Eberhards im Bart von Württemberg (1449–1496)." *Blätter für deutsche Landesgeschichte* 129 (1993): 165–93.

Grand, Roger. *Les Cent-jours dans l'Ouest: La Chouannerie de 1815.* Paris, 1942.

Granqvist, Hilma. *Marriage Conditions in a Palestinian Village.* Vols. 1 and 2. Helsingfors, 1931, 1935. Reprinted, New York, 1975.

Grassby, Richard. *The English Gentleman in Trade: The Life and Works of Sir Dudley North, 1641–1691.* Oxford, 1994.

Greif, Avner. *Institutions and the Path to the Modern Economy: Lessons from Medieval Trade.* Cambridge, 2006.

Gresset, Maurice. "Les Franc-Comtois entre la France et l'Empire." In *Régions et régionalisme en France du XVIIIe siècle à nos jours,* edited by Christian Gras and Georges Livet, 87–101. Paris, 1977.

Gribaudi, Maurizio. *Itinéraires ouvriers. Espaces et groupes sociaux à Turin au début du XXème siècle.* Paris, 1987.

Groebner, Valentin. "Ausser Haus. Otto Brunner und die 'Alteuropäische Ökonomik'." *Geschichte in Wissenschaft und Unterricht* 2 (1995): 69–80.

Guerreau-Jalabert, Anita. "Sur les structures de parenté dans l'Europe médiévale (Note Critique)." *Annales ESC* 36 (1981): 1028–49.

Guiomar, Jean-Yves. *Le bretonisme: Les historiens bretons au XIXe siècle.* Mayenne, 1987.

Haak, Wolfgang, et al. "Ancient DNA, Strontium Isotopes, and Osteological Analyses Shed Light on Social and Kinship Organization of the Later Stone Age." *Proceedings of the National Academy of Science of the United States of America* 105, no. 47 (2008): 18226–31.

Haarscher, André-Marc. *Les Juifs du Comté de Hanau-Lichtenberg entre le XIVe siècle et la fin de l'Ancien Régime.* Strasbourg, 1997.

Halbwachs, Maurice. *Das kollektive Gedächtnis.* Stuttgart, 1967.

Hamilston, Alastair, Alexander H. de Groot, and Mauritius H. van den Boogert, eds. *Friends and Rivals in the East: Studies in Anglo-Dutch Relations in the Levant from the Seventeenth to the Early Nineteenth Century.* Leiden, 2000.

Hammer-Purgstall, Joseph. *Histoire de l'Empire ottoman, depuis son origine jusqu'a nos jours.* 18 vols. Paris, 1835–1843.

Hancock, David. *Citizens of the World: London Merchants and the Integration of the British Atlantic Community, 1735–1785.* Cambridge, 1995.

Hansmann, Henry, Reinier Kraakman, and Richard Squire. "Law and the Rise of the Firm." *Harvard Law Review* 119 (2006): 1333–1403.

Harbsmeier, Michael. *Wilde Völkerkunde: Andere Welten in deutschen Reiseberichten der Frühen Neuzeit.* Frankfurt, 1994.

Hardenberg, Herman. "Les divisions politiques des Ardennes et des Pays d'Outremeuse avant 1200." In *Etudes sur l'Histoire du Pays Mosan au Moyen Age. Mélanges Félix Rousseau.* Brussels, 1958.

Hardiman, David. *Peasant Nationalists of Gujarat: Kheda District 1917–1934.* Delhi, 1981.

Harlaftis, Gelina. *History of Greek-Owned Shipping: The Making of an International Tramp Fleet, 1830 to the Present.* Athens, 1996.

———. "Mapping the Greek Maritime Diaspora from the Early Eighteenth to the Late Twentieth Centuries." In McCabe, Harlaftis, and Pepelasis Minoglou, *Diaspora Entrepreneurial Networks,* 147–71.

Harrison, Carol. *The Bourgeois Citizen in Nineteenth-Century France: Gender, Sociability, and the Uses of Emulation.* Oxford, 1999.

Hart, Oliver D. *Firms, Contracts, and Financial Structure.* Oxford, 1995.

Hathaway, Jane. *A Tale of Two Factions.* Albany, 2003.

———. *Politics of Households in Ottoman Egypt: The Rise of the Qazdaglis.* Cambridge, 1997.

———. "The Military Household in Ottoman Egypt." *International Journal of Middle East Studies* 27 (1995): 39–52.

Hegel, Carl, ed. *Die Chroniken der deutschen Städte vom 14. bis ins 16. Jahrhundert.* Vol. 11. Leipzig, 1874.

Heintzenberg, Friedrich, ed. *Aus einem reichen Leben: Werner von Siemens in Briefen an seine Familie und Freunde.* 2nd ed. Stuttgart, 1953.

Helfferich, Carl. *Georg von Siemens: Ein Lebensbild aus Deutschlands großer Zeit.* 2nd ed., 3 vols. Berlin, 1923.

Helweg, Arthur W. "Sikh Identity in England, Its Changing Nature." In *Sikh History and Religion in the Twentieth Century,* edited by Joseph T. O'Connell, Milton Israel, and Willard G. Oxtoby, 356–75. Delhi, 1990.

———. "Why Leave India for America? A Case Study Approach to Understanding Migrant Behaviour." *International Migration* 25 (1987): 165–78.

Henriques, Fernando. *Family and Colour in Jamaica*. London, 1953.

Herold, Jürgen. "Der Aufenthalt des Markgrafen Gianfrancesco Gonzaga zur Erziehung an den Höfen der fränkischen Markgrafen von Brandenburg 1455–1459: Zur Funktionsweise und zu den Medien der Kommunikation zwischen Mantua und Franken im Spätmittelalter." In *Principes: Dynastien und Höfe im späten Mittelalter: Interdisziplinäre Tagung des Lehrstuhls für allgemeine Geschichte des Mittelalters und Historische Hilfswissenschaften in Greifswald in Verbindung mit der Residenzen-Kommission der Akademie der Wissenschaften zu Göttingen vom 15.–18. Juni 2000*, edited by Cordula Nolte, Karl-Heinz Spiess, and Ralf-Gunnar Werlich, 199–234. Stuttgart, 2002.

Herskovits, Melville. *The Myth of the Negro Past*. Boston, 1941.

Herzfeld, Michael. *The Poetics of Manhood: Contest and Identity in a Cretan Mountain Village*. Princeton, NJ, 1985.

Herzig, Edmund. "Borrowed Terminology and Techniques of the New Julfa Armenian Merchants, A Study in Cultural Transmission." Presented Paper, Sixth Biennial Conference on Iranian Studies, London, 3–5 August 2006.

———. "The Armenian Merchants of New Julfa, Isfahan, A Study in Premodern Trade." PhD dissertation, Oxford University, 1991.

———. "The Family Firm in the Commercial Organization of the Julfa Armenians." In *Études Safavides*, edited by Jean Calmard, 287–304. Paris and Louvain, 1993.

———. "The Iranian Silk Trade and European Manufacture in the XVIIth and XVIIIth Centuries." *Journal of European Economic History* 19 (1990): 73–89.

———. "The Volume of Iranian Raw Silk Exports in the Safavid Period." *Iranian Studies* 25 (1992): 61–79.

———. "Venice and the Julfa Armenian Merchants." In *Gli armeni e Venezia: Dagli Sceriman a Mechitar: Il momento culminante di una consuetudine millenaria*, edited by Boghos Levon Zekiyan and Aldo Ferrari, 141–64. Venice, 2004.

Higman, Barry. *Slave Population and Economy in Jamaica 1807–1834*. Cambridge, 1976.

Hobsbawm, Eric. *The Age of Revolution, 1789–1851*. New York, 1975.

Hodson, Simon. "Politics of the Frontier, Henri IV, the Maréchal-Duc de Bouillon and the Sovereignty of Sedan." *French History* 19, no. 4 (2005): 413–39.

———. "The Power of Female Dynastic Networks, A Brief Study of Louise de Coligny, Princess of Orange, and Her Stepdaughters." *Women's History Review* 16, no. 3 (2007): 335–51.

Höh, Marc von der. "Zwischen religiöser Memoria und Familiengeschichte, Das Familienbuch des Werner Overstolz." In *Haus- und Familienbücher in der städtischen Gesellschaft des Spätmittelalters und der frühen Neuzeit*, edited by Birgit Studt, 33–60. Cologne, 2007.

Hohkamp, Michaela. "Do Sisters Have Brothers? Or the Search for the 'rechte Schwester,' Brothers and Sisters in Aristocratic Society at the Turn of the Sixteenth Century." In Christopher H. Johnson and David Warren Sabean, *Sibling Relations and the Transformations of European Kinship*. New York, 2011.

———. "Eine Tante für alle Fälle, Tanten-Nichten-Beziehungen und ihre politische Bedeutung für die reichsfürstliche Gesellschaft der Frühen Neuzeit (16. bis 18. Jahrhundert)." In *Politiken der Verwandtschaft*, edited by Margareth Lanzinger and Edith Saurer, 149–71. Vienna, 2007.

———. "Sisters, Aunts, and Cousins, Familial Architectures and the Political Field in Early Modern Europe." In Sabean, Teuscher and Mathieu, *Kinship in Europe*, 91–104.

———. "Tanten, Vom Nutzen einer verwandtschaftlichen Figur für die Erforschung familiärer Ökonomien in der Frühen Neuzeit." *WerkstattGeschichte* 46 (2007): 5–12.

———. "Transmission von Herrschaft und Verwandtschaft in der reichsfürstlichen Gesellschaft vom 15. bis zum 18. Jahrhundert." Habilitation thesis, Freie Universität Berlin, 2007.

Holt, Peter M. *Studies in the History of the Near East.* London, 1973.

Hourani, Albert. "Ottoman Reform and the Politics of Notables." In *Beginnings of Modernization in the Middle East: The Nineteenth Century,* edited by William R. Polk and Richard L. Chambers, 41–68. Chicago, 1968.

Howell, Martha C. *The Marriage Exchange: Property, Social Place, and Gender in Cities of the Low Countries 1300–1550.* Chicago, 1998.

Huber, Eugen. *System und Geschichte des Schweizerischen Privatrechts.* 4 vols. Basel, 1886–1893.

Huchet, Patrick. *1795: Quiberon, ou le destin de la France.* Rennes, 1995.

Hughes, Diane Owen. "From Brideprice to Dowry in Mediterranean Europe." *Journal of Family History* 3 (1978): 262–96.

Hunt, Lynn. *The Family Romance of the French Revolution.* London, 1992.

"Hüsrev Paışa." In *Islâm ansiklopedisi: Islâm âlemi coğrafya, etnografya ve biyografya lügatı* [Encyclopedia of Islam, A Geographical, Ethnographical, and Biographical Dictionary of the Islamic World]. Ankara, 1940–1988.

Imhaus, Brunehilde. *Le minoranze orientali a Venezia, 1300–1510.* Rome, 1997.

Inalcik, Halil. "Centralization and Decentralization in Ottoman Administration." In *Studies in Eighteenth-Century Islamic History,* edited by Thomas Naff and Roger Owen. Carbondale, IL, 1977.

———. "The Khan and the Tribal Aristocracy." In *Studies in Ottoman Social and Economic History.* London, 1985.

Iorga, Nicolae. *Byzance après Byzance.* Paris, 1992.

Isenburg, Wilhelm Karl, Prinz zu. *Stammtafeln zur Geschichte der europäischen Staaten.* 17 vols. Marburg, 1961–1978.

Isenmann, Eberhard. *Die deutsche Stadt im Spätmittelalter, 1250–1500: Stadtgestalt, Recht, Stadtregiment, Kirche, Gesellschaft, Wirtschaft.* Stuttgart, 1988.

Israel, Jonathan I. "Diaspora Jewish and Non-Jewish and the World Maritime Empires." In McCabe, Harlaftis, and Pepelasis Minoglou, *Diaspora Entrepreneurial Networks,* 3–26.

———. *Diasporas within a Diaspora: Jews, Crypto-Jews, and the World of Maritime Empires, 1540–1740.* Leiden, 2002.

Jain, Ravindra K. *Indian Communities Abroad: Themes and Literature.* Delhi, 1993.

James, Carolyn. "Friendship and Dynastic Marriage in Renaissance Italy." *Literature and History* 17 (2008): 4–18.

James, Susan Craig. "Intertwining Roots." *Journal of Caribbean History* 25, no. 2 (1992): 216–18.

James, Winston. *Holding Aloft the Banner of Ethiopia: Caribbean Radicalism in Early Twentieth Century America.* London, 1998.

Janos, Damien. "Panaiotis [*sic*] Nicousios and Alexander Mavrocordatos, The Rise of the Phanariots and the Office of Grand Dragoman in the Ottoman Administration in the Second Half of the Seventeenth Century." *Archivum Ottomanicum* 23 (2005): 177–96.

Jansen, Dorothea. *Einführung in die Netzwerkanalyse.* Opladen, 1999.

Janssens, Paul, ed. *La Belgique au XVIIe siècle.* Brussels, 2006.

Janssens, Paul, and Luc Duerloo. *Armorial de la noblesse belge du XVe au XXe siècle.* Brussels, 1992.

Jeannin, Pierre. *Les marchands au XVIe siècle.* Paris, 1967.

Jochens, Jenny. *Old Norse Images of Women*. Philadelphia, 1996.

Johnson, Christopher H. "Capitalism and the State, Capital Accumulation and Proletarianization in the Languedocian Woolens Industry, 1700–1789." In *The Workplace before the Factory: Artisans and Proletarians, 1500–1800*, edited by Thomas Max Safley and Leonard N. Rosenband, 37–62. Ithaca, NY, 1993.

———. "Das Geschwister Archipel, Bruder-Schwester-Liebe und Klassenformation im Frankreich des 19. Jahrhunderts." *L'Homme: Zeitschrift für feministische Geschichtswissenschaft* 13, no. 1 (2002): 50–67.

———. "Kinship, Civil Society, and Power in Nineteenth-Century Vannes." In Sabean, Teuscher and Mathieu, *Kinship in Europe*, 258–83.

Johnson, Christopher H. and David Warren Sabean. "From Siblingship to Siblinghood, Kinship and the Shaping of European Society (1300–1900)." In Johnson and Sabean, *Sibling Relations and the Transformations of European Kinship*. New York, 2011.

———, eds. *Sibling Relations and the Transformations of European Kinship, 1300–1900*. New York: 2011.

Jollivet, René M. *Discours prononcé par M. le Président du Collège électoral de l'arrondissement de Vannes à l'ouverture de sa session, le 14 août 1815*. Vannes, 1815.

Joris, Elisabeth. "Kinship and Gender, Property, Enterprise, and Politics." In Sabean, Teuscher, and Mathieu, *Kinship in Europe*, 231–257.

Kafadar, Cemal. *Between Two Worlds: The Construction of the Ottoman State*. Berkeley, CA, 1995.

"Kallimachis." In *Megale Hellenike Enkyklopaideia*. Vol. 17, 572. Athens, 1956–1965.

Karnoouh, Claude. "Penser 'maison', penser 'famille': Residence domestique et parenté dans les sociétés rurales de l'est de la France." *Études rurales* 75 (1979): 33–75.

Kasdan, Leonard. "Family Structure, Migration and the Entrepreneur." *Comparative Studies in Society and History* 7 (1965): 345–57.

Kasinitz, Philip. *Caribbean New York: Black Immigrants and the Politics of Race*. Ithaca, NY, 1992.

Katsiardi-Herring, Olga. "He hellenike diaspora, He geographia kai he typologia tes" ["The Greek Diaspora, Its Geography and Typology"] In *Hellenike Oikonomike Historia* [Greek Economic History, Sixteenth to Nineteenth Centuries]15os-19os aionas, edited by Spyros I. Asdrachas, 237–47. Athens, 2003.

Kellner, Beate. "Genealogien." In *Höfe und Residenzen im spätmittelalterlichen Reich: Hof und Schrift*, edited by Werner Paravicini, 347–60. Ostfildern, 2007.

Kerviler, René, ed. *Répertoire général de Bio-Bibliographie bretonne*. Rennes, 1904. Reprinted, 1978.

Kévonian, Kéram. "Marchands Arméniens au XVIIe siècle, À propos d'un livre arménien à Amsterdam en 1699." *Cahiers du monde russe et soviétique* 16 (1975): 199–244.

Khachikian, Levon. "The Ledger of the Merchant Hovhannes Joughayetsi." *Journal of the Asiatic Society* 8 (1966): 153–86.

Khater, Akram Fouad. *Inventing Home: Emigration, Gender, and the Middle Class in Lebanon, 1870–1920*. Berkeley, CA, 2001.

Khera, Sigrid. "An Austrian Peasant Village under Rural Industrialization." *Behavior Science Notes* 7 (1972): 29–36.

Khoury, Dina Rizk. *State and Provincial Society in the Ottoman Empire: Mosul, 1540–1834*. Cambridge, 2002.

Klapisch-Zuber, Christiane. "L'invention du passé familial." In *La maison et le nom: Stratégies et rituels dans l'Italie de la renaissance*, edited by Christiane Klapisch-Zuber, 19–35. Paris, 1990.

Klein, W. *De Trippen in de 17e eeuw*. Assen, 1965.

Klein, W., and J. W. Veluwenkamp. "The Role of the Entrepreneur in the Economic Expansion of the Dutch Republic." In *The Dutch Economy in the Golden Age: Nine Studies*, edited by Karel Davids and Leo Noordegraaf, 27–53. Amsterdam, 1993.

Kmec, Sonja. "'A Stranger Born': Female Usage of International Networks in Times of War." In *The Contending Kingdoms: France and England, 1420–1700*, edited by Glenn Richardson, 147–60. Aldershot, UK, 2008.

Köbler, Gerhard. "Das Familienrecht in der spätmittelalterlichen Stadt." In *Haus und Familie in der spätmittelalterlichen Stadt*, edited by Alfred Haverkamp, 136–60. Cologne, 1984.

Koch, Elisabeth. "Die Frau im Recht der Frühen Neuzeit, Juristische Lehren und Begründungen." In *Frauen in der Geschichte des Rechts: Von der Frühen Neuzeit bis zur Gegenwart*, edited by Ute Gerhard, 73–93. Munich, 1997.

Kohler, Alfred. "'Tu Felix Austria Nube…': Vom Klischee zur Neubewertung dynastischer Politik in der neueren Geschichte Europas." *Zeitschrift für historische Forschung* 21 (1994): 461–82.

Komnenos Hypsilantes, Athanasios. *Ekklesiastikon kai politikon ton eis dodeka biblion E' Th' kai I' etoi Ta Meta ten Alosin (1453–1789)* [Ecclesiastical and Political Events after the Fall of Constantinople in Twelve Books]. Athens, 1972.

Krüger, Bernhard. *The Pear Tree Blossoms: A History of the Moravian Mission Stations in South Africa 1737–1869*. Genadenthal, 1966.

Kunisch, Johannes, ed. *Der dynastische Fürstenstaat: Zur Bedeutung von Sukzessionsordnungen für die Entstehung des frühmodernen Staates*. Berlin, 1982.

Kunt, Metin. *The Sultan's Servants: The Transformation of Ottoman Provincial Government, 1550–1650*. New York, 1983.

Kuper, Adam. "Incest, Cousin Marriage, and the Origin of the Human Sciences in Nineteenth-Century England." *Past and Present* 174 (2002): 153–83.

Lachenicht, Susanne. "Huguenot Immigrants and the Formation of National Identities, 1548–1787," *Historical Journal* 50, no. 2 (2007): 309–31.

La Condamine, Pierre de. *Salm en Vosges—une principauté de conte de fées*. Paris, 1974.

Lane, Frederic C. "Family Partnerships and Joint Ventures in the Venetian Republic." *Journal of Economic History* 4 (1944): 178–96.

Lapeyre, Henri. *Une famille des marchands: Les Ruiz*. Paris, 1955.

Latte Abdallah, Stéphanie. *Femmes réfugiées palestiniennes*. Paris, 2006.

———. "Le débat sur la criminalité liée à l'honneur en Jordanie, Le genre comme enjeu politique et question sociale." *Monde arabe Maghreb-Machrek: Les constructions sociales de la question féminine* 179 (2004): 29–45.

———. "Les femmes des camps à l'avant-garde de la contestation du système patriarcal en Jordanie." *Les Cahiers de l'Orient: Le Royaume Hachémite. De Abdallah Ier à Abdallah II. Un demi-siècle d'histoire* 75 (2004): 77–100.

———. "Subvertir le consentement, Itinéraires sociaux des femmes des camps de réfugiés palestiniens en Jordanie 1948–2001." *Annales ESC* 60 (2005): 53–89.

Lazzarini, Isabella. *Fra un principe e altri stati: Relazioni di potere e forme di servizio a Mantova nell'età di Ludovico Gonzaga*. Rome, 1996.

Le Goff, Timothy. *Vannes and Its Region: A Study of Town and Country in the Eighteenth Century*. Oxford, 1981.

Leguay, Jean-Pierre. *Histoire de Vannes et sa region*. Toulouse, 1988.

Lehmann, Hartmut. "Horizonte pietistischer Lebenswelten." In *Protestantische Weltsichten: Transformationen seit dem 17. Jahrhundert*, edited by Hartmut Lehmann, 11–28. Göttingen, 1998.

Lenders, Piet. "Trois façons de gouverner dans les Pays-Bas autrichiens." In *Unité et diversité de l'Empire des Habsbourg à la fin du XVIIIe siècle,* edited by Roland Mortier and Hervé Hasquin, 41–86. Brussels, 1988.

Lepeux, Georges. *Gallia typographique ou Répertoire biographique … de tous les imprimeurs de France.* Paris, 1914.

Le Play, M. Frédéric. *L'organisation de la famille selon le vrai modèle signalé par l'histoire de toutes les races et tous les temps.* Paris, 1871.

Lesger, Clé, and Leo Noordegraaf, eds. *Entrepreneurs and Entrepreneurship in Early Modern Times: Merchant and Industrialists within the Orbit of the Dutch Staple Market.* The Hague, 1995.

Lever, Evelyne. *Louis XVIII.* Paris, 1988.

Lévy-Bruhl, Henri. *Histoire juridique des sociétés de commerce en France aux XVIIe et XVIIIe siècles.* Paris, 1938.

Lewis, Bernard. *The Muslim Discovery of Europe.* New York, 1982.

Lipp, Carola. "Verwandtschaft. Ein negiertes Element in der politischen Kultur des 19. Jahrhunderts." *Historische Zeitschrift* 283 (2006): 31–77.

Litchfield, R. Burr. "Demographic Characteristics of Florentine Patrician Families from the Sixteenth to the Nineteenth Centuries." *Journal of Economic History* 29 (1969): 191–205.

———. "Les investissements commerciaux des patriciens florentins au XVIIIe siècle." *Annales ESC* 24 (1969): 685–721.

Long, Edward. *The History of Jamaica.* Vol. 2. London, 1774.

Loomie, Albert. *Spain and the Early Stuarts, 1585–1655.* Aldershot, UK, 1996.

Louden, Irvine. *Death in Childbirth: An International Study of Maternal Care and Maternal Mortality, 1800–1950.* Oxford, 1992.

Ludwig, Theodor. *Die deutschen Reichstände im Elsass und der Ausbruch der Revolutionskriege.* Strasbourg, 1898.

Lyon, Michael H., and Bernice J. M. West. "London Patels, Caste and Commerce." *New Community* 21–23 (1995): 399–419.

Malanima, Paolo. "I commerci del mondo del 1674 visti da Amsterdam e da Livorno." In *Ricerche di storia moderna in onore di Mario Mirri,* edited by Giuliana Biagioli, 153–80. Pisa, 1995.

Malkki, Liisa. *Purity and Exile: Violence, Memory, and National Cosmology among Hutu Refugees in Tanzania.* Chicago, 1995.

Manning, Patrick. *Migration in World History.* New York, 2005.

Mansel, Philip. *Prince of Europe: The Life of Charles Joseph de Ligne, 1735–1814.* London, 2003.

Markovits, Claude. *The Global World of Indian Merchants, 1750–1947: Traders of Sind from Bukhara to Panama.* Cambridge, 2000.

Mason, John C. S. *The Moravian Church and the Missionary Awakening in England 1760–1800.* Suffolk, UK, 2001.

Matschoß, Conrad, ed. *Werner Siemens: Ein kurzgefaßtes Lebensbild nebst einer Auswahl seiner Briefe: Aus Anlaß der 100. Wiederkehr seines Geburtstages.* Berlin, 1916.

Matthee, Rudolph P. *The Politics of Trade in Safavid Iran: Silk for Silver 1600–1730.* Cambridge, 1999.

McCabe, Ina Baghdiantz. "Global Trading Ambitions in Diaspora: The Armenians and Their Eurasian Silk Trade, 1530–1750." In McCabe, Harlaftis, and Pepelasis Minoglou, *Diaspora Entrepreneurial Networks,* 27–48.

McCabe, Ina Baghdiantz, Gelina Harlaftis, and Ioanna Pepelasis Minoglou, eds. *Diaspora Entrepreneurial Networks: Four Centuries of History.* Oxford, 2005.

McClure, Ellen. *Sunspots and the Sun King: Sovereignty and Mediation in Seventeenth-Century France.* Urbana, IL, 2006.

McDonald, Roderick A., ed. *Between Slavery and Freedom. Special Magistrate John Anderson's Journal of St. Vincent during the Apprenticeship.* Kingston, 2001.

McGowan, Bruce. "The Age of the Ayans, 1699–1812." In *An Economic and Social History of the Ottoman Empire,* edited by Suraiya Faroqhi, Bruce McGowan, Donald Quataert, and Sevket Pamuk. Vol. 2, 637–758. Cambridge, 1994.

McKeown, Adam. "Global Migrations, 1846–1940." *Journal of World History* 15, no. 2 (2004): 155–89.

Medick, Hans, and David Warren Sabean, eds. *Interest and Emotion: Essays on the Study of Family and Kinship.* Cambridge, 1984. Translated as *Emotionen und materielle Interessen: Sozialanthropologische und historische Beiträge zur Familienforschung.* Göttingen, 1984.

Meriwether, Margaret. *The Kin Who Count: Family and Society in Ottoman Aleppo, 1770–1840.* Austin, TX, 1999.

Mertens, Arnout. "Noble Independence, Monarchical Power and Early Modern State Building. Pedigreed Nobles from Brabant in the Age of Absolutism." Unpublished conference paper. Antwerp, 2008.

Mettam, Roger. "The Role of the Higher Aristocracy in France under Louis XIV, with Special Reference to the Faction of the Duke of Burgundy and Provincial Governors." PhD dissertation, Cambridge University, 1967.

Mettele, Gisela. "Bürgerinnen und Schwestern, Weibliche Lebensentwürfe in bürgerlicher Gesellschaft und religiöser Gemeinschaft." *Unitas Fratrum* 45/46 (1999): 113–40.

———. "Entwürfe des pietistischen Körpers, Die Herrnhuter Brüdergemeine und die Mode." In *Das Echo Halles: Kulturelle Wirkungen des Pietismus,* edited by Rainer Lächele, 291–314. Tübingen, 2001.

———. "Kommerz und fromme Demut, Wirtschaftsethik und Wirtschaftspraxis im 'Gefühlspietismus.'" *Vierteljahrschrift für Sozial- und Wirtschaftsgeschichte* 92 (2005): 301–32.

———. *Weltbürgertum oder Gottesreich: Die Herrnhuter Brüdergemeine als globale Gemeinschaft 1727–1857.* Göttingen, 2009.

Meyer, Dietrich. *Zinzendorf und die Herrnhuter Brüdergemeine, 1700–2000.* Göttingen, 2000.

Meyer, Paul, ed. *L'histoire de Guillaume le Maréchal comte de Striguil et de Pembroke régent d'Angleterre de 1216 à 1219.* 3 vols. Paris, 1891–1901.

Michaelson, Maureen. "The Relevance of Caste amongst East African Gujaratis in Britain." *New Community* 7 (1978–1979): 350–60.

Midelfort, H. C. Erik. *Mad Princes of Renaissance Germany.* Charlottesville, VA, 1994.

Mintz, Sidney. "The Caribbean as a Socio-Cultural Area." *Journal of World History* 9 (1966): 916–41.

Mintz, Sidney, and Richard Price. *An Anthropological Approach to the African-American Past: A Caribbean Perspective.* Philadelphia, 1976.

Mitterauer, Michael. *Warum Europa? Mittelalterliche Grundlagen eines Sonderwegs.* Munich, 2003.

Moch, Leslie Page. "Bretons in Paris, Regional Ties and Urban Networks in an Age of Urbanization." *Quaderni storici* 86 (2001): 177–99.

———. "Migration and the Nation, The View from Paris." *Social Science History* 28 (2004): 1–18.

———. "Networks among Bretons? The Evidence from Paris." *Continuity and Change* 18 (2003): 431–55.

Moisse-Daxhelet, Geneviève. "La Principauté de Stavelot-Malmédy sous le règne du cardinal Guillaume-Egon de Fürstenberg, Problèmes politiques et institutionnels, 1682–1704." *Anciens pays et assemblées d'états XXIX* (1963): 1–224.

Moors, Annelies. *Women, Property and Islam: Palestinian Experiences 1920–1990*. Cambridge, 1995.

Moraw, Peter. "Das Heiratsverhalten im hessischen Landgrafenhaus ca. 1300–1500: Auch vergleichend betrachtet." In *Hundert Jahre Historische Kommission für Hessen 1897–1997*, edited by Walter Heinemeyer, 115–40. Marburg, 1997.

———. "Conseils princiers en Allemagne au XIVème et au XVème siècle." In *Powerbrokers in the Late Middle Ages: The Burgundian Low Countries in a European Context*, edited by Robert Stein, 165–76. Turnhout, 2001.

Mordenti, Raul. *I libri di famiglia in Italia*. Vol. 2, *Geografia e storia*. Rome, 2001.

Morgan, Kenneth. "Business Networks in the British Export Trade to North America, 1750–1800." In *The Early Modern Atlantic Economy*, edited by John J. McCusker and Kenneth Morgan, 36–62. Cambridge, 2000.

Morris, Harold S. *The Indians in Uganda*. London, 1968.

Morsel, Joseph. "Geschlecht als Repräsentation, Beobachtungen zur Verwandtschaftskonstruktion im fränkischen Adel des späten Mittelalters." In *Die Repräsentation der Gruppen: Texte, Bilder, Objekte*, edited by Otto Gerhard Oexle and Andrea von Hülsen-Esch, 259–325. Göttingen, 1998.

———. *L'aristocratie médiévale Ve–XVe siècle*, 253–60. Paris, 2006.

Moser, Franz, and Ritter Wilhelm von Diesbach. *Schultheiss von Bern 1442–1517*. Bern, 1930.

"Mourouzis." In *Megale Hellenike Enkyklopaideia*. Vol. 18: 426. Athens, 1956–1965.

Moya, Jose C. "A Continent of Immigrants, Postcolonial Shifts in the Western Hemisphere." *Hispanic American Historical Review* 86, no. 1 (2006): 1–28.

———. *Cousins and Strangers: Spanish Immigrants in Buenos Aires, 1850–1930*. Berkeley, CA, 1998.

———. "Domestic Service in a Global Perspective, Gender, Migration, and Ethnic Niches." *Journal of Ethnic and Migration Studies* 33, no. 4 (2007): 559–79.

Müller-Wille, Staffan, and Hans-Jörg Rheinberger, eds. *Heredity Produced: At the Crossroads of Biology, Politics, and Culture, 1500–1870*. Cambridge, MA: 2007.

Nagata, Yuzo. *Tarihte ayanlar: Karaosmanoğulları üzerine bir inceleme* [Ayans in History, A Study of the Karaosmanogullari]. Ankara, 1997.

Nascimento Raposo, José de. "Don Gabriel de Silva, A Portuguese-Jewish Banker in Eighteenth-Century Bordeaux." PhD dissertation, York University, 1989.

Newitt, Malyn. *A History of Portuguese Overseas Expansion, 1400–1668*. New York, 2005.

Newton, Velma. *The Silver Men*. Kingston, 1987.

Niederkorn, Jan Paul, ed. *Le corti come luogo di comunicazione: Gli Asburgo e l'Italia (secoli XVI–XIX) / Höfe als Orte der Kommunikation: Die Habsburger und Italien (16.–19. Jh.): Tagungsband zur gleichnamigen Tagung in Trento 8.–10. November 2007*. Berlin, 2010.

Niemeier, Wolf-Dietrich. "Archaic Greeks in the Orient, Textual and Archaeological Evidence." *Bulletin of the American Schools of Oriental Research* 322 (2001): 11–32.

Nijsten, Gerard. *In the Shadow of Burgundy: The Court of Guelders in the Late Middle Ages*. Translated by Tania Guest. Cambridge, 2004.

Noiriel, Gérard. *The French Melting Pot: Immigration, Citizenship, and National Identity*. Translated by Geoffroy de Laforcade. Minneapolis, 1996.

Nolde, Dorothea. "Die Assimilation des Fremden, Nahrung und Kulturkontakt in de Brys 'America.'" *Historische Anthropologie* 3 (2004): 355–72.

Nolte, Cordula. "'Ir seyt ein fremds weib, das solt ihr pleiben, dieweil ihr lebt': Beziehungsgeflechte in fürstlichen Familien des Spätmittelalters." In *Geschlechterdifferenz im interdisziplinären Gespräch: Kolloquium des interdisziplinären Zentrums für Frauen- und Geschlechterstudien an der Ernst-Moritz-Arndt-Universität Greifswald*, edited by Doris Ruhe, 11–41. Würzburg, 1998.

Nolte, Theodor. *'Lauda post mortem': Die deutschen und niederländischen Ehrenreden des Mittelalters.* Bern, 1983.

Nordman, Daniel. *Frontières de France, de l'espace au territoire XVIe–XIXe siècle.* Paris, 1998.

Noy, David. *Foreigners at Rome: Citizens and Strangers.* London, 2000.

Nusteling, H. H. "The Jews in the Republic of the United Provinces, Origins, Numbers and Dispersion." In *Dutch Jewry: History and Secular Culture (1500–2000)*, edited by Jonathan Israel and Reinier Salverda, 43–62. Leiden, 2002.

Ohlemacher, Jürgen. *Das Reich Gottes in Deutschland bauen: Ein Beitrag zur Vorgeschichte von Theologien der deutschen Gemeinschaftsbewegung.* Göttingen, 1986.

Oliel-Grausz, Evelyne. "Networks and Communication in the Sephardi Diaspora, An Added Dimension to the Concept of Port Jews and Port Jewries." In *Jews and Port Cities, 1590–1990: Commerce, Community and Cosmopolitanism*, edited by David Cesarani and Gemma Romain, 61–76. London, 2006.

Olwig, Karen Fog. *Caribbean Journeys: An Ethnography of Migration and Home in Three Family Networks.* Durham, NC, 2007.

———. "Constructing Lives, Migration Narratives and Life Stories among Nevisians." In Chamberlain, *Caribbean Migration*, 63–80.

Opitz, Claudia. "Neue Wege der Sozialgeschichte? Ein kritischer Blick auf Otto Brunners Konzept des 'Ganzen Hauses'." *Geschichte und Gesellschaft* 20 (1994): 88–98.

Oresko, Robert. "The Marriages of the Nieces of Cardinal Mazarin, Public Policy and Private Strategy in Seventeenth-Century Europe." In *Frankreich im Europäischen Staatensystem der Frühen Neuzeit*, edited by Rainer Babel, 109–51. Sigmaringen, 1995.

Osterhammel, Jürgen. "Transnationale Gesellschaftsgeschichte: Erweiterung oder Alternative?" In *Geschichte und Gesellschaft* 27 (2001): 464–79.

Osterhammel, Jürgen, and Niels Peterson. *Geschichte der Globalisierung.* Munich, 2003.

Padgett, John F., and Paul D. McLean. "Organizational Invention and Elite Transformation: The Birth of Partnership Systems in Renaissance Florence." *American Journal of Sociology* 111 (2006): 1463–1568.

Palmer, Ransford, ed. *In Search of a Better Life: Perspectives on Migration from the Caribbean.* New York, 1990.

Palriwala, Rajni, and Patricia Uberoi. "Marriage and Migration in Asia: Gender Issues." *Indian Journal of Gender Studies* 12, no. 2–3 (2005): 5–29.

Panaite, Viorel. *The Ottoman Law of War and Peace: The Ottoman Empire and Tribute-Payers.* New York, 2000.

Papelasis Minoglou, Ioanna. "The Greek Merchant House of the Russian Black Sea, A 19th-Century Example of a Traders' Coalition." *International Journal of Maritime History* 10 (1998): 61–104.

Papelasis Minoglou, Ioanna. "Toward a Typology of Greek Diaspora Entrepreneurship." In McCabe, Harlaftis, and Pepelasis Minoglou, *Diaspora Entrepreneurial Networks.*

Paravicini Bagliani, Agostino, Eva Pibiri, and Denis Reynard, eds. *L'itinérance des seigneurs (XIVe–XVIe siècles).* Lausanne, 2003.

Paravicini, Werner. *Europäische Reiseberichte des späten Mittelalters: Eine analytische Bibliographie.* 3 vols. Frankfurt a. M.: 1994–2001.

———. "Seigneur par itinérance? Le cas du patricien bernois Conrad de Scharnachtal." In *L'itinérance des seigneurs (XIVe–XVIe siècles)*, edited by Agostino Paravicini Bagliani, Eva Pibiri, and Denis Reynard, 27–71. Lausanne, 2003.

———. "The Court of the Dukes of Burgundy. A Model for Europe?" In *Princes, Patronage and the Nobility,* edited by Ronald G. Asch and Adolf M. Birke. Oxford, 1991.

———. "Von der Heidenfahrt zur Kavalierstour, Über Motive und Formen adligen Reisens im späten Mittelalter." In *Wissensliteratur im späten Mittelalter.* Vol. 13, 91–130. Wiesbaden, 1993.

———. "Fahrende Ritter, Literarisches Bild und gelebte Wirklichkeit im Spätmittelalter." In *Mittelalterliche Menschenbilder,* edited by Martina Neumeyer, 205–54. Regensburg, 2000.

Pariset, Jean-Daniel. "La Lorraine dans les relations internationals au XVIe siècle." In *Les Habsbourg et la Lorraine,* edited by Jean-Paul Bled, Eugène Faucher, and René Taveneaux. Nancy, 1988.

Parisse, Michel. "La Lorraine, la maison de Salm et les archives d'Anholt." *Annales de l'Est* 5, no. 26 (1975): 148–57.

———. "Les comtes de Salm et l'évêché de Metz, XIème–XIIème siècles." In *Histoire des terres de Salm*, 23–35. Saint Dié-des-Vosges, 1994.

Parker, Geoffrey. *Europe in Crisis, 1598–1648.* London, 1979.

Parrott, David. "The Mantuan Succession, 1627–1631: A Sovereignty Dispute in Early Modern Europe." *English Historical Review* 112 (1997): 20–65.

Pasetti, Giovanni, and Gianna Pinotti. "La camera in luce, La camera degli Sposi di Andrea Mantegna in Palazzo Ducale a Mantova—redazione 1999." http,//xoomer.alice.it/gpasett/luce.htm (accessed 10 July 2008).

Patterson, Orlando. *The Sociology of Slavery.* London, 1967.

Peach, Ceri. *The Caribbean in Europe: Contrasting Patterns of Migration and Settlement in Britain, France and the Netherlands.* Warwick, UK, 1991.

Peirce, Leslie. *The Imperial Harem: Women and Sovereignty in the Ottoman Empire.* New York, 1993.

Peltre, Jean, and Maurice Noël. "Les Mercy en Europe aux XVIIe et XVIIIe siècles. De la Lorraine au Banat." *Le Pays Lorrain* 77, no. 3 (1996): 185–98.

Perréon, Stéphane. *L'armée en Bretagne au XVIIIe siècle.* Rennes, 2005.

Peteet, Julie. *Gender in Crisis: Women and the Palestinian Resistance Movement.* New York, 1991.

Petiot, Alain. *Au service des Habsbourg: Officiers, ingénieurs, savants et artistes lorrains en Autriche.* Paris, 2000.

Petropoulos, John A. *Politics and Statecraft in the Kingdom of Greece.* Princeton, NJ, 1965.

Petropoulous, Jonathan. *Royals and the Reich: The Princes von Hessen in Nazi Germany.* Oxford, 2006.

Peucker, Paul. "Heerendijk—Link in the Moravian Network, Moravian Colonists Destined for Pennsylvania." *Transactions of the Moravian Historical Society* 30 (1998): 9–21.

Peyer, Hans Conrad. "Die Anfänge der Schweizerischen Aristokratien." In *Luzerner Patriziat: Sozial- und Wirtschaftsgeschichtliche Studien zur Entwicklung im 16. und 17. Jahrhundert: Mit einer Einführung von Hans Conrad Peyer,* edited by Kurt Messmer and Peter Hoppe, 1–28. Luzern, 1976.

Philliou, Christine. *Biography of an Empire: Practicing Ottoman Governance in the Age of Revolution.* Berkeley, CA, 2010.

———. "Breaking the Tetrarchy and Saving the Kaymakam: To Be an Ambitious Ottoman Christian in 1821." In *Ottoman Rule and the Balkans, 1760–1850: Conflict, Transformation, Adaptation: Proceedings of an International Conference Held in Rethymno, Greece, 13–14 December 2003*, edited by Antonis Anastasopoulos and Elias Kolovos, 181–94. Rethymno, 2007.

———. "Communities on the Verge: Unraveling the Phanariot Ascendancy in Ottoman Governance." *Comparative Studies in Society and History* 51 (2009): 151–81.

———. "Worlds Old and New: Phanariot Networks and the Remaking of Ottoman Governance, 1800–1850." PhD dissertation, Princeton University, 2004.

Photeinos, Dionysios. *Historia tes Palai Dakias* [History of the Former Dacia]. 3 vols. Vienna, 1819.

Pieterse, Jan Nederveen. "Globalisation as Hybridisation." *International Sociology* 9 (1994): 161–84.

Piterberg, Gabriel. *An Ottoman Tragedy.* Berkeley, CA, 2003.

———. "The Formation of an Ottoman Egyptian Elite in the 18th Century." *International Journal of Middle East Studies* 22 (1990): 275–89.

Plaza, Dwaine. "Transnational Grannies: The Changing Family Responsibility of Elderly African Caribbean-Born Women Resident in Britain." *Social Indicators Research Journal* 11, no. 7 (2000): 180–201.

Pocock, David F. *Kanbi and Patidar: A Study of the Patidar Community of Gujarat.* Oxford, 1972.

———. "Preservation of the Religious Life; Hindu Immigrants in England." *Contributions to Indian Sociology* 10 (1976): 341–65.

Pole, William. *The Life of Sir William Siemens.* London, 1888.

Pouzol-Ershaidat, Valérie. "La nation contestée: Luttes féministes, combat pour la paix des femmes palestiniennes et israéliennes (1948–1998)." PhD dissertation, L'École des Hautes Etudes en Sciences Sociales, Paris, 2001.

Price, Jacob M. *Perry of London: A Family and a Firm on the Seaborne Frontier, 1615–1753.* Cambridge, MA, 1992.

———. "The Great Quaker Business Families of Eighteenth-Century London: The Rise and Fall of a Sectarian Patriciate." In *The World of William Penn*, edited by Richard S. Dunn and Mary Maples Dunn, 363–99. Philadelphia, 1986.

———. "Transaction Costs: A Note on Merchant Credit and the Organization of Private Trade." In *The Political Economy of Merchants Empires*, edited by James Tracy, 276–97. Cambridge, 1991.

Price, Jacob, and Paul G. E. Clemens. "A Revolution of Scale in Overseas Trade: British Firms in the Chesapeake Trade, 1675–1775." *Journal of Economic History* 47 (1987): 1–43.

Price, T. Douglas, et al. "Isotopic Evidence for Mobility and Group Organization among Neolithic Farmers at Talheim, Germany, 5000 BC." *European Journal of Archaeology* 9, no. 2–3 (2006): 259–84.

Price, T. Douglas, et al. "Strontium Isotopes and Prehistoric Human Migration: The Bell Beaker Period in Central Europe." *European Journal of Archaeology* 7, no. 1 (2004): 9–40.

Primi Visconti, Giovanni-Battista, conte di San Maiolo. *Mémoires sur la Cour de Louis XIV, 1673–1681*, edited by Jean-François Solnon. Paris, 1988.

Quéniart, Jean. *Culture et société urbaines dans la France de l'ouest au XVIIIe siècle.* Paris, 1978.

Raabe, Paul, ed. *Pietas Hallensis Universalis. Weltweite Beziehungen der Franckeschen Stiftungen im 18. Jahrhundert.* Halle a.d. Saale, 1995.

Ram, Sodhi. *Indian Immigrants in Great Britain.* Delhi, 1989.

Ravel, Jeffrey S. "The Coachman's Bare Rump: An Eighteenth-Century French Cover-Up." In *Eighteenth-Century Studies* 40, no. 2 (2007): 279–308.

Reichert, Dagmar. "Räumliches Denken als Ordnen der Dinge." In *Räumliches Denken,* edited by Dagmar Reichert, 15–45. Zürich, 1996.

Reif, Heinz. *Westfälischer Adel 1770–1860: Vom Herrschaftsstand zur regionalen Elite.* Göttingen, 1979.

Revel, Jacques, ed. *Jeux d'échelles. La micro-analyse à l'expérience.* Paris, 1996.

Richardson, Bonham. *Caribbean Migrants, Environment and Human Survival on St. Kitts and Nevis.* Knoxville, TN, 1983.

———. *Panama Money in Barbados, 1900–1920.* Knoxville, TN, 1985.

Riehl, Wilhelm. *Die Naturgeschichte des Volks als Grundlage einer deutschen Social-Politik.* Vol. 3, *Die Famille.* 3rd ed. Stuttgart, 1855.

Rigogne, Thierry. *Between State and Market: Printing and Bookselling in Eighteenth-century France.* Oxford, 2008.

Robert, Adolphe, and Gaston Couguy. *Dictionnaire des Parlementaires français.* Paris, 1889.

Roberts, George. "Emigration from the Island of Barbados." *Social and Economic Studies* 4, no. 3 (1955): 245–87.

Robotham, Don. "Transnationalism in the Caribbean: Formal and Informal." AES distinguished lecture series, 2, *American Ethnologist* 25 (1996): 307–21.

Roche, Daniel. *France in the Enlightenment.* Translated by Arthur Goldhammer. Cambridge, MA, 1998.

Rodríguez-Salgado, Maria-Jose. "Terracotta and Iron: Mantuan Politics (ca. 1450–ca. 1550)." In *La corte di Mantova nell'età di Andrea Mantegna, 1450–1550* [The Court of the Gonzaga in the Age of Mantegna, 1450–1550]. Atti del convegno (Londra, 6–8 marzo 1992; Mantova, 28 marzo 1992), edited by Cesare Mozzarelli, Robert Oresko, and Leandro Ventura, 15–59. Rome, 1997.

Romani, Marina. *Una città in forma di Palazzo: Potere signorile e forma urbana nella Mantova medievale e moderna.* Mantova, 1995.

Roover, Raymond de. *Money, Banking and Credit in Medieval Bruges: Italian Merchant-Bankers, Lombards and Money-Changers: A Study in the Origins of Banking.* Cambridge, MA, 1948.

———. "The Organization of Trade." In *The Cambridge Economic History of Europe.* Vol. 3, *Economic Organization and Policies in the Middle Ages,* edited by M. M. Postan, E. E. Rich, and Edward Miller, 42–118. Cambridge, 1963.

———. *The Rise and Decline of the Medici Bank, 1397–1494.* Cambridge, MA, 1963.

Rosenfeld, Henry. "An Analysis of Marriage and Marriage Statistics for a Muslim and Christian Arab Village." *International Archive of Archaeology and Ethnography* 68 (1957): 32–52.

———. "Social and Economic Factors in Explanation of the Increased Rate of Patrilineal Endogamy in the Arab Village in Israel." In *Mediterranean Family Structures,* edited by J. G. Peristiany, 115–36. Cambridge, 1976.

Rosenfeld, Paul. "The Provincial Governors from the Minority of Charles V to the Revolt." *Anciens pays et assemblées d'états XVII* (1959): 3–63.

Rothman, Ella-Natalie. "Between Venice and Istanbul: Trans-Imperial Subjects and Cultural Mediation in the Early Modern Mediterranean." PhD dissertation, University of Michigan, 2006.

Runciman, Sir Stephen. *Great Church in Captivity: A Study of the Patriarchate of Constantinople from the Even of the Turkish Conquest to the Greek War of Independence.* London, 1968.

Ruppel, Sophie. "Geschwisterbeziehungen im Adel und Norbert Elias' Figurationssoziologie: Ein Anwendungsversuch." In *Höfische Gesellschaft und Zivilisationsprozeß: Norbert Elias' Werk in kulturwissenschaftlicher Perspektive*, edited by Claudia Opitz, 207–24. Cologne, 2005.

———. *Verbündete Rivalen: Geschwisterbeziehungen im Hochadel des 17. Jahrhunderts.* Cologne, 2006.

Ruspio, Federica. *La Nazione Portoghese: Ebrei ponentini e nuovi cristiani a Venezia*. Turin, 2007.

Rutten, Mario. *Farms and Factories: Social Profile of Large Farmers and Rural Industrialists in West India*. Delhi, 1995.

Sabean, David Warren. "Kinship and Issues of the Self in Europe around 1800." In Johnson and Sabean, *Sibling Relations and the Transformations of European Kinship.*

———. "From Clan to Kindred: Kinship and the Circulation of Property in Premodern and Modern Europe." In Müller-Wille and Rheinberger, *Heredity Produced*, 37–59.

———. "Inzestdiskurse vom Barock bis zur Romantik." *L'Homme: Zeitschrift für feministische Geschichtswissenschaft* 13 (2002): 7–28.

———. *Kinship in Neckarhausen, 1700–1870*. Cambridge, 1998.

———. *Property, Production and Family in Neckarhausen, 1700–1870*. Cambridge, 1990.

Sabean, David Warren, and Simon Teuscher. "Kinship in Europe: A New Approach to Long-Term Development." In Sabean, Teuscher and Mathieu, *Kinship in Europe*, 1–32.

Sabean, David Warren, Simon Teuscher, and Jon Mathieu, eds. *Kinship in Europe: Approaches to Long-Term Development (1300–1900)*. Oxford, 2007.

Sablonier, Roger. "The Aragonese Royal Family around 1300." In Medick and Sabean, *Interest and Emotion*. Translated as "Die Aragonesische Königsfamilie um 1300." In *Emotionen und materielle Interessen*, 282–317.

Sadat, Deena. "Rumeli Ayanlari: The Eighteenth Century." *The Journal of Modern History* 44 (1972): 346–63.

Salzmann, Ariel. "An Ancien Regime Revisited: 'Privatization' and Political Economy in the 18th Century Ottoman Empire." *Politics and Society* 21 (1993): 393–423.

———. *Tocqueville in the Ottoman Empire: Rival Paths to the Modern State.* Leiden, 2005.

Santarelli, Umberto. *Per la storia del fallimento nelle legislazioni italiane dell'età intermedia.* Padua, 1964.

Sayigh, Rosemary. "Engendered Exile: Palestinian Camp Women Tell Their Lives." *Oral History* (Autumn 1997): 39–48.

———. "Palestinian Camp Women's Narratives of Exile: Self, Gender, National Crisis." PhD dissertation, University of Hull, 1994.

Schib, Karl, ed. *Hans Stockars Jerusalemfahrt 1519 und Chronik 1520–1529*. Basel, 1949.

Schijf, Huibert. "Jewish Bankers 1850–1914: Internationalization along Ethnic Lines." In McCabe, Harlaftis, and Pepelasis Minoglou, *Diaspora Entrepreneurial Networks*, 191–216.

Schiller, Nina Glick, and Georges Fouron. *Georges Woke Up Laughing: Long Distance Nationalism*. London, 2001.

Schmugge, Ludwig. "Kollektive und individuelle Motivstrukturen im mittelalterlichen Pilgerwesen." In *Migration in der Feudalgesellschaft*, edited by Gerhard Jaritz and Albert Müller, 263–89. Frankfurt, 1988.

Schöpflin, Johann Daniel. *Historia Zaringo Badensis.* 7 vols. Karlsruhe, 1763–1766.

Schrader, Hans-Jürgen. *Literaturproduktion und Büchermarkt des radikalen Pietismus. Johann Heinrich Reitz' "Historie der Wiedergebohrnen" und ihr geschichtlicher Kontext.* Göttingen, 1989.

Schröder, Brigitte. "Der Weg zur Eisenbahnschiene: Geschichte der Familie Remy und ihre wirtschaftliche und kulturelle Bedeutung." *Deutsches Familienarchiv: Ein genealogisches Sammelwerk* 91 (1986): 3–158.

Schubert, Ernst. *Einführung in die Grundprobleme der deutschen Geschichte im Spätmittelalter.* Darmstadt, 1992.

Schwab, Dieter. "Familie." In *Geschichtliche Grundbegriffe: Historisches Lexikon zur politisch-sozialen Sprache in Deutschland,* edited by Otto Brunner, Werner Conze, and Reinhart Kosellek, 253–301. Stuttgart, 1975.

Schwartz, Olivier. *Le monde privé des ouvriers. Hommes et femmes du Nord.* Paris, 1990.

Schwennicke, Detlev. *Europäische Stammtafeln: Neue Folge.* Vol. 1.1. Frankfurt a. M.: 1998.

Schwinges, Rainer Christoph, ed. *Neubürger im späten Mittelalter: Migration und Austausch in der Städtelandschaft des alten Reiches (1250–1550).* Berlin, 2002.

Scott, John D. *Siemens Brothers 1858–1958: An Essay in the History of Industry.* London, 1958.

Scott, Tom. *Regional Identity and Economic Change. The Upper Rhine, 1450–1600.* Oxford, 1997.

Sebald, Peter. "Christian Jakob Protten Africanus (1715–1769): Erster Missionar einer deutschen Missionsgesellschaft in Schwarzafrika." In *Kolonien und Missionen,* edited by Wilfried Wagner, 109–21. Münster, 1994.

Selzer, Stephan. *Deutsche Söldner im Italien des Trecento.* Tübingen, 2001.

———. "Die Iberische Halbinsel als Ziel bewaffneter Mobilität deutschsprachiger Edelleute im 14. Jahrhundert, Eine Skizze." In *'Das kommt mir spanisch vor': Eigenes und Fremdes in den deutsch-spanischen Beziehungen des späten Mittelalters,* edited by Klaus Herbers and Nikolas Jaspert, 185–216. Münster, 2004.

Sensbach, John. *Rebecca's Revival: Creating Black Christianity in the Atlantic World.* Cambridge, MA, 2005.

Serman, William. *Les origines des officiers français (1848–1870).* Paris, 1979.

Severidt, Ebba. *Familie, Verwandtschaft und Karriere bei den Gonzaga: Struktur und Funktion von Familie und Verwandtschaft bei den Gonzaga und ihren deutschen Verwandten (1444–1519).* Leinfelden-Echterdingen, 2002.

Shepherd, Verene A., and Glen L. Richards, eds. *Questioning Creole: Creolisation Discourses in Caribbean Culture.* Kingston, 2002.

Shinn, Terry. *L'École polytechnique, 1794–1914.* Paris, 1980.

Shryock Andrew. "Une politique de 'maison' dans la Jordanie des tribus: Réflexions sur l'honneur, la famille et la nation dans le royaume hashémite." In *Émirs et présidents: Figures de la parenté et du politique dans le monde arabe,* edited by Pierre Bonte, Édouard Conte, and Paul Dresch, 331–52. Paris, 2001.

Sieber-Lehmann, Claudius. *Spätmittelalterlicher Nationalismus: Die Burgunderkriege am Oberrhein und in der Eidgenossenschaft.* Göttingen, 1995.

Siemens, Georg. *History of the House of Siemens.* 2 vols. Freiburg, 1952.

Siemens, Hermann Werner. *Stammbaum der Familie Siemens.* Munich, 1935.

———. "Über das Erfindergeschlecht Siemens." *Archiv für Rassen- und Gesellschaftsbiologie* 12 (1916–1918): 162–92.

Siemens, Werner von. *Personal Recollections.* London, 1893.

Signorini, Rodolfo. *La più bella camera del mondo: La camera dipinta di Andrea Mantengna detta "degli Sposi."* 2nd ed. Mantua, 2002.

———. *Opus hoc tenue: La camera dipinta di Andrea Mantegna; Lettura storica iconografica iconologia.* Parma, 1985.

Simey, Thomas. *Welfare and Planning in the West Indies.* Oxford, 1946.

Simon, Jules. *Premières années.* Paris, n.d. [1901].

Simon, Kate. *A Renaissance Tapestry: The Gonzaga of Mantua.* New York, 1988.

Singerman, Diane. *Avenues of Participation: Family, Politics, and Networks in Urban Quarters of Cairo.* Princeton, NJ, 1995.

Sinner, Karl Ludwig von. "Versuch einer diplomatischen Geschichte der Edlen von Scharnachthal." *Der Schweizer Geschichtforscher* 3 (1820): 33–204.

Smaby, Beverly. *The Transformation of Moravian Bethlehem: From Communal Mission to Family Economy.* Philadelphia, 1988.

Smedt, Raphaël de, ed. *Les chevaliers de l'Ordre de la Toison d'or au XVe siècle. Notices bio-bibliographiques.* Frankfurt, 1994.

Smith, Raymond T. *The Negro Family in British Guiana.* London, 1956.

Smyrnelis, Marie-Carmen. "Les arméniens catholiques de Smyrne aux XVIIIe et XIXe siècle." *Revue du monde arménien moderne et contemporaine* 2 (1995): 25–44.

Sommer, Elisabeth. "Gambling with God: The Use of the Lot by the Moravian Brethren in the 18. Century." *Journal of the History of Ideas* 59 (1998): 267–86.

———. *Serving Two Masters: Authority, Faith and Community among the Moravian Brethren in Germany and North Carolina in the 18th Century.* Lexington, KY, 2000.

Sourches, Louis-François du Bouchet, marquis de. *Mémoires sur le règne de Louis XIV,* edited by Gabriel-Jules, comte de Cosnac, and Arthur Bertrand. 13 vols. Paris, 1882.

Spagnoletti, Angelantonio. *Le dinastie italiane nella prima età moderna.* Bologna, 2003.

Spangler, Jonathan. *The Society of Princes: The Lorraine-Guise and the Conservation of Power and Wealth in Seventeenth-Century France.* Farnham, UK, 2009.

Spanheim, Ezéchiel. *Relation de la Cour de France en 1690,* edited by Emile Bourgeois. Paris, 1973.

Sperling, Jutta Gisela. *Convents and the Body Politic in Late Renaissance Venice.* Chicago, 1999.

Spielman, John. *Leopold I of Austria.* London, 1977.

Spiess, Karl-Heinz. "Europa heiratet: Kommunikation und Kulturtransfer im Kontext europäischer Königsheiraten des Spätmittelalters." In *Europa im späten Mittelalter: Politik, Gesellschaft, Kultur,* edited by Rainer Christoph Schwinges, Christian Hesse, and Peter Moraw, 435–64. Munich, 2006.

———. *Familie und Verwandtschaft im deutschen Hochadel des Spätmittelalters, 13. bis Anfang des 16. Jahrhunderts.* Stuttgart, 1993.

———. "Fremdheit und Integration der ausländischen Ehefrau und ihres Gefolges bei internationalen Fürstenheiraten." In *Fürstenhöfe und ihre Außenwelt: Aspekte gesellschaftlicher und kultureller Identität im deutschen Spätmittelalter,* edited by Thomas Zotz, 267–90. Würzburg, 2004.

———. "Lordship, Kinship, and Inheritance among the German High Nobility in the Middle Ages and Early Modern Period." In Sabean, Teuscher, and Mathieu, *Kinship in Europe,* 57–75.

———. "Unterwegs zu einem fremden Ehemann: Brautfahrt und Ehe in europäischen Fürstenhäusern des Spätmittelalters." In *Fremdheit und Reisen im Mittelalter,* edited by Irene Erfen and Karl-Heinz Spiess, 17–36. Stuttgart, 1997.

Srbik, Heinrich Ritter von. *Wien und Versailles, 1692–1697: Zur Geschichte von Strassburg, Elsass und Lothringen.* Munich, 1944.

Stamatiades, Epameinondas. *Viographiai ton Hellenon megalon diermeneon tou Othomanikou kratous* [Biographies of the Greek Grand Dragomans of the Ottoman State]. Thessaloniki, 1865. Reprinted, 1973.

Stein, Robert, ed. *Powerbrokers in the Late Middle Ages: The Burgundian Low Countries in a European Context.* Turnhout, 2001.

Steingass, Francis Joseph. *A Comprehensive Persian-English Dictionary Including the Arabic Words and Phrases to be Met with in Persian Literature.* London, 1892. Reprinted, 1930.

Stettler, Karl. *Ritter Niklaus von Diesbach 1430–1475.* Bern, 1924.

Studnicki-Gizbert, David. *A Nation upon the Ocean Sea: Portugal's Atlantic Diaspora and the Crisis of the Spanish Empire, 1492–1640.* New York, 2007.

Studt, Birgit, ed. *Haus- und Familienbücher in der städtischen Gesellschaft des Spätmittelalters und der frühen Neuzeit.* Cologne, 2007.

Sturdza, Mihail-Dimitri. *Dictionnaire historique et généalogique de grandes familles de Grèce, d'Albanie et de Constantinople.* Paris, 1983.

Sutherland, Donald. *Les Chouans: Les origines sociales de la Contre-Révolution populaire en Bretagne, 1770–1796.* Rennes, 1990.

Sutton, Constance R. "Celebrating Ourselves: The Family Reunion Rituals of African Caribbean Transnational Families." *Global Networks* 4, no. 3 (2004): 243–58.

Sutton, Constance R. and Elsa M. Chaney, eds. *Caribbean Life in New York City: Socio-Cultural Dimensions.* New York, 1994.

Swetschinski, Daniel M. *Reluctant Cosmopolitans: The Portuguese Jews of Seventeenth-Century Amsterdam.* Oxford, 2000.

Taddei, Elena. "Anna Caterina Gonzaga und ihre Zeit. Der italienische Einfluss am Innsbrucker Hof." In *Der Innsbrucker Hof: Residenz und höfische Gesellschaft in Tirol vom 15. bis 19. Jahrhundert,* edited by Heinz Noflatscher and Jan Paul Niederkorn, 213–40. Vienna, 2005.

Tamalio, Raffaele. *La memoria dei Gonzaga: Repertorio bibliografico Gonzaghesco 1473–1999.* Mantua, 1999.

Tambs-Lyche, Harald. *London Patidars: A Case Study in Urban Ethnicity.* London, 1980.

Tanner, Fritz. *Die Ehe im Pietismus.* Zürich, 1952.

Teuscher, Simon. *Bekannte, Klienten, Verwandte: Soziabilität und Politik in der Stadt Bern um 1500.* Cologne, 1998.

———. "Parenté, politique et comptabilité: Chroniques familiales du Sud de l'Allemagne et de la Suisse autour de 1500." *Annales: Histoire, Sciences Sociales* 59 (2003): 847–58.

———. "Politics of Kinship in the City of Bern at the End of the Middle Ages." In Sabean, Teuscher and Mathieu, *Kinship in Europe,* 76–90.

Thomas-Hope, Elizabeth. *Explanation in Caribbean Migration.* London, 1992.

Tindale, Norman B. "Tribal and Intertribal Marriage among the Australian Aborigines." *Human Biology* 25, no. 3 (1953): 169–90.

Toaff, Renzo. *La nazione ebrea a Livorno e Pisa (1591–1700).* Florence, 1990.

Todd, Christopher. *Voltaire's Disciple: Jean-François de La Harpe.* London, 1972.

Togliani, Carlo, ed. *Gazzuolo, Belforte: Storia, arte e cultura.* Mantua, 2007.

Tölölyan, Khachig. "The Nation-State and Its Others: In Lieu of a Preface." *Diaspora: Journal of Transnational Studies* 1 (1991): 3–7.

Trausch, Gilbert. "Les Habsbourg, incarnation de l'Empire au Luxembourg à la fin du XVIIIe siècle: Fidélité dynastique et manque de conscience impériale." In *Unité et diversité de l'Empire des Habsbourg à la fin du XVIIIe siècle,* edited by Roland Mortier and Hervé Hasquin, 133–48. Brussels, 1988.

Trenard, Louis. "Provinces et départements des Pays-Bas français aux départements du Nord et du Pas-de-Calais." In *Régions et régionalisme en France du XVIIIe siècle à nos jours,* edited by Christian Gras and Georges Livet, 55–85. Paris, 1977.

Tricoupes, Spyridon. *Historia tes Hellenikes Epanastaseos* [History of the Greek Revolution]. 4 vols. Athens, 1888. Reprinted, 1968.

Trivellato, Francesca. *The Familiarity of Strangers: The Sephardic Diaspora, Livorno, and Cross-Cultural Trade in the Early Modern Period.* New Haven, CT, 2009.

Trochu, Jules. *L'armée en 1867.* Paris, 1867.

Trossbach, Werner. "Das 'Ganze Haus'—Basiskategorie für das Verständnis ländlicher Gesellschaften in der Frühen Neuzeit." *Blätter für deutsche Landesgeschichte* 129 (1993): 277–314.

Tucker, Judith E. "Marriage and Family in Nablus 1720–1856: Toward a History of Arab Marriage." *Journal of Family History* 13, no. 2 (1988).

———. "The Arab Family in History: 'Otherness' and the Study of the Family." In *Arab Women: Old Boundaries. New Frontiers,* edited by J. E. Tucker, 195–207. Bloomington, IN, 1993.

Tudesq, Jean-André. *Les grands notables en France, 1840–1849.* Paris, 1964.

Umbach, Maiken, ed. *German Federalism: Past, Present and Future.* Basingstoke, UK, 2002.

Uttendörfer, Otto. *Wirtschaftsgeist und Wirtschaftsorganisation Herrnhuts und der Brüdergemeine von 1743 bis zum Ende des Jahrhunderts.* Herrnhut, 1926.

Vaini, Mario. *Ricerche Gonzaghesche (1189-inizi sec. XV).* Florence, 1994.

Van den Boogert, Maurits H. *The Capitulations and the Ottoman Legal System: Qadis, Consuls and Beratlis in the 18th Century.* Leiden, 2005.

Van der Linden, Herman. *Belgium. The Making of a Nation.* Translated by Sybil Jane. Oxford, 1920.

Van Rooy, Silvio. "Armenian Habits as Mirrored in 17–18th Century Amsterdam Documents." *Revue des études arméniennes* 3 (1966): 347–57.

Vedder, Ulrike. "Continuity and Death: Literature and the Law of Succession in the Nineteenth Century." In Müller-Wille and Rheinberger, *Heredity Produced,* 85–102.

Veliman, Valeriu. *Relatiile Romano-Otomane 1711–1821: Documente turcesti.* Bucharest, 1984.

Vertovec, Steven. *The Hindu Diaspora: Comparative Patterns.* London, 2000.

Villari, Rosario. *The Revolt of Naples.* Cambridge, 1993.

Vogt, Peter. "A Voice of Themselves: Women as Participants in Congregational Discourse in the 18th Century Moravian Movement." In *Women Preachers and Prophets through Two Millennia of Christianity,* edited by Beverly Mayne Kienzle and Pamela J. Walker, 227–47. Berkeley, CA, 1998.

———. "Des Heilands Ökonomie: Wirtschaftsethik bei Zinzendorf." *Unitas Fratrum. Zeitschrift für Geschichte und Gegenwartsfragen der Brüdergemeine,* 49/50 (2002): 157–72.

Vorst, Claudia. *Familie als Erzählkosmos: Phänomen und Bedeutung der Chronik.* Münster, 1995.

Vowinckel, Gerhard. *Verwandtschaft, Freundschaft und die Gesellschaft der Fremden: Grundlagen menschlichen Zusammenlebens.* Darmstadt, 1995.

Vuorela, Ulla. "Transnational Families: Imagined and Real Communities." In Bryceson and Vuorela, *Transnational Family,* 63–82.

Ward Swain, Elisabeth. "My Most Excellent and Singular Lord: Marriage in a Noble Family of Fifteenth-Century Italy." *Journal of Medieval and Renaissance Studies* 16 (1986): 171–95.

Watkins-Owens, Irma. *Blood Relations. Caribbean Immigrants and the Harlem Community.* Bloomington, IN, 1996.

Weber, Eugene. *Peasants into Frenchmen: The Modernization of Rural France, 1870–1914.* Stanford, CA, 1976.

Weber, Max. *Economy and Society: An Outline of Interpretative Sociology*, edited by Guenther Roth and Claus Wittich. 2 vols. Berkeley, CA, 1978.

———. *The History of Commercial Partnerships in the Middle Ages*, edited by Lutz Kaelber. Lanham, MD: 2003.

Weibel, Thomas. *Erbrecht und Familie: Fortbildung und Aufzeichnung des Erbrechts in der Stadt Zürich, vom Richtebrief zum Stadtrecht von 1716*. Zürich, 1986.

Wellenreuther, Hermann, and Carola Wessel, eds. *Herrnhuter Indianermission in der Amerikanischen Revolution: Die Tagebücher von David Zeisberger 1772 bis 1781*. Berlin, 1995.

Weller, Tobias. *Die Heiratspolitik des deutschen Hochadels im 12. Jahrhundert*. Vienna, 2004.

Wessel, Carola. "Connecting Congregations: The Net of Communication among the Moravians as Exemplified by the Interaction Between Pennsylvania, the Upper Ohio Valley, and Germany (1772–1774)." In *The Distinctiveness of Moravian Culture*, edited by Craig Atwood and Peter Vogt, 153–72. Nazareth, PA: 2003.

Weyer, Johannes, ed. *Soziale Netzwerke: Konzepte und Methoden der sozialwissenschaftlichen Netzwerkforschung*. Munich, 2000.

White, Donald Maxwell. *Zaccaria Seriman (1709–1784) and the Viaggi di Enrico Wanton: A Contribution to the Study of the Enlightenment in Italy*. Manchester, UK, 1961.

White, Mary E. "Greek Colonization." *The Journal of Economic History* 2, no. 4 (1961): 443–54.

Williams, Raymond Brady. *A New Face of Hinduism: The Swaminarayan Religion*. Cambridge, 1984.

Wilson, A. J. N. *Emigration from Italy in the Republican Age of Rome*. Manchester, UK, 1966.

Wilson, Peter H. *From Reich to Revolution: German History, 1558–1806*. Basingstoke, UK, 2004.

Wobst, H. Martin. "Boundary Conditions for Paleolithic Social Systems, A Sociological Approach." *American Antiquity* 39, no. 2 (1974): 147–78.

Wolloch, Isser. *The New Regime: Transformations of the French Civic Order 1789–1820s*. New York, 1994.

Woods, John E. *The Aqquyunlu*. Minneapolis, 1976.

Wunder, Heide. *"Er ist die Sonn', sie ist der Mond": Frauen in der Frühen Neuzeit*. Munich, 1992.

Würgler, Andreas. "Boten und Gesandte an der eidgenössischen Tagsatzung: Diplomatische Praxis im Spätmittelalter." In *Gesandtschafts- und Botenwesen im spätmittelaterlichen Europa*, edited by Rainer Christoph Schwinges and Klaus Wriedt, 287–312. Ostfildern, 2003.

Wymans, Gabriel. *Inventaire des archives des ducs de Croÿ*. Brussels, 1977.

Yanagisako, Sylvia J. "Bringing it All Back Home: Kinship Theory in Anthropology." In Sabean, Teuscher and Mathieu, *Kinship in Europe*, 33–48.

Yogev, Gedalia. *Diamonds and Coral: Anglo-Dutch Jews and Eighteenth-Century Trade*. Leicester, UK, 1978.

Zahnd, Urs Martin. "Ludwig von Diesbach." In *Historisches Lexikon der Schweiz*. Vol. 3, 714. Basel, 2004.

———. *Die autobiographischen Aufzeichnungen Ludwig von Diesbachs: Studien zur spätmittelalterlichen Selbstdarstellung im oberdeutschen und schweizerischen Raume*. Bern, 1986.

Zallony, Marc-Philippe. *Essai sur les Phanariotes, ou l'on voit les causes primitives de leur élévation aux hospodariats de la Valachie et la Moldavie, leur mode d'administration, et les causes principales de leur chute; suivi de quelques réflexions sur l'état actuel de la Grèce.* Marseille, 1824.

Zekiyan, Boghos Levon. "Le colonie armene del Medio Evo in Italia e le relazioni culutrali italo-armene." In *Atti del primo simposio internazionale di arte armena (Bergamo, 28–30 giugno 1975)*, 803–929. Venice, 1978.

Zens, Robert. "The Ayanlik and Pasvanoğlu Osman Paşa of Vidin in the Age of Ottoman Social Change, 1791–1815." PhD dissertation, University of Wisconsin–Madison, 2005.

Zilfi, Madeline. *Politics of Piety: The Ottoman Ulema in the Postclassical Age (1600–1800).* Minneapolis, 1988.

Zimmermann, Reinhard. *The Law of Obligations: Roman Foundations of the Civil Traditions.* Oxford, 1996.

Zunkel, Friedrich. *Der Rheinisch-Westfälische Unternehmer 1834–1879: Ein Beitrag zur Geschichte des deutschen Bürgertums im 19. Jahrhundert.* Cologne, 1962.

Notes on Contributors

Christina Antenhofer is Assistant Professor of Medieval History at the University of Innsbruck (Austria). She was visiting professor at the University of New Orleans in 2011. She studied history and Germanic and Romance languages and literature at the University of Innsbruck and the Sorbonne (Paris IV), graduating in 2004. Since 2005, she has been a member of the international doctoral program "Political Communication from the Ancient World to the Twentieth Century" (Universities of Frankfurt, Innsbruck, Trento, Bologna, and Pavia). Her main research field is the late medieval and Renaissance period and the contact zone between the German and Italian areas. She is interested in the history of communication, gender studies, family systems, and cultural studies. So far, she has published a book on the relationship between the Gonzaga family and the counts of Görz (*Briefe zwischen Süd und Nord: Die Hochzeit und Ehe von Paula de Gonzaga und Leonhard von Görz im Spiegel der fürstlichen Kommunikation (1473–1500)* [Innsbruck, 2007]); together with Mario Müller she has edited a comparative study on letters as historical sources (*Briefe in politischer Kommunikation vom Alten Orient bis ins 20. Jahrhundert* [Göttingen, 2008]); she has also published several essays on the Gonzaga family and their correspondence with princely relatives, including "Letters Across the Borders: Strategies of Communication in an Italian-German Renaissance Correspondence," in Jane Couchman and Ann Crabb, eds., *Women's Letters Across Europe, 1400–1700: Form and Persuasion* (Aldershot, UK, and Burlington, 2005), 103–22.

Mary Chamberlain is emeritus Professor of Caribbean History at Oxford Brookes University. She was one of the pioneers of oral history, with her study of rural women in England, *Fenwomen* (1975, 2011). Since then she has published widely on women's history, oral history, and, most recently, on twentieth-century Caribbean history, in particular on migration and families. Recent relevant publications include *Narratives of Exile and Return* (London, 1997); *Family Love in the Diaspora: Migration and the Anglo-Caribbean Experience* (New Brunswick, NJ, 2006); *Empire and Nation-building in the Caribbean: Barbados 1937–1966* (Manchester, UK, 2010). She has also edited *Caribbean Migration: Globalised Identities* (London, 1997); with Paul Thompson, *Narrative and Genre* (London, 1997); with Harry Goulbourne, *Caribbean Families in Britain and the Transatlantic World* (London, 2001). She has held visiting professorships at New York University and the University of the West Indies, is a Fellow of the Royal Historical Society, a founding and former principal editor of *Memory and Narrative*, and has served on a number of advisory and editorial boards, as consultant to the Barbados Government's National Oral History Project (1999) and as a member of the UK Government's Caribbean Advisory Group (1998–2002).

Michaela Hohkamp is a professor at the Free University Berlin. A graduate of the University of Göttingen, where she studied under Rudolf Vierhaus, she was a research assistant at the Max Planck Institute for History in Göttingen and a research fellow at the European University Institute. Her interests span from European rural society to court society, aristocratic power and kinship, issues of gender and power in early modern Europe, and the history of early modern historiography. Her writings include: "Sisters, Aunts, and Cousins: Familial Architectures and the Political Field in Early Modern Europe," in David Warren Sabean, Simon Teuscher, and Jon Mathieu, eds., *Kinship in Europe: Approaches to Long-Term Developments (1300–1900)* (New York, 2007), 128–45; "Eine Tante für alle Fälle: Tanten-Nichten-Beziehungen und ihre politische Bedeutung für die reichsfürstliche Gesellschaft der Frühen Neuzeit (16. bis 18. Jahrhundert)," in Margareth Lanzinger and Edith Saurer, eds., *Politiken der Verwandtschaft* (Vienna, 2007), 149–71; "Grausamkeit blutet–Gerechtigkeit zwackt: Überlegungen zu Grenzziehungen zwischen legitimer und nicht-legitimer Gewalt," in Barbara Krug-Richter and Magnus Eriksson, eds., *Streitkultur(en): Studien zu Gewalt, Konflikt und Kommunikation in der ländlichen Gesellschaft (16. bis 19. Jh.)* (Cologne, 2003), 59–79; *Herrschaft in der Herrschaft: Die vorderösterreichische Obervogtei Triberg von 1737 bis 1780* (Göttingen, 1998). Currently, she is engaged in a study of the transmission of kinship and power in European aristocracies from the sixteenth to the eighteenth century and of representations of kinship in early modern European historiography.

Christopher H. Johnson is Professor Emeritus of History and member of the Academy of Scholars at Wayne State University. He has held fellowships from the Leverhulme and the Guggenheim Foundations as well as the Social Science Research Council and the National Endowment for the Humanities. He is currently engaged in research on the history of kinship and the family. He has published "Die Geschwister Archipel: Bruder-Schwester Liebe und Klassenformation im Frankreich des 19. Jahrhunderts," in *L'Homme: Zeitschrift für feministische Geschichtswissenschaft* 13 (2002): 50–67, and "Kinship, Civil Society, and Power in Nineteenth-Century Vannes," in David Warren Sabean, Simon Teuscher, and Jon Mathieu, eds., *Kinship in Europe: Approaches to Long-Term Developments (1300–1900)* (New York, 2007), 258–83. His book manuscript on kinship and bourgeois class formation in Vannes is nearing completion. Johnson is also at work on a study of family conflict and women's rights in eighteenth-century Paris. His earlier publications include *Utopian Communism in France: Cabet and the Icarians, 1839–1851* (Ithaca, NY, 1974; nominated for a National Book Award in 1975); *Maurice Sugar: Law, Labor, and the Left in Detroit, 1912–1950* (Detroit, 1989), and *The Life and Death of Industrial Languedoc, 1700–1920: The Politics of De-Industrialization* (Oxford, 1995).

Stéphanie Latte Abdallah is a historian and political scientist and holds a research position at the Institut de recherches et d'études sur le monde arabe et musulman (IREMAM-CNRS) in Aix-en-Provence. She is a lecturer at the University of Provence and at the Institut d'études de l'islam et des sociétés du monde musulman (IISMM-EHESS) in Paris. She first specialized in Palestinian refugee social history and in issues of gender, political activism, and feminisms in the Near East. She is working on the connection between images and politics in the Israeli-Palestinian conflict. She is currently coordinating a collective research program on borders in the Israeli-Palestinian spaces and is researching on political imprisonment of Palestinians in Israel since 1967. Among her publications are *Femmes réfugiées palestiniennes* (Paris, 2006), "Subvertir le consentement: itinéraires sociaux des femmes des camps de réfugiés palestiniens en Jordanie 1948–2001," *Annales ESC* 60 (2005); "Regards, visibilité historique et politique des images des réfugiés palestiniens depuis 1948," *Le Mouvement social* 219–20 (2007); "Incarcération des femmes palestiniennes et engagement (1967–2009)," in (ed. with Leyla Dakhli), *Des engagements féminins au Moyen Orient (XXè–XXIè siècles)*, *Le Mouvement social* 231 (2010); and "Fragile Intimacies: Marriage and Love in the Palestinian Camps of Jordan (1948–2001)," in *Journal of Palestine Studies* 38, 4 (2009): 47–62. She has edited several collections of articles on Islamic feminisms: *Images aux frontières. Représentations et constructions sociales et politiques. Palestine, Jordanie 1948–2000* (Beirut, 2005); and (with Cédric Parizot) *A l'ombre du Mur. Israéliens et Palestininiens entre séparation et occupation* (Arles, 2011).

Gisela Mettele is Professor of Gender History at Friedrich-Schiller-University Jena, Germany. Before joining the University at Jena in 2010, she was a Lecturer at the Centre for Urban History, University of Leicester. From 2005 to 2007, she was a Research Fellow and, in 2007, Acting Director of the German Historical Institute Washington, D.C. From 1994 to 2005 she taught at the Technical University of Chemnitz, in Germany. In 1999–2000 she was a Senior Fellow at the Center for the Study of World Religions at Harvard University. She received her PhD from the Johann Wolfgang-Goethe University of Frankfurt-am-Main in 1994, where she worked in the research project "City and Middle Classes in the Nineteenth Century." Her monograph, *Bürgertum in Köln: Gemeinsinn und Freie Association 1775–1870*, was published by Oldenbourg in 1998. In her Habilitation she analyzed the collective identity of a transnational religious group. Her book, *Weltbürgertum oder Gottesreich? Die Herrnhuter Brüdergemeine als globale Gemeinschaft 1727–1856* appeared with Vandenhoeck and Ruprecht in 2009. She has published widely in the field of transnational and transatlantic history, most recently an edited volume with Karen Hagemann und Jane Rendall, *Gender, War, and Politics: The Wars of Revolution and Liberation; Transatlantic Comparisons (1775–1815)* (New York, 2009).

Jose C. Moya is Professor Emeritus at UCLA and Professor of history at Barnard College, Columbia University where he also directs the Forum on Migration. He has been a visiting professor at the Universidad de San Andres in Buenos Aires, the Universidad de Santiago de Compostela in Spain, and the Université de Paris VII. His book, *Cousins and Strangers: Spanish Immigrants in Buenos Aires, 1850–1930* (Berkeley, CA, 1998), received five awards and the journal *Historical Methods* (Winter 2001) devoted a forum to its theoretical contributions to migration studies. He has been a Fulbright Fellow in Buenos Aires (three times), a Burkhardt Fellow at the American Academy in Rome, a Del Amo Fellow in Madrid, and held a fellowship from the National Endowment for the Humanities. Among his more recent publications are: "Domestic Service in a Global Perspective: Gender, Migration, and Ethnic Niches," *Journal of Ethnic and Migration Studies* 33 (2007): 559–79; "Modernization, Modernity, and the Trans/formation of the Atlantic World in the Nineteenth Century," in Jorge Canizares-Esguerra and Erik Seeman, eds., *The North and*

South Atlantics and Global History (Upper Saddle River, NJ, 2006); and "A Continent of Immigrants: Postcolonial Shifts in the Western Hemisphere," *Hispanic American Historical Review* 86 (2006): 1–28.

Pravin J. Patel is a sociologist. He did his postdoctoral research at Columbia University. He has won several awards and honors including a Fulbright Fellowship in the United States, a Charles Wallace Fellowship in the United Kingdom, a visiting professorship at Charles Gordon University, and several University Grants Commission's visiting professorships/fellowships at various universities in India. His publications include, with N. R. Sheth, *Industrial Sociology in India* (Rawat, 1979), *Sociology of Robert K. Merton* (in Gujarati, 1976) and a number of research papers. He is on the editorial boards of several academic journals including the British Sociological Society's *Work, Employment and Society.* He was Professor of Sociology and Dean of the Faculty of Arts at M.S. University of Baroda and Vice Chancellor of Sardar Patel University, Gujarat, India.

Christine Philliou, of Columbia University's Department of History, specializes in the political and social history of the Ottoman Empire, particularly in the eighteenth and nineteenth centuries. Her book, *Biography of an Empire: Governing Ottomans in an Age of Revolution* (University of California Press, 2010), examines the changes in Ottoman governance leading up to the Tanzimat reforms of the mid-nineteenth century. It does so using the vantage point of Phanariots, an Orthodox Christian elite that was intimately involved in the day-to-day work of governance even though structurally excluded from the Ottoman state.

Gabriel Piterberg is Professor of History at UCLA. He teaches the history of the Ottoman Empire and the Mediterranean in the early modern period, and modern themes such as Zionism, colonialism, and the Palestinian-Israel conflict. He published *An Ottoman Tragedy* (Berkeley, CA, 2003) and *The Returns of Zionism* (London, 2008). He writes for the *New Left Review* and the *London Review of Books.*

Mario Rutten is Professor of Comparative Sociology of Asia in the Department of Anthropology and Sociology at the University of Amsterdam and Fellow of the Amsterdam Institute for Social Science Research. He has extensive research experience in rural entrepreneurship and labor relations in India, Indonesia, and Malaysia, and on Indian migrants in Europe. He has been a research fellow at the Royal Netherlands Academy of Arts and Sciences, at the Nordic Institute of Asian Studies in Copenhagen, Denmark, and at the Asia Research Institute, National University of Singapore. His book publications include *Asian Capitalists in the European Mirror* (Amsterdam, 1994); *Farms and Factories* (New York, 1995); coedited with Carol Upadhya, *Small Business Entrepreneurs in Asia and Europe* (Delhi, 1997); *Rural Capitalists in Asia: A Comparative Analysis of India, Indonesia, and Malaysia* (London, 2003); coedited with Srilata Ravi and Beng-Lan Goh, *Asia in Europe, Europe in Asia* (Singapore, 2004); coedited with K. P. Kannan, *Labour and Capitalist Transformation in Asia* (special issue of *Indian Journal of Labour Economics* 47 [2004]), and *You Had a Nice Holiday? Stories about Anthropological Fieldwork* [in Dutch] (Amsterdam, 2007). Closely related to his academic research, Mario Rutten codirected, together with Sanderien Verstappen and Isabelle Makay, a documentary on Gujarati youngsters in London and their families in India, entitled "Living Like a Common Man" (2011). Currently he is codirector of the program *Provincial Globalisation: The Impact of Reverse Transnational Flows in India's Regional Towns* (2010–2015).

David Warren Sabean is Henry J. Bruman Professor of German History at the University of California, Los Angeles. A graduate of the University of Wisconsin, where he studied under George Mosse, Sabean has taught at the University of East Anglia, University of Pittsburgh, and Cornell University. He has been a Fellow at the Max Planck Institute for History in Göttingen, the Maison des Science de l'Homme in Paris, the Wissenschaftskolleg zu Berlin, the American Academy in Berlin, the National Humanities Center, and the International Research Center Work and Human Lifecycle in Global History, Humboldt University in Berlin. He is a Fellow of the American Academy of Arts and Sciences. His publications include: *Power in the Blood: Popular Culture and Village Discourse in Early Modern Germany* (Cambridge, 1984); *Property, Production, and Family in Neckarhausen, 1700–1870* (Cambridge, 1990); *Kinship in Neckarhausen, 1700–1870* (Cambridge, 1998). He is coeditor with Simon Teuscher and Jon Mathieu of *Kinship in Europe: Approaches to Long-Term Development (1300–1900)* (New York, 2007). Currently, he is engaged in an extensive study on the history of incest and other fields of European cultural history.

Jonathan Spangler is a Senior Lecturer in history at Manchester Metropolitan University in England. His doctoral research focused on the foreign princes in seventeenth-century France, notably the Lorraine-Guise, about whom he has published articles in *French History* and *Proceedings of the Western Society for French History*, and a recent monograph, *The*

Society of Princes (Ashgate, UK, 2009). He has also looked at the relationship between the Guise and the Stuarts, with particular reference to Stirling Palace (with a recent article in *Court Historian*). Future research will include a more in-depth exploration of transregional princely families, with a particular focus on the Southern Netherlands. Spangler is a native of Virginia and did his first degree in history and anthropology at the College of William & Mary. He worked for several years in Washington, DC, and New York as a museum exhibition designer, before completing a DPhil at Oxford University. He held a postdoctoral post at Glasgow University and moved to Manchester in 2009. He is coeditor of the journal *The Court Historian*.

Simon Teuscher is Professor of Medieval History at the University of Zurich, where he also earned his doctoral degree in 1996. From 2000 to 2006, he taught at the University of California, Los Angeles. He was also an assistant professor at the University of Basel, a visiting professor at the École des Hautes Études en Sciences Sociales in Paris and at the Université de Neuchâtel, as well as a member of the Institute for Advanced Study, School of Historical Studies, at Princeton. His research interests include kinship and other personal relationships, rural society, and administrative culture during the late Middle Ages in western and northern Europe. Together with David Sabean and Jon Mathieu, he edited *Kinship in Europe: Approaches to Long-Term Development (1300–1900)* (New York, 2007). His publications include *Erzähltes Recht: Lokale Herrschaft, Verschriftlichung und Traditionsbildung im Spätmittelalter* (Frankfurt a. M., 2007) and *Bekannte—Verwandte—Klienten: Soziabilität und Politik in Bern um 1500* (Cologne, 1998).

Francesca Trivellato is Professor of History at Yale University. She earned a PhD in economic and social history at the Luigi Bocconi University in Milan (1999) and a PhD in history at Brown University (2004). She received fellowships from the American Council of Learned Societies and the Radcliffe Institute for Advanced Study at Harvard University, and was a visiting professor at the École des Hautes Études en Sciences Sociales in Paris. Her publications include *Fondamenta dei Vetrai: Lavoro, tecnologia e mercato a Venezia tra Sei e Settecento* (Rome, 2000), and *The Familiarity of Strangers: The Sephardic Diaspora, Livorno, and Cross-Cultural Trade in the Early Modern Period* (New Haven, CT, 2009).

Index

Q

R